DIGITAL SERVICES IN INTERNATIONAL TRADE LAW

Digitisation has significantly impacted international trade. This book explains the impact of digitisation on trade in services, the ensuing concept of 'digital services' and the different types of trade barriers these services face. This book establishes that the legal framework that applies to trade in services also applies to digital services. It elaborates on the scope of the General Agreement on Trade in Services (GATS) and how to classify digital services. The relevant GATS obligations are subsequently applied to several case studies that illustrate the barriers to digital services trade. These case studies demonstrate the impact of the applicability of GATS to digital services on countries' international obligations. Finally, the book maps the electronic commerce–related provisions in regional trade agreements (RTAs). Six extensive e-commerce RTAs are compared in depth and it is considered whether they add substantially to the existing multilateral obligations applicable to digital services trade.

INES WILLEMYNS is an associate at Sidley Austin LLP in Brussels, focussing her practice on international and European trade law. Before joining Sidley, Ines was a research assistant at KU Leuven and interned at the AB Secretariat of the WTO. Her research has been published in leading journals on international trade law. The views expressed in this book do not represent the views of Sidley Austin LLP or its clients. This book has been prepared for informational purposes only and does not constitute legal advice.

CAMBRIDGE INTERNATIONAL TRADE AND ECONOMIC LAW

Series editors

Processes of economic regionalisation and globalisation have intensified over the last decades, accompanied by increases in the regulation of international trade and economics at the levels of international, regional and national laws. At the same time, significant challenges have arisen with respect to economic liberalization, rule-based systems of trade and investment, and their political and social impacts. The subject matter of this series is international economic law, in this contemporary context. Its core is the regulation of international trade, investment, finance and cognate areas such as intellectual property and competition policy. The series publishes books on related regulatory areas, in particular human rights, labour, environment and culture, as well as sustainable development. These areas are horizontally interconnected and vertically linked at the international, regional and national levels. The series also includes works on governance, dealing with the structure and operation of international organisations related to the field of international economic law, and the way they interact with other subjects of international and national law. The series aims to include excellent legal doctrinal treatises, as well as cutting-edge interdisciplinary works that engage law and the social sciences and humanities.

Books in the series

Digital Services in International Trade Law
Ines Willemyns

Energy in International Trade Law: Concepts, Regulation and Changing Markets
Anna-Alexandra Marhold

Essential Interoperability Standards: Interfacing Intellectual Property and Competition in International Economic Law
Simon Brinsmead

Shareholders' Claims for Reflective Loss in International Investment Law
Lukas Vanhonnaeker

Transparency in the WTO SPS and TBT Agreements: The Real Jewel in the Crown
Marianna B. Karttunen

Emerging Powers in International Economic Law: Cooperation, Competition and Transformation
Sonia E. Rolland and David M. Trubek

Commitments and Flexibilities in the WTO Agreement on Subsidies and Countervailing Measures
José Guilherme Moreno Caiado

The Return of the Home State to Investor-State Disputes: Bringing Back Diplomatic Protection?
Rodrigo Polanco

The Public International Law of Trade in Legal Services
David Collins

Industrial Policy and the World Trade Organization: Between Legal Constraints and Flexibilities
Sherzod Shadikhodjaev

The Prudential Carve-Out for Financial Services: Rationale and Practice in the GATS and Preferential Trade Agreements
Carlo Maria Cantore

Preferential Services Liberalization: The Case of the European Union and Federal States
Johanna Jacobsson

Judicial Acts and Investment Treaty Arbitration
Berk Demirkol

Distributive Justice and World Trade Law: A Political Theory of International Trade Regulation
Oisin Suttle

Freedom of Transit and Access to Gas Pipeline Networks under WTO Law
Vitaliy Pogoretskyy

Reclaiming Development in the World Trading System, 2nd edition
Yong-Shik Lee

Developing Countries and Preferential Services Trade
Charlotte Sieber-Gasser

WTO Dispute Settlement and the TRIPS Agreement: Applying Intellectual Property Standards in a Trade Law Framework
Matthew Kennedy

Establishing Judicial Authority in International Economic Law Edited by Joanna Jemielniak, Laura Nielsen and Henrik Palmer Olsen

Trade, Investment, Innovation and Their Impact on Access to Medicines: An Asian Perspective
Locknie Hsu

The Law, Economics and Politics of International Standardisation Edited by Panagiotis Delimatsis

The WTO and International Investment Law: Converging Systems
Jürgen Kurtz

Export Restrictions on Critical Minerals and Metals: Testing the Adequacy of WTO Disciplines
Ilaria Espa

Optimal Regulation and the Law of International Trade: The Interface between the Right to Regulate and WTO Law
Boris Rigod

The Social Foundations of World Trade: Norms, Community, and Constitution
Sungjoon Cho

Public Participation and Legitimacy in the WTO
Yves Bonzon

The Challenge of Safeguards in the WTO
Fernando Piérola

General Interests of Host States in International Investment Law Edited by Giorgio Sacerdoti, with Pia Acconci, Mara Valenti and Anna De Luca

The Law of Development Cooperation: A Comparative Analysis of the World Bank, the EU and Germany
Philipp Dann

WTO Disciplines on Subsidies and Countervailing Measures: Balancing Policy Space and Legal Constraints
Dominic Coppens

Domestic Judicial Review of Trade Remedies: Experiences of the Most Active WTO Members Edited by Müslüm Yilmaz

The Relevant Market in International Economic Law: A Comparative Antitrust and GATT Analysis
Christian A. Melischek

International Organizations in WTO Dispute Settlement: How Much Institutional Sensitivity?
Marina Foltea

Public Services and International Trade Liberalization: Human Rights and Gender Implications
Barnali Choudhury

The Law and Politics of WTO Waivers: Stability and Flexibility in Public International Law
Isabel Feichtner

African Regional Trade Agreements as Legal Regimes
James Thuo Gathii

Liberalizing International Trade after Doha: Multilateral, Plurilateral, Regional, and Unilateral Initiatives
David A. Gantz

Processes and Production Methods (PPMs) in WTO Law: Interfacing Trade and Social Goals
Christiane R. Conrad

Non-Discrimination in International Trade in Services: 'Likeness' in WTO/GATS
Nicolas F. Diebold

The Law, Economics and Politics of Retaliation in WTO Dispute Settlement
Edited by Chad P. Bown and Joost Pauwelyn

The Multilateralization of International Investment Law
Stephan W. Schill

Trade Policy Flexibility and Enforcement in the WTO: A Law and Economics Analysis
Simon A. B. Schropp

Law and Politics on Export Restrictions: WTO and Beyond
Chien-Huei Wu

DIGITAL SERVICES IN INTERNATIONAL TRADE LAW

INES WILLEMYNS

CAMBRIDGE
UNIVERSITY PRESS

CAMBRIDGE
UNIVERSITY PRESS

University Printing House, Cambridge CB2 8BS, United Kingdom

One Liberty Plaza, 20th Floor, New York, NY 10006, USA

477 Williamstown Road, Port Melbourne, VIC 3207, Australia

314–321, 3rd Floor, Plot 3, Splendor Forum, Jasola District Centre,
New Delhi – 110025, India

103 Penang Road, #05–06/07, Visioncrest Commercial, Singapore 238467

Cambridge University Press is part of the University of Cambridge.

It furthers the University's mission by disseminating knowledge in the pursuit of education, learning, and research at the highest international levels of excellence.

www.cambridge.org
Information on this title: www.cambridge.org/9781108837538
DOI: 10.1017/9781108946353

First published 2021

A catalogue record for this publication is available from the British Library.

Library of Congress Cataloging-in-Publication Data
Names: Willemyns, Ines, author.
Title: Digital services in international trade law / Ines Willemyns, Sidley Austin LLP, Brussels.
Description: Cambridge, United Kingdom ; New York, NY : Cambridge University Press, 2021. | Series: Cambridge international trade and economic law | Includes bibliographical references and index.
Identifiers: LCCN 2021023087 (print) | LCCN 2021023088 (ebook) | ISBN 9781108837538 (hardback) | ISBN 9781108931038 (paperback) | ISBN 9781108946353 (ebook)
Subjects: LCSH: Foreign trade regulation – Data processing. | Transborder data flow – Law and legislation. | Electronic commerce – Law and legislation.
Classification: LCC K3943 .W539 2021 (print) | LCC K3943 (ebook) | DDC 343.08/7538433–dc23
LC record available at https://lccn.loc.gov/2021023087
LC ebook record available at https://lccn.loc.gov/2021023088

ISBN 978-1-108-83753-8 Hardback

Voor Philip en Goedele

CONTENTS

FIGURES

TABLES

WTO CASES

Short title	Full case title	Dispute no.
Argentina – Financial Services	*Argentina – Measures Relating to Trade in Goods and Services*	DS453
Brazil – Retreaded Tyres	*Brazil – Measures Affecting Imports of Retreaded Tyres*	DS332
Brazil – Taxation	*Brazil – Certain Measures Concerning Taxation and Charges*	DS472, DS497
Canada – Autos	*Canada – Certain Measures Affecting the Automotive Industry*	DS139, DS142
Canada – Dairy	*Canada – Measures Affecting the Importation of Milk and the Exportation of Dairy Products*	DS103, DS113
Canada – Periodicals	*Canada – Certain Measures Concerning Periodicals*	DS31
Canada – Renewable Energy	*Canada – Certain Measures Affecting the Renewable Energy Generation Sector/Canada – Measures Relating to the Feed-in Tariff Program*	DS412, DS426
Canada – Wheat Exports and Grain Imports	*Canada – Measures Relating to Exports of Wheat and Treatment of Imported Grain*	DS276
China – Electronic Payment Services	*China – Certain Measures Affecting Electronic Payment Services*	DS413

(*cont.*)

Short title	Full case title	Dispute no.
China – Publications and Audiovisual Products	*China – Measures Affecting Trading Rights and Distribution Services for Certain Publications and Audiovisual Entertainment Products*	DS363
China – Raw Materials	*China – Measures Related to the Exportation of Various Raw Materials*	DS394, DS395, DS398
Colombia – Textiles	*Colombia – Measures Relating to the Importation of Textiles, Apparel and Footwear*	DS461
EC – Asbestos	*European Communities – Measures Affecting Asbestos and Asbestos-Containing Products*	DS135
EC – Bananas III	*European Communities – Regime for the Importation, Sale and Distribution of Bananas*	DS27
EC – Chicken Cuts	*European Communities – Customs Classification of Frozen Boneless Chicken Cuts*	DS269
EC – Computer Equipment	*European Communities – Customs Classification of Certain Computer Equipment*	DS62, DS67, DS68
EC – IT Products	*European Communities and its Member States – Tariff Treatment of Certain Information Technology Products*	DS375, DS376, DS377
EC – Seal Products	*European Communities – Measures Prohibiting the Importation and Marketing of Seal Products*	DS401
EC – Tariff Preferences	*European Communities – Conditions for the Granting of Tariff Preferences to Developing Countries*	DS246

(*cont.*)

Short title	Full case title	Dispute no.
EU – Biodiesel (Argentina)	*European Union – Anti-Dumping Measures on Biodiesel from Argentina*	DS473
Japan – Alcoholic Beverages II	*Japan – Taxes on Alcoholic Beverages*	DS8, DS10, DS11
Korea – Various Measures on Beef	*Korea – Measures Affecting Imports of Fresh, Chilled and Frozen Beef*	DS161, DS169
Mexico – Taxes on Soft Drinks	*Mexico – Tax Measures on Soft Drinks and Other Beverages*	DS308
Mexico – Telecoms	*Mexico – Measures Affecting Telecommunications Services*	DS204
US – 1916 Act	*United States – Anti-Dumping Act of 1916*	DS136, DS162
US – Anti-Dumping and Countervailing Duties (China)	*United States – Definitive Anti-Dumping and Countervailing Duties on Certain Products from China*	DS379
US – Carbon Steel	*United States – Countervailing Duties on Certain Corrosion-Resistant Carbon Steel Flat Products from Germany*	DS213
US – Corrosion-Resistant Steel Sunset Review	*United States – Sunset Review of Anti-Dumping Duties on Corrosion-Resistant Carbon Steel Flat Products from Japan*	DS244
US – Gambling	*United States – Measures Affecting the Cross-Border Supply of Gambling and Betting Services*	DS285
US – Gasoline	*United States – Standards for Reformulated and Conventional Gasoline*	DS2
US – Oil Country Tubular Goods Sunset Reviews	*United States – Sunset Reviews of Anti-Dumping Measures on Oil Country Tubular Goods from Argentina*	DS268

(*cont.*)

Short title	Full case title	Dispute no.
US – Tuna II (Mexico)	*United States – Measures Concerning the Importation, Marketing and Sale of Tuna and Tuna Products*	DS381
Russia – Traffic in Transit	*Russia – Measures Concerning Traffic in Transit*	DS512
Saudi Arabia – Protection of IPRs	*Saudi Arabia – Measures Concerning the Protection of Intellectual Property Rights*	DS567

E-COMMERCE RTAS

ID	RTA	Year entry into force	Signatories
01	ASEAN – Australia – New Zealand	2010	Australia; New Zealand; Brunei Darussalam; Myanmar; Cambodia; Indonesia; Lao People's Democratic Republic; Malaysia; Philippines; Singapore; Viet Nam; Thailand
02	Australia – Chile	2009	Australia; Chile
03	Australia – China	2015	Australia; China
04	Canada – Colombia	2011	Canada; Colombia
05	Canada – Costa Rica	2002	Canada; Costa Rica
06	Canada – Honduras	2014	Canada; Honduras
07	Canada – Jordan	2012	Canada; Jordan
08	Canada – Korea, Republic of	2015	Canada; Korea, Republic of
09	Canada – Panama	2013	Canada; Panama
10	Canada – Peru	2009	Canada; Peru
11	Canada – Ukraine	2017	Canada; Ukraine
12	Caribbean Community and Common Market (CARICOM)	2002	Antigua and Barbuda; Bahamas; Barbados; Belize; Dominica; Grenada; Guyana; Haiti; Jamaica; Montserrat; Saint Kitts and Nevis; Saint Lucia; Saint Vincent and the Grenadines; Suriname; Trinidad and Tobago

(*cont.*)

ID	RTA	Year entry into force	Signatories
13	Central European Free Trade Agreement (CEFTA)	2007	Albania; Bosnia and Herzegovina; Moldova, Republic of; The former Yugoslav Republic of Macedonia; UNMIK/Kosovo; Serbia; Montenegro
14	Chile – Colombia	2009	Chile; Colombia
15	Chile – Thailand	2015	Chile; Thailand
16	China – Georgia	2018	China; Georgia
17	China – Hong Kong, China	2003	China; Hong Kong, China
18	China – Korea, Republic of	2015	China; Korea, Republic of
19	China – Macao, China	2003	China; Macao, China
20	Colombia – Northern Triangle (El Salvador, Guatemala, Honduras)	2009	Colombia; El Salvador; Guatemala; Honduras
21	Costa Rica – Colombia	2016	Colombia; Costa Rica
22	Costa Rica – Singapore	2013	Costa Rica; Singapore
23	Dominican Republic – Central America – United States Free Trade Agreement (CAFTA-DR)	2006	Costa Rica; Dominican Republic; El Salvador; Guatemala; Honduras; Nicaragua; United States of America
24	EFTA – Central America (Costa Rica and Panama)	2014	Costa Rica; Panama; Iceland; Liechtenstein; Norway; Switzerland
25	EFTA – Colombia	2011	Colombia; Iceland; Liechtenstein; Norway; Switzerland
26	EFTA – Peru	2011	Peru; Iceland; Liechtenstein; Norway; Switzerland

(*cont.*)

ID	RTA	Year entry into force	Signatories
27	EU – Canada (CETA)	2017	Canada; European Union; Austria; Belgium; Bulgaria; Croatia; Cyprus; Czech Republic; Denmark; Estonia; Finland; France; Germany; Greece; Hungary; Ireland; Italy; Latvia; Lithuania; Luxembourg; Malta; Netherlands; Poland; Portugal; Romania; Slovak Republic; Slovenia; Spain; Sweden; United Kingdom
28	EU – CARIFORUM States EPA	2008	Antigua and Barbuda; Bahamas; Barbados; Belize; Dominica; Dominican Republic; Grenada; Guyana; Jamaica; Saint Kitts and Nevis; Saint Lucia; Saint Vincent and the Grenadines; Suriname; Trinidad and Tobago; European Union; Austria; Belgium; Bulgaria; Croatia; Cyprus; Czech Republic; Denmark; Estonia; Finland; France; Germany; Greece; Hungary; Ireland; Italy; Latvia; Lithuania; Luxembourg; Malta; Netherlands; Poland; Portugal; Romania; Slovak Republic; Slovenia; Spain; Sweden; United Kingdom
29	EU – Central America	2013	Costa Rica; El Salvador; Guatemala; Honduras; Nicaragua; Panama; European Union; Austria; Belgium; Bulgaria; Croatia; Cyprus; Czech Republic; Denmark; Estonia; Finland; France; Germany; Greece; Hungary; Ireland; Italy; Latvia; Lithuania; Luxembourg; Malta; Netherlands; Poland; Portugal; Romania; Slovak Republic; Slovenia; Spain; Sweden; United Kingdom

(*cont.*)

ID	RTA	Year entry into force	Signatories
30	EU – Chile	2005	Chile; European Union; Austria; Belgium; Bulgaria; Croatia; Cyprus; Czech Republic; Denmark; Estonia; Finland; France; Germany; Greece; Hungary; Ireland; Italy; Latvia; Lithuania; Luxembourg; Malta; Netherlands; Poland; Portugal; Romania; Slovak Republic; Slovenia; Spain; Sweden; United Kingdom
31	EU – Colombia and Peru	2013	Colombia; Peru; European Union; Austria; Belgium; Bulgaria; Croatia; Cyprus; Czech Republic; Denmark; Estonia; Finland; France; Germany; Greece; Hungary; Ireland; Italy; Latvia; Lithuania; Luxembourg; Malta; Netherlands; Poland; Portugal; Romania; Slovak Republic; Slovenia; Spain; Sweden; United Kingdom
32	EU – Eastern and Southern Africa States Interim EPA	2012	Madagascar; Mauritius; Seychelles; Zimbabwe; European Union; Austria; Belgium; Bulgaria; Croatia; Cyprus; Czech Republic; Denmark; Estonia; Finland; France; Germany; Greece; Hungary; Ireland; Italy; Latvia; Lithuania; Luxembourg; Malta; Netherlands; Poland; Portugal; Romania; Slovak Republic; Slovenia; Spain; Sweden; United Kingdom
33	EU – Georgia	2014	Georgia; European Union; Austria; Belgium; Bulgaria; Croatia; Cyprus; Czech Republic; Denmark; Estonia; Finland; France; Germany; Greece; Hungary; Ireland; Italy; Latvia; Lithuania; Luxembourg; Malta;

(*cont.*)

ID	RTA	Year entry into force	Signatories
			Netherlands; Poland; Portugal; Romania; Slovak Republic; Slovenia; Spain; Sweden; United Kingdom
34	EU – Ghana	2016	Ghana; European Union; Austria; Belgium; Bulgaria; Croatia; Cyprus; Czech Republic; Denmark; Estonia; Finland; France; Germany; Greece; Hungary; Ireland; Italy; Latvia; Lithuania; Luxembourg; Malta; Netherlands; Poland; Portugal; Romania; Slovak Republic; Slovenia; Spain; Sweden; United Kingdom
35	EU – Korea, Republic of	2011	Korea, Republic of; European Union; Austria; Belgium; Bulgaria; Croatia; Cyprus; Czech Republic; Denmark; Estonia; Finland; France; Germany; Greece; Hungary; Ireland; Italy; Latvia; Lithuania; Luxembourg; Malta; Netherlands; Poland; Portugal; Romania; Slovak Republic; Slovenia; Spain; Sweden; United Kingdom
36	EU – Moldova, Republic of	2014	Moldova, Republic of; European Union; Austria; Belgium; Bulgaria; Croatia; Cyprus; Czech Republic; Denmark; Estonia; Finland; France; Germany; Greece; Hungary; Ireland; Italy; Latvia; Lithuania; Luxembourg; Malta; Netherlands; Poland; Portugal; Romania; Slovak Republic; Slovenia; Spain; Sweden; United Kingdom
37	EU – Ukraine	2014	Ukraine; European Union; Austria; Belgium; Bulgaria; Croatia; Cyprus; Czech Republic; Denmark; Estonia; Finland; France; Germany; Greece;

(*cont.*)

ID	RTA	Year entry into force	Signatories
			Hungary; Ireland; Italy; Latvia; Lithuania; Luxembourg; Malta; Netherlands; Poland; Portugal; Romania; Slovak Republic; Slovenia; Spain; Sweden; United Kingdom
38	Eurasian Economic Union (EAEU) – Viet Nam	2016	Viet Nam; Armenia; Belarus; Kazakhstan; Kyrgyzstan; Russia
39	European Economic Area (EEA)	1994	Iceland; Liechtenstein; Norway; European Union; Austria; Belgium; Bulgaria; Croatia; Cyprus; Czech Republic; Denmark; Estonia; Finland; France; Germany; Greece; Hungary; Ireland; Italy; Latvia; Lithuania; Luxembourg; Malta; Netherlands; Poland; Portugal; Romania; Slovak Republic; Slovenia; Spain; Sweden; United Kingdom
40	Gulf Cooperation Council (GCC)	2003	Bahrain, Kingdom of; Kuwait, the State of; Oman; Qatar; Saudi Arabia, Kingdom of; United Arab Emirates
41	Gulf Cooperation Council (GCC) – Singapore	2013	Singapore; Bahrain, Kingdom of; Kuwait, the State of; Oman; Qatar; Saudi Arabia, Kingdom of; United Arab Emirates
42	Hong Kong, China – New Zealand	2011	Hong Kong, China; New Zealand
43	India – Singapore	2005	India; Singapore
44	Japan – Australia	2015	Australia; Japan
45	Japan – Mongolia	2016	Japan; Mongolia
46	Japan – Philippines	2008	Japan; Philippines
47	Japan – Singapore	2002	Japan; Singapore
48	Japan – Switzerland	2009	Japan; Switzerland
49	Japan – Thailand	2007	Japan; Thailand

(*cont.*)

ID	RTA	Year entry into force	Signatories
50	Jordan – Singapore	2005	Jordan; Singapore
51	Korea, Republic of – Colombia	2016	Colombia; Korea, Republic of
52	Korea, Republic of – Australia	2014	Australia; Korea, Republic of
53	Korea, Republic of – Singapore	2006	Korea, Republic of; Singapore
54	Korea, Republic of – United States	2012	Korea, Republic of; United States of America
55	Korea, Republic of – Viet Nam	2015	Korea, Republic of; Viet Nam
56	Malaysia – Australia	2013	Australia; Malaysia
57	Mexico – Central America	2012	Costa Rica; El Salvador; Guatemala; Honduras; Mexico; Nicaragua
58	Mexico – Panama	2015	Mexico; Panama
59	New Zealand – Chinese Taipei	2013	Chinese Taipei; New Zealand
60	New Zealand – Singapore	2001	New Zealand; Singapore
61	Nicaragua – Chinese Taipei	2008	Chinese Taipei; Nicaragua
62	Pacific Alliance	2016	Chile; Colombia; Mexico; Peru
63	Panama – Singapore	2006	Panama; Singapore
64	Peru – Korea, Republic of	2011	Korea, Republic of; Peru
65	Peru – Singapore	2009	Peru; Singapore
66	Singapore – Australia	NA	Australia; Singapore
67	Singapore – Chinese Taipei	2014	Chinese Taipei; Singapore
68	Thailand – Australia	2005	Australia; Thailand
69	Thailand – New Zealand	2005	New Zealand; Thailand
70	Turkey – Malaysia	2015	Malaysia; Turkey

(cont.)

ID	RTA	Year entry into force	Signatories
71	United States – Australia	2005	Australia; United States of America
72	United States – Bahrain	2006	Bahrain, Kingdom of; United States of America
73	United States – Chile	2004	Chile; United States of America
74	United States – Colombia	2012	Colombia; United States of America
75	United States – Jordan	2001	Jordan; United States of America
76	United States – Morocco	2006	Morocco; United States of America
77	United States – Oman	2009	Oman; United States of America
78	United States – Panama	2012	Panama; United States of America
79	United States – Peru	2009	Peru; United States of America
80	United States – Singapore	2004	Singapore; United States of America
81	EU – Singapore	2019	Singapore; European Union; Austria; Belgium; Bulgaria; Croatia; Cyprus; Czech Republic; Denmark; Estonia; Finland; France; Germany; Greece; Hungary; Ireland; Italy; Latvia; Lithuania; Luxembourg; Malta; Netherlands; Poland; Portugal; Romania; Slovak Republic; Slovenia; Spain; Sweden; United Kingdom
82	Comprehensive and Progressive Agreement for Trans-Pacific Partnership (CPTPP)	2018	Australia: Brunei; Canada; Chile; Japan; Malaysia; Mexico; New Zealand; Peru; Singapore; Viet Nam

(*cont.*)

ID	RTA	Year entry into force	Signatories
83	EU – Japan (JEEPA)	2019	Japan; European Union; Austria; Belgium; Bulgaria; Croatia; Cyprus; Czech Republic; Denmark; Estonia; Finland; France; Germany; Greece; Hungary; Ireland; Italy; Latvia; Lithuania; Luxembourg; Malta; Netherlands; Poland; Portugal; Romania; Slovak Republic; Slovenia; Spain; Sweden; United Kingdom
84	EU – Mexico	NA	Mexico; European Union; Austria; Belgium; Bulgaria; Croatia; Cyprus; Czech Republic; Denmark; Estonia; Finland; France; Germany; Greece; Hungary; Ireland; Italy; Latvia; Lithuania; Luxembourg; Malta; Netherlands; Poland; Portugal; Romania; Slovak Republic; Slovenia; Spain; Sweden; United Kingdom
85	EU – Viet Nam	NA	Viet Nam; European Union; Austria; Belgium; Bulgaria; Croatia; Cyprus; Czech Republic; Denmark; Estonia; Finland; France; Germany; Greece; Hungary; Ireland; Italy; Latvia; Lithuania; Luxembourg; Malta; Netherlands; Poland; Portugal; Romania; Slovak Republic; Slovenia; Spain; Sweden; United Kingdom
86	USCMA	2020	Canada; Mexico; United States
87	Hong Kong – Georgia	2019	Hong Kong, China; Georgia
88	EU – Côte d'Ivoire	2016	Côte d'Ivoire; European Union; Austria; Belgium; Bulgaria; Croatia; Cyprus; Czech Republic; Denmark; Estonia; Finland; France; Germany; Greece; Hungary; Ireland; Italy; Latvia;

(*cont.*)

ID	RTA	Year entry into force	Signatories
			Lithuania; Luxembourg; Malta; Netherlands; Poland; Portugal; Romania; Slovak Republic; Slovenia; Spain; Sweden; United Kingdom
89	China – Chile	2019	China; Chile
90	Singapore – Sri Lanka	2018	Singapore; Sri Lanka
91	Singapore – Turkey	2017	Singapore; Turkey
92	EFTA – GCC	2014	Iceland; Liechtenstein; Norway; Switzerland; United Arab Emirates; Bahrain; Saudi Arabia; Oman; Qatar; Kuwait
93	EU – Armenia	2018	Armenia; European Union; Austria; Belgium; Bulgaria; Croatia; Cyprus; Czech Republic; Denmark; Estonia; Finland; France; Germany; Greece; Hungary; Ireland; Italy; Latvia; Lithuania; Luxembourg; Malta; Netherlands; Poland; Portugal; Romania; Slovak Republic; Slovenia; Spain; Sweden; United Kingdom
94	Trans-Pacific Strategic Economic Partnership Agreement	2006	Brunei; Chile; New Zealand; Singapore
95	EU – Cameroon	2014	Cameroon; European Union; Austria; Belgium; Bulgaria; Croatia; Cyprus; Czech Republic; Denmark; Estonia; Finland; France; Germany; Greece; Hungary; Ireland; Italy; Latvia; Lithuania; Luxembourg; Malta; Netherlands; Poland; Portugal; Romania; Slovak Republic; Slovenia; Spain; Sweden; United Kingdom

(*cont.*)

ID	RTA	Year entry into force	Signatories
96	EU – Algeria	2005	Algeria; European Union; Austria; Belgium; Bulgaria; Croatia; Cyprus; Czech Republic; Denmark; Estonia; Finland; France; Germany; Greece; Hungary; Ireland; Italy; Latvia; Lithuania; Luxembourg; Malta; Netherlands; Poland; Portugal; Romania; Slovak Republic; Slovenia; Spain; Sweden; United Kingdom
97	EU – Bosnia and Herzegovina	2015	Bosnia and Herzegovina; European Union; Austria; Belgium; Bulgaria; Croatia; Cyprus; Czech Republic; Denmark; Estonia; Finland; France; Germany; Greece; Hungary; Ireland; Italy; Latvia; Lithuania; Luxembourg; Malta; Netherlands; Poland; Portugal; Romania; Slovak Republic; Slovenia; Spain; Sweden; United Kingdom
98	Australia – Peru	2020	Australia; Peru
99	Argentina – Chile	2019	Argentina; Chile
100	Brazil – Chile	NA	Brazil; Chile
101	Australia – Indonesia	2020	Australia; Indonesia
102	Chile – Uruguay	NA	Chile; Uruguay
103	DEPA	NA	Chile; New Zealand; Singapore
104	US – Japan Digital Trade Agreement	2020	Japan; United States
105	Australia – Hong Kong	2020	Australia; Hong Kong

ABBREVIATIONS

AB	Appellate Body
ADA	Agreement on Implementation of Article VI of the General Agreement on Tariffs and Trade 1994 (Anti-dumping Agreement)
AVMSD	Audiovisual Media Services Directive (European Union)
BPM	Balance of Payments Manual (International Monetary Fund)
CAD	computer-aided design
CEFTA	Central European Free Trade Agreement
CETA	Comprehensive Economic and Trade Agreement between Canada and the European Union
CPC	Central Product Classification
CPTPP	Comprehensive and Progressive Agreement for Trans-Pacific Partnership
CTS	Council for Trade in Services (World Trade Organization)
CUP	China UnionPay Co. Ltd
DNS	domain name system
DLR	data localisation requirement
DSM	dispute settlement mechanism
DST	digital services tax
DSU	Understanding on Rules and Procedures Governing the Settlement of Disputes (Dispute Settlement Understanding)
EBOPS	Extended Balance of Payments Services Classifications
e-commerce	electronic commerce
EEA	European Economic Area
EPS	electronic payment services
ESA	Eastern and Southern Africa
EU	European Union
eWTP	electronic world trade platform
FCC	(US) Federal Communications Commission
FDI	foreign direct investment
FED	Friends of E-commerce for Development (WTO negotiation group)
GATS	General Agreement on Trade in Services
GATT	General Agreement on Tariffs and Trade (1994)

GCC	Gulf Cooperation Council
GDPR	General Data Protection Regulation
GVC	global value chain
IaaS	infrastructure as a service
ICANN	The Internet Corporation for Assigned Names and Numbers
ICP	Internet content provider
IGF	Internet Governance Forum
ICT	Information and Communications Technology
IoT	Internet of Things
IP	intellectual property
IPR	intellectual property rights
ISIC	International Standard Industrial Classification of All Economic Activities (United Nations)
ISP	Internet service provider
ITA	Information Technology Agreement
ITU	International Telecommunication Union
KORUS	Korea–United States free trade agreement
LDC	least developed country
MFN	most-favoured-nation
MLEC	Model Law on Electronic Commerce
MRA	mutual recognition agreement
MSITS	Manual on Statistics of International Trade in Services
(M)SME	(micro-), small- and medium-sized enterprise
NAP	network access point
NIST	National Institute of Standards and Technology (United States)
NTB	non-tariff barrier
NTM	non-tariff measures
OECD	Organisation for Economic Co-operation and Development
OED	Oxford English Dictionary
OTT	over-the-top services
PaaS	platform as a service
R&D	research and development
RTA	regional trade agreement
SaaS	software as a service
SCA	Stored Communications Act (United States)
SCM	Agreement on Subsidies and Countervailing Measures
STRI	Services Trade Restrictiveness Index
SNA	System of National Accounts
SOE	state-owned enterprise
TBT	Agreement on Technical Barriers to Trade
TFA	Trade Facilitation Agreement
TiSA	Trade in Services Agreement

TRIPS	WTO Agreement on Trade-Related Intellectual Property Rights
UN	United Nations
UNCITRAL	United Nations Commission on International Trade Law
UNCTAD	United Nations Conference on Trade and Development
US	United States
USITC	United States International Trade Commission
USMCA	United States–Mexico–Canada Agreement
USTR	United States Trade Representative
VCLT	Vienna Convention on the Law of Treaties
VOD	video on demand
VoIP	Voice over Internet Protocol
VPN	virtual private network
WPEC	Work Programme on Electronic Commerce (World Trade Organization)
WTO	World Trade Organization
W3C	World Wide Web Consortium

Introduction

The Uruguay Round and the Advent of the Internet

The emergence of the Internet and the phenomenon of the digitisation of traditional goods and services has had a major impact on global trade. In the same way as digital goods and services have seeped into every aspect of our daily lives, digitisation has permeated international trade, heavily impacting cross-border trade in goods and services. Goods need no longer be bought in brick-and-mortar stores but can now be ordered online with minimal effort. Goods produced on the other side of the world are only one click away and consumers are spoiled with endless choice in virtual marketplaces. The rise of electronic commerce has caused the creation of so-called multi-sided platforms, whose business model is built on enabling transactions between two or more distinct types of customers (e.g. sellers and buyers). Some of these platforms have gained immense market shares and are starting to dominate the economic landscape in various sectors.

The terms Internet and electronic commerce (or e-commerce) mainly evoke images of mighty platforms that enable immediate access to thousands of foreign sellers, Amazon's patented '1-Click' ordering and the delivery of countless packages through courier services. However, trade in physical goods that are ordered online is only a part of what e-commerce encompasses. Services have actually been affected most by the rise of the Internet, as it allows them to be traded increasingly across borders, it blurs the distinction between goods and services and it allows for a general growth in services trade.[1] Through use of the Internet, most types of services can now be provided without requiring any physical proximity between service provider and consumer. This has caused a significant surge in global trade in (digital) services.

[1] Joshua P Meltzer, 'Maximizing the Opportunities of the Internet for International Trade' (International Centre for Trade and Sustainable Development (ICTSD) 2016) 12 <https://e15initiative.org/publications/maximizing-opportunities-internet-international-trade/>.

This book deals with the phenomenon of digital services from the perspective of international trade law. As part of the international economic law framework, international trade law regulates trade between countries. International trade law instruments have all been created under the auspices of the World Trade Organization (WTO). This work analyses relevant international trade law instruments applicable to digital services trade, assessing *how* they apply to these digital services. The book therefore centres on an in-depth study of the General Agreement on Trade in Services (GATS), at the multilateral level, as well as regional trade agreements (RTAs) that contain provisions relevant to digital services trade, at the regional level.

The WTO Agreements were negotiated during the Uruguay Negotiation Round, which lasted from 1986 to 1994. This means that the GATS, the agreement dealing with international trade in services, also dates back to the early nineties. Its obligations have thus been negotiated around the same time that Tim Berners-Lee invented the World Wide Web (the most common way to access data online). Even though the technology on which the Internet is based dates back to the 1970s, commercial use of the Internet only became commonplace by the end of the 1990s, early 2000s. Whereas the technology behind the Internet definitely already existed when the WTO Agreements were negotiated, the remark that the technologies that are now used to trade digitally were in their infancy holds true to some extent.[2] At the same time, what we now consider as quintessential digital trade often already existed in an offline form. For example, information (or data) used to be circulated on floppy disks, whereas now, data mainly flows digitally.

The agreements resulting from the Uruguay Negotiation Round did not anticipate the way in which the Internet would impact international trade. This has prompted the question whether agreements that date back to 1994 can be applied unencumbered to this 'new way of trading'. Due to the proliferation of digital services trade, the need for appropriate regulation has arisen. Adequate provisions should allow for necessary regulation of electronic commerce, while at the same time avoiding protectionism through the creation of unnecessary (regulatory) barriers to trade in services.

The possible issues created by electronic commerce in relation to the WTO legal framework already came to the fore in 1998. The establishment

[2] Amazon and eBay, as prime examples of large global e-commerce platforms, were both established in the United States in 1995.

of the Work Programme on Electronic Commerce (WPEC) was supposed to provide for a forum in which WTO Members could clarify, *inter alia*, the applicability of the existing framework. The Council for Trade in Services (CTS) was explicitly asked to examine and report on the treatment of electronic commerce in the GATS legal framework.[3] For the last twenty years, Members have held discussions on electronic commerce within the context of not only the CTS but also the Council for Trade in Goods, the Council for TRIPS and the Committee on Trade and Development. However, so far, progress has been extremely limited. The WPEC's main achievement to date is that it has successfully highlighted the diverging opinions of WTO Members on how the existing framework applies (or should apply) to electronic commerce.

Even though scholarship on the position of electronic commerce within the international trade law framework is slowly increasing, there is only a handful of scholars that have started to address the legal questions surrounding digital services and the barriers these services are confronted with. It therefore remains unclear, on the one hand, how the GATS can be applied to barriers to digital services trade, and on the other hand, how RTAs are addressing possible lacunae in the multilateral framework.

This book was written with the aim to answer a specific question: can the specific barriers to digital services trade be addressed within the existing international legal framework applicable to services trade? A legal analysis is conducted to determine to what extent WTO Agreements and RTAs are applicable to digital services and what obligations arise from commitments made or provisions agreed to, in order to assess whether the specific barriers that digital services trade is confronted with can be addressed.

This book is divided into four parts. Part I introduces the issues related to the unclear legal framework applicable to digital services trade. It discusses the phenomenon of digitisation, which has contributed significantly towards the prevalence of digital services trade nowadays. The increased trade in digital services also raises questions as to the applicable legal framework. By sketching the context in which digital services have emerged, this part aims to clarify the importance of digital services in twenty-first-century trade, thereby intensifying the need to map the legal framework applicable to trade in such services. This part also elaborates

[3] WTO, 'Work Programme on Electronic Commerce – Adopted by the General Council on 25 September 1998', WT/L/274, 30 September 1998, para 2.1.

on what is understood under 'digital services' and what types of barriers trade in digital services is confronted with.

Part II of the research deals with the applicability of the GATS to digital services and the classification of digital services within the GATS' existing classification system Classification of services within the GATS is necessary to determine what specific obligations apply to each WTO Member. This part of the research lays the groundwork for the analysis of the WTO consistency of the identified barriers in Part III. Once the applicability of the GATS is established and the services are adequately classified, the GATS can be applied to the barriers to digital services trade.

Part III of the research sets out the relevant GATS obligations and applies them to four case studies. It additionally frames the other barriers in the context of the GATS. First, the different obligations under the GATS and their applicability to digital services trade are discussed. These obligations are subsequently applied to four specific case studies: Russia's amended Law on Personal Data, the EU's General Data Protection Regulation, China's Great Firewall and the US' Restoring Internet Freedom Order.

In the fourth and final part of the book, I discuss the electronic commerce provisions in RTAs. First, a general study of e-commerce RTAs is conducted. I use descriptive statistics methods to map historical, geographical and income level-related evolutions of electronic commerce-related provisions in RTAs. Second, an in-depth analysis of six RTAs that contain significant provisions on e-commerce is conducted. It compares the approaches that have been taken in these different agreements regarding digital services trade: how they define digital services, how they delineate the scope of their e-commerce chapter and how they address the specific barriers to digital services trade.

PART I

Digitisation and International Trade

Twenty-first-century trade is characterised by two developments: first, the fragmentation of production into global value chains (GVCs), crossing various borders, and second, the digitisation of production and trade, which has led to a growing electronic cross-border delivery of services and the increased trade in digital products. Both evolutions help explain the proliferation of digital services trade and consequently also the importance of enacting a clear and comprehensive international legal framework for digital services. In many ways, the consequences and problems faced due to digitisation are symptomatic of the position of services within GVCs and the ensuing barriers these services are faced with.

These two phenomena are interlinked to a high degree. The effective use of GVCs requires a constant flow of large amounts of data across borders.[4] The economic dimension of the Information and Communications Technology (ICT) revolution is reflected in both the transformation of supply and demand chains and the internal restructuring of organisations.[5] Digital trade encompasses not only digital services, which constitute the focus of this book, but also trade that is enabled through growing connectivity.[6] Even though not all trade is necessarily digitally delivered, it is nowadays all digitally enabled in one way or another.

For the purpose of this book, 'digitisation' is understood to refer to the increased incorporation of digital technologies and digitised processes in global trade. This phenomenon is one of the main causes of the increased cross-border flows of data. Even though it is difficult to measure the amount of cross-border data flows, it has become clear that Internet population, Internet usage and cross-border Internet traffic

[4] Meltzer, 'Maximizing the Opportunities of the Internet for International Trade' (n 1) 8.

[5] Rolf Weber and Mira Burri, *Classification of Services in the Digital Economy* (Springer 2013) 2.

[6] Javier Lopez-Gonzalez and Janos Ferencz, 'Digital Trade and Market Openness' (OECD 2018) Working Party of the Trade Committee TAD/TC/WP (2018)3/FINAL 25–26.

have all increased immensely in the last two decades.[7] With the evolution of the 'Web 2.0',[8] the Internet has developed into a space of open innovation and collaboration, with a focus on user-generated content.[9] This evolution increased the Internet's contribution to economic growth and international trade as it allows for a new range of economic activities.

In addition, the analysis and management of big data have become an essential part of the Internet in the twenty-first century.[10] Big data is defined as 'data sets with sizes that are beyond the ability of commonly used software tools to capture, curate, manage and process within a tolerable degree of time'.[11] It is also this data and its flow across borders that allow for the potential economic growth and increased use of the Internet in all kinds of service sectors (including healthcare, education and tourism).

This part first focusses on providing a clear explanation of what is understood under 'digitisation', what digital platforms are, how servicification and the rise of digital products have blurred the distinction between goods and services (which underpins the existing international trade rules), what cross-border data flows entail and how the Internet functions. Furthermore, the impact of digitisation on international trade in general, and trade in services specifically, is explained, highlighting both the benefits and issues related to it. Finally, the barriers that digital services trade faces are explained, which provides the basis for the rest of the legal analysis conducted in this book.

[7] Susan Lund and James Manyika, 'How Digital Trade Is Transforming Globalisation' (International Centre for Trade and Sustainable Development (ICTSD) 2016) 2 <https://e15initiative.org/publications/how-digital-trade-is-transforming-globalisation/>.

[8] The difference with 'Web 1.0' lies in the fact that people using the Internet used to be limited to passively viewing content available on the Internet. The transition to 'Web 2.0' is not linked to technical changes or upgrades but was merely prompted by the different *use* of this platform.

[9] Joshua P Meltzer, 'Supporting the Internet as a Platform for International Trade Opportunities for Small and Medium-Sized Enterprises and Developing Countries' (Brookings 2014) Working Paper 69, 3 <https://papers.ssrn.com/sol3/papers.cfm?abstract_id=2400578>.

[10] ibid.

[11] ibid 1.

1

Digitisation and Its Terminology

Part of the confusion surrounding digital services trade specifically, but also e-commerce in general, is caused by the fact that digital trade comes with its own terminology, which is often unfamiliar to the average trade lawyer. Not only does the WTO itself not make use of the term 'digital services', other terms have popped up in the debate without Members reaching consensus on their meaning. Such terms include 'digital platforms', 'digital product', 'digital content', 'data' and 'data flows'. I will analyse these terms and determine their position in relation to the definition of digital services as used in this book.

The creation of the Internet has allowed for the emergence of new business models, bringing users and information together, hosting user-generated content and promoting social and commercial connections, connecting buyers and sellers and creating new platforms for businesses in other sectors of the economy.[12] This results in the Internet affecting the global economy in two ways: (i) by making business more competitive, through the use of the Internet and data as enablers of economic activity;[13] and (ii) by granting businesses unprecedented access to consumers worldwide, thereby directly enabling international trade.[14] The productivity gains from digitisation are manifold and include access to competitive online services, as well as access to online market information.[15] The Internet allows for transactions that were previously impossible due to prohibitive costs.[16] The World

[12] ibid.

[13] Important to note is that this is an economy-wide phenomenon, affecting various service sectors across the economy and not only those directly related to the information technology (IT) sector.

[14] Joshua P Meltzer, 'The Internet and International Data Flows in the Global Economy' (International Centre for Trade and Sustainable Development (ICTSD) 2016) <http://e15initiative.org/blogs/the-internet-and-international-data-flows-in-the-global-economy/>.

[15] ibid.

[16] By removing information asymmetries, the Internet promotes a more inclusive trading environment. Digitisation entails market creation effects. World Bank, 'Digital Dividends' (The World Bank 2016) World Development Report 9–10.

Bank highlights the inclusiveness of the Internet and how it promotes inclusion of firms in the world economy in different ways. The Internet is a means to expand trade, raise productivity of capital or intensify competition by inducing innovation.[17] Moreover, digital trade has allowed companies to branch out into other service sectors, thereby breaking down traditional sector divides.[18]

As shown by Lopez-Gonzalez and Ferencz, there is a clear positive relationship between trade openness and digital connectivity. However, the direction in which the causality applies is less straightforward. Does digital connectivity foster trade openness or does a country's openness to trade stimulate its adoption of digital technologies?[19] Digitisation has transformed global trade through the creation of three different phenomena: (i) digital platforms, which allow for unprecedented international connections by driving down costs of cross-border transactions; (ii) the virtual and immediate trading of purely digital goods and services; and (iii) access to cross-border data flows, which has become crucial for the functioning of modern economies as well as GVCs.[20] These three phenomena are discussed in more depth in the following sections.

17 ibid 11.

18 For example, e-commerce platforms like Amazon not only enable the sale of physical goods but have also branched out to cloud services, streaming services, and so on.

19 Lopez-Gonzalez and Ferencz (n 6) 61. They refer to various other studies that have shown the positive relationship between digitisation and trade: Caroline Freund and Diana Weinhold, 'The Internet and International Trade in Services' (2002) 92 American Economic Review 236; Caroline Freund and Diana Weinhold, 'The Effect of the Internet on International Trade' (2004) 62 Journal of International Economics 171; George RG Clarke and Scott Wallsten, 'Has the Internet Increased Trade? Developed and Developing Country Evidence' (2006) 44 Economic Inquiry 465; Vijay K Vemuri and Shadid Siddiqi, 'Impact of Commercialization of the Internet on International Trade: A Panel Study Using the Extended Gravity Model' (2009) 23 The International Trade Journal 458; Changkyu Choi, 'The Effect of the Internet on Service Trade' (2010) 109 Economics Letters 102; David Riker, 'Internet Use and Openness to Trade' (US International Trade Commission 2014) Office of Economics Working Paper 2014–12c; Sebastian Benz, Anupam Khanna and Hildegunn Kyvik Nordas, 'Services and Performance of the Indian Economy: Analysis and Policy Options' (OECD Publishing 2017) OECD Trade Policy Papers 196.

20 James Manyika and others, 'Digital Globalization: The New Era of Global Flows' (McKinsey Global Institute 2016) 33 <www.mckinsey.com/business-functions/digital-mckinsey/our-insights/digital-globalization-the-new-era-of-global-flows>. The McKinsey report refers to the third phenomenon as 'the use of digital wrappers to enhance the value of traditional products'. Digital wrappers will be discussed later as a specific examples of data flows as an added value to GVCs (*infra*, Section 1.3.2).

1.1 Digital Platforms

The digital economy is characterised by a platform-based ecosystem of digital products and services.[21] Digital platforms facilitate cross-border transactions, enabling a broad range of 'micro-exchanges'.[22] The Internet cuts search costs and harmonises prices as well as improving global marketing opportunities. This not only enables multinational firms to trade globally but also allows small companies to participate in global exporting.[23] Manyika et al. provide some examples of different digital platforms that are widely used, including e-market places (e.g. eBay and Amazon), operating systems (e.g. Android and iOS), social networks (e.g. Facebook, Twitter and Instagram) and digital media platforms (e.g. YouTube, Netflix and Spotify). Various other platforms allow for immediate contact between employers and jobseekers (e.g. LinkedIn), borrowers and lenders (e.g. Upwork, Kiva), creative projects and funders (e.g. Kickstarter) and travellers with accommodation (e.g. Airbnb). This allows for unprecedented international trade in (digital) services.[24] For example, e-commerce marketplaces create new global markets and enable micro-, small- and medium-sized enterprises (MSMEs) to export globally through the provision of inter alia payment infrastructure, logistics support and global visibility.[25] Additionally, digital platforms successfully match tasks across the whole skills spectrum, thereby considerably transforming labour markets.[26] Digital platforms constitute an integral part of the digital landscape. There are many different types of platforms but no universally agreed upon classification.[27]

Some platforms have been referred to as 'multisided platforms'. Such platforms have two defining traits: first, they take on the role of intermediary between two or more types of users; and second, the value of the platform for one user type depends on the number of users of the other

[21] UNCTAD, 'The Value and Role of Data in Electronic Commerce and the Digital Economy and Its Implications for Inclusive Trade and Development' (United Nations Conference on Trade and Development 2019) Note by the UNCTAD Secretariat TD/B/EDE/3/2, 2.

[22] This includes small/low-value transactions of goods, services, finance and labour. See Lund and Manyika (n 7) 5.

[23] ibid.

[24] Manyika and others (n 20) 33.

[25] ibid 34.

[26] UNCTAD, 'Fostering Developments Gains from E-Commerce and Digital Platforms' (United Nations Conference on Trade and Development 2018) TD/B/EDE/2/2, para 36.

[27] ibid 10.

types.[28] This creates a network effect: the more parties there are on either side, the more the other side benefits. Benefit to users grows significantly with the size of the network. Consequently, it can be economically optimal for multisided platforms to charge their customers below the marginal cost (or not at all).[29] An example of such a multisided platform is Android – an economic platform which creates value by bringing together four different parties: consumers, device makers, app developers and service providers.[30] In a market with network effects, consumers benefit from common standards as they allow for interoperability, variety and certainty.[31]

In its 2018 note, the UNCTAD Secretariat distinguishes different types of platforms on various bases: whether they are profit oriented, whether they deal in goods or services, whether they are incumbent or third-party platforms, etc. For each of the identified different types of platforms, examples are provided. It should, however, be kept in mind that many platforms are multipurpose. For example, Facebook is a social media platform which at the same time qualifies as a service e-commerce platform for advertising services. Platforms can additionally be distinguished based on the agents or users involved in the transaction: peer-to-peer, consumer-to-consumer, business-to-business, business-to-consumer or business-to-government.[32] The UNCTAD Secretariat identifies the following characteristics of platforms: (i) they provide infrastructure to intermediate between agents and users; (ii) they rely on network effects (which leads to monopolistic trends); (iii) they use cross-subsidisation; and (iv) they tend to outsource jobs and services.[33] It distinguishes between two general types of platforms: nonprofit-oriented digital platforms (including exchange platforms, donation platforms, free services platforms and other 'true' sharing economy platforms) and profit-oriented digital platforms (including electronic payment platforms, crowdfunding platforms, social media and e-commerce platforms). E-commerce platforms can further be divided into incumbent companies' e-commerce platforms and

[28] Oxera, 'Android in Europe: Benefits to Consumers and Businesses' (Oxera 2018) <www.oxera.com/wp-content/uploads/2018/10/Android-in-Europe-1.pdf>.

[29] ibid.

[30] More specifically, Android provides to consumers a user interface; to developers, an open source code base; to device makers, an industry standard; and to service providers, access to a large, global user base. ibid 4, 6.

[31] ibid 5.

[32] UNCTAD, 'Fostering Developments Gains from E-Commerce and Digital Platforms' (n 26) para 14.

[33] ibid 18.

third-party e-commerce platforms (which can be goods e-commerce platforms, services e-commerce platforms or a combination of both).[34]

1.2 Digital Products

In the context of this book, digital products are understood as commodities that solely consist of bits and bytes. The invention of computers and the advent of the Internet has allowed for the creation of such digital products, which are not always easily linked back to previously existing goods or services. A classic example of a digital product is a mobile application (or 'app'), which takes on various functions. The economic importance of these apps cannot be overestimated, as they enable all mobile phone holders to have access to information on transport, health, weather and to many other relevant data.[35]

Other examples of digital products include e-books, online games, MP3 music files, cloud services and streamed audiovisual products.[36] Due to their digital nature, these products are instantaneously tradable. Online access to digital products allows for easy and immediate transactions, with the additional benefit of the ability to create an 'international buzz' in promoting products.[37] The amount of digital products is expanding rapidly, with prospects of an even more differentiated range due to inventions like the 3D printer.[38] This printer allows for purely digital communication between the designer of the product and the consumer as the blueprints of the design can digitally be sent to a 3D printer located anywhere in the world and manufactured immediately.[39]

Internet of Things (IoT) products are another example of how technological advancements have made it increasingly difficult to distinguish between goods and services. IoT products like smartwatches, self-driving cars and intelligent thermostats and fridges consist of both the physical hardware and the personalised services that they enable. For example, when a consumer buys a smartwatch, they are not simply buying a watch with a built-in computer. Rather, they purchase the watch with the expectation that it will provide them with personalised information on their health and fitness. The software linked to the smartwatch might also

[34] For examples of the different types identified, see the figure at ibid 5.
[35] Meltzer, 'The Internet and International Data Flows in the Global Economy' (n 14).
[36] Manyika and others (n 20) 35.
[37] ibid.
[38] Lund and Manyika (n 7) 3.
[39] ibid 4.

allow for personalised fitness plans, and provide health data to their doctor as well as localisation services.

There is, however, considerable lack of clarity surrounding the concept of 'digital products' and whether they constitute goods or services. This classification is important as international trade rules are built on the goods versus services dichotomy.[40] Several elements should be considered in this debate.

1.2.1 *The Classification of Digital Products*

Many products that consist of content used to be distributed using a physical carrier and were therefore treated as goods (examples include books, movies on VCR and DVD, music on LP, cassette and CD, and software on floppy disks and CD). In recent decades, these products are, however, increasingly being distributed in electronic form (over the Internet).[41] Everyone is familiar with the concept of e-books, online access to movies and music as well as purchasing and downloading software online. It is, however, less clear how these products, often dubbed 'digital products', fit within the WTO framework. Should they still be classified as goods, even though they have become intangible and no longer physically cross borders? Does their mode of delivery (from physical distribution to electronic distribution) change their nature and should they therefore be considered as services? How does this impact the application of WTO obligations? Considering the limited obligations of the GATS,[42] would this entail that the distribution of, for example, physical films is subject to different obligations than its electronic counterpart?

When reference is made to 'digital products', this can in principle refer to both digital goods and digital services. The panel in *China – Publications and Audiovisual Products* has clarified that the contemporary use of the word 'product' refers to services as well as goods.[43] The

[40] The WTO's international trade rules are based on the clear distinction between trade in goods and services, as is apparent from the clear divide between rules applicable to trade in goods (the GATT and its annexed agreements) and the rules applicable to trade in services (the GATS).

[41] Or, put differently, 'products that are digitally encoded and that – before the rise of the Internet – were traditionally traded as part of a physical carrier medium' in Sacha Wunsch-Vincent, 'WTO, E-Commerce, and Information Technologies – From the Uruguay Round through the Doha Development Agenda' (Markle Foundation 2004) 10.

[42] See *infra* Section 6.1.2.

[43] The panel made this analysis in the context of its interpretation of the term 'audiovisual products'. It referred to both the dictionary meaning of the term 'product' as well as the

panel avoided going into the specific relationship between the importation of hard-copy sound recordings and further electronic distribution of these recordings.[44] It simply concluded that the measures affected the electronic distribution of sound recordings, and not the importation of the hard-copy sound recordings, and that therefore the GATT was not applicable. In this context, the panel denounced the United States' ambiguous use of the term 'products', as the United States used this term to refer both to the imported physical product as well as the electronic content. The Panel stated that such use unjustly blurred the distinction between hard-copy sound recordings and electronic sound recordings.[45] It additionally clarified that digital distribution or communication, based on the dictionary meaning of 'digital', can also include other means than the Internet. Digital distribution is therefore broader than distribution over the Internet, including, for example, mobile phone networks.[46] The Appellate Body confirmed that the term 'product' is used to refer to both tangible and intangible goods as well as services.[47]

In the context of the debate on whether digital products qualify as goods or services, two elements have so far been (implicitly) agreed on.[48] First, goods that are ordered over the Internet but delivered physically still qualify as trade in goods (which entails applicability of the GATT). Second, online services that do not implicate downloaded or stored content are still services (which entails applicability of the GATS). One of the main interpretative problems is, however, caused by those products which used to be traded on physical carriers but that can now be traded over the Internet, without ever being transferred to a physical carrier.

An example of such a problematic product is 'software'. In 1998, the WTO Secretariat noted that computer software does not seem to be covered by the existing services classification list, considering that computer and related services are mainly concerned with consultancy

usage of the term in the CPC as referenced by China and many other WTO Members in their services schedules. See Panel Report, *China – Publications and Audiovisual Products*, para 7.1188.

44 Panel Report, *China – Publications and Audiovisual Products*, paras 7.1641–7.1653. This issue was not appealed.

45 Panel Report, *China – Publications and Audiovisual Products*, para 7.1642.

46 ibid para 7.1152.

47 AB Report, *China – Publications and Audiovisual Products*, para 364; see also ibid para 7.1188.

48 Tim Wu, 'The World Trade Law of Censorship and Internet Filtering' (2006) 7 Chicago Journal of International Law 263, 268.

services.[49] Some Members, however, disagreed and suggested that software that consists of 'sets of instructions to make computers work and communicate' falls within the GATS computer and related services sector.[50] Considering that the creation of custom-made software or the customisation of existing software is covered in the services classification list,[51] can it be inferred that the development of all forms of software would equally be covered? So far, the status of software within the WTO remains an outstanding question.[52] It was reported that a Member stressed that the service of making software and the classification of software should not be confused.[53] The WTO Secretariat reported that some national and international statistical groups are looking into classifying certain standardised software products within a new service sector, named 'software publishing'.[54] In its 2003 submission to the Work Programme on Electronic Commerce (WPEC), the United States clarified that a change in the means of delivery of a product does not change that product's functional characteristics (which is an expression of the principle of technological neutrality[55]). However, it also stated that the focus should not be on how to classify 'software' but rather on how to treat software for trade purposes 'with the goal being the most liberal treatment irrespective of how such products are classified'.[56] This last

[49] WTO Council for Trade in Services, 'Computer and Related Services' Background Note by the Secretariat, S/C/W/45, 14 July 1998, paras 2 and 9.

[50] WTO Council for Trade in Services, 'Understanding on the Scope of Coverage of CPC 84 – Computer Services' Communication from Albania, Australia, Canada, Chile, Colombia, Croatia, the European Communities, Hong Kong China, Japan, Mexico, Norway, Peru, the Separate Customs Territory of Taiwan Penghu, Kinmen and Matsu, Turkey and the United States, TN/S/W/60, S/CSC/W/51, 26 January 2007, fn 2.

[51] More specifically, in subsector 1.B.b. (software implementation services – CPC 843).

[52] As also noted by the Chairman of the Committee on Specific Commitments: WTO Committee on Specific Commitments, 'Computer and Related Services Overview of Classification Issues' Informal Note by the Secretariat, JOB/SERV/39, 4 March 2011, para 11; WTO Committee on Specific Commitments, 'Informal Discussion of Classification Issues on Computer and Related Services (CRS) on 10 March 2011 – Summary by the Chairperson', JOB/SERV/44, 4 April 2011, para 12, and in the context of the Secretariat's Background Note: WTO Council for Trade in Services, 'Computer and Related Services' Background Note by the Secretariat, S/C/W/300, 22 June 2009, para 6.

[53] WTO Committee on Specific Commitments, 'Informal Discussion of Classification Issues on Computer and Related Services (CRS) on 10 March 2011 – Summary by the Chairperson', JOB/SERV/44, 4 April 2011, para 13.

[54] WTO Council for Trade in Services, 'Computer and Related Services' Background Note by the Secretariat, S/C/W/300, 22 June 2009, para 7.

[55] This principle is explained and elaborated upon in Section 4.2.3.

[56] WTO Work Programme on Electronic Commerce, 'Submission from the United States', WT/GC/W/493/Rev.1, 8 July 2003, para 7.

statement cannot simply be agreed with. Even though liberalisation of trade in digital products arguably benefits consumers, the liberalisation objective should not unreservedly dictate the classification debate.

1.2.2 The EU–US Juxtaposition

When considering this issue in more detail, it becomes clear that no consensus exists between WTO Members on what these products constitute and, consequently, what WTO Agreements apply to them. In its 1999 special progress report, the General Council acknowledged that several delegations expressed the view that all digital products are services. Other delegations, however, signalled that to them it wasn't entirely clear that all electronically delivered products are services.[57] In 2004, Mueller already noted that 'the line between "product" and "service" will erode'.[58] It has been put forward that neither GATT nor GATS is comprehensive enough to cover e-commerce issues and that merely extending the concepts (which are based on territorial and geographical notions, i.e. modes of supply) does not suffice.[59]

In 1998, the WTO WPEC was set up to try to deal with some of these issues. In the context of this work programme, a clear juxtaposition regarding the classification of digital media emerged between the European and US view. Whereas the EU (then, European Communities) classifies all electronic deliveries as '*supplies of services which fall within the scope of the GATS*' (arguably allowing it to classify digital media as 'audiovisual services', entailing limited commitments),[60] the United States focusses on the principle of technological neutrality, stating that the classification should focus on the digital products themselves regardless of whether they have been delivered electronically or

[57] WTO Council for Trade in Services, 'Work Programme on Electronic Commerce – Progress Report to the General Council' Adopted by the Council for Trade in Services on 19 July 1999, S/L/74, 27 July 1999, para 6.

[58] Milton Mueller, 'Convergence: A Reality Check' in Damien Geradin and David Luff (eds), *The WTO and Global Convergence in Telecommunications and Audio-Visual Services* (Cambridge University Press 2004) 321.

[59] Farrokh Farrokhnia and Cameron Richards, 'E-Commerce Products under the World Trade Organization Agreements: Goods, Services, Both or Neither?' (2016) 50 Journal of World Trade 793, 816.

[60] WTO Work Programme on Electronic Commerce, 'Communication from the European Communities and their Member States', S/C/W/183, 30 November 2000, 3.

not.[61] The EU responded that the principle of technological neutrality is not a WTO principle requiring the classification of digitised products as goods covered by the GATT.[62]

In its 1999 Communication, the EU acknowledged that electronic commerce involves two types of deliveries, with different agreements applying to these types: (i) the online ordering but physical delivery of goods, to which the GATT applies; and (ii) the electronic delivery of services, to which the GATS applies.[63] In a 2000 communication, the EU asserted that Members had already agreed that the majority of digital products are services and that the disagreement was limited to a small number of unidentified electronically delivered products.[64] In 2003, the EU went even further and elaborated on why electronically delivered products do not classify as goods.[65] It stated that the GATT schedules do not cover 'digitised information'.[66] The EU has also made clear that the transmission of digitised information is covered by the GATS, regardless of the fact that such information can be stored on a physical carrier.[67] In the same submission, the EU went on to explain the applicability of GATS to any 'digitised product'.[68]

The United States does not agree with the EU on many of these points, raising the argument that a general classification of digital products as being services is incorrect because (i) digital products retain permanence,

[61] WTO Work Programme on Electronic Commerce, Submission by the United States, WT/GC/16, G/C/2, S/C/7, IP/C/16, WT/COMTD/17, 12 February 1999, 5.

[62] WTO Work Programme on Electronic Commerce, Submission for the European Communities, 'Classification Issue', WT/GC/W/497, 9 May 2003, 3. The principle of technological neutrality in the context of the GATS is discussed in more detail below, at Section 4.2.3.

[63] WTO General Council, 'Possible List of Trade Principles on Electronic Commerce', part of Communication from the European Communities and their Member States, WTO Work Programme on Electronic Commerce, preparations for the 1999 Ministerial Conference, WT/GC/W/306, 9 August 1999.

[64] It called on those Members disagreeing with a general services classification to identify the specific digital products that according to them did not classify as a service. See WTO Work Programme on Electronic Commerce, 'Communication from the European Communities and their Member States', S/C/W/183, 30 November 2000, para 5.

[65] WTO Work Programme on Electronic Commerce, Submission for the European Communities, 'Classification Issue', WT/GC/W/497, 9 May 2003, paras 5–9; see also WTO Council for Trade in Services, 'The Work Programme on Electronic Commerce' Note by the Secretariat, S/C/W/68, 16 November 1998, 10.

[66] WTO Work Programme on Electronic Commerce, Submission for the European Communities, 'Classification Issue', WT/GC/W/497, 9 May 2003, para 8.

[67] ibid paras 7–9.

[68] One of the arguments raised by the EU is that the physical outcome of certain services does not render the service itself a good. ibid paras 10–18.

(ii) other intangible products have been classified as goods (e.g. electricity) and (iii) the functional characteristics do not change because of a different means of delivery (the United States thereby argues that one should focus on the nature of the product, rather than the means through which it is provided).[69] Australia seems to approach more the EU position, arguing that there is more commonly an attribute of services rather than goods in digital products.[70] These discussions in the context of the WPEC have so far not reached a unanimously carried conclusion. Attempts to reinvigorate this debate at the WPEC have been undertaken by both the EU and the United States, proposing general principles intended to function as a basic harmonisation framework. So far to no avail, as the WTO Members have not subscribed to these principles.[71]

1.2.3 Practical Considerations in This Debate

In assessing whether digital products should be classified as goods or services, Mattoo and Schuknecht point out three considerations to be taken into account: (i) the applicability of the national treatment obligation; (ii) the applicability of customs duties; and (iii) the availability of quantitative restrictions (quotas).[72] The fact that there is no generally applicable national treatment obligation under the GATS gives countries more leeway to enact restrictive measures in uncommitted sectors, if digital products were to be classified as services. It can, however, also be noted that the national treatment obligation under the GATS has a broader scope[73] and that any type of discriminatory restriction (including taxes) is not allowed where Members

69 Rohan Kariyawasam, *International Economic Law and the Digital Divide: A New Silk Road?* (Edward Elgar Publishing 2007) 149–150.

70 WTO Council for Trade in Services, 'Work Programme on Electronic Commerce' Communication from Australia, S/C/W/108, 18 May 1999, paras 21–22.

71 WTO Council for Trade in Services, 'Contribution to the Work Programme on Electronic Commerce' Communication from the European Union and the United States, S/C/W/338, 13 July 2011; WTO Council for Trade in Services, 'Work Programme on Electronic Commerce: Ensuring that Trade Rules Support Innovative Advances in Computer Applications and platforms, such as Mobile Applications and the Provision of Cloud Computing Services' Communication from the United States, S/C/W/339, 20 September 2011. For more information on these principles, see Mira Burri, 'The International Economic Law Framework for Digital Trade' (2015) 135 Zeitschrift für Schweizerisches Recht 10, 45.

72 Aaditya Mattoo and Ludger Schuknecht, 'Trade Policies for Electronic Commerce' (World Bank 2000) 2380, 11–12 <https://elibrary.worldbank.org/doi/abs/10.1596/1813-9450-2380>.

73 Applying to all measures affecting trade in services (GATS), instead of only internal measures (GATT).

have undertaken national treatment commitments.[74] Whereas the GATT only allows for customs duties up to a Member's bound levels, the GATS requires a Member's tax regime to be consistent with its national treatment commitments. Finally, the GATT generally does not allow for quantitative restrictions. Under the GATS, quantitative restrictions are only prohibited where Members have undertaken market access commitments.

Kariyawasam defines the term 'electronic intangibles' (equivalent to the term digital product as used in this book) as '*digital combinations of binary code*'.[75] He also brings up the argument related to the applicability of market access and MFN obligations, which differs between the GATT and GATS, as well as the difficulty of enforcing customs duties on intangible products.[76] He adds that a classification of electronic intangibles as goods would lead to the applicability of many other agreements, including the Anti-dumping Agreement (ADA), the Agreement on Technical Barriers to Trade (TBT), the Agreement on Subsidies and Countervailing Measures (SCM) and the Import Licensing Agreement, arguably complicating the applicable framework. Another interesting argument raised by Kariyawasam relates to the scope of application of the GATT and the GATS. He argues that whereas the GATT would focus on the digital products themselves, in order to distinguish the different products and to be able to impose tariffs to these products, the GATS regulates measures that (in)directly restrict trade in (digital) services.[77] Taking that into account, it will prove easier and more straightforward to use the GATS to deal with these intangibles. Additionally, whereas the GATT focusses on cross-border trade, applying the GATS to digital products would imply not only cross-border trade, but also consumption abroad. He additionally points out that the characteristics of electronic intangibles point towards a services classification: the fact that many of them can be customised to the consumer's preference and the fact that many of them can be consumed on demand. Contrariwise, it has been argued that those digital products that can be locally stored and are transferable between buyers should be classified as goods.[78]

[74] Mattoo and Schuknecht (n 72) 12.

[75] Kariyawasam, *International Economic Law and the Digital Divide: A New Silk Road?* (n 69) 70–71.

[76] ibid 121–133.

[77] ibid 127, 135, 140.

[78] Other elements that can be considered here are whether ownership rights can be established, whether production output is owned and whether the use of the product is separate in time from its production.

Weber and Burri define 'digital products' as '*products that are digitally encoded and transmitted electronically*', which includes computer programs, texts, videos, images and sound recordings.[79] They do not go into this discussion in much depth, but note that as consumers are generally more interested in the content of the product, regardless of its physical carrier, digital products will generally be classified as communication services.[80] However, they also rightly point out that a common classification of all digital products is impossible, as the classification as a good or a service will depend on the characteristics of that specific digital product.[81]

An important consideration in trying to resolve the classification issue is indeed the fact that if a product is classified under the GATT while its electronically supplied equivalent is classified under the GATS, different national treatment and market access obligations would apply to what might be seen as 'like' products.[82] Wu argues for the classification of downloaded traditional goods (software, audio, video, newspapers, electronic books) as goods because of (i) the risk of backsliding of commitments, considering the limited commitments Members have undertaken under the GATS; and (ii) the possibility of different treatment of like products (those online and those offline). He indicates that the main argument to treat such products as services lies in the preservation of regulatory autonomy on audiovisual content.[83]

The abovementioned consequences of the applicability of either WTO Agreement are important elements in the debate. I, however, argue that the qualification of whether a digital product is a good or a service should be based on the specific characteristics of the product and not on what would be most convenient from a liberalisation standpoint. The

[79] Weber and Burri (n 5) 37.

[80] That is, sector 2 in the Services Sectoral Classification List (W/120), including *inter alia* telecommunications services and audiovisual services; ibid 4. The same position is taken by Zacharias, who defines 'digital products' as '*those products which can be stored as data*', see Diana Zacharias, 'Article I General Agreement on Trade in Services (GATS): Scope and Definition' in Rüdiger Wolfrum, Peter-Tobias Stoll and Clemens Feinäugle (eds), *Max Planck Commentaries on World Trade Law, Vol. 6: WTO – Trade in Services* (Martinus Nijhoff 2008) 43.

[81] Weber and Burri (n 5) 37.

[82] See Farrokhnia and Richards, (n 59) 813; WTO Council for Trade in Services, 'The Work Programme on Electronic Commerce' Note by the Secretariat, S/C/W/68, 16 November 1998, para 10.

[83] He argues that this concern reflects a different problem: the fact that the GATT does not include a general exception on the protection of culture. He notes, however, '*It's a mistake to suggest, for this reason alone, that all Internet content should be considered a service*'. Wu (n 48) 269.

abovementioned considerations are therefore duly noted but will not determine the subsequent classification of these products.

1.2.4 Change in Means of Delivery or Change in Nature of the Product?

The classification issue related to digital products is critical for digital trade.[84] Even though it has been confirmed by the Appellate Body in *EC – Bananas III* and *Canada – Autos* that the GATT and the GATS are not mutually exclusive, the uncertainty regarding the goods and services classification remains.[85] The most straightforward difference between both agreements as to their scope is that the GATT is allegedly limited to physical products (or '*tradeable items with actual or potential tariff classification*'),[86] whereas the GATS covers all services, regardless of the means of delivery.[87]

Neither the GATT nor the GATS contain a limitative definition of what a good or a service entails,[88] but the GATT Secretariat did issue an indicative list of 'relevant services' in 1991 in drafting document W/120.[89] In *Canada – Periodicals*, the Appellate Body focussed on the tangible and material nature of the product for classifying it as a good, regardless of the (limited) material importance of the tangible component to the value or economic reality of the good.[90] The Secretariat noted

[84] Burri, 'The International Economic Law Framework for Digital Trade' (n 71) 42.

[85] This, however, also entails the possibility of a product having both a good and a services component. ibid 40; Joost Pauwelyn, 'Squaring Free Trade in Culture with Chinese Censorship: The WTO Appellate Body Report on China – Audiovisuals' (2010) 11 Melbourne Journal of International Law 1, 8.

[86] Farrokhnia and Richards (n 59) 801–802; Pauwelyn (n 85) 8.

[87] Thereby implementing the principle of technological neutrality, which is elaborated on in Section 4.2.3.

[88] The GATS does provide some guidance on what is understood by 'supply of a service', Article XXVIII(b) GATS states that it '*includes the production, distribution, marketing, sale and delivery of services*'. Other guidance can be found in the definitions provided for service suppliers ('*any person that supplies a service*' in Article XXVIII(g) GATS, with person meaning '*either a natural person or a juridical person*' (Article XXVIII(j) GATS)) and for service consumers ('*any person that receives or uses a services*' (Article XXVIII(i) GATS)).

[89] See *infra* Section 5.1.1. WTO Council for Trade in Services, 'The Work Programme on Electronic Commerce' Note by the Secretariat, S/C/W/68, 16 November 1998, para 37.

[90] AB Report, *Canada – Periodicals*, 17. In *China – Publications and Audiovisual Products* the Appellate Body came to a different conclusion, finding that China's commitments re. 'sound recording distribution services' encompassed the distribution of both physical and non-physical products: AB Report, *China – Publications and Audiovisual Products*, paras 364–372; See also Pauwelyn (n 85) 9.

in 1998 that '*there is no classification which would permit us to say that all intangible products, or even all electronically delivered products, are services by definition*'.[91] It additionally clarified that the legal regime applicable to transactions is determined by the *nature* of the product being traded, rather than its means of delivery.[92]

The increased blurring between goods and services due to digitisation is aptly illustrated in a recent OECD working paper, which stated that '*goods are being substituted by services – for instances, printed books and DVDs are being replaced by e-books and movie downloading or streaming services [. . .]*'.[93] This observation raises the question of whether it is the nature of the products that change or merely their means of delivery. Is a novel or a movie a different product based on the means through which it is delivered to the consumer? Considering the WTO Secretariat's focus on the nature of the product rather than the means of delivery in classifying products, it could be argued that we are still dealing with the same product, it being either a good or a service, regardless of whether it is being delivered on a physical carrier or through the Internet.

A digitally traded product could therefore fall within the scope of either the GATT or GATS and it is impossible to make a blanket statement as to the nature of all digital products. As noted *supra* (Section 1.2.1), there should be no discussion on the nature of products ordered online and delivered physically (classified as goods) or of online services that are not downloaded or stored content (classified as services). When it comes to the contested category of digital products (those that used to be solely delivered on digital carriers but that can now be traded electronically), the focus should be on the *nature* of these products. Whether a book is sold on paper or in electronic form does not change its nature as a good. The same consideration applies to movies and packaged software.[94]

Here, it should be recalled that the GATT applies to *measures affecting trade in goods* and the GATS applies to *measures affecting the supply of services*. Whether we are, *in abstracto*, dealing with a good or a service is of relatively little practical significance. Rather, the focus should be on whether the measure at issue regulates the trade of goods or the supply of

91 WTO Council for Trade in Services, 'The Work Programme on Electronic Commerce' Note by the Secretariat, S/C/W/68, 16 November 1998, para 37.

92 ibid.

93 Lopez-Gonzalez and Ferencz (n 6) 34.

94 Packaged software is non-customised software that can be bought and used by a wide variety of consumers.

a service/the behaviour of service suppliers. This is also the approach taken by the Appellate Body in both *EC – Bananas III* and *Canada – Periodicals*.[95] I therefore submit that the classification of e-books, digital movies or packaged software as goods should not be accorded undue weight. The focus should rather be on what type of measure affects these products, to determine the applicable agreement in a dispute.

Burri rightfully notes that the debate on the classification of digital products is highly political.[96] The assessment of whether the GATT or GATS applies will always have to be done on a case-by-case basis.[97] The examples provided further in this study all clearly amount to services being supplied digitally.[98]

1.2.5 Digital Content

A final term that plays a role in this debate should be addressed. 'Digital content' constitutes a large part of products digitally traded. This term has been used to distinguish the (physical) carrier from its content when it comes to digital services. For example, the panel in *China – Publications and Audiovisual Services* clarified that the classification of sound recordings as a service is determined by its nature as 'content'.[99] In doing so, it distinguished between the content and the (physical) medium on which it is embedded or transferred.[100]

In the classification of services, WTO Members traditionally distinguish between the telecommunications service sector and the audiovisual service sector based on the dichotomy between transmission and content.[101] Whereas telecommunications services are linked to the transmission of information, audiovisual services represent the content that is being provided to end users via telecommunication transmission

[95] AB Report, *EC – Bananas III*, para 226 and AB Report, *Canada – Periodicals*, 18. Anupam Chander, 'The Internet of Things: Both Goods and Services' (2019) 18 World Trade Review 9, 19–20; RS Neeraj, 'Trade Rules for the Digital Economy: Charting New Waters at the WTO' (2019) 18 World Trade Review 121, 128.

[96] Mira Burri, 'Designing Future-Oriented Multilateral Rules for Digital Trade' in Pierre Sauvé and Martin Roy (eds), *Research Handbook on Trade in Services* (Edward Elgar Publishing 2016) 341.

[97] AB Report, *EC – Bananas*, para 221.

[98] See also the analysis as carried out in the AB Report, *Canada – Periodicals*, 17–20.

[99] Panel Report, *China – Publications and Audiovisual Services*, para 7.1176.

[100] ibid para 7.1175.

[101] This dichotomy is elaborated upon in Section 5.3.2.

services.[102] Peng already flags that this classic dichotomy feels significantly outdated when considering digital services. Various digital services consist of 'content' being transferred via the Internet, no longer requiring the traditional telecoms transmission.[103] Services that deliver content through an Internet platform have been labelled 'Over-the-Top (OTT) services'.[104] These OTT services are being provided without direct involvement of the transmission service supplier, while at the same time using the latter's networks and infrastructure.[105] Additionally, the classic dichotomy between the service suppliers of content and those of transmission is fading, as we see traditional telecom suppliers venturing beyond mere transmission of audiovisual products, also providing OTT services themselves.[106]

Regarding the use of the term 'content', Mueller notes that this '*strips programming capabilities of any particular form or medium, collapsing literature and journalism, music, paintings, movies and interactive games into a single category*'.[107] The largest factor in the widespread use of the term 'content' is the fact that, nowadays, various media forms can be stored, transmitted and manipulated on a single end-user platform.[108] Whereas different media used to have different carriers (and thus be technologically isolated), this is less and less the case as computers of all types can now deal with almost all media forms (books, music, video).[109] The term digital content has thus become seemingly all-encompassing.

It can therefore be argued that the term 'digital content' is too vague and does not aid in clarifying their position within the WTO legal

102 Shin-yi Peng, 'GATS and the Over-the-Top Services: A Legal Outlook' (2016) 50 Journal of World Trade 21, 22.

103 ibid 22–25.

104 'OTT services' is a commercial term, used to refer to services and applications that are offered by third parties and that allow service consumers (free) access to communications and information services that consumers would ordinarily be charged for by the underlying communication network. Examples of these OTT services include chat applications, streaming video services as well as voice calling services.

105 Peng illustrates this by stating '*consumers generally access the OTT content via an Internet connection independently of his or her contract with a telecom company*'. Moreover, many of these OTT services are in direct competition with the services offered by that telecom company. Peng, 'GATS and the Over-the-Top Services: A Legal Outlook' (n 102) 25.

106 Lee Tuthill and Martin Roy, 'GATS Classification Issues for Information and Communication Technology Services' in Mira Burri and Thomas Cottier (eds), *Trade Governance in the Digital Age* (Cambridge University Press 2012) 161.

107 Mueller (n 58) 313.

108 ibid.

109 ibid 314.

framework. Moreover, Members have voiced differing views on how digital content fits within the WTO framework. Australia stated that it supported the principle of technological neutrality, requiring a distinction to be made between 'carriage' and 'content' services. The former refers to the transmissions service, whereas the latter is the service that is being transmitted. Therefore, '*an audiovisual content service would not need to be reclassified because it was delivered in a different way – for example by using an Internet delivery service*'.[110] Japan opined that GATS disciplines should apply to the acts of supplying digital content electronically, while the GATT principles should apply to digital content.[111] It is clear that, so far, there is no consensus on the classification of digitisable media content.[112] Arguably, 'digital content' encompasses too broad a category of products to allow for a constructive contribution to the classification debate.

1.3 Cross-border Data Flows

One of the effects of the digitisation of the economy is the fact that very few transactions (if any) can be made without data crossing borders.[113] For a GVC to function, a continuous cross-border movement of large quantities of data is necessary. UNCTAD illustrates the exponential growth of data flows by looking into global Internet protocol (IP) traffic growth. Whereas Internet networks carried 100 GB of data per day in 1992, this has grown to 100 GB per second in 2002 and 45,000 GB per second in 2017.[114]

1.3.1 What Is Data?

So far, neither the term 'data' nor its characteristics have been defined in the context of the WTO. Looking at other sources, various definitions can

[110] These statements by Australia are made in the context of its reiteration of the importance of culture within its society, wanting to preserve policy space in the audiovisual services sector. WTO Council for Trade in Services, 'Report of the Meeting held on 9 to 12 July 2001' Note by the Secretariat, S/CSS/M/10, 21 September 2001, para 221.

[111] WTO General Council, 'Preparations for the 1999 Ministerial Conference – Electronic Commerce' Communication from Japan, WT/GC/W/253, 14 July 1999, para 10.

[112] Neeraj (n 95) 125.

[113] National Board of Trade, 'Data Flows. A Fifth Freedom for the Internal Market?' (National Board of Trade 2016), 9.

[114] UNCTAD, 'The Value and Role of Data in Electronic Commerce and the Digital Economy and Its Implications for Inclusive Trade and Development' (n 21) 2.

be found. The OECD defines data as '*characteristics or information, usually numerical, that are collected through observation*'.[115] Aaronson and Leblond clarify the different functions of data as '*a means of production, an asset that can be traded, and the means through which some services are traded and global value chains (GVCs) are organized*'.[116] Elsewhere, data has been defined as '*the raw material of which information and knowledge is produced*'.[117] Looking into its dictionary definition, Sen defines data as '*information in digital form*' and data flows as '*movement of information in digital form*', enabled through the technology of the Internet.[118] Data is increasingly becoming an essential input into decision-making and production processes, transactions and management in various service sectors.[119]

The Oxford English Dictionary (OED) defines 'data' as '*information in digital form*'. Data is created through the use of physical or digital devices, including sensors, webpages and applications. Any data that is gathered through Internet-based platforms is stored on servers, a kind of computing device that is directly connected to the Internet. As with more classic information sources, data creates its worth through being used by the owner of the data itself to gain a competitive advantage through information asymmetry and/or being sold to interested parties. Monetising data will most often require the (global) movement of data, or cross-border data flows.

Of course, data, or information, comes in various forms, with different characteristics. The different approaches taken in scholarship attest to the fact that there is no internationally agreed categorisation of data. Sen distinguishes between social data, business data, company data, personal data and sensitive data. These categories overlap in various places.[120] Aaronson identifies personal data, public data, confidential business data,

[115] The OECD refers to the International Statistical Institute's *The Oxford Dictionary of Statistical Terms*, edited by Yadolah Dodge (Oxford University Press 2003) as its source.

[116] Susan Ariel Aaronson and Patrick Leblond, 'Another Digital Divide: The Rise of Data Realms and Its Implications for the WTO' (2018) 21 Journal of International Economic Law 245, 248.

[117] National Board of Trade, 'Data Flows. A Fifth Freedom for the Internal Market?' (n 113) 10.

[118] Nivedita Sen, 'Understanding the Role of the WTO in International Data Flows: Taking the Liberalization or the Regulatory Autonomy Path?' (2018) 21 Journal of International Economic Law 323, 325.

[119] UNCTAD, 'The Value and Role of Data in Electronic Commerce and the Digital Economy and Its Implications for Inclusive Trade and Development' (n 21) 5.

[120] Sen (n 118) 343–345.

machine-to-machine data and metadata.[121] The protection of data will depend on its category: personal data will be protected more stringently than social data (which comprises large volumes of anonymised personal data, enabling study of behavioural patterns of large social units).[122] Concerns surrounding usage and movement of data will also depend on that data's category.[123]

The Internet has created increased possibilities for the collection and processing of data. This has also led to increased importance of data in production and provision of various goods and services. We are increasingly aware of the fact that data can be monetised.[124] Global digital platforms create value by aggregating and analysing data. The value of (big) data lies in the worth that businesses and researchers put on the ability to gain insights from large amounts of data.[125] As stated by the UNCTAD secretariat: '*data have [...] become a valuable extractable resource in the digital economy*'.[126] The emergence of the IoT, which extends the connectivity beyond people to objects and devices, enables a continuous real-time collection of data based on the sensors embedded in these objects.[127] IoT products involve transfer of data, storage of data, processing of data and provision of data services.[128]

The classification of data as a service or a good has recently attracted considerable discussion. So far, it remains unclear what position 'data' takes in the international economic law framework. Does it qualify as goods or rather services? Can it be argued that data is a *sui generis* commodity? Due to the limited focus of this book, data will only be

[121] As reproduced in Aaronson and Leblond (n 116) 249–250.
[122] Sen (n 118) 344.
[123] ibid 344–345.
[124] Monetising data can be done through targeted advertising, fostering innovation, providing better services and selling the service, infrastructure or software to be able to operate in the data-driven economy. See UNCTAD, 'The Value and Role of Data in Electronic Commerce and the Digital Economy and Its Implications for Inclusive Trade and Development' (n 21) 5; See also Alessio Botta, Nunzio Digiacomo and Kevin Mole, 'Monetizing Data: A New Source of Value in Payments' (McKinsey 2017) <www.mckinsey.com/industries/financial-services/our-insights/monetizing-data-a-new-source-of-value-in-payments>.
[125] Lee Tuthill, 'Cross-Border Data Flows: What Role for Trade Rules?' in Pierre Sauve and Martin Roy (eds), *Research Handbook on Trade in Services* (Edward Elgar Publishing 2016) 361.
[126] UNCTAD, 'Fostering Developments Gains from E-Commerce and Digital Platforms' (n 26) para 18.
[127] UNCTAD, 'The Value and Role of Data in Electronic Commerce and the Digital Economy and Its Implications for Inclusive Trade and Development' (n 21) 3.
[128] Chander (n 95) 14.

considered to the extent that it is ancillary to or necessary for the supply of digital services. Regulation of data that is a crucial input in the supply of digital services will fall within the scope of the GATS as it will qualify as 'a measure affecting trade in services'.[129] Chapter 3 will elaborate on the impact of restrictions on cross-border data flows on the supply of digital services.

1.3.2 Cross-border Data Flows

It is the constant cross-border flows of data that keep complex and geographically spread value chains functioning. The movement of data underpins the digital trade environment.[130] Access to the Internet and the continuous amount of data being gathered and shared is what makes twenty-first-century businesses competitive. Where cross-border flows of data are hampered, foreign firms are put at a competitive disadvantage as they can no longer engage in activities necessary to stay competitive (e.g. analyse consumer behaviour, provide payment and delivery methods).[131] This impacts both consumers as well as downstream producers.[132] Policymakers should be aware of the fact that even though not all international data flows are trade transactions, the restrictions put on them do significantly impact trade.[133]

Researchers and policymakers, however, disagree on how to characterise cross-border data flows. Porges and Enders divide cross-border data flows into three categories: (i) information and company data that are used to support production, marketing, sales, after-market services and the functionality of goods (this also includes personal data); (ii) trade (import as well as export) of digitally enabled services and goods, as well as e-commerce;[134] and (iii) the trade (import and export) of digitised content.[135] An example of the latter is the electronic delivery of digital

129 Article I.1 GATS.
130 Lopez-Gonzalez and Ferencz (n 6) 36; Tuthill (n 125) 357.
131 National Board of Trade, 'Data Flows. A Fifth Freedom for the Internal Market?' (n 113) 10.
132 ibid 11.
133 Lopez-Gonzalez and Ferencz (n 6) 36.
134 Regarding the delineation of e-commerce and the position of digitally enabled services within this context, see *infra* Section 2.4.
135 Amy Porges and Alice Enders, 'Data Moving Across Borders: The Future of Digital Trade Policy' (International Centre for Trade and Sustainable Development (ICTSD) 2016) <https://e15initiative.org/publications/data-moving-across-borders-the-future-of-digital-trade-policy/>.

files, including music, films, literature, games and software, directly to the consumer.[136]

They go even further in explaining the importance of cross-border data flow for trade, stating that '*in the 21st century, all enterprises that trade depend on the ability to move data*'.[137] Compiling and analysing data all over the world allows firms to mitigate supply chain risks, improve business performance and lower product prices.[138] Cross-border data flows are one of the hallmarks of twenty-first-century globalisation by reducing costs of transaction and allowing instant exchange of digital products.[139] It has been reported that country participation in global flows has had both short- (cyclical) as well as long-term (structural) impact on countries' GDP. The importance of data flows is emphasised by the fact that data flows now have a larger impact on global GDP than flows of goods.[140] The concept of data flows is, however, not exclusive to twenty-first-century trade. Already in 1980, the OECD issued Guidelines Governing the Protection of Privacy and Transborder Flows of Personal Data.[141]

An example of the increased incorporation of digital functionality in manufacturing and services production, as well as in the goods or services output, is the concept of 'digital wrappers'. 'Digital wrappers' are an important element in twenty-first-century trading since long and complex supply chains require a continuous flow of up-to-date data to be able to function. Various types of 'digital wrappers' exist, including: (i) data related to self-driving capabilities, hazard reaction and preventative maintenance alert in 'intelligent cars'; (ii) data obtained in the shipment of goods, through sensors tracking location and monitoring temperatures, humidity and light exposure;[142] and (iii) online user-generated

[136] ibid.

[137] ibid.

[138] Kati Suominen, *Fuelling Trade in the Digital Era: Policy Roadmaps for Developing Countries*, Issue Paper (Geneva: International Centre for Trade and Sustainable Development (ICTSD) 2017) 6 <www.ictsd.org/sites/default/files/research/suominen_fuelling_trade_in_the_digital_era_0.pdf>.

[139] Manyika and others (n 20) 30.

[140] ibid 73.

[141] OECD Guidelines on the Protection of Privacy and Transborder Flows of Personal Data as Annexed to the Recommendation of the Council Concerning Guidelines Governing the Protection of Privacy and Transborder Flows of Personal Data, 23 September 1980, available at <www.oecd.org/sti/ieconomy/oecdguidelinesontheprotectionofprivacyandtransborderflowsofpersonaldata.htm>. These Guidelines were last updated in 2013.

[142] Often through the use of radio-frequency identification (RFID) technology. This technology uses wireless radio communication to identify certain objects or persons and to collect information on product, place, time or transaction. Lund and Manyika (n 7) 4.

reviews and ratings, which raise much-required trust among (potential) consumers.[143] Digital wrappers have various uses, from improving inventory management (and thereby reducing inventory costs, as well as reducing losses in transit) to increasing efficiency of shipping and transport and improving tracking of exports (high potential value in emerging economies with underdeveloped infrastructure).[144]

Another example of the importance of data flows for the economy is the rise of the 'app economy'. This economy depends on '*access to cloud-based distributed data processing*'.[145] Without the aggregated, stored and processed data, many applications (including apps like Waze, Uber, YouTube and Twitter) would not function. The app economy[146] should not be underestimated as it already accumulated a worth of 1.3 trillion US dollars in 2016, with significant growth projected for the future.[147] An important part of their revenue does not derive from the classic sale of goods or services but is linked to online advertising.[148]

At the same time, it should be recognised that international data flows can raise important concerns. The widespread supply of digital services and IoT products has opened up the possibility for many actors to collect personal data throughout the supply process. As pointed out by Mattoo and Meltzer, the global nature of the Internet has led to the high tradability of personal data, with instant and easy transfer of data all over the world.[149] Countries have expressed legitimate concern about possible violations of their citizens' right to privacy when data is transferred to countries with low(er) privacy protection frameworks. It is such concerns that have prompted various WTO Members to enact barriers to cross-border data flows. The current international regulatory framework on the

143 Manyika and others (n 20) 37.

144 Lund and Manyika (n 7) 4.

145 Porges and Enders (n 135) 3.

146 The app economy refers to the range of economic activity surrounding mobile applications.

147 Laurie Beaver, 'The Global App Economy is Poised to Explode', *Business Insider UK* (29 June 2017) <http://uk.businessinsider.com/the-global-app-economy-is-poised-to-explode-2017-6>.

148 Well-known examples of companies that derive their revenue almost entirely from online advertising include Facebook, YouTube and Alphabet (the parent company of Google). This aspect is further discussed *infra* Section 5.4.4.

149 Aaditya Mattoo and Joshua P Meltzer, 'International Data Flows and Privacy: The Conflict and Its Resolution' (World Bank 2018) Policy Research Working Paper 8431, 770 <https://documents.worldbank.org/en/publication/documents-reports/documentdetail/751621525705087132/international-data-flows-and-privacy-the-conflict-and-its-resolution>.

protection of data is, however, highly fragmented.[150] Countries have difficulty striking a balance between supporting the free flow of data (as it fuels the digital economy and creates new sources of employment, innovation and economic growth) and the protection of privacy and security.[151]

1.4 The Internet as a Network of Networks

In order to understand the concept of digital services, and digital trade more generally, it is important to acquire a basic understanding of how the Internet functions. This section will provide a brief introduction into the functioning of the Internet, but interested readers are strongly encouraged to turn to specialised literature to broaden their knowledge.[152]

The Internet is a packet network, or a network of networks. It allows for sending information in individualised packets through a large and changing collection of networks.[153] Every host that is connected to the Internet is assigned a unique IP address, which allows it to be identified by incoming and outgoing data packets. Different networks are connected through gateways which route packets from one network to another. As with any function of the Internet, this routing relies on protocols and standards. The Internet in itself is 'dumb', merely transferring information (or 'data') from one location/computer to another, without interfering with its contents. The intelligence lies at the end points of the data transmission, which is different from classic telecommunication networks, where telephone and cable companies were required to maintain the network. This increased independence has forced carriers of mobile telephone networks to limit the derivation of revenue from carrying the data (and to no longer supply certain services themselves).[154]

[150] UNCTAD, 'The Value and Role of Data in Electronic Commerce and the Digital Economy and Its Implications for Inclusive Trade and Development' (n 21) 9.

[151] ibid 10–11.

[152] This basic explanation of what the Internet is and how it functions is based on the excellent handbook of Brian W Kernighan, *Understanding the Digital World. What You Need to Know about Computers, the Internet, Privacy, and Security* (Princeton University Press 2017).

[153] This is where the Internet differs from classic telecommunication networks (e.g. telephone system), where each conversation required a dedicated circuit.

[154] However, as will be explained later on, carriers are more and more venturing into the supply of digital services, competing with the 'intelligence at the end of the transmission'.

Internet service providers (ISPs) are all entities that provide connections to the Internet. These are often cable and telephone companies. ISPs can use various technologies to provide Internet access, including dial-up,[155] DSL,[156] cable modem,[157] wireless[158] or dedicated high-speed connections.[159] ISPs are connected to one another through network access points (NAPs), which are public network facilities on the Internet backbone.[160] The Internet backbone consists of fibre-optic cables that physically transmit data and many companies operate their own high-capacity backbone. These backbones are interconnected through NAPs and it is the agreement between companies to intercommunicate freely that effectively constitutes what we call 'the Internet'. It is this unique constellation that causes the Internet to face some specific trade barriers, of which some are described *infra*.

1.4.1 *Competition Aspects of the Internet*

The Internet being a network of networks, ISPs have to deal with various network management issues, both in the short and the long term. An example of a short-term network management issue can be found in the fact that usage patterns, due to a small number of users that account for the majority of the traffic on these networks, negatively affect the operation of the ISP and the experience of other users.[161] Such short-term network management issues are often addressed by ISPs through anti-competitive behaviour.[162]

[155] Dial-up Internet consists of using the existing wired telephone system to transmit data. Due to its low speed and need for dedicated phone line, this way of accessing the Internet is largely outdated. Internet data transmission is much more efficient than via conventional phone lines. Mattoo and Schuknecht (n 72) 6.

[156] Digital Subscriber Loop (DSL) sends data over telephone wire but does not interfere with the voice signal, allowing for simultaneous use of one telephone line for calling and surfing.

[157] Cable modem uses the cable that carries cable television, converting signals into computer bits and back to signals that can be transported over the cable.

[158] Wireless Internet uses electromagnetic radiation to carry signals at a particular frequency.

[159] Definition as provided by Technopedia, available at <www.techopedia.com/definition/2510/Internet-service-provider-isp>.

[160] Definition as provided in the Encyclopaedia Britannica, available at <www.britannica.com/technology/Internet-service-provider>.

[161] Disproportionate amounts of traffic are caused by, for example, peer-to-peer networking, online video games and distribution of high-quality videos.

[162] For examples, see Pierre Larouche, 'Network Neutrality: The Global Dimension' in Mira Burri and Thomas Cottier (eds), *Trade Governance in the Digital Age* (Cambridge University Press 2012) 92–93.

In various ways, the Internet is similar to other content delivery networks, such as postal delivery or other transport networks.[163] Similar to these other content delivery networks, the Internet allows for the possibility of differentiated quality of services. Such differentiated quality of services would, in case of the Internet, entail the option to pay a surplus for a higher-speed Internet connection. The peculiarity of the Internet as a delivery network is that it is a two-sided market, where the ISP can charge both the users as well as the content providers.[164] In such two-sided markets, the benefit for both sides of the market is directly related to the number of users/parties on the other side of the market. Internet users, on the one hand, benefit from a large amount of content suppliers, as this will allow for a competitive offering of content services. Content suppliers, on the other hand, benefit from a large group of consumers to provide their content to.

Even though theoretically possible, the technical implementation of differentiated quality of service requires coordination between the ISPs and the network operators managing the facilities.[165] This need for coordination can be illustrated by the fact that differentiated quality of service over the Internet needs to be provided end-to-end, requiring both the ISP offering differentiated quality as well as its contenders to enable, for example, high-quality streaming services. The coordination problem is caused by the fact that often not the whole of the transmission process is done over networks that are under the ISP's control. Additionally, differentiated quality of service can be applied both to the user and the content provider, which requires another form of coordination as the preferences of both users and content providers must be reconciled.

1.4.2 Interoperability

Gasser and Palfrey define interoperability as '*the ability to transfer and render useful data and other information across systems, applications or components*'.[166] Ensuring interoperability entails both benefits and hazards. On the one hand, transfer and optimal use of data helps to achieve

[163] ibid 95.
[164] ibid.
[165] ibid 97–98.
[166] Urs Gasser and John Palfrey, 'Fostering Innovation and Trade in the Global Information Society: The Different Facets and Roles of Interoperability' in Mira Burri and Thomas Cottier (eds), *Trade Governance in the Digital Age* (Cambridge University Press 2012) 125.

economic growth through innovation, competition and trade and it enhances user choice and autonomy in choosing systems, applications and components. On the other hand, the widespread exchange of data creates privacy and security concerns. Additionally, Gasser and Palfrey refer to the fact that interoperability does not always encourage innovation, especially where companies are incentivised to compete for the entire market, instead of for a share of it. ICT interoperability should be distinguished from legal interoperability, enabling the flow of services and data across jurisdictions. Legal interoperability addresses the issue of regulatory divergence, leading to a decrease in the cost of cross-border trade, driving innovation, competition, trade and economic growth and (potentially) fostering fundamental values and rights.[167]

In achieving ICT interoperability, both the private sector as well as the government have a role to play. Whereas it is often felt that the private sector is best suited to establish interoperability, the government still has a key role in those instances where a dominant player blocks the achievement of interoperability.[168] Legal interoperability can be approached from a top-down perspective, setting up an international body dedicated to creating international law on Internet regulation or tasking an existing international organisation, like the International Telecommunications Union (ITU), with this exercise. Alternatively, a bottom-up approach can be pursued through international cooperation in standard-setting processes.[169] Regulatory cooperation exists on a broad spectrum, ranging from exchanging views on new regulation, mutual recognition and harmonisation to enacting the same measures.

[167] ibid 132–134.
[168] ibid 129.
[169] ibid 134–135.

2

The Impact of Digitisation on International Trade

Value in the global economy is increasingly being created digitally and it is estimated that this will rise to 50 per cent of all value created in 2025.[170] UNCTAD estimates the global value of e-commerce in 2017 already at 29 trillion dollars, with trade still relatively domestic but increasingly becoming international.[171] Between 2005 and 2021, global internet traffic is estimated to increase 127-fold.[172] The flow of data contributed an estimated $2.8 trillion to the global economy in 2014 and this number is only expected to have grown in recent years.[173]

It has been asserted that the Internet has a direct impact on economic growth and international trade; however, limited data is available to back this up.[174] Adding to the difficulty in measuring digital trade is the fact

[170] Suominen (n 138).

[171] Value can be broken down into 25.5 trillion dollars for business to business (B2B) commerce and 3.8 trillion dollars for business to consumer (B2C) commerce. See UNCTAD, 'Global E-Commerce Sales Surged to $29 Trillion', *United Nations Conference on Trade and Development* (29 March 2019) <https://unctad.org/en/pages/PressRelease.aspx?OriginalVersionID=505>.

[172] Joshua P Meltzer, 'Governing Digital Trade' (2019) 18 World Trade Review 23, 26.

[173] On why the value of data is very difficult to measure, see Manyika and others (n 20) 39; See OECD, *Measuring the Digital Economy: A New Perspective* (OECD Publishing 2014) 62.

[174] Meltzer, 'Supporting the Internet as a Platform for International Trade Opportunities for Small and Medium-Sized Enterprises and Developing Countries' (n 9) 4. See also Nina Czernich and others, 'Broadband Infrastructure and Economic Growth' (2011) 121 The Economic Journal 505; Matthieu Pélissié du Rausas and others, 'Internet Matters: The Net's Sweeping Impact on Growth, Jobs and Prosperity' (McKinsey Global Institute 2011) <www.mckinsey.com/industries/high-tech/our-insights/internet-matters>; Christine Zhen-Wei Qiang, Carlo M Rossotto and Kaoru Kimura, 'Economic Impacts of Broadband', *2009 Information and Communications for Development: Extending Reach and Increasing Impact* (World Bank 2009) <https://openknowledge.worldbank.org/handle/10986/2636>.

that different institutions have different definitions and measuring cross-border data flows is susceptible to inaccuracies.[175]

Use of the Internet entails significant potential for productivity growth in many different service sectors.[176] Whereas services were long considered non-tradable because of the temporal coinciding of provision and consumption and the need for physical proximity and interaction between consumer and producer, the Internet has done away with these practical hindrances.[177] The Internet has increased the tradability of certain services (including legal, accounting and engineering services).[178] A way in which digitisation boosted international trade in services is by enabling producers in developing countries, who traditionally exported commodities and low-value manufactured goods, to shift focus to the more valuable provision of services.[179] Developing countries increased their export of commercial services significantly in the last decade.[180]

Moreover, the Internet can increase productivity growth in several ways: improving business process efficiency through low-cost communication, reducing IT infrastructure, improving supply chain management and reducing costs of services through use of cloud computing,[181] achieving more efficient and well-functioning markets and improving resource allocation through collection and processing of data.[182]

[175] Including the United States International Trade Commission (USITC), the US Bureau of Economic Analysis and the Organisation for Economic Co-operation and Development (OECD), as found in Lund and Manyika (n 7) 3.

[176] Meltzer, 'Supporting the Internet as a Platform for International Trade Opportunities for Small and Medium-Sized Enterprises and Developing Countries' (n 9) 21.

[177] Mira Burri, 'The Governance of Data and Data Flows in Trade Agreements: The Pitfalls of Legal Adaptation' (2017) 51 UC Davis Law Review 65, 81.

[178] Meltzer, 'Supporting the Internet as a Platform for International Trade Opportunities for Small and Medium-Sized Enterprises and Developing Countries' (n 9) 5.

[179] Suominen (n 138) 5.

[180] World Trade Organization, *World Trade Statistical Review 2016* (Geneva: World Trade Organization 2016) 56 <www.wto.org/english/res_e/statis_e/wts2016_e/wts2016_e.pdf>.

[181] IBM defines 'cloud computing' (often referred to as 'the cloud') as '*the delivery of on-demand computing resources – everything from applications to data centers – over the Internet on a pay-for-use basis*'. It lists several characteristics: (i) elastic resources, allowing quick and easy scaling up or down to meet demand, (ii) metered services (pay what you use) and (iii) self-service access to IT resources. See IBM, 'What is cloud computing?', available at <www.ibm.com/cloud-computing/learn-more/what-is-cloud-computing/>.

[182] Meltzer, 'Supporting the Internet as a Platform for International Trade Opportunities for Small and Medium-Sized Enterprises and Developing Countries' (n 9) 4.

Moreover, digital trade has been recognised as fostering intra-firm connections and overall linking to GVCs.[183] GVCs increasingly rely on digital solutions to work smoothly.[184]

2.1 The Benefits of Digitisation

Several benefits to digitisation can easily be identified. The main advantage being the – seemingly complete – removal of practical barriers to cross-border trade, especially related to trade in services. For example, the servicification of production could only be achieved through the coordination of the services inputs via digital networks.[185] Countries with higher Internet use seem to export more goods to more markets and have a more diverse export basket.[186] Several studies have demonstrated the clearly positive effect of broadband introduction or Internet access to the increase of GDP.[187] An important caveat here is that, even after digitisation, a significant degree of regionalisation can still be perceived, both in the trade of services and in data flows.[188] Even in e-commerce transactions, volume reduces when distance increases.[189]

Consumers are benefitting from digitally enabled trade as it allows them to access many more (online) suppliers, it widens their choice and it allows them to easily compare price and quality. Because of digitisation, consumers can more directly participate in international trade.[190] For business in general, the constraints of the domestic or regional market are lifted, allowing for unprecedented access to markets around the world. This allows them not only to access new consumers, but also to source their inputs (whether goods or services) from new suppliers.[191] 'Digital businesses' also have specific characteristics compared to more traditional businesses: (i) their value is created differently (often through

[183] Lopez-Gonzalez and Ferencz (n 6) 36.

[184] UNCTAD, 'Fostering Developments Gains from E-Commerce and Digital Platforms' (n 26) para 45.

[185] Servicification is the process of corporate transformation towards services, as discussed *infra* (Section 2.3). Lopez-Gonzalez and Ferencz (n 6) 11.

[186] ibid 6.

[187] Czernich and others (n 174); OECD, *Measuring the Digital Economy: A New Perspective* (n 173); Pélissié du Rausas and others (n 174); Qiang, Rossotto and Kimura (n 174).

[188] Manyika and others (n 20) 39; OECD, *Measuring the Digital Economy: A New Perspective* (n 173) 62.

[189] However, this is to a significantly smaller extent (50 per cent) compared to regular transactions.

[190] Lopez-Gonzalez and Ferencz (n 6) 12.

[191] Porges and Enders (n 135) 2.

monetisation of user data); (ii) they conduct all of their activities remotely; (iii) intangible assets are increasingly important to them; (iv) the end users of the service contribute in the value creation; and (v) they operate in a winner-takes-most market structure.[192]

Digitisation allows for large-scale globalisation by small retailers. The global digital market is more inclusive as it erases many of the barriers these companies were traditionally confronted with.[193] This illustrates the more inclusive nature of the global digital market. MSMEs that are able to embrace the digital environment can more easily create new business and trade opportunities. Through the Internet, small companies have access to inputs required to compete internationally (e.g. global advertisement, consumer communication and access to IT services anywhere in the world).[194] Additionally, MSMEs are given the ability to deliver services online, eliminating the need of physical presence in the countries of export (often a prohibitive cost). By lowering the cost of export entry, digitisation has had a transformative impact on the economics of trade, increasing export volumes, export diversification and the number of small traders who can export.[195] In their communication to the WTO General Council in 2017, the ASEAN countries highlighted the benefits for MSMEs that have arisen from e-commerce as it lowers barriers to entry and operating costs for MSMEs wanting to branch out into foreign markets.[196] They also identified several outstanding challenges: lack of infrastructure and knowledge, regulatory barriers, limited access to enabling services, online privacy and security concerns, consumer confidence and the digital divide.

Implications for businesses and economies have been most significant in developing countries, where digitisation impacts economic

[192] European Commission, Proposal for a Council Directive on the common system of a digital services tax on revenues resulting from the provision of certain digital services, Brussels, 21 March 2018, COM(2018) 148 final, 2.

[193] Manyika and others (n 20) 43; Lopez-Gonzalez and Ferencz (n 6) 12; Meltzer, 'Supporting the Internet as a Platform for International Trade Opportunities for Small and Medium-Sized Enterprises and Developing Countries' (n 9) 1; Suominen (n 138) 3.

[194] Meltzer, 'Supporting the Internet as a Platform for International Trade Opportunities for Small and Medium-Sized Enterprises and Developing Countries' (n 9) 6.

[195] Suominen (n 138) 4.

[196] WTO General Council, 'ASEAN Reflections on Lunch Panel on "Can E-Commerce Trade Rules Help MSMEs from Developing Countries?" Held During the UNCTAD E-Commerce Week, 27 April 2017', JOB/GC/126, JOB/CTG/6, JOB/SERV/260, JOB/IP/23, JOB/DEV/44, 2 June 2017, 1.

growth, facilitates small transactions and helps merchants to sell internationally.[197] However, Internet connectivity over traditional telecommunication networks has been limited due to a lack of infrastructure in many developing countries. This shortcoming was partly remedied by the increased use of mobile devices that use wireless networks for Internet connectivity.[198] This increased access to the Internet and the development of applications for smartphones that provide access to financial services, health care information and data on various topics (including market pricing, weather forecasts, etc.) allow for unprecedented access to global markets for developing country enterprises.[199] Services trade is therefore a '*key component of Internet-enabled international trade and economic growth*'.[200] Despite this cautiously positive trend, the World Bank stated in its 2016 world development report that the Internet '*remains unavailable, inaccessible, and unaffordable to a majority of the world's population*'.[201]

Various studies have found that data flows positively impact world GDP. The combined direct and indirect impact of data flows has a larger impact on world GDP growth than physical trade flows.[202] The importance of digitisation for economic growth becomes quite apparent when considering the importance of cross-border data flows for specific industries. Castro and McQuinn indicate that the cross-border movement of data not only allows companies to gain competitive advantages, but that it is also used as part of normal business operations in various traditional industries.[203] They explain how various companies in different traditional industries rely on cross-border trade to conduct their business (including multi-

[197] Manyika and others (n 20) 43–44; Meltzer, 'Supporting the Internet as a Platform for International Trade Opportunities for Small and Medium-Sized Enterprises and Developing Countries' (n 9) 1.

[198] Mobile phones provide the main gateway to the Internet in developing countries. World Bank (n 16) 6.

[199] Meltzer, 'Supporting the Internet as a Platform for International Trade Opportunities for Small and Medium-Sized Enterprises and Developing Countries' (n 9) 7.

[200] Furthermore, Internet-enabled trade opens up employment opportunities in the form of microwork, in the form of small digital tasks.

[201] World Bank (n 16) 8.

[202] Indirect impact refers to the fact that data flows enable trade flows, FDI and people flows. Manyika and others (n 20) 76.

[203] Daniel Castro and Alan McQuinn, 'Cross-Border Data Flows Enable Growth in All Industries' (Information Technology and Innovation Foundation 2015) 2 <www2.itif.org/2015-cross-border-data-flows.pdf.

national companies in the sector of mining,[204] manufacturing,[205] oil and gas,[206] retail,[207] banking[208] and airplane manufacturing[209]).[210] Meijers finds that high Internet penetration leads to more international trade, causing economic growth.[211] He also asserts this effect to be more pronounced for non-high-income countries.

Lastly, the Internet has also been described as '*the key driver of innovation and productivity growth because it reduces transaction costs and enables businesses to better utilize existing resources*'.[212] Additionally, the Internet fosters human capital as it provides individuals with an easy way to acquire new skills. New digital technologies have also been credited with the potential of creating new ecosystems for trade.[213]

2.2 Issues Faced by the Digital Economy

Unfortunately, digitisation has not had only positive effects on global markets, companies and consumers, but has also created or enlarged

[204] Mining companies use data obtained during mining activities to identify size, location and the quality of ore. This information allows companies *inter alia* to be more environmentally friendly and promote safe mining conditions.

[205] Manufacturing companies invest in cross-border data flows in order to be able to use consumer analytics from all over the world and to provide the ability to business users to use standard reporting from any location. This allows for unprecedented access to consumers and allows the personalised provision of services.

[206] Oil and gas companies analyse data collected from their wells to estimate depletion, but also to discover new oil and gas reserves.

[207] Retail companies are increasingly collecting and analysing data (e.g. through the issuing of loyalty cards) allowing them to anticipate stock depletion (and reorder in time), to instantly change national prices (through the use of digital price indicators in store) and overall provide a better service and fresher ingredients and limit food waste.

[208] Banks use cross-border provided data not only to analyse their financial data, but also to monitor website interactions, consumer service calls and user feedback. This allows them to segment consumers (thereby tailoring customer services), use predictive marketing, ensure increased cyber security and lower interest rates.

[209] Aircraft manufacturers use data gathered mid-flight and transmitted in real time to allow for immediate repairs and targeted check-ups upon touch-down. Access to this (international) data allows for better safety and less delays, saves costs and reduces waiting times.

[210] Castro and McQuinn (n 203) 2–7.

[211] He does, however, also recognise that the direct link between the Internet and economic growth is less straightforward to establish. He identifies growth in international trade as the crucial intermediate step. Huub Meijers, 'Does the Internet Generate Economic Growth, International Trade, or Both?' (2014) 11 International Economics and Economy Policy 137, 161–162.

[212] Meltzer, 'Supporting the Internet as a Platform for International Trade Opportunities for Small and Medium-Sized Enterprises and Developing Countries' (n 9).

[213] Lopez-Gonzalez and Ferencz (n 6) 12.

problems. First, globalisation has the effect of exposing local industries to international competition, sometimes to the detriment of these industries, displacing them and their workers. This effect is arguably enlarged by digitisation, with the risk of losing entire industries to globalised and digitised trade.[214]

Second, the gains from digital trade, as set out *supra*, are not automatically extended to or accessible in developing countries.[215] In that context, we have observed the emergence of a new cause of economic inequality, the 'digital divide', which affects much of the global population. The digital divide has been defined as '*[separating] those who are connected to the digital revolution in ICTs and those who have no access to the benefits of the new technologies*'.[216] In 2018, 48.8 per cent of the world's population (more than 4 billion people) remained offline, lacking access to the Internet.[217] This share of the global population can therefore neither directly benefit from nor participate in the digitisation of the global economy. Moreover, in some developing countries less than 5 per cent of the population engages in e-commerce.[218] Manyika et al. rightly note that access to digital platforms and communication becomes an urgent development issue as data flows become more central to the global economy.[219] The 2009 UNCTAD Information Technology Report contains a study on the various aspects of the digital divide and discusses the main outstanding issues (e.g. the 'broadband challenge').[220] The message in the report is clear: '*[d]espite positive trends in ICT diffusion, much more needs to be done to achieve an information society for all. Important gaps remain within economies and societies (e.g. due to language of content; rural versus urban; gender; generation) that affect the demand for and the ability to use ICT*'.[221] The importance of connectivity for development has also been highlighted in the WTO's 2017 study on the Information Technology Agreement (ITA), which states that

214 Manyika and others (n 20) 79.

215 Suominen (n 138) 1; World Bank (n 16) 50.

216 As defined at the UN's World Summit on the Information Society, see <www.itu.int/net/wsis/basic/faqs.asp>.

217 UNCTAD, 'The Value and Role of Data in Electronic Commerce and the Digital Economy and Its Implications for Inclusive Trade and Development' (n 21) 4.

218 UNCTAD, 'Fostering Developments Gains from E-Commerce and Digital Platforms' (n 26) 47.

219 Manyika and others (n 20) 100.

220 UNCTAD, '2009 Information Economy Report. Trends and Outlook in Turbulent Times' (United Nations Publications 2009) UNCTAD/IER/2009, 16–28.

221 ibid 19.

affordable access to the Internet has a considerable impact on firms, consumers and border authorities, affecting their ability to utilise the benefits of e-commerce.[222] Interestingly, it also concluded that the majority (approximately 80 per cent) of economic benefits from technology derive from the widespread use of technology, rather than from production.[223] UNCTAD highlights that the lag in use of ICT by MSMEs creates a considerable barrier to their effective integration in GVCs.[224]

Developing countries should therefore strive to unlock access to telecommunication networks as well as digital mobile networks to allow for their consumers as well as businesses to benefit from using the Internet. This requires investment in adequate physical infrastructure combined with supportive government policies.[225] Suominen distinguishes between two elements of the digital divide: the lack of broadband connectivity on the one hand, and the differences in ability of countries to use the Internet for economic and social gains on the other hand.[226] The World Bank points to both policy failures[227] as well as monopoly control being causes of the digital divide.[228] Moreover, a 'gender digital divide' also exists, with women (entrepreneurs) in developing countries having considerably less access to the Internet.[229] Finally, Chander points to the uneven distribution of smart objects (including IoT) as another element of the digital divide.[230]

222 World Trade Organization, '20 Years of the Information Technology Agreement. Boosting Trade, Innovation and Digital Connectivity' (World Trade Organization 2017) 81. The 2017 joint OECD/WTO report on Aid for Trade comes to similar conclusions, listing the key economic efficiency gains from digital connectivity, see OECD and WTO, 'Aid for Trade at a Glance 2017. Promoting Trade, Inclusiveness and Connectivity for Sustainable Development' (WTO/OECD Publishing 2017) 57.

223 Stephen J Ezell and Robert D Atkinson, 'The Good, The Bad, and The Ugly (and The Self-Destructive) of Innovation Policy: A Policymaker's Guide to Crafting Effective Innovation Policy' (Information Technology and Innovation Foundation 2010) 32 <https://itif.org/publications/2010/10/07/good-bad-and-ugly-innovation-policy>.

224 UNCTAD, 'Fostering Developments Gains from E-Commerce and Digital Platforms' (n 26) para 45. This was also repeated in UNCTAD, 'Agreed policy recommendations of the Intergovernmental Group of Experts on E-commerce and the Digital Economy at its first session', 4–6 October 2017, available at <https://unctad.org/en/Pages/Meetings/Group-of-Experts-Ecommerce-Digital-Economy.aspx>.

225 Suominen (n 138) 1.

226 ibid 8–9.

227 This includes regulatory captures, troubled privatisation and excessive taxation.

228 World Bank (n 16) 25.

229 UNCTAD, 'The Value and Role of Data in Electronic Commerce and the Digital Economy and Its Implications for Inclusive Trade and Development' (n 21) 4.

230 Chander (n 95) 10.

MSMEs face critical barriers in cross-border e-commerce: (i) inadequate ICT infrastructure; (ii) unreliable and costly power supply; (iii) limited use of credit cards; (iv) lack of purchasing power; and (v) underdeveloped logistics and financial systems.[231] Additionally, companies from developing countries have difficulty accessing existing global e-commerce platforms due to the difficulty for the platforms to assess the quality of the companies, their production processes and products or because of the inflexible and poorly integrated domestic payment solutions.[232]

In the Panel report of *Brazil – Taxation*, circulated on 30 August 2017, the WTO panel recognised that Brazil is confronted with a problem of 'digital divide', which has implications for its population's standard of living.[233] In its written submission, Brazil defined the digital divide as a '*gap between demographics and regions that have access to modern information and telecommunications technology and those that do not have access or have restricted access*'.[234] It highlights the advantages of closing this gap, stating that access to high-speed, high-quality connections would improve literacy, democracy, social mobility, economic quality and growth.[235] The panel found that 'bridging the digital divide' was a public morals objective for Brazil, which fell within the scope of Article XX(a) of the GATT, allowing for a justification of otherwise GATT-inconsistent (discriminatory) measures.[236] This finding highlights that the importance of bridging the digital divide is becoming widely recognised. In applying the other elements in the test of Article XX GATT, the panel, however, found that Brazil's measure was not necessary to protect the public moral objective as various less trade-restrictive alternatives were available.[237]

In its 2017 communication in the context of the WPEC, the African group voiced its concerns regarding the disruption of economies around the world through digital technologies.[238] It pointed out that there is an

[231] UNCTAD, 'Fostering Developments Gains from E-Commerce and Digital Platforms' (n 26) 13.

[232] ibid 40.

[233] Panel Report, *Brazil – Certain Measures Concerning Taxation and Charges*, para 7.565.

[234] Brazil's first written submissions, paras 408 (DS472) and 346 (DS497). See ibid para 7.544.

[235] Panel Report, *Brazil – Certain Measures Concerning Taxation and Charges*, para 7.544.

[236] ibid para 7.567.

[237] ibid para 7.622.

[238] WTO General Council, 'Report of Panel Discussion on "Digital Industrial Policy and Development" – Communication from the African Group', JOB/GC/133, 21 July 2017.

unequal distribution of international bandwidth and that the digital divide is growing persistently. The group argued that developed countries have had the opportunity to foster domestic industries through the use of digital trade barriers, which those same countries now want to prohibit through multilateral negotiations, constraining countries' ability to implement industrial policy and catch up. It moreover cautioned developing countries to start thinking of how to start using the raw material that is data to their economic advantage, rather than giving it away for free to multilateral companies from developed countries. This communication aptly illustrates the very different outlook some countries have on digitisation, which makes multilateral discussions on this topic significantly more difficult.

Third, another pressing and persistent issue in the global digital economy is the tendency of parts of that economy to develop natural monopolies.[239] Large digital platforms have '*enormous network effects and low marginal costs*' because of their size.[240] This creates the potential for anticompetitive practices and abuse of this dominant position.[241] A company that controls a digital platform also controls its distribution channels, which puts this company in a position of considerable market power.[242] It is difficult for governments to balance the aversion to this kind of market power (held by foreign companies) with the need for their citizens and businesses to participate in these platforms.

Fourth, the use of IoT devices raises security and privacy concerns, due to the uninterrupted collection of (personal) data.[243] Cybersecurity is another major issue related to the digitisation phenomenon. This problem not only poses public safety and possibly national security threats, but also entails substantial business costs.[244] Additionally, because of the lack of face-to-face transaction,

[239] Manyika and others (n 20) 102.

[240] ibid; see also European Parliament, 'Challenges for Competition Policy in a Digitalised Economy' (Directorate General for Internal Policies 2015) IP/A/ECON/2014-12, 25 <www.europarl.europa.eu/RegData/etudes/STUD/2015/542235/IPOL_STU%282015%29542235_EN.pdf>.

[241] UNCTAD, 'Fostering Developments Gains from E-Commerce and Digital Platforms' (n 26) para 29.

[242] UNCTAD, 'The Value and Role of Data in Electronic Commerce and the Digital Economy and Its Implications for Inclusive Trade and Development' (n 21) 8.

[243] UNCTAD, '2009 Information Economy Report. Trends and Outlook in Turbulent Times' (n 220) 7.

[244] Manyika and others (n 20) 102.

the consumer bears more risks related to disclosure and transparency, data protection and responsibility of platforms. It has already been noted that a harmonised approach across countries is vital in policing such issues, but the current system for, for example, data protection is very fragmented.[245]

Finally, because of the vastly different nature of digital trade, specific regulatory challenges emerged, including: the challenge of protecting privacy without overly limiting cross-border data flows; the incomplete intellectual property frameworks;[246] a lack of regulation of online platforms; market access impediments to digital products; and censorship of foreign websites.[247] Additionally, prominent barriers to digital services trade were enacted by various countries. Several examples of such barriers, including limitations on cross-border data flows, web filtering and content control, lack of access to infrastructure and digital services taxes, will be discussed throughout this book.

2.3 Impact on Services Trade Specifically

'Servicification' has been referred to as the steadily ongoing process of corporate transformation towards services. For example, in the production of garments, sophisticated global networks of suppliers of various goods and services work together to allow for just-in-time supply at the retail end.[248] Another concrete example of servicification is the increased presence of services in a company such as Apple. Whereas Apple started out as a company manufacturing personal computers and small handheld devices for playing digital audio and video files (iPods), it only started outgrowing its competition when it added services to its core business. This was done in the form of the creation of the online music store iTunes

245 Lund and Manyika (n 7) 9; UNCTAD, 'Fostering Developments Gains from E-Commerce and Digital Platforms' (n 26) paras 30–32.

246 These frameworks are incomplete in the sense that they are not adjusted to IP infringements in the course of digital trade.

247 For a more complete analysis, Suominen (n 138) 8.

248 Jane Drake-Brockman and Sherry Stephenson, 'Implications for 21st Century Trade and Development of the Emergence of Services Value Chains' (International Centre for Trade and Sustainable Development (ICTSD) 2012) 14 <https://ictsd.iisd.org/themes/services/research/implications-for-21st-century-trade-and-development-of-the-emergence-of>.

in 2003 and the launch of the iPhone with all of its digital applications (software) in 2007 together with the launch of its own operating software (iOS). Nowadays, Apple gains the second biggest part of its revenue (the biggest part being revenue derived from iPhone sales) from the services it provides. These services include App Store (sale of apps), iCloud (online storing of data), Apple Music (sale of music and music-streaming service) and AppleCare (customer support).[249]

Servicification is thus the phenomenon of increasing dependence on services by manufacturing firms, which encompasses an increased buying,[250] producing[251] and selling[252] of services.[253] Goods and services are progressively complementary and can no longer function completely without one another.[254] Put differently, manufacturers of all kinds of goods make greater use of services inputs.[255]

On top of the changes brought about by servicification, the phenomenon of digitisation has a significant impact on trade in services in particular. The impact is two-fold: first, specific services derive from the development of information technology and the Internet (so-called IT services[256] or digital infrastructure services); and second, digitisation enables cross-border supply of previously existing service sectors ('ICT-enabled services'[257] or digitally

[249] Mike Murphy, 'What to Expect from Apple's Fourth-Quarter Earnings Tomorrow', *Quartz* (24 October 2016) <http://qz.com/816174>.

[250] Purchasing services inputs for the manufacturing of certain goods: can be 'bought services inputs' or 'service value added' with the former being a directly acquired service and the latter the accumulation of value added by different service providers throughout the value chain.

[251] The production of services in manufacturing firms is measured through service employment.

[252] Also referred to as 'services output'.

[253] National Board of Trade, 'The Servicification of EU Manufacturing – Building Competitiveness in the Internal Market' (National Board of Trade 2016) 8.

[254] Hosuk Lee-Makiyama, 'Future-Proofing World Trade in Technology: Turning the WTO IT Agreement (ITA) into the International Digital Economy Agreement (IDEA)' (Ecipe 2011) ECIPE Working Paper 04/2011, 17 <https://ecipe.org/publications/future-proofing-world-trade-in-technology-turning-the-wto-it-agreement-ita-into-the-international-digital-economy-agreement-idea/>.

[255] Lopez-Gonzalez and Ferencz (n 6) 11.

[256] Examples given by UNCTAD include '*programming, systems integration, application design, IT infrastructure management and maintenance, IT consulting, software development and implementation services, data processing and database services, IT support services, data warehousing, and content management and development*'. UNCTAD, '2009 Information Economy Report. Trends and Outlook in Turbulent Times' (n 220) 74.

[257] Examples given by UNCTAD include '*call centres and customer contact centres (inbound and outbound); data entry, human resources, payroll, finance and accounting, procurement, transcription; financial analysis, data mining, engineering, research and*

enabled services).[258] These developments changed the landscape of international trade in services, which raises questions as to the applicable legal framework. This question is dealt with in Part II of this book. It can, however, already be raised that these services are not necessarily 'new' in WTO terms. The main difference is that services that used to require proximity between the supplier and consumer to be supplied in the territory of a WTO Member can now be supplied over the Internet, from a distance. The interlinkage between the rise of global trade in services and the emergence of digitisation is no coincidence. The digitisation phenomenon has been crucial for the growth in digital services trade.

The increased possibility of cross-border supply of services enables producers to offshore some of the 'tasks' in the value chains to other locations. Digitisation therefore caused an increased offshoring of services, which is expected to expand both geographically and sectorally.[259] Offshoring can be done in two ways: either through relocation of the production to an own foreign affiliate ('captive offshoring') or through the offshore outsourcing to a third-party provider abroad.[260] It should be noted that not all digital services are subject to the same level of offshoring, with IT services being offshored most. The increasing popularity of offshoring digital services is (partly) due to the fact that this is seen as a way to reduce production costs and to enhance competitiveness.

Whereas many large companies increasingly offshore services, other (generally smaller) companies in various sectors are embracing the opportunities offered by digitisation to specialise and internationalise their services.[261] They are reaping the benefits of this evolution by specialising in services that can, with increasing ease, be traded globally and therefore more easily offshored.

development, insurance claims processing, architectural design, remote education and publishing, medical diagnostics, journalism'. ibid.

258 As mentioned in Panel Report, *China – Publications and Audiovisual Services*, para 7.1180: '*nowadays technology allows an increasing range of intangible products to be distributed in a commercial sense. These intangible products, such as digitised content, often involve services, and can be distributed to consumers.*' Section 2.4 discussed the double definition of digital services trade and its implications for digital services regulation.

259 UNCTAD, '2009 Information Economy Report. Trends and Outlook in Turbulent Times' (n 220) 73.

260 ibid 73–74.

261 ibid 73.

2.4 The Digital Economy Framework and Digital Services

This book studies a specific part of e-commerce: trade in digital services. Whereas the term e-commerce mainly evokes images of large e-commerce platforms, like eBay, Amazon or Alibaba, shipping low-cost goods to anywhere in the world, this term also encompasses a vast array of digital services. Digital services play a substantial role in twenty-first-century trade. Not only are consumers surrounded by digital services in their everyday life,[262] so are the goods that are being traded all over the world.[263] In fact, digitisation principally impacts trade in services, enabling the widespread use of IT services and allowing for unprecedented cross-border supply of services (digital supply).

2.4.1 Delineating the Digital Economy

The introduction to the 2017 UNCTAD Information Economy Report acknowledged that '*The world is on the cusp of a new digital era. With dramatically reduced costs of collecting, storing and processing data, and greatly enhanced computing power, digitalization is transforming economic activities around the world. It is expected to affect value chains, skill requirements, production and trade, and will require adaptations of existing legal and regulatory frameworks in various areas.*'[264] It thereby articulates the premise that this book is based on: the currently existing international digital trade law framework should be clarified and updated where necessary. As a first step in the analysis, the definition of 'digital services' in the context of the digital economy is expounded upon.

Several international organisations have provided some kind of (partial) definition or view on the digital economy. Table 2.1 lists and compares the definitions found for the terms 'digital economy', 'e-commerce' and 'digital services'. The comparison's aim is to provide a clearer image of how the digital economy is perceived in the context of international trade. The dictionary meaning of these terms is also added to provide for a linguistic benchmark.

[262] Consumers not only order goods and services online, their attachment to their smartphones entails an almost unwavering stream of digital services being supplied to them throughout the day.

[263] Traded goods are equipped with a 'digital wrapper' service.

[264] UNCTAD, '2017 Information Economy Report. Digitalization, Trade and Development' (United Nations Publications 2017) xiii UNCTAD/IER/2017/Corr.1.

Table 2.1 *Definitions and interrelatedness of the concepts 'digital economy', 'e-commerce' and 'digital services'*

	Digital economy	E-commerce	Digital services
Oxford English Dictionary	An economy which functions primarily by means of digital technology, especially electronic transactions made using the Internet	A sector of the digital economy; A commercial activity conducted via electronic media, especially on the Internet	-
UNCTAD	Digitalised economy > digital economy > digital sector; All extensive applications of digital technologies and their production; Economic output derived from digital technologies with a business model based on digital goods or services	Part of the 'digitalised economy'	Part of the 'digital economy'
OECD	Comprised of markets based on digital technologies that facilitate the trade of goods and services through e-commerce	An e-commerce transaction is the sale or purchase of goods or services, conducted over computer networks by methods specifically designed for the purpose of receiving or placing of orders	-
G20	Economic activities that use digitised information and knowledge, modern information networks and ICT	A service sector within the digital economy	-

Table 2.1 (*cont.*)

	Digital economy	E-commerce	Digital services
WTO	-	The production, distribution, marketing, sale or delivery of goods and services by electronic means	-
IMF	Narrow: online platforms and activities that owe their existence to such platforms Broad: all activities that use digitised data are part of the digital economy: in modern economies, the entire economy[265]	-	-

UNCTAD[265] states that '*there is no widely accepted definition for "digital economy"*',[266] but refers to a study by Bukht and Heeks which provides a useful overview of some of the definitions given to 'digital economy' so far.[267] The authors distinguish between the broad scope

265 UNCTAD, '2017 Information Economy Report. Digitalization, Trade and Development' (n 264) 3.

266 Rumana Bukht and Richard Heeks, 'Defining, Conceptualising and Measuring the Digital Economy' (Manchester: Centre for Development Informatics, Global Development Institute, SEED, University of Manchester 2017) Development Informatics Working Paper Series 68, 6–10 <www.gdi.manchester.ac.uk/research/publications/di/di-wp68/> .

267 In using this wording, the authors go back to the difference between the concept of digitisation (the conversion of data from analogue to digital) and that of digitalisation (the application of digitisation to organisational and social processes). ibid 12. See also Scott Brennen and Daniel Kreiss, 'Digitalization and digitization', *Culture Digitally* (8 September 2014) <http://culturedigitally.org/2014/09/digitalization-and-digitization/>.

(defined as the digitalised economy,[268] including all digitally enabled economic activity), the narrow scope (defined as the digital economy) and the core (defined as the digital sector[269]). Bukht and Heeks propose that the term 'digital economy' encompasses all extensive applications of digital technologies and the production of those technologies.[270] More concretely, they define the digital economy as '*that part of economic output derived solely or primarily from digital technologies with a business model based on digital goods or services*'.[271] Moreover, digital services are explicitly identified as constituting part of the digital economy.[272] This is different for e-commerce, which is identified as being a part of the broader scope (i.e. digitalised economy).

In the 2012 report on the Digital Economy by the OECD, the digital economy is described as '*comprised of markets based on digital technologies that facilitate the trade of goods and services through e-commerce*'.[273] In its definition of e-commerce, the OECD Glossary of Statistical Terms refers to transactions conducted 'over computer networks'.[274] It clarifies that the defining trait of e-commerce is the *ordering* online, as payment and delivery do not have to be conducted online. The OECD provides a narrow definition of electronic commerce, focussing solely on the online ordering of products. It does not define 'digital services' nor does it explicitly set out the relationship between the three different terms.

The G20 describes the digital economy as '*a broad range of economic activities that include using digitized information and knowledge as the key factor of production, modern information networks as an important*

[268] International Monetary Fund, 'Measuring The Digital Economy' (International Monetary Fund 2018) 7 <www.imf.org/en/Publications/Policy-Papers/Issues/2018/04/03/022818-measuring-the-digital-economy>.

[269] They consider the 'digital sector' to encompass the following service sectors: manufacture of computer, electronic and optical products (ISIC rev 4 26), software publishing (ISIC rev 4 582), telecommunications (ISIC rev 4 61), computer programming, consultancy and related activities (ISIC rev 4 62) and information service activities (ISIC rev 4 63). See ibid 11.

[270] 'Extensive applications of digital technologies' refers to the technologies that have arisen due to the development of information technology (i.e. new technologies). ibid 12.

[271] This does not include all digitised activity. ibid 13.

[272] See the diagram at ibid.

[273] OECD Directorate for Financial and Enterprise Affairs, 'The Digital Economy' (Paris: OECD 2012) Hearings Competition Committee DAF/COMP(2012)22, 5 <www.oecd.org/daf/competition/The-Digital-Economy-2012.pdf>.

[274] OECD Glossary of Statistical Terms, 'Electronic Commerce', available at <https://stats.oecd.org/glossary/detail.asp?ID=4721>.

activity space, and the effective use of information and communication technology (ICT) as an important driver of productivity growth and economic structural optimization'.[275] Since 2017, the G20 organises ministerial meetings on trade and the digital economy, recognising that '*the digital economy is an increasingly important driver of global inclusive economic growth and plays a significant role in accelerating economic development, enhancing productivity of existing industries, cultivating new markets and industries and achieving inclusive sustainable growth and development*'.[276] It does not define e-commerce specifically, but seems to perceive e-commerce as a service sector that is part of the digital economy, alongside e-government, e-logistics, online tourism, Internet finance and the sharing economy.[277] This implies a narrow scope. The G20 does not explicitly address digital services.

The WTO itself does not refer to the term 'digital economy'. Rather, it uses the term 'electronic commerce', which it defines as '*the production, distribution, marketing, sale or delivery of goods and services by electronic means*'.[278] Interesting to note is the US's statement that it prefers to use the term 'digital trade' rather than the WTO's preferred term 'electronic commerce', due to the former being clearer and broader.[279] The alleged limitedness of the term 'electronic commerce' is, however, based on the conventionally used term 'e-commerce' to refer to the online ordering of goods (see the OECD and G20 definitions), not the broad definition given by the WTO. It is the WTO definition which is used throughout this book. This definition and the work of the WPEC require a more elaborate introduction, as they provide the foundation for the international legal framework on trade in digital services.

2.4.2 *Defining Digital Services*

E-commerce encompasses a vast array of digital services. It is the seemingly new nature of these services that has caused confusion and anxiety

275 G20 Digital Economy Task Force, 'G20 Digital Economy Development and Cooperation Initiative' (G20 2016) para 2 <www.g20.utoronto.ca/2016/g20-digital-economy-development-and-cooperation.pdf>.

276 G20, 'G20 Digital Economy Ministerial Declaration. Shaping Digitalisation for an Interconnected World' (G20 2017) para 2 <http://unctad.org/meetings/en/Contribution/dtl_eWeek2017c02-G20_en.pdf>.

277 G20 Digital Economy Task Force (n 275) 5.

278 WTO, 'Work Programme on Electronic Commerce – Adopted by the General Council on 25 September 1998', WT/L/274, 30 September 1998.

279 WTO General Council, 'Joint Statement on Electronic Commerce Initiative – Communication from the United States', JOB/GC/178, 12 April 2018, fn 1.

among WTO Members. It is therefore worthwhile to take a closer look at what these services entail.

The WTO neither refers to nor defines the terms digital trade, digital products or digital services. The lack of reference to the term 'digital service' does not mean that the WTO is of limited relevance to these services. To the contrary, a large part of the work conducted on electronic commerce in the WTO is done through submissions and discussion in the Council for Trade in Services. Chapter 4 elaborates on the applicability of the GATS to digital services, illustrating that digital services fall within the scope of the WTO rules.

For this research, digital services are understood to be *services that are supplied digitally*. This includes both more 'classic services', like legal services or consulting services that can now easily be provided over the Internet (including counselling over e-mails or voice-over-Internet Protocols [VoIP]), and 'new-generation services', like Internet telephony, blogs, social networks and search engines. The unifying trait of all of these services is their digital supply, which entails the use of the Internet and requires cross-border data flows.

Digital trade entails both online and offline elements, which makes capturing and regulating difficult.[280] Additional confusion is caused by the increased integration of goods and services (servicification), which makes it harder to distinguish and regulate both.[281] Moreover, because of the increased digitisation of products (e.g. the increased prevalence of digital content not fixed on a physical carrier), the distinction between goods and services increasingly blurs, provoking intense discussions on whether these 'digital products' fall into either one of these categories.[282]

2.4.3 Two Groups of Digital Services for Sake of Classification

Digital services make up a large part of e-commerce. The concept of 'digital services' encompasses a wide variety of different services. To facilitate classification, this research distinguishes two groups of digital services: digital infrastructure services and digitally enabled services.[283]

[280] Burri, 'The International Economic Law Framework for Digital Trade' (n 71) 10.
[281] ibid 13. *Supra* Section 2.3.
[282] Weber and Burri (n 5) 4; Zacharias (n 80).
[283] Note that this same distinction was already made by the WTO Secretariat in its 1998 note on 'WTO Agreements and electronic commerce' where it specified that electronic commerce related to services comprises three groups of transactions: (i) provision of Internet access services; (ii) electronic delivery of services (form of digitised information

This distinction is not a legal one and should not be interpreted that way. It aims at drawing a distinction between two 'kinds' of services which aids in the subsequent classification of these 'digital services' subgroups.[284]

2.4.3.1 Digital Infrastructure Services

With the development and widespread use of the Internet, distant delivery of services is no longer dependent on transmissions over telecommunication networks in the classic sense.[285] Digital infrastructure services are the services necessary for/incidental to the network that is the Internet. This includes data processing services, cloud computing, carrier services, hosting and IT infrastructure provisioning services and network management services. These services will be classified as either telecommunication or computer services, considering their nature.[286]

In light of technological advances and the fact that the Services Sectoral Classification List (W/120) was conceived in the early 1990s, WTO

flows); and (iii) online purchase of services which are delivered offline. This research only discusses the first two types of transactions as the third type of transaction does not entail the supply of a digital service as the services are provided offline. The former two types of transactions coincide with the distinction I make here. WTO General Council, 'WTO Agreements and Electronic Commerce' Note by the Secretariat, WT/GC/W/90, 14 July 1998, para 2 Wunsch-Vincent, 'Trade Rules for the Digital Age' (n 458) in M. Panizzon, N. Pohl and P. Sauvé (eds.), GATS and the International Regulation of Trade in Services (Cambridge University Press, 2008).

284 A similar approach seems to be taken in the ongoing negotiations on trade-related aspects of e-commerce. In their statement to the General Council, Argentina, Colombia and Costa Rica refer to '*sectors which form the enabling infrastructure for e-commerce*' and '*sectors of services that are deliverable online*'. WTO General Council, WTO Negotiations on Trade-related Aspects of E-commerce, 'Elements of a Potential Approach under the Framework of the Joint Statement on Electronic Commerce – Joint Communication from Argentina, Colombia and Costa Rica', JOB/GC/174, 6 April 2018, 2. See also: WTO General Council, 'Joint Statement on Electronic Commerce Initiative – Proposal for the Exploratory Work by Japan', JOB/GC/177, 12 April 2018, para 3.12. This approach is also proposed in Tuthill (n 125) 375.

285 Transmission over telecommunication networks in the classic sense required dedicated phone lines and had a tight limit on the amount of data that could be sent over these telephone lines. Nowadays, it is uncommon to use wired telephones to connect to the Internet.

286 As the introductory notes for the CPCprov clarify, its classification is based on the *nature* of the products. See CPCprov, full publication, available at <www.mauritiustrade.mu/ressources/pdf/UN_CPC_Codes.pdf>, para 25. Interestingly in its April 2018 non-paper, Brazil distinguished between services related to new business models based on digital environment (classifiable under computer and related services) and services related to the infrastructure of the digital environment (classifiable under telecommunications services). WTO General Council, 'Exploratory Work on Electronic Commerce – Non-paper from Brazil', JOB/GC/176, 12 April 2018, paras 4.1–4.3.

Members have taken a disparate approach in trying to create more certainty when it comes to such 'new' services. An example can be found in Vietnam's (relatively recent) GATS Schedule, which contains commitments on 'Internet Access Services' as a value-added telecom service under 'o. other'. It defines these services as '*services providing Internet access to the end users*'.[287] The EU has created and circulated a list of these electronic commerce infrastructure services, including telecommunications services, computer-related services, distribution services, advertising services and some banking services.[288]

Because these are the services that are required for the electronic delivery of services, it is important that extensive commitments are undertaken by WTO Members in the relevant service sectors and that market access is facilitated. This same consideration formed the basis for the adoption of the GATS Annex on Telecommunications,[289] which successfully led to increased market access for other service sectors that require access to and use of communication networks and services to work effectively.[290] Regardless of their exact classification, the focus should be on the liberalisation of these service sectors as this will facilitate the supply of any digital service.

2.4.3.2 Digitally Enabled Services

Digitally enabled services are those services that are supplied over the Internet. This encompasses a wide range of services, including: online lending services, online legal services, video-on-demand services, search engines, general over-the-top (OTT) services, e-payment services and Internet telephony. Any service that can be supplied over the internet or 'digitally' will fit within this category of digital services. Digitally enabled services can, in theory, be classified in any of the twelve service sectors contained in the GATS' sectoral classification list.

[287] WTO Trade in Services, 'Viet Nam – Schedule of Specific Commitments', GATS/SC/142, 19 March 2007, 30.

[288] WTO Work Programme on Electronic Commerce, 'Communication from the European Communities and their Member States', S/C/W/183, 30 November 2000, 4–5.

[289] This Annex is elaborated upon in Chapter 6 of this book.

[290] These included banking, insurance and other financial services. Weber and Burri (n 5) 62.

3

Barriers to Digital Services Trade

Having defined 'digital services' for the purpose of this research, the next step is to identify the barriers that such services are confronted with. This chapter first explains the general barriers to services trade that also impact digital trade and subsequently focusses on three specific barriers to digital services. In the subsequent parts of this book, the consistency of these specific barriers with international trade rules will be assessed.

Recital 3 of the preamble of the WTO Agreement identifies '*the reduction of tariffs and other barriers to trade*' as contributing to achieving the objectives of the WTO. From this objective, it can be deduced that barriers include both tariffs and 'other barriers'. These other barriers are not defined in the context of the WTO. The OED defines 'barrier' as '*a fence or material obstruction of any kind erected (or serving) to bar the advance of persons or things, or to prevent access to a place*'. In the context of trade, barriers should be understood as government interventions (or lack of action) which prevent goods or services from accessing consumers.[291]

Barriers to trade in services are generally high and, because of the proliferation of (digital) services trade, increasingly significant.[292] Examples of such barriers include, but are not limited to, licensing requirements, prior authorisation requirements, local content requirements and outdated rules of origin.[293] The economic impact of these barriers is exacerbated by the fact

[291] Or '*all government imposed and sponsored actions or omissions that act as prohibitions or restrictions on trade, other than ordinary customs duties and other duties and charges on imports and exports*' in Peter Van den Bossche and Werner Zdouc, *The Law and Policy of the World Trade Organization. Text, Cases and Materials* (4th edn, Cambridge University Press 2017) 479. For more references, see Roy Santana and Lee Ann Jackson, 'Identifying Non-Tariff Barriers: Evolution of Multilateral Instruments and Evidence from the Disputes (1948–2011)' (2012) 11 World Trade Review 462, 462.

[292] Joshua P Meltzer, 'A New Digital Trade Agenda' (International Centre for Trade and Sustainable Development (ICTSD) 2015) 5 <https://e15initiative.org/publications/a-new-digital-trade-agenda/>.

[293] Generally, see National Board of Trade, 'E-Commerce – New Opportunities, New Barriers: A Survey of e-Commerce Barriers in Countries Outside the EU' (n 283).

that access to online services is crucial for companies to function in GVCs and to expand their market.[294] Firms have identified the following issues as affecting their operations the most: (i) data flows; (ii) trade facilitation; (iii) consumer protection; (iv) payments; (v) digital identity; (vi) competition policy; (vii) access to services; and (viii) interoperability.[295] Many of these issues are closely related to the digital economy.

Worryingly, the number of significant barriers to digital services trade seems to have increased in recent years. Ferracane and Lee-Makiyama observe that, for example, most of China's restrictions on Internet access and digital services have been enacted in the last decade.[296] These barriers not only target cross-border data flows, but also deal with Internet content access, national standards, intellectual property rights (IPRs), restrictions on tariffs and trade defence measures.[297]

A major contributing factor to the proliferation of barriers to digital services trade is the historically unregulated nature of the Internet. It is felt by governments that this unregulated nature creates issues of national security, transparency and national sovereignty. Digital services quite easily cross borders undetected, lacking the tangibility that characterises trade in physical goods. Moreover, due to their digital supply, services can be traded internationally at an unprecedented pace. Therefore, in protecting various regulatory objectives, national governments have created barriers to the free flow of digital services. Reasons for restrictive regulation are manifold and include limiting freedom of speech, addressing threats to national security, ensuring law enforcement, threats to consumer privacy and freedom of speech, and responding to competitive challenges faced by domestic businesses.[298]

[294] Meltzer, 'Supporting the Internet as a Platform for International Trade Opportunities for Small and Medium-Sized Enterprises and Developing Countries' (n 9) 13.

[295] Lopez-Gonzalez and Ferencz (n 6) 30. However, they also point out that large digital firms are still concerned by traditional trade issues such as international standards, shipping, tariffs, etc.

[296] 54 measures were enacted after 2007 out of a total of 76 measures. Martina F Ferracane and Hosuk Lee-Makiyama, 'China's Technology Protectionism and Its Non-Negotiable Rationales' (ECIPE 2017) <http://ecipe.org/publications/chinas-technology-protectionism/>.

[297] ibid.

[298] Usman Ahmed and Grant Aldonas, 'Addressing Barriers to Digital Trade' (International Centre for Trade and Sustainable Development (ICTSD) 2015) 2 <http://e15initiative.org/publications/addressing-barriers-to-digital-trade/>; Mark Wu, 'Digital Trade-Related Provisions in Regional Trade Agreements: Existing Models and Lessons for the Multilateral Trade System' (ICTSD and IDB 2017) 1 <http://e15initiative.org/publications/digital-trade-related-provisions-in-regional-trade-agreements-existing-models-and-lessons-for-the-multilateral-trade-system/>.

Various barriers to digital services exist and this research does not aim to give an exhaustive description of the regulations that create barriers to trade in digital services. The objective of this Chapter is to provide the reader with a clear understanding of several types of barriers that hamper digital services trade. When considering the barriers discussed in this Chapter, their implications beyond the affected digital service should be considered. For example, the barriers' impact on GVCs, considering that digital services are crucial for the functioning of GVCs.

It should nevertheless be noted that regulation can also enable digital trade in various ways, including through provisions that provide both businesses and consumers confidence to trade digitally,[299] regulation that prevents harmful information from being available online, regulation that allows for the cross-border transfer of data and, more generally, regulation that '*addresses the impact of regulatory externalities and counteracts restrictions on digital services*'.[300] However, domestic regulation does have its limits, as it generally does not allow for the governing of service suppliers located in other jurisdictions, leading to regulatory divergence.[301]

In this Chapter, different types of trade barriers are elaborated upon that are of particular interest for the digital economy, based on their characteristics and specific impact on digital services trade. This typology will also structure the analysis of these barriers under the WTO framework and under WTO Members' RTAs.[302] One important barrier to digital service trade that cannot easily be classified within the typology but is worth mentioning nonetheless is the trade finance gap. This refers to the fact that it is considerably harder for MSMEs to gain the required finance in comparison to their multinational counterparts.[303] Additionally, e-commerce is hampered by certain border measures

299 Various elements affect this confidence: lack of harmonisation or mutual recognition, security concerns, inadequate logistics networks, access to international payment mechanisms and the non-profitability of taking disputes on trade in low-value goods to a dispute settlement mechanism. Meltzer, 'Maximizing the Opportunities of the Internet for International Trade' (n 1) 15–16.

300 ibid 14.

301 Defined as 'out of regulatory reach'. Peng, 'GATS and the Over-the-Top Services: A Legal Outlook' (n 102) 41.

302 Not necessarily every type of barrier will be discussed in depth in every section of the book. However, the continued use of this typology allows for a more structured approach throughout this study.

303 Suominen (n 138) 11.

(which are less relevant to digital services): cumbersome customs procedures as well as low *de minimis* values disproportionally affect small and medium-sized e-commerce traders.[304]

In a study conducted by the USITC, business pointed to five non-tariff measures (NTMs) that operate as barriers to digital trade: (i) localisation measures; (ii) data privacy and protection measures; (iii) IPRs-related measures; (iv) censorship measures; and (v) border measures and limits on immigration.[305] Wu identifies several barriers affecting digital trade: (i) impediments to free flow of data and requirements to store data locally (including limitations on digital finance); (ii) market access restrictions for digital services and goods related to IoT; (iii) limitations on investment or conditions for provision of digital products (e.g. disclosure of source code); and (iv) traditional barriers which also affect digital trade (e.g. customs duties, licensing procedures).[306] I use a different typology of barriers to digital services trade, but most of the NTMs identified *supra* will fit within one of the types of barriers described in this chapter.

3.1 General Services Barriers Impacting Trade in Digital Services

The advent of a new means to supply services also caused the rise of barriers to digitally enabled services. The rise of new opportunities for trade often comes with new types of impediments to this trade. Barriers to trade in services take the form of prohibitions, quantitative restrictions and burdensome (and/or unnecessary) government regulation.[307] Such barriers also affect digital services trade.

There is, however, one general barrier to services trade with specific ramifications for trade in digital services that deserves a mention here, as it closely relates to the phenomena of GVCs and digitisation: regulatory

[304] Meltzer, 'Supporting the Internet as a Platform for International Trade Opportunities for Small and Medium-Sized Enterprises and Developing Countries' (n 9) 13; USITC, 'Digital Trade in the U.S. and Global Economies, Part 1' (US International Trade Commission 2013) USITC Publication 4415, 5–23.

[305] USITC (n 304). The second part of that study focusses on the economic effects of these barriers to digital industries in the US and the US economy as a whole. USITC, 'Digital Trade in the U.S. and Global Economies, Part 2' (US International Trade Commission 2014) USITC Publication 4485.

[306] Wu (n 298) 1.

[307] Bernard Hoekman, 'Tentative First Steps: An Assessment of the Uruguay Round Agreement on Services' (World Bank 1995) WPS1455, 4; Andrew D Mitchell and Neha Mishra, 'Data at the Docks: Modernizing International Trade Law for the Digital Economy' (2018) 20 Vanderbilt Journal of Entertainment & Technology Law 1073, 1091–1092.

divergence.[308] Barriers created by regulatory divergence affect both trade in goods and trade in services. However, it can be put forward that some of the regulatory objectives prompting this type of barrier are closely related to digital services trade. These regulatory objectives particularly include the protection of consumers, privacy, public morals and (national) security.[309] For example, Brazil noted that: '*the use of electronic payment systems depends, to a large extent, upon a proper domestic regulatory environment*'.[310] A similar observation was made by Japan, which emphasised the importance of access to various online payment solutions, while at the same time ensuring security.[311]

Trade in digital services is considerably affected by regulatory differences and this divergence lowers incentives to enter markets and negatively impacts services trade flows.[312] Different regulations applying to the supply of the same digital service(s) in different countries raise costs for both businesses and consumers.[313] The limiting effect of regulatory divergence on free movement of digital services is especially pronounced in intra-industry and intra-firm trade, which impacts value chains.[314] Regulatory divergence is fostered by a lack of international standards, leading to a wide range of technical standards or licensing requirements that have been enacted for the same purpose but that impose particular

308 Regulatory barriers are often mentioned in the context of digital trade. For example: WTO General Council, WTO Negotiations on Trade-related Aspects of E-commerce, 'Elements of a Potential Approach under the Framework of the Joint Statement on Electronic Commerce – Joint Communication from Argentina, Colombia and Costa Rica', JOB/GC/174, 6 April 2018.

309 These regulatory objectives lead to restrictions to online content for public morals, privacy regimes, restrictions on online advertising, etc. Generally, see National Board of Trade, 'E-Commerce – New Opportunities, New Barriers: A Survey of e-Commerce Barriers in Countries Outside the EU' (n 283).

310 WTO General Council, 'Exploratory Work on Electronic Commerce – Non-paper from Brazil', JOB/GC/176, 12 April 2018, para 4.10.

311 WTO General Council, 'Joint Statement on Electronic Commerce Initiative – Proposal for the Exploratory Work by Japan', JOB/GC/177, 12 April 2018, paras 3.4 and 3.5.

312 Lopez-Gonzalez and Ferencz (n 6) 33–37; Hildegunn Kyvik Nordas, 'Services Trade Restrictiveness Index (STRI): The Trade Effect of Regulatory Differences' (OECD Publishing 2016) 189 <www.oecd-ilibrary.org/trade/services-trade-restrictiveness-index_5jlz9z022plp-en>.

313 The higher cost for companies lies, for example, in the obligation to comply with multiple certification requirements and approval processes and the requirement to meet different standards (e.g. related to privacy or consumer protection) in different countries. This cost is often passed on to the consumer. Simon Lester and Inu Barbee, 'The Challenge of Cooperation: Regulatory Trade Barriers in the Transatlantic Trade and Investment Partnership' (2013) 16 Journal of International Economic Law 847, 849, 852.

314 ibid 850.

obligations on digital service suppliers, differing from country to country. Examples were raised in the Council for Trade in Goods, where reference was made to technical standards affecting interconnectivity, compatibility of protocols and hardware and resulting interoperability problems.[315] Another example can be found in different countries enacting different privacy protection frameworks, which jeopardises the cross-border delivery of electronic services.[316] Lastly, the lack of transparency in regulation often leads to market access barriers, especially for MSMEs trying to expand their operations to foreign markets.[317]

There is, however, not a complete lack of international guidance. In 1996, the United Nations Commission on International Trade Law (UNCITRAL) adopted the Model Law on Electronic Commerce (MLEC).[318] The MLEC incorporates a set of '*internationally acceptable rules*' that aim to remove obstacles to electronic commerce, with particular focus on providing equal treatment to paper-based and electronic information. This Model Law merely serves as inspiration for countries wanting to enact legal measures on electronic commerce, as it does not itself create any legal obligations. UNCITRAL additionally created the Model Law on Electronic Signatures, which sets out criteria of technical reliability for the equivalence between electronic and offline signatures.[319] More recently, in 2017, UNCITRAL adopted the Model Law on Electronic Transferable Records.[320] Other related guidelines can be found within the OECD Privacy Framework that includes its 2013 Privacy Guidelines. These guidelines further the basic principles of free flow of data and proportionate restrictions.[321] Finally, APEC's Privacy

[315] WTO Council for Trade in Goods, 'Interim Review of Progress in the Implementation of the Work Programme on Electronic Commerce – Communication from the Chairman of the Council for Trade in Goods', WT/GC/24, 12 April 1999.

[316] Rolf Weber, 'Regulatory Autonomy and Privacy Standards under the GATS' (2012) 7 Asian Journal of WTO & International Health Law and Policy 25, 31. This divergence exists even though the Madrid Resolution contains a set of international standards for data protection and privacy: Madrid Resolution, adopted on 5 November 2009 at the International Conference of Data Protection and Privacy Commissioners, Madrid, available at <https://icdppc.org/wp-content/uploads/2015/02/The-Madrid-Resolution.pdf>.

[317] WTO General Council, 'Joint Statement on Electronic Commerce Initiative – Proposal for the Exploratory Work by Japan', JOB/GC/177, 12 April 2018, para 3.16.

[318] UNCITRAL, 'Model Law on Electronic Commerce with Guide to Enactment 1996 with Additional Article 5 Bis as Adopted in 1998' (United Nations Publications 1999).

[319] UNCITRAL, 'Model Law on Electronic Signatures with Guide to Enactment' (United Nations Publications 2001).

[320] UNCITRAL, 'Model Law on Electronic Transferable Records' (United Nations Publications 2017).

[321] OECD, 'The OECD Privacy Framework' (OECD 2013).

Framework was enacted to provide clear guidance and direction to businesses in APEC economies on common privacy issues and the impact of privacy issues on the way in which legitimate businesses are conducted.[322] None of these documents constitute binding international standards.

The barrier of regulatory divergence becomes particularly apparent when considering the importance of *trust* in international digital transactions. Because of certain risks related to digital trade that are not present in brick-and-mortar stores,[323] consumers require a certain degree of reassurance and trust to allow the Internet to develop its capacity as a driver of international trade.[324] Diverging regulation, even if enacted to ensure trust, can add to a lack of trust and lead to legal uncertainty. Regulatory cooperation in consumer and privacy protection helps foster the necessary trust for consumers to conduct international transactions online. In the context of the plurilateral negotiations on e-commerce, there is a clear need for a discussion on standardisation and focus on interoperability.[325] The interoperability of differing regulatory regimes and technologies has been recognised as a major challenge for digital trade.[326]

3.2 Restrictions on Cross-border Data Transfer

The continuous flow of data across borders is inseparable from the digital supply of services. Restrictions on the cross-border transfer of data are hence very disruptive of digital services trade as they contradict the borderless society created by digital technologies.[327] The term 'data' in

322 Paragraph 7 of the Preamble to Asian-Pacific Economic Cooperation, *APEC Privacy Framework* APEC#205-SE-01.2, December 2005, available at <http://publications.apec.org/Publications/2005/12/APEC-Privacy-Framework>.

323 This includes inability to inspect the merchandise, see the store and meet the vendor, the inability to return the goods to a physical store and the transmission of sensitive financial information. Meltzer, 'Supporting the Internet as a Platform for International Trade Opportunities for Small and Medium-Sized Enterprises and Developing Countries' (n 9) 12.

324 Meltzer also notes that it is the entirety of the online experience that determines consumer trust. '*Failure in one step in the commerce chain can undermine trust in the entire business*'.

325 WTO General Council, 'Joint Statement on Electronic Commerce Initiative – List of the Key Elements and Ideas on Electronic Commerce – Communication from Japan', JOB/GC/180, 13 April 2018.

326 Lopez-Gonzalez and Ferencz (n 6) 39.

327 Chan-Mo Chung, 'Data Localization: The Causes, Evolving International Regimes and Korean Practices' (2018) 52 Journal of World Trade 187, 193.

itself is not uncontested and trade lawyers have grappled with the concept of data and its position in international trade.[328] In recent years, it has become clear that data is a valuable commodity, often relinquished without much thought by users of 'free' digital services. There is no precedent in international trade law on how to deal with this kind of commodity. Members have also signalled the need for clarification of this term.[329]

The cross-border transfer of data is crucial for the Internet to function as a platform for international trade. Cross-border data flows can either constitute the object that is being traded themselves (e.g. purchasing of digital files, i.e. music, movies, books) or enable economic activity on the Internet (that might result in international trade).[330] Japan noted that limiting the international transferability of data through government policies encumbers cross-border business operations, hindering their development, and makes it more difficult for MSMEs worldwide to participate in GVCs.[331] For MSMEs, especially, the cost of complying with data localisation requirements (DLRs) can be prohibitive.[332] Additionally, barriers to data flows create the risk of balkanisation of cyberspace.[333]

Ferracane defines restrictions on data flows as '*those measures that raise the cost of conducting business across borders by either mandating companies to keep data within a certain border or by imposing additional requirements for data to be transferred abroad*'.[334] This entails a heterogeneous group of measures, all of which force firms to store their data locally or which make them incur higher costs in sending or processing data abroad.[335] These cross-border data flow restrictions seem to be

[328] For an in-depth analysis of the position of data within the WTO Framework see Sen (n 118).

[329] Including Taiwan in the context of the plurilateral e-commerce negotiations. See WTO General Council, 'Joint Statement on Electronic Commerce Initiative – Communication from the Separate Customs Territory of Taiwan, Penghu, Kinmen and Matsu', JOB/GC/182, 16 April 2018, 2.

[330] Meltzer, 'Supporting the Internet as a Platform for International Trade Opportunities for Small and Medium-Sized Enterprises and Developing Countries' (n 9) 12.

[331] WTO General Council, 'Joint Statement on Electronic Commerce Initiative – Proposal for the Exploratory Work by Japan', JOB/GC/177, 12 April 2018, para 3.7.

[332] Tuthill (n 125) 365.

[333] Sen (n 118) 324.

[334] Martina Ferracane, 'Restrictions on Cross-Border Data Flows: A Taxonomy' (ECIPE 2017) ECIPE Working Paper 1/2017, 2 <https://ecipe.org/publications/restrictions-to-cross-border-data-flows-a-taxonomy/>.

[335] ibid 3.

arranged along a spectrum, ranging from a little to very trade restrictive. Some 'types' or degrees of restrictions of free flow of data have been identified by various authors. Peng and Liu discuss three types of restrictions: type 1 being outright localisation requirements, type 2 including a combination of general cross-border data restrictions and industry-specific localisation requirements and type 3 constituting general cross-border data flow restrictions that do not require localisation.[336] Within the type 1 restrictions, a distinction can be drawn between local data storage requirements and local data processing requirements.[337] The former require companies to store data collected in one country within the borders of that country, necessitating the maintenance of data storage infrastructure.[338] The latter require companies to localise data processing within the territory of the country where the data was gathered.[339] Ferracane proposes a slightly different classification, distinguishing between strict restrictions on cross-border data flows on the one hand and conditional restrictions to cross-border data flows on the other hand. The former group consists of three types of restrictions: (i) local storage requirements; (ii) local storage and processing requirements; and (iii) ban on data transfer (i.e. local storage, local processing and local access requirements).[340] The latter group contains both conditional flow regimes where conditions apply to the recipient country and those regimes where conditions apply to the data controller or data processor. Even though these different types of restrictions could be arranged according to level of trade restrictiveness, Ferracane cautions that the trade restrictiveness of barriers to cross-border data flows will depend on the type of data that is affected as well as the service sectors covered.[341] Chung classifies national practices on data localization in five categories,

336 Shin-yi Peng and Han-wei Liu, 'The Legality of Data Residency Requirements: How Can the Trans-Pacific Partnership Help?' (2017) 51 Journal of World Trade 183, 193.

337 Daniel Crosby, 'Analysis of Data Localization Measures under WTO Services Trade Rules and Commitments' (International Centre for Trade and Sustainable Development (ICTSD) 2016) 2 <https://e15initiative.org/publications/analysis-of-data-localization-measures-under-wto-services-trade-rules-and-commitments/>.

338 Put differently, data cannot be transferred unless a copy of the data is stored within the exporting country's borders. Ferracane (n 334) 4.

339 Local data processing requirements limit in two ways, limiting not only the core service of data processing but also the attendant service of data processing required for many international (digital) business transactions. Crosby (n 337) 2.

340 It could be argued that the combination of a local storage and local processing requirement amounts to a *de facto* data transfer ban. Ferracane (n 334) 4.

341 ibid 3.

based on the strength of the requirements: (i) sector-specific; (ii) mild; (iii) partial; (iv) de facto; and (v) strong.[342]

Restrictions affecting cross-border data transfer are one of the most specific barriers to digital (services) trade. They take the form of, inter alia, DLRs, provisions preventing access to certain online content and data transfer restrictions.[343] Because the transfer of data is required for the provision of many (if not all) digital services, it makes an easy target for domestic regulatory policy.[344]

Various rationales lie at the basis of restrictions on cross-border data transfer: digital industrial policy, economic protectionism, protection of citizen's privacy, protection of public order/morals and national security interests.[345] An additional reason for barriers to cross-border data flows can be found in the inclination to preserve jurisdiction and the ability to enforce national law.[346] Even though some of these restrictions can be considered 'legitimate' and necessary, many others are simply protectionist measures under the guise of justifiable regulatory objectives. The domestic regulation of data flows has created considerable barriers to digital trade.[347] It is therefore crucial to strike a balance between ensuring the free flow of digital data and allowing for the necessary regulatory space to protect various policy objectives.

3.2.1 Data Localisation Requirements

The most prominent example of barriers to cross-border data flows is the requirement of data localisation, often maintained for privacy and national security reasons.[348] Data localisation rules can take different

342 Explaining the limitations as restrictions (i) tailored to specific service sectors (examples include location data (Greece), health records (Australia, Canada) and financial data (Argentina, China, Indonesia, Venezuela)); (ii) on international data transfer under certain conditions; (iii) applying to e.g. certain domain names or requiring the individual's consent; (iv) that create barriers to data transfer across borders; and (v) explicit requirements that data is stored on domestic servers. Chung (n 327) 189.

343 Andrew D Mitchell and Jarrod Hepburn, 'Don't Fence Me In: Reforming Trade and Investment Law to Better Facilitate Cross-Border Data Transfer' (2018) 19 Yale Journal of Law and Technology 182, 188–195.

344 As stated in National Board of Trade (n 283), at 16: '*The ability to transfer data across borders is a prerequisite for the utilisation of, so called, cloud services*'.

345 Crosby (n 337) 2.

346 WTO General Council, 'Exploratory Work on Electronic Commerce – Non-paper from Brazil', JOB/GC/176, 12 April 2018, para 4.16.

347 Wu (n 298) 5.

348 Also characterised as part of the larger group of barriers caused by 'state controls'. See Mitchell and Hepburn (n 343) 186; National Board of Trade, 'E-Commerce – New

forms, some being more onerous than others, but all of them limit efficiency and raise costs, often to be borne by the consumers.[349]

Data localisation measures have been defined as '*measures that require businesses to locate data servers within the host country for which they provide services [or] that require either the original data or a copy of it to be located in the territory concerned [or] that make the flow of data to other countries difficult*'.[350] This three-pronged definition fittingly illustrates the broad scope of this concept. BusinessEurope defines data localisation measures as '*[forcing] data to be geographically located in a certain location when processed or stored*'.[351] Tuthill defines DLRs as '*a collection of regulations that typically mandate where companies or their data must reside and whether [data] may cross borders at all*'.[352] Meltzer explains data localisation measures as '*any law that limits the ability for data to move globally and to remain local*'.[353] This includes commercial presence requirements, local content requirements and domestic regulations.

Regardless of its exact definition, it should be noted that localisation is not always involuntary; companies can choose to localise data servers for various reasons.[354] DLRs imposed by governments can nonetheless have significant negative effects: they increase the costs of providing digital services and entail the risk of certain markets being bypassed, leading to a balkanised Internet.[355] They reduce the productivity of services, increase prices for consumers and lead to inefficiently expended government resources.[356] Measures requiring data localisation hurt GDP,

Opportunities, New Barriers: A Survey of e-Commerce Barriers in Countries Outside the EU' (n 283) 17.

349 Including the requirements to: physically place a server in a country, store local consumer data within a country or process all data locally (from less to more onerous); See ibid 6; Others are domestic content requirements for government procurement contracts or subsidies, and compliance with country-specific requirements instead of national standards. Porges and Enders (n 135) 5.

350 Chung (n 327) 188–189.

351 BusinessEurope, 'The Proposal for a Free Flow of Data Regulation' (BusinessEurope 2017) Position Paper 2 <www.businesseurope.eu/publications/proposal-free-flow-data-regulation-businesseurope-position-paper>.

352 Tuthill (n 125) 363.

353 Meltzer, 'A New Digital Trade Agenda' (n 292) 5.

354 Chung (n 327) 189.

355 Meltzer, 'The Internet and International Data Flows in the Global Economy' (n 14).

356 Neha Mishra, 'Privacy, Cybersecurity, and GATS Article XIV: A New Frontier for Trade and Internet Regulation?' (2019) 19 World Trade Review 341, 5.

exports and foreign FDI and essentially impose a tax on local companies.[357] Japan equally reiterated the threat posed by DLRs to market access for foreign companies.[358] The USITC qualified data localisation as a primary barrier to digital trade.[359]

Various regulatory approaches exist to controlling cross-border data transfer.[360] Aaronson and Leblond identify three 'data realms', each with their own approach to developing a different enabling environment for cross-border data flows.[361] While the US realm imposes few limits on cross-border data flows, the EU subjects cross-border data flows to limitations for reasons of privacy protection (which it identifies as its top priority), and China almost completely restricts the free flow of data, both cross-border and domestically. They identify the existence of these three different data realms and the impact they have on other countries (bringing those into their realm through incentives or coercion) as a new digital divide.[362] The approaches to cross-border data flows taken by the three realms notably reflect their views on personal data protection. Whereas the United States is of the opinion that countries should establish a privacy floor without going into detail on how personal data should be protected as a consumer right solely, the EU has recognised (online) privacy as a human as well as a consumer right.[363] China goes much further in its desire to control information, in that it controls not only information that flows out of China, but also data that circulates within the country.[364]

Members have voiced their concerns regarding barriers to cross-border data flows in various instances. Brazil requested discussing the ownership of data produced in different jurisdictions and the issue of content responsibility in the negotiations on the trade-related aspects of e-commerce.[365] In its request for guidelines on regulating the cross-

[357] Matthias Bauer and others, 'The Costs of Data Localisation: Friendly Fire on Economic Recovery' (ECIPE 2014) ECIPE Occasional Paper 3/2014, 10 <https://ecipe.org/publications/dataloc/>.

[358] WTO General Council, 'Joint Statement on Electronic Commerce Initiative – Proposal for the Exploratory Work by Japan', JOB/GC/177, 12 April 2018, para 3.8.

[359] USITC (n 304).

[360] Ferracane (n 334) 6; Peng and Liu (n 336) 187–192.

[361] Aaronson and Leblond (n 116).

[362] ibid 247.

[363] ibid 256. Through instruments with extraterritorial application like the General Data Protection Regulation (GDPR) and the e-Privacy Directive, the EU is imposing its values upon foreign suppliers and consumers of data.

[364] ibid 263.

[365] WTO General Council, 'Exploratory Work on Electronic Commerce – Non-paper from Brazil', JOB/GC/176, 12 April 2018, paras 4.19 and 4.20.

border transmission of data, Taiwan discussed (i) the exceptionality of the circumstances under which restrictions should be allowed; (ii) providing examples of legitimate and recognised policy objectives that allow regulatory restrictions; (iii) avoiding the creation of unnecessary obstacles to electronic commerce; and (iv) developing and applying regulatory measures on a transparent and non-discriminatory basis.[366] The United States focussed on the reduced costs, improvement of quality of service and strengthened cybersecurity due to the economies of scale afforded by digitally enabled services. They further trade rules which ensure that companies are not required to build or employ local infrastructure '*to better serve their customers*'.[367] They have called for the abolishment of localisation barriers in order to further the digital economy, as these barriers '*add unnecessary costs and burdens on providers and consumers alike*'.[368] Chung argues that in addressing security concerns, rather than exporting a brick-and-mortar idea of location-based requirements, Members should opt for a risk-based approach with appropriate administrative, physical and technical safeguards.[369]

The business perspective on DLRs can partly be found in BusinessEurope's 2017 position paper on the European Commission's proposal for a Free Flow of Data Regulation. The paper requests the European Commission to require Member States to remove DLRs.[370] As more and more data will move across borders, trade and innovation will be increasingly hindered. Industry, however, also distinguishes between personal and non-personal data, as it supports the principle of free movement of non-personal data and only includes personal data in that principle when it is too difficult or costly to unbundle both types of data.[371]Additionally, it requested the Commission to clarify the scope of public security as a justification and urged it not to include new security requirements. Not only does BusinessEurope request more transparency and a reporting duty for all new DLRs, it also calls for a clarification of the powers of the European Commission to determine the legality of new

366 WTO General Council, 'Joint Statement on Electronic Commerce Initiative – Communication from the Separate Customs Territory of Taiwan, Penghu, Kinmen and Matsu', JOB/GC/182, 16 April 2018.

367 WTO General Council, 'Joint Statement on Electronic Commerce Initiative – Communication from the United States', JOB/GC/178, 12 April 2018, para 2.1.

368 WTO General Council, 'Work Programme on Electronic Commerce – Non-Paper from the United States', JOB/GC/94, 4 July 2016, para 2.5.

369 Chung (n 327) 194.

370 BusinessEurope (n 351) 2.

371 ibid 3.

DLRs in light of the single market principle. Finally, an industry-led initiative should draft codes of conduct on data portability (so-called 'porting') to ensure effective competition and to make it easier to switch providers and port data.[372]

Similarly, DigitalEurope, representing the digital technology industry in Europe, reacted with alarm to the European Commission's February 2018 proposal on horizontal provisions for cross-border data flows in EU Trade and Investment Agreements. It warned that such provisions could facilitate and legitimise forced data localisation and that they would significantly hinder cross-border data flows.[373] It warned that it is important for these provisions to find the right balance between EU law and well-established trade disciplines.[374]

Associations of US digital companies have sent similar messages regarding the undesirability of DLRs. They warn that DLRs are often imposed for protectionist reasons, with the aim of developing a local IT sector.[375] At the same time, these restrictions on cross-border data flows considerably increase the cost of doing business in other markets. US industry has spoken out against DLRs enacted by foreign governments as well as actively supported the inclusion of DLR prohibitions in US trade agreements.[376]

Various reasons exist for countries to want to enact DLRs. Countries justify their DLRs arguing that they want to secure data privacy from surveillance of foreign companies or governments, that they want to facilitate taxation and law enforcement, to protect the domestic industry (from an economic point of view) or merely to exercise its rights as a sovereign state (from a political point of view).[377] Other objectives of data localisation include cybersecurity, national security and public order.[378] Establishing jurisdiction is another important reason for mainly developing countries to require localisation of data. Jurisdiction over data

[372] ibid 5.

[373] See Peng and Liu (n 336) 199.

[374] ibid 3.

[375] Richard Adler, 'Towards a Better Understanding of Internet Economics' (Internet Association 2018) <https://internetassociation.org/publications/towards-better-understanding-internet-economics/>.

[376] See, for example, 'U.S. Tech Giants Plan to Fight India's Data Localisation Plans', *Reuters*, 18 August 2018 and 'Toward a State-of-the-Art U.S.-UK Trade Agreement', *Information Technology Industry Trade Council (ITI)*, 5 May 2020.

[377] For example, the objectives invoked by Russia for its amended Law on Personal Data were protection of privacy and security interests.

[378] Ferracane (n 334) 6.

can be based on various elements: the nationality of the Internet user, the location of the Internet service supplier or the location of the data. It is this latter basis which is being furthered more and more by governments as the most straightforward method to establish jurisdiction over data.[379] Whereas extraterritorial application of laws is feasible for large countries, this is less the case for developing countries, which address this legitimate concern through the enactment of DLRs.[380] DLRs not only allow access to data stored domestically, but also avoid foreign law enforcement.[381]

3.2.2 *Examples of Members Restricting Cross-border Data Flows*

The example that will be used as a case study and discussed in more detail in this book is Russia's 2014 amendment of the Law on personal data, which imposes a DLR on service suppliers wanting to supply their services in the Russian territory.[382] Other examples of DLRs can be found in Vietnam's Decree 72[383] and its recently approved cybersecurity law,[384] India's Reserve Bank's proposal to require storing payment systems' data locally,[385] Indonesia's requirement on providers of 'public services' to establish local data centres,[386] Malaysia's Personal Data Protection Act,[387] Nigeria's requirement on ICT companies to host

[379] Peng and Liu (n 336) 199.

[380] Chung (n 327) 195.

[381] Peng and Liu (n 336) 200.

[382] Federal Law No. 242-FZ (Russia, 2014). Under Federal Statute of 5 May 2014 No.97-FZ (Russia, 2014), data operators in Russia are '*required to ensure that the collection, recording, systematization, accumulation, storage updating, amending, and retrieval of any information about Russian citizens [is] done via servers located in its territory and that competent authorities [are] notified regarding the location of storage facilities where such data is stored*'.

[383] This decree bans the online sharing of materials that are considered harmful to national security, social order or safety and requires ISPs to maintain at least one local server to facilitate inspection. Article 24 of Decree No. 72/2013/ND-CP of 15 July 2013, on the management, provision and use of Internet services and online information (Decree 72), available at <www.vnnic.vn/en/about/legaldocs/decree-no-72–2013-nd-cp-july-15–2013-management-provision-and-use-Internet?lang=en>.

[384] Mai Nguyen, 'Vietnam Lawmakers Approve Cyber Law Clamping Down on Tech Firms, Dissent' *Reuters* (Hanoi, 12 June 2018).

[385] Reserve Bank of India Notification, 'Storage of Payment Systems Data', RBI/2017–18/153.

[386] United States Trade Representative, 'Key Barriers to Digital Trade', Fact Sheets (Washington DC: USTR 2017).

[387] Article 129 of the Personal Data Protection Act, Act 709, 2 June 2010, prohibits the transfer of 'any personal data' outside of Malaysia.

government data locally,[388] Australia's Privacy Principles[389] and its ban on the transfer of health data,[390] and Canadian provinces' ban on transfer of personal data from public institutions.[391]

The most important European example of conditional flow regimes is the General Data Protection Regulation (GDPR).[392] Under the GDPR, the processing of personal data may in principle only be done in countries with an adequate level of protection. The GDPR provides several (restrictive) bases for the transfer of personal data to third countries: (i) transfers to countries for which an adequacy decision has been adopted;[393] (ii) the company that transfers the data has provided appropriate safeguards;[394] and (iii) derogations for specific situations.[395] The GDPR will be discussed in more detail in Chapter 7.

In 2016, Turkey enacted the 'Law on the Protection of Personal Data', which limits the cross-border flow of personal data out of Turkey.[396] This law is based on the principles of the EU's GDPR.[397] Cross-border transmission of personal data is only possible upon the data subject's consent or if the data will be adequately protected in the country it is being

388 Section 14.1 of the Guidelines for Nigerian Content Development in Information and Communications Technology (ICT), 3 December 2013, available at <https://nlipw.com/wp-content/uploads/Guidelines-for-Nigerian-Content-Development-in-Information-and-Communications-Technology-ICT.pdf>.

389 The Australian Privacy Principles (APPs) only allow disclosing personal information to a foreign recipient if reasonable steps are taken to ensure that this recipient does not breach the privacy principles. Privacy principle 8.1 prohibits entities from disclosing personal information to an overseas recipient unless reasonable effort is undertaken to ensure that the recipient respects the APPs. The principle, however, foresees in exceptions allowing transfer when the recipient is governed by substantially equivalent law as the APPs, the data subject has provided informed consent or if the transfer is otherwise permitted. The APPs can be found in schedule 1 of the (amended) Privacy Act 1988, Act No. 119 of 1988, 14 December 1988.

390 Section 77 of the Personally Controlled Electronic Health Record Act of 2012, Act No. 63, 26 June 2012.

391 Freedom of Information and Protection of Privacy Act, R.S.B.C. 1996, c 165, s 30.1 (British Columbia) and Personal Information International Disclosure Protection Act, S. N.S. 2006, c 3, s 5(a), November 2006 (Nova Scotia).

392 Regulation (EU) 2016/679 of the European Parliament and of the Council of 27 April 2016 on the protection of natural persons with regard to the processing of personal data and on the free movement of such data and repealing Directive 95/46/EC, OJ L 119, 4 May 2016, 1.

393 Article 45 of the GDPR.

394 Articles 46 and 47 of the GDPR

395 Article 49 of the GDPR

396 Law on Protection of Personal Data, 7 April 2016, no. 6698.

397 Burak Ozdagistanli, 'Data Protection in Turkey: Overview' (Thomson Reuters 2018) Country Q&A <https://uk.practicallaw.thomsonreuters.com/7-520-1896>.

transferred to.[398] These obligations are enforced through criminal penalties.[399] In 2018, Brazil passed the General Data Protection Law, which was said to have been inspired by the EU's GDPR. Like the European Regulation, the General Data Protection Law restricts cross-border transfers of personal data to instances where (i) the country of destination is deemed to provide an adequate level of data protection or (ii) standard contractual clauses or other mechanisms approved by the data protection authority are used.[400] The Law is enforced through fines.

South Korea enacted DLRs throughout various pieces of legislation and applying to different types of data: the Personal Information Protection Act prohibits cross-border transfer of personal information, unless consent is given by the data subject;[401] the Information and Communications Network Act enacts data protection provisions that are applicable to the information and communications sector;[402] the Act on Establishment, Management, etc. of Spatial Data restricts cross-border transfer of mapping data;[403] South Korea's pre-announced standards for cloud computing require cloud computing service suppliers to locate public sector servers within Korean territory; and the Regulation on Financial Institutions' Delegation of Data Processing Business and IT Facilities only allows data processing of financial data by affiliated companies.

China also considerably limits cross-border data flows. Since the early 1990s, companies have been under a *de facto* obligation to store any data they collect in China on servers located within the country.[404] The 2016 Cybersecurity Law, however, formalised barriers to cross-border data flows by setting out that personal data of Chinese citizens and 'important data' that is collected by 'key infrastructure operators' must be stored within China.[405] The 2015 Counterterrorism law submits the transfer of

398 Article 9 of the Law on Protection of Personal Data, 7 April 2016, no. 6698.

399 Articles 17 and 18 of the Law on Protection of Personal Data, 7 April 2016, no. 6698.

400 Article 33 of Law No. 13.709, of 14 August 2018 – Provides for the protection of personal data and changes Law No. 12.965, of 23 April 2014.

401 Personal Information Protection Act, No. 10465, 30 September 2011. The law does not specify a penalty for violation of these provisions. Chung (n 327) 203.

402 Act on Promotion of Information and Communication Network Utilization and Information Protection, Etc., No. 5986, 31 December 2001.

403 Act on the Establishment, Management, etc. of Spatial Data, No. 12738, 3 June 2014.

404 Ferracane and Lee-Makiyama (n 296) 13.

405 Article 37 of Standing Committee of the National People's Congress, *Cybersecurity Law of the People's Republic of China,* Order No. 53 of the President of the People's Republic of China, 7 November 2016 (2016 Cybersecurity Law).

personal data abroad not only to the subject's explicit consent but also government approval or explicit regulatory approval.[406] Additionally, China requires data localisation (storing, processing and handling) for some specific types of data: personal information collected by banks and health information. This data cannot be transferred abroad.[407] Also, providing online maps in China requires an official certificate and the data must be stored locally.[408] In its 2017 communication to the Council for Trade in Services, the United States argues that China's measures disrupt, deter and prohibit cross-border transfers of information.[409] That year, China also enacted limitations to cross-border data flows through leased lines and virtual private networks (VPNs).[410] VPNs allow companies and consumers to bypass China's Great Firewall as they disguise data/traffic flowing through the firewall, making it seems as if they are (permitted) data flows with destinations in other parts of the world. China no longer allows companies operating in China to create or hire dedicated lines (including VPNs) to conduct cross-border business activities. The use of authorised VPNs is limited to internal office use and lines cannot be used to connect to domestic or overseas data centres or operation platforms to conduct telecom operation business activities. The United States has argued that China's measures restrict cross-border information transfers exclusively to information flows for internal office purposes. This arguably puts constraints on market access opportunities for cross-border service suppliers and could also violate Section 5 (c) of the Telecoms Annex as it directly and significantly affects the ability of cross-border service suppliers to access and use public telecommunications services (including VPNs and leased lines).[411] Ferracane and Lee-Makiyama note that, whereas many countries impose restrictions to

406 Standing Committee of the National People's Congress, *Counterterrorism Law of the People's Republic of China*, Order No. 36 of the President of the People's Republic of China, 27 December 2015; Ferracane and Lee-Makiyama (n 296) 14.

407 ibid 13.

408 Ferracane (n 334) 13.

409 WTO Council for Trade in Services, 'Communication from the United States – Measures Adopted and under Development by China Relating to its Cybersecurity Law', S/C/W/374, 26 September 2017.

410 China Ministry of Industry and Information Technology, 'MIIT notice on Cleaning Up and Regulating the Internet Access Service Market', MIIT Telecom. Dept. Doc. No. [2017] 32, 17 January 2017.

411 WTO Council for Trade in Services, 'Measures Adopted and under Development by China Relating to its Cybersecurity Law' Communication from the United States, S/C/W/376, 23 February 2018, paras 6 and 7.

cross-border data flows similar to China's, they do not impose these restrictions simultaneously nor so disproportionally or opaquely.[412]

3.3 Web Filtering and Content Control

Governments can limit access to the Internet in various ways. Most often, this is done through the simple blocking of foreign web pages or applications.[413] Content or language quotas enacted to preserve national identities can equally act as market access barriers to digital (audiovisual) services.[414] Other examples include restrictions on online advertising and Internet access and measures to divert searches for online goods and services.[415] Erixon et al. identify two ways to block foreign websites: either by centralising and supervising all exit points of Internet communications or by preventing ISPs operating in their country from accessing certain websites.[416] However, censorship is not only exercised through restrictions on cross-border supply of services. Censorship can equally take the form of a restriction on foreign equity ownership in businesses, denial of trading rights or denial of access to distributors.[417]

Contrary to the complete blocking of web pages, governments can also filter selectively, censoring only individual pages or sections of websites. Selective filtering can also be based on keyword inputs by users, for example in search engines.[418] For user-generated content, the emphasis is often laid on self-censorship by the platforms or ISPs, in order to avoid complete blocking of their services.[419] The textbook example of a government engaging in web filtering is the Chinese government through its so-called 'Chinese firewall'. This web filtering system will be used as a case study and discussed in more detail in Chapter 7 of this book.

The most extreme example of web blocking seen so far was the complete disconnection of the Xinjiang province from the Internet in

412 Ferracane and Lee-Makiyama (n 296) 15.

413 Fredrik Erixon, Brian Hindley and Hosuk Lee-Makiyama, 'Protectionism Online: Internet Censorship and International Trade Law' (ECIPE 2009) ECIPE Working Paper 12/2009, 4; Wu (n 48) 275 <https://ecipe.org/publications/protectionism-online-internet-censorship-and-international-trade-law/>.

414 Wunsch-Vincent, 'Trade Rules for the Digital Age' (n 283) 29.

415 Meltzer, 'Supporting the Internet as a Platform for International Trade Opportunities for Small and Medium-Sized Enterprises and Developing Countries' (n 9) 13.

416 Erixon, Hindley and Lee-Makiyama (n 413) 4–5.

417 ibid 7.

418 For example, in China and Iran searching for specific terms does not yield results. ibid 6.

419 ibid.

2009.[420] This geographical region was not granted access to the Internet for more than 6 months after ethnic riots in July 2009. Even though Internet access was restored, users in Xinjiang can still not access foreign websites and only have access to filtered versions of official Chinese news and information websites.

Many reasons exist for governments to filter the websites that their citizens have access to. The political motivation is most obvious (curbing critical ideas, opposition groups and regime criticism), but reasons of morality and even commercial purposes have also been cited.[421] Additionally, Tuthill refers to protection of privacy and security of Internet users, suppression of fraud and money laundering, copyright infringement and threats to health and safety as possible policy objectives leading to web filtering.[422]

3.4 Other Barriers and Obstacles to Digital Services Trade

Of course, not all barriers to digital services trade fit within the above-mentioned three types of barrier. The different barriers that digital services can be faced with are so varied and changeable that it would be difficult to map all of them exhaustively. Moreover, any taxonomy will be a snapshot of the current situation as new business models will likely give rise to new kinds of barriers. This book limits itself to an in-depth study of the digital-trade-specific barriers mentioned *supra*, and a more succinct analysis of three additional barriers that do not exclusively affect digital services trade, but are especially relevant for this type of trade. These additional barriers are briefly discussed in this section.

3.4.1 Limited Access to Infrastructure

As digital traders require access to the Internet as a platform to trade internationally, hindered access to mobile networks, broadband or reliable power supply inhibits trade in digital services. It is important to acknowledge here that limited access to infrastructure can be caused by anti-competitive practices by incumbent firms, by governmental (protectionist) policies or as a consequence of what is known as the 'digital

420 Cynthia Liu, 'Internet Censorship as a Trade Barrier: A Look at the WTO Consistency of the Great Firewall in the Wake of the China-Google Dispute' (2011) 42 Georgetown Journal of International Law 1199, 1211.

421 Erixon, Hindley and Lee-Makiyama (n 413) 4.

422 Tuthill (n 125) 364.

divide'. The term 'digital divide' refers to the gap between those who have ready access to computers and the Internet and those who do not. This divide exists among the least-developed, the developing and the developed parts of the world, reporting figures of Internet penetration of, respectively, 19, 47 and 87 per cent in 2019.[423] In the context of the WPEC, developing Members have referred to the continuing digital divide between the developed and many developing countries to denounce the uneven playing field.[424] Where the central components necessary for e-commerce are lacking (power supply, connectivity, bandwidth or access to the Internet[425]), developing countries cannot participate in global digital trade. The problem of the digital divide is exacerbated by the fact that Internet access allows for a range of economic growth opportunities for developing countries.[426] The WTO Secretariat recognised the importance of efforts to enhance infrastructure investments, especially in broadband.[427]

Tackling the digital divide requires the combined solving of various simultaneous problems, including lowering broadband costs, avoiding monopolies or duopolies in the telecommunications market, providing a reliable power supply and improving English proficiency.[428] Therefore, a pro-competitive regulatory environment in the telecommunications market is crucial. Such regulations will not only avoid abuse of monopoly positions but should equally ensure adequate allocation of spectrum and increase price competition.[429] Burri characterises the digital divide as multi-layered, consisting not only of divergence in Internet access but also in a social divide as well as a democratic divide.[430]

[423] International Telecommunications Union, 'Facts and figures 2019 – Measuring digital development', available at <https://itu.foleon.com/itu/measuring-digital-development/offline-population/>.

[424] WTO News, 'WTO Members Discuss the Role of E-Commerce in Fostering Development' (14 March 2017) <www.wto.org/english/news_e/news17_e/devel_14mar17_e.htm>.

[425] ibid.

[426] Meltzer, 'Maximizing the Opportunities of the Internet for International Trade' (n 1) 11; UNCTAD, '2015 Information Economy Report' (United Nations Publications 2015) UNCTAD/IER/2015.

[427] WTO Council for Trade in Services, 'Computer and Related Services' Background Note by the Secretariat, S/C/W/300, 22 June 2009, para 28.

[428] This last point is a problem not to be underestimated, as the majority of online content is in English. Meltzer, 'Supporting the Internet as a Platform for International Trade Opportunities for Small and Medium-Sized Enterprises and Developing Countries' (n 9) 12.

[429] ibid 18.

[430] Mira Burri, 'The Global Digital Divide as Impeded Access to Content' in Mira Burri and Thomas Cottier (eds), *Trade Governance in the Digital Age* (Cambridge University Press 2012) 396.

It is important to keep in mind that the digital divide continues to exist also in developed countries, where the ICT penetration is high. The continuous introduction of new technologies and new tools in the market keeps generating new lines of division.[431] As a first step to overcome the digital divide by fostering competitive telecoms markets, the United States has proposed the adoption of the Reference Paper on basic telecoms into GATS schedules and to provide market access to telecoms investors and cross-border suppliers.[432] It should, however, be kept in mind that there is no one-size-fits-all solution to the problems created by the digital divide. The developing countries that are confronted with these issues are widely diverging and many will require a specific pragmatic approach.[433]

The issues caused by the digital divide are also aptly illustrated by the initial refusal by the African Group and certain LDCs to engage in negotiations on the liberalisation of e-commerce. In its submission to the General Council of July 2017, the African Group warned that the development of new digital technologies will seriously disrupt economies.[434] It pointed out the unequal distribution of international bandwidth, the fact that 75 per cent of the African population is not using the Internet and that the digital divide is only widening.[435] Bandwidth is still unequally distributed and there is a clear need for developing countries to assess the impact of the lack of digital and technological capabilities on the digital divide, as it will most likely widen. Moreover, the African Group urged developing countries to think about the way in which they treat data as it will determine the development path they take in the digital age. It pointed out that Members have been using barriers to digital services to nurture and develop domestic industries and that regulating digital trade now would seriously curtail the policy space of developing countries. It argued that such curtailing prevents closing the digital divide.[436] Kelsey rightly warns that the technologies that have transformed services trade are not development neutral and that the

431 ibid 403.

432 WTO General Council, 'Joint Statement on Electronic Commerce Initiative – Communication from the United States', JOB/GC/178, 12 April 2018, para 7.1.

433 Burri, 'The Global Digital Divide as Impeded Access to Content' (n 430) 403.

434 WTO General Council, 'Report of Panel Discussion on "Digital Industrial Policy and Development" – Communication from the African Group', JOB/GC/133, 21 July 2017.

435 ibid paras 1.3 and 1.4.

436 ibid paras 1.7 and 1.8.

digital domain is not a level playing field.[437] It is crucial to make sure that measures support developing countries to integrate better into the digital economy.[438]

Noam identifies three kinds of digital gaps: (i) the gap of telecommunications connectivity, (ii) the gap of Internet access and (iii) the gap of e-commerce. He states the first gap can quite easily be addressed through investment in infrastructure and liberalising policy reform.[439] The second requires a similar solution, focussing on specific policies to encourage Internet usage (once the infrastructure itself is in place).[440] The third gap he identifies relates to how the vast majority of companies active in e-commerce are based in developed countries, where they form economies of scale.[441]

Other examples of obstacles include lack of access to technology distribution channels and information networks as well as new online market structures and the subsequent potential market dominance of a handful of companies. The treatment of large online platforms is also an important policy consideration in the negotiations on data flows, as many of them strongly resemble natural monopolies. Brazil has proposed discussions on new approaches to competition policy, including the concepts of data portability and non-discriminatory access.[442] A lack of Internet access is not limited to a lack of access to physical infrastructure but also encompasses a lack of a regulatory framework to ensure a free and open Internet. Access to services on the Internet for consumers and provision of

[437] Jane Kelsey, 'How a TPP-Style E-Commerce Outcome in the WTO Would Endanger the Development Dimension of the GATS Acquis (and Potentially the WTO)' (2018) 21 Journal of International Economic Law 273, 294.

[438] Mitchell and Mishra (n 307) 1125.

[439] Eli Noam, 'Overcoming the Three Digital Divides' in Damien Geradin and David Luff (eds), *The WTO and Global Convergence in Telecommunications and Audio-Visual Services* (Cambridge University Press 2004) 425.

[440] ibid.

[441] He notes the difficulty of engaging in e-commerce, based on the fact that doing e-commerce well is expensive. It often requires '*supply chain EDI, payment systems, integration with financial institutions, fulfilment systems, customer data mining, production, customisation, community creation and the creation of consumer lock-in by additional features*'. ibid 425–426. It could be argued that part of these costs is taken away by the creation of e-commerce platforms (e.g. eBay, Etsy) that allow MSMEs to access global consumers, depend on trustworthy payment systems, etc.

[442] WTO General Council, 'Exploratory Work on Electronic Commerce – Non-paper from Brazil', JOB/GC/176, 12 April 2018, para 4.21.

services on the Internet by suppliers should be ensured, both domestically and cross-border.[443]

It is important to indicate that Internet access does not only take the form of access to classic telecommunication infrastructure, but also that of availability of mobile phones and mobile networks.[444] This development is due to the decreasing costs of mobile phones as well as the fact that fixed-line networks turned out to be more expensive to build than telecommunications networks for mobile devices.[445] The obstacles to mobile phone access are mainly found in the cost of the devices and the interconnection charges.[446] Mobile networks hold the potential for improving trading conditions in developing countries, but this will still require considerable investment into mobile towers, telecommunication infrastructure and data centres.[447]

Another important obstacle to digital services trade is the lack of network neutrality. Network neutrality or 'net neutrality' refers to the principle that all data sent over networks should be treated in a non-discriminatory way, be it based either on the user, content, website, platform, application or another distinguishing feature. Or put differently, it means that '*broadband service providers charge consumers only once for Internet access, don't favor one content provider over another, and don't charge content providers for sending information over broadband lines to end users*'.[448] As mentioned by Brazil in its April 2018 non-paper, ISPs '*should not be allowed to discriminate data packages by its content, origin and destination, service, terminal or application, through public networks, except for emergency communications and for technical requirements indispensable to the adequate provision of services and applications*'.[449]

443 WTO General Council, 'Joint Statement on Electronic Commerce Initiative – Proposal for the Exploratory Work by Japan', JOB/GC/177, 12 April 2018, para 3.9.

444 Meltzer, 'Supporting the Internet as a Platform for International Trade Opportunities for Small and Medium-Sized Enterprises and Developing Countries' (n 9) 10.

445 ibid. Porges and Enders explain the preference for mobile broadband over classic telecommunication infrastructure '*because mobile towers cover an entire area without any need to build out last-mile access lines and mobile network upgrades generally pay for themselves*'. Porges and Enders (n 135) 3.

446 Meltzer, 'Supporting the Internet as a Platform for International Trade Opportunities for Small and Medium-Sized Enterprises and Developing Countries' (n 9) 11.

447 Porges and Enders (n 135) 3.

448 Robert W Hahn and Scott Wallsten, 'The Economics of Net Neutrality' (American Enterprise Institute and Brooking Institution 2006) RP06-13 <www.cato.org/sites/cato.org/files/serials/files/regulation/2012/6/v34n4-4.pdf>.

449 WTO General Council, 'Exploratory Work on Electronic Commerce – Non-paper from Brazil', JOB/GC/176, 12 April 2018, para 4.3.

Absence of net neutrality rules can, depending on the specific market situation, lead to abuse of dominant position and significantly increase costs for consumers. More generally, anti-competitive behaviour has been recognised within the WPEC as a barrier to e-commerce. Members noted that monopolies and restrictive business practices can hinder electronic commerce and that these issues should be addressed within the WPEC's context.[450] China has raised the importance of digital inclusion and asks Members to take into account the specific demands of developing countries and LDCs.[451] The case study on limited access to infrastructure in Chapter 7 of this book will focus on the US abolishment of net neutrality rules.

3.4.2 Ban on Cross-border Supply through Electronic Means

Other barriers also include the imposition of a complete ban to provide a certain service through cross-border supply. For example, similar to what was done by the United States in the *US – Gambling* dispute, Vietnam prohibits the cross-border supply of online advertising services. Foreign websites that want to advertise to Vietnamese citizens have to outsource these advertising services to a Vietnamese service supplier.[452] Similarly, Indonesia requires providers of OTT services to establish locally and use local IP numbers.[453] Because the cross-border supply of these services is practically only done through the Internet, via electronic supply, this amounts to a *de facto* ban on the digital supply of these services.

3.4.3 Digital Taxes

Even though it is steeply on the rise, taxation of digital services was still relatively rare at the time of writing. Due to their intangibility and the fact that they do not physically cross borders, services in general are rarely subject to import duties. Some are, however, subject to internal taxation, which is also the case for digital services. Due to the new business models

450 WTO Council for Trade in Services, 'Work Programme on Electronic Commerce – Progress Report to the General Council' Adopted by the Council for Trade in Services on 19 July 1999, S/L/74, 27 July 1999, para 13.

451 WTO General Council, 'E-commerce Elements for MC11' Communication from China, JOB/GC/142, JOB/CTG/9, JOB/ SERV/271, JOB/DEV/49, 19 October 2017.

452 United States Trade Representative (n 386).

453 ibid.

created by digitisation, taxation of digital services faces challenges in two ways: (i) with regard to direct taxation, the question can be raised whether a country has the right to tax a company that has no physical presence in its territory; and (ii) with regard to indirect taxation, tax authorities are struggling with the growing volume of goods and services that are purchased online from foreign suppliers, making it difficult to impose, for example, value-added tax or services taxes.

The possibility of taxation of digitally enabled services was anticipated by the WTO membership early on. In the context of the establishment of the WPEC, Members agreed to continue their practice of not imposing customs duties on electronic transmissions (the so-called e-commerce moratorium or moratorium on electronic transmissions).[454] The question of whether customs duties could apply to services and/or electronic transmissions was already raised in the WPEC's 1999 progress report to the General Council.[455] Even though Members were unable to answer this question, they did agree on the fact that such duties are detrimental. The permanent extension of the current standstill on customs duties on electronic transmissions has been proposed repeatedly,[456] but so far Members have limited themselves to temporary extensions, of which the latest example can be found in the General Council Decision of 10 December 2019.[457] In this discussion, it should be kept in mind that the duty-free moratorium is a political commitment, but that it is not legally binding within the WTO framework.[458]

Recently, some WTO Members have, however, started questioning the nature of the moratorium and its meaning. Whereas some Members are convinced that the moratorium on electronic transmission only prevents Members from imposing taxes on the electronic transmission itself, others see the moratorium as a commitment not to impose duties, not only on electronic transmission but also on the content that is being

454 WTO Ministerial Conference Geneva, 'Declaration on Global Electronic Commerce' Adopted 20 May 1998, WT/MIN(98)/DEC/2, 25 May 1998.

455 WTO Council for Trade in Services, 'Work Programme on Electronic Commerce – Progress Report to the General Council' Adopted by the Council for Trade in Services on 19 July 1999, S/L/74, 27 July 1999, para 22.

456 See e.g. ibid para 23, but also more recently, WTO General Council, 'Joint Statement on Electronic Commerce Initiative – Communication from the United States', JOB/GC/178, 12 April 2018, para 3.1.

457 WTO Work Programme on Electronic Commerce, General Council Decision, Adopted on 10 December 2019, WT/L/1079, 11 December 2019.

458 Kariyawasam, *International Economic Law and the Digital Divide: A New Silk Road?* (n 69) 133.

transmitted. Whereas the former position is prompted by a textual interpretation of the wording used to set out the moratorium, the latter is driven by the *effet utile* doctrine, which requires provisions to be interpreted in a way that would not reduce them to redundancy or inutility.[459] Most Members argue that interpreting the moratorium as only applying to the transmission but not the content would disregard the true meaning of 'customs duty'. Taxes imposed on transmission will qualify as internal taxes as they cannot be imposed at the border, upon importation. Taxes on content that is being transmitted electronically and imported into a Member could, however, be a border tax (regardless of where it is being collected). However, it should also be noted that the content of a digital product is represented by digital codes transmitted via the Internet and that it might be almost impossible to distinguish a taxation on the content from that on the transmission.[460]

Additional challenges are posed for tax authorities that want to tax digital production services that are incorporated into goods (i.e. services supplied through the '5th mode of supply', see *infra* Section 4.2.2). Apart from their underrepresentation in trade statistics, the main problem mode 5 services are confronted with, compared to services supplied through the traditional modes of supply, are the disparate duties and non-tariff barriers.[461] Mode 5 services that cross the border incorporated in goods are subject to the duties paid on the importation of these goods, while the same service imported on its own, through one of the four traditional modes of supply, would be free from duties. This convergence between goods and services and the resulting application of duties is similar to the ongoing discussion as to the nature of digital products. Moreover, several digital services could possibly classify as 'mode 5 services' where they are incorporated into manufactured goods: data collection through IoT products, the software in cars or on laptops, the personalised functioning of IoT products, etc. The issue of incorporated services was anticipated by Members, as Article 8(1)(b)(iv) of the Customs Valuation Agreement allows for duty-free importation of the

[459] As applied by the Appellate Body in e.g. *US – Gasoline, Japan – Alcoholic Beverages II* and *Canada – Dairy*. See also, AB Report, *United States – Standards for Reformulated and Conventional Gasoline*, 23; AB Report, *Japan – Taxes on Alcoholic Beverages*, 12; AB Report, *Canada – Measures Affecting the Importation of Milk and the Exportation of Dairy Products*, para 133.

[460] Mitchell and Mishra (n 307) 1093.

[461] Alessandro Antimiani and Lucian Cernat, 'Liberalizing Global Trade in Mode 5 Services: How Much Is It Worth?' (2018) 52 Journal of World Trade 65, 80.

value of certain incorporated services (engineering, development, artwork and design services) provided that they originate in the country of importation.[462] This provision does, however, not cover software or other types of digital services, which leads to an inconsistency in how these services are traded based on whether they are supplied across borders or through 'mode 5'.

Several examples exist of digital taxes, of which one of the most prominent is France's Digital Services Tax, which prompted a Section 301 investigation by the US Trade Representative (USTR).[463] The French Digital Services Tax was signed on 24 July 2019.[464] The law imposes a 3 per cent tax on revenue generated in France from two sources: (i) digital information services and (ii) targeted advertising services. The tax only applies to companies that meet a double revenue threshold.

The law defines 'digital information services' as the provision of a digital interface that allows users to connect, including buying and selling products. This scope encompasses digital content providers, telecom providers and financial service suppliers. However, digital interface providers that sell goods or services that they own to a user are excluded from the scope. 'Targeted advertising services' are services to advertisers to place targeted advertisements on digital interfaces. The revenue threshold is based on (i) all amounts paid by users minus the value of the delivered goods and services for 'digital information services' and (ii) all amounts paid by advertisers in return for placement of ads for 'targeted advertising services'. The double threshold is set at more than €750 million revenue worldwide and more than €25 million revenue in France. The requirement of revenue generated in France is understood as revenue derived from (i) users of digital interfaces located in France (or with a user account opened in France) and (ii) data collected/used/sold from users located in France or targeted advertising based on data from users located in France.

462 ibid 74.

463 Office of the United States Trade Representative, 'Initiation of Section 301 Investigations of France's Digital Services Tax', 16 July 2019, 84 FR 347042. Section 301 of the U.S. Trade Act 1974 (19 U.S. Code §2411) is the principal authority under which the US may impose trade sanctions on foreign countries that either violate trade agreements or otherwise maintain laws or practices that are unjustifiable and restrict US commerce.

464 LOI n° 2019-759 du 24 juillet 2019 portant création d'une taxe sur les services numériques et modification de la trajectoire de baisse de l'impôt sur les sociétés, JORF n°0171, 25 July 2019, 1 ('French Digital Services Tax'). France agreed to suspend collection of the digital services tax until December 2020 in exchange for the US agreeing to hold off retaliatory tariffs on French goods.

On 5 June 2020, the USTR initiated a new Section 301 investigation into (proposals on) digital services taxes in Austria, Brazil, Czech Republic, EU, India, Indonesia, Italy, Spain, Turkey and the United Kingdom.[465]

3.4.4 Restrictions on Intellectual Property Rights

Restrictions on IPRs related to digital services take many forms. It is especially the digital companies themselves that see intellectual property barriers as one of the main barriers to their operations.[466] Such barriers include: differing rules of third-party liability regarding intellectual property of copyrighted material on the Internet, lack of information on how to purchase licenses for copyright-protected materials, obscure information about IPRs in specific countries and requirements of IPR transfer.[467] In the Joint Statement on Electronic Commerce released in the context of the 2017 Buenos Aires Ministerial, mention was made of various barriers to digital trade, including: requirements to share source code, trade secrets or algorithms as a condition for market access, conditioning market access on forced transfers of technology and arbitrary mandates to use national technology.[468] Another reported trade barrier was the mandatory requirement on the use of particular technologies like encryption. It was argued that this impedes development of new technologies and business opportunities as well as prevents market access.[469]

The negative effects of the requirement of transfer of IPRs may not seem as obvious a barrier to market access as the other types of barriers discussed in this Chapter. However, these negative effects take several forms: decreased access to cheap or advanced foreign inputs (thereby hurting the domestic industry), adversely affected productivity and

465 Office of the United States Trade Representative, 'Initiation of Section 301 Investigations of Digital Services Taxes', 5 June 2020, 85 FR 34710.

466 National Board of Trade, 'E-Commerce – New Opportunities, New Barriers: A Survey of e-Commerce Barriers in Countries Outside the EU' (n 283) 12. But Members are also aware of the importance of this type of barrier: the United States called for stronger protection of IPRs for 'Internet-delivered products' in 2003. WTO Work Programme on Electronic Commerce, 'Submission from the United States', WT/GC/W/493/Rev.1, 8 July 2003, para 6.

467 ibid 12–15.

468 WTO General Council, 'Joint Statement on Electronic Commerce Initiative – Communication from the United States', JOB/GC/178, 12 April 2018, para 4.1.

469 WTO General Council, 'Joint Statement on Electronic Commerce Initiative – Proposal for the Exploratory Work by Japan', JOB/GC/177, 12 April 2018, para 3.14.

innovation due to the 'network effect'[470] and adversely affected high-tech industries because of higher costs of cross-border flows.[471] Additionally, mandated technology transfers create considerable barriers to doing business in specific markets.[472]

Another IPR issue raised in the context of digital trade concerns the limitations and exceptions to IP liability applying to Internet providers and platforms.[473] Here, the balance must be struck between effectively protecting IPRs against abuse while at the same time not overburdening Internet providers and platforms as it is difficult to assess all user-generated content for copyright infringements. In this context, the United States calls for trade rules that guarantee that intermediaries are not legally liable for the content of data they store, process or transmit.[474] Internet intermediaries '*give access to, host, transmit, and index content, products and services originated by third parties on the Internet or provide Internet-based services to third parties*'.[475] This includes online portals for buying and selling, payment apps, search engines, web hosting facilities and social networks. None of these intermediaries provide or produce own content.[476] An interesting example of such liability can be found in Article 17 of the EU's Directive on Copyright in the Digital Single Market. The original proposal required 'information society service providers' to ensure the enforcement of IPRs, including removing works that have been shared by the users of the information society platform in violation of IPRs.[477] The proposal was heavily criticised by 'the inventors of the Internet' for transforming the Internet from an open

470 The network effect is the effect that one user of a good or a service has on the value of that product to other people. When this effect is present, the value of the service will depend on the number of users.

471 Claude Barfield, 'When Trade and Tech Collide. Digital Policy Challenges and Solutions for 2016 and Beyond' (American Enterprise Institute 2015) AEI Technology Policy Working Paper, 12–13 <www.aei.org/research-products/report/when-trade-and-tech-collide/>.

472 China requires in various instances the sharing of software or hardware as a prior requirement for entering or continuing competition in the Chinese market. ibid 12.

473 Meltzer, 'Supporting the Internet as a Platform for International Trade Opportunities for Small and Medium-Sized Enterprises and Developing Countries' (n 9) 13.

474 WTO General Council, 'Joint Statement on Electronic Commerce Initiative – Communication from the United States', JOB/GC/178, 12 April 2018, para 6.1.

475 Karine Perset, 'The Economic and Social Role of Internet Intermediaries' (OECD 2010) OECD Digital Economy Papers No. 171, 4 <www.oecd.org/sti/ieconomy/44949023.pdf>.

476 Tuthill (n 125) 362.

477 Proposal for a Directive of the European Parliament and of the Council on Copyright in the Digital Single Market, Brussels, 14 September 2016, COM (2016) 593 Final.

platform into a controlled environment. They argued that the obligations in Article 17, even though well intended, would mainly burden start-ups and MSMEs rather than the large social media companies, with the ultimate price being paid by the users of Internet platforms.[478] In the final version of the Directive, the obligations on 'online content-sharing service providers' were reduced. These service suppliers are now required to perform an act of communication to the public when they give public access to copyright-protected works and to obtain authorisation from the relevant rightsholders.[479] Where they do not obtain authorisation, online content-sharing service providers are liable for unauthorised making available to the public copyright-protected works and other subject matter, unless they (a) made best efforts to obtain authorisation; (b) made best efforts to ensure unavailability of specific works if requested by the rightsholder; and (c) acted expeditiously to disable access to, or to remove from their websites, the notified works or other subject matter, and made best efforts to prevent their future uploads.[480]

IPRs are protected for good reasons, a fact that is recognised in the preamble to the TRIPS agreement.[481] Potential violations of intellectual property are abundant not only in the offline world but also particularly in the realm of digital trade. The online supply of services makes it increasingly difficult to police copyrights and patents.[482] The peculiar nature of digital products (their intangibility and instant global delivery) makes IP piracy a distinct issue for these products.[483] For example, 'cybersquatting' is an exclusively digital IP issue.[484] This term refers to the practice of registering the domain names that use the names of well-known brands, with the aim of reselling them to the original brands at

[478] Vint Cerf, Tim Berners-Lee and Anriette Esterhuysen, 'Article 13 of the EU Copyright Directive Threatens the Internet' (12 June 2018) <www.eff.org/files/2018/06/12/article13letter.pdf>.

[479] Article 17.1 of Directive (EU) 2019/790 of the European Parliament and of the Council of 17 April 2019 on copyright and related rights in the Digital Single Market, OJ L 130, 17 May 2019, 92–125.

[480] Article 17.3 of Directive (EU) 2019/790 of the European Parliament and of the Council of 17 April 2019 on copyright and related rights in the Digital Single Market, OJ L 130, 17 May 2019, 92–125.

[481] The preamble *inter alia* states 'Taking into account the need to promote effective and adequate protection of intellectual property rights'.

[482] WTO Council for Trade in Services, 'Computer and Related Services' Background Note by the Secretariat, S/C/W/300, 22 June 2009, para 29.

[483] Meltzer, 'Supporting the Internet as a Platform for International Trade Opportunities for Small and Medium-Sized Enterprises and Developing Countries' (n 9) 14.

[484] ibid 13.

a high price. Also, counterfeit goods are omnipresent on the Internet. Additionally, through e-commerce, the unwilling purchasing of pirated goods becomes a heightened risk.[485] Combatting these IPR violations should be an important priority for governments aiming to regulate digital trade.

3.5 Summary

Digitisation has raised a number of questions in the context of international trade law, including how to classify digital products and digital content and what the role of data flows is. The introduction of the Internet has had an enormous impact on the way we trade, including the creation of digital platforms and ever-extending GVCs. Digital services, the topic of this book, play an important role in the digital landscape.

Various technological advancements have enabled the emergence of digital services trade in two respects.[486] First, the emergence of digital services was caused by the creation of the Internet.[487] The Internet allows for unprecedented access to distant markets and creates enhanced productivity through the elimination of communication costs, the availability of outsourcing, access to new business models and global consumers, and the digitisation of various products.[488] Importantly, the development of the Internet has also allowed for global competition by MSMEs through a lowering of entry, information and infrastructure costs.[489] The existence of the Internet specifically impacts and creates opportunities for trade in services. It enables the online (and therefore remote) provision of services, it blurs the distinction between goods and services, and it allows for a general growth in services trade.[490]

A second element in the proliferation of digital services is the emergence of GVCs as the prevalent mode of '21st-century trading'. For these new trade patterns to function optimally, the cross-border flow of data is required. Only where data from different locations can be supplied across

[485] ibid 14.

[486] Farrokhnia and Richards (n 59) 794.

[487] Wunsch-Vincent, 'Trade Rules for the Digital Age' (n 283) 497.

[488] Barfield (n 471) 4–5; Meltzer, 'Maximizing the Opportunities of the Internet for International Trade' (n 1) 10.

[489] Barfield (n 471) 6; Meltzer, 'Maximizing the Opportunities of the Internet for International Trade' (n 1) 11.

[490] Meltzer, 'Maximizing the Opportunities of the Internet for International Trade' (n 1) 12.

borders will GVCs be able to function.[491] Additionally, GVCs create an ever-increasing demand for data-driven services, including financial services, distribution services and management services.[492] The existence of GVCs encourages companies, but specifically MSMEs, to specialise in specific tasks in GVCs, often concentrating on digital services.[493] The cross-border flows of data are crucial for the provision of digital services. Following this line of reasoning, it becomes clear that GVCs can only function if the provision of certain services and the required flow of (non-personal) data is unhampered.

This part of the book aimed to clarify the digital trade landscape by explaining important terms, providing an overview of how digitisation impacts trade and elaborating on the role of digital services. Not only do digital services entail a new way of supplying services all over the world, they also come with their own set of trade barriers. These first chapters have set the scene for the subsequent legal analysis.

Trade has transformed considerably in the last decades, which raises the question whether international trade regulation has kept up with these changes. The subsequent parts of this book will answer this question for digital services trade specifically. Part II analyses the scope of the GATS and assesses the classification of digital services within the existing legal framework. Part III analyses the applicability of the GATS obligations to digital services and whether these obligations can address the barriers to digital services trade as explained in Chapter 3. Finally, Part IV maps evolutions in e-commerce-related provisions in RTAs and analyses whether the obligations that WTO Members have included in their most extensive e-commerce RTAs go beyond these GATS obligations and are able to address the barriers to digital services trade.

[491] Supplying cross-border data services is crucial for the functioning of GVCs in various ways: it allows exercising overarching control and coordination, it ensures efficient supply chain management, it allows for management of the production and to deliver post-sales services. National Board of Trade, 'No Transfer, No Production – a Report on Cross-Border Data Transfers, Global Value Chains, and the Production of Goods' (National Board of Trade 2015), 9.

[492] Barfield (n 471) 9.

[493] Meltzer, 'Maximizing the Opportunities of the Internet for International Trade' (n 1) 11.

PART II

Classification of Digital Services

Having explained the position of digital services within the digital economy and their impact on international trade, the question arises what, if any, international trade rules apply to digital services. An obvious candidate is the WTO's General Agreement on Trade in Services (GATS), which sets out the legal framework applicable to international trade in services. The seemingly new nature of digital services has caused confusion and anxiety among WTO Members. It is therefore worthwhile to take a closer look at what these services entail and whether, from the perspective of the GATS, we are actually dealing with a new phenomenon.

The application of the GATS to digital services raises several difficult questions as to the nature and classification of digital services, including: Does electronic cross-border supply of a service qualify as a mode 1 or mode 2 service? What is the role of the principle of technological neutrality? What considerations should determine the classification of digital services and what weight should be given to the means of delivery?[494] These unanswered questions and considerations lead to uncertainty and confusion in an increasingly important part of international trade. The second part of this book will clarify the scope of the GATS and its applicability to digital services, and propose a way to classify digital services in a consistent and predictable manner.

Many trade policymakers have taken the view that WTO rules are increasing outdated in the digital era.[495] Through a thorough legal analysis of the GATS framework in the next chapters, I disprove that perception. Chapter 4 explains the scope of the GATS and analyses its

[494] Farrokhnia and Richards (n 59) 812.
[495] As observed in Wu (n 298) 1.

applicability to digital services. Additionally, the history of the WTO's work on digital services in the context of the Work Programme on E-commerce (WPEC)[496] is discussed. In a second step, the classification of these digital services within the GATS framework is addressed in Chapter 5.

[496] WTO, 'Work Programme on Electronic Commerce – Adopted by the General Council on 25 September 1998', WT/L/274, 30 September 1998.

4

Digital Services and the GATS

As the second annex to the WTO's Marrakesh Agreement, the GATS contains the basic principles that govern trade in services. The GATS incorporates the principle of non-discrimination as well as market access obligations, transparency obligations and provisions applicable to domestic regulation of services.

Wunsch-Vincent and Hold identified eight 'key unresolved questions related to digital trade' and the GATS: (i) no agreement on a permanent duty-free moratorium on electronic transmissions; (ii) the application of general GATS rules and specific commitments to the electronic delivery of services; (iii) whether electronically traded services fall under mode 1 or mode 2; (iv) the classification and scheduling of new services in the context of e-commerce; (v) the classification of digital products; (vi) whether services provided offline and those provided online are 'like'; (vii) application of Article VI GATS, on domestic regulation, to digital services; (viii) application of Article XIV GATS, containing the general exceptions, to digital services.[497] Whereas questions (i) and (v) were already addressed in the first chapter of this book, the subsequent chapters will delve into the remaining seven issues. Questions (ii) and (iii) will be addressed in this chapter, Chapter 5 will answer question (iv) on classification of digital services and Chapter 6 will address questions (vi) – (viii).

4.1 Peculiarities of the GATS: Modes of Supply and Schedules of Specific Commitments

Two core elements that distinguish the GATS from its 'goods' counterpart, the General Agreement on Tariffs and Trade (GATT), determine

[497] Sacha Wunsch-Vincent and Arnold Hold, 'Towards Coherent Rules for Digital Trade: Building on Efforts in Multilateral versus Preferential Trade Negotiations' in Mira Burri and Thomas Cottier (eds), *Trade Governance in the Digital Age* (Cambridge University Press 2012) 182–185.

the discussions on the scope of the GATS. First, international trade in goods can be characterised relatively straightforwardly as goods being delivered from the producer in one country to the consumer in another, thereby crossing (multiple) borders. Services are, however, intangible and can therefore not physically be seen to cross borders. More importantly, trade in services was traditionally perceived as often requiring physical proximity between the service supplier and the consumer in order to deliver the service. Examples of services provided through physical proximity include health services (e.g. surgery), education services (e.g. teaching), transport services (e.g. passenger railway transport services) and other services (e.g. hairdressing services).

To account for this requirement of proximity and the different ways in which physical proximity can be achieved, the GATS distinguishes between four modes of supplying services.[498]

(i) *Cross-border supply* (mode 1): the service is supplied from the territory of one Member into the territory of any other Member.
(ii) *Consumption abroad* (mode 2): the service is supplied in the territory of one Member to the service consumer of any other Member.
(iii) *Commercial presence* (mode 3): the service is supplied by a service supplier of one Member, through commercial presence in the territory of any other Member.
(iv) *Presence of natural persons* (mode 4): the service is supplied by a service supplier of one Member, through presence of a natural person of that Member in the territory of any other Member.

To facilitate determination of the relevant mode of supply, the Scheduling Guidelines[499] contain additional information on what the four modes encompass. The mode of supply is determined by the origin of the service supplier and that of the consumer and the degree and type of territorial presence they have at the moment the service is being delivered, as illustrated in Table 4.1.[500]

498 The four modes of supply are defined in Article I:2 GATS.

499 The GATT and WTO Secretariat respectively drafted the 1993 and 2001 Scheduling Guidelines to assist Members in the scheduling of their commitments and the interpretation of existing Schedules. These Scheduling Guidelines are not binding on WTO Members, but they do provide common language and structure. They have widely been used and relied upon by WTO Members.

500 WTO Trade in Services, 'Guidelines for the Scheduling of Specific Commitments under the General Agreement on Trade in Services (GATS)' Adopted by the Council for Trade in Services on 23 March 2001, S/L/92, 28 March 2001, para 26 and GATT Multilateral

Table 4.1 *Movement of service suppliers and consumers in four modes of supply*

Mode of supply	Who moves
Mode 1	*No one*, the service supplier and consumer remain in their respective Members' territories
Mode 2	The *consumer* moves to another Member's territory to receive the service
Mode 3	The *service supplier* has established commercial presence in another Member's territory in order to supply the service
Mode 4	The *service supplier* (either the supplier him/herself, as a natural person, or an employee) travels to another Member's territory to supply the service

A second important feature of the GATS is its distinction between general obligations and obligations subject to specific commitments. Whereas the general obligations apply to all WTO Members and for all service sectors, the second type of obligations has a more limited application. The general obligations include the most-favoured-nation (MFN) treatment obligation as contained in Article II GATS and the transparency obligation articulated in Article III GATS. Under the MFN obligation, all WTO Members are prohibited from differentiating in their treatment between foreign services and service suppliers.

The two most prominent obligations subject to Members' specific commitments are the market access and national treatment obligations.[501] For each of these obligations, WTO Members are required to formulate their commitments in so-called Schedules of Specific Commitments (or 'Services Schedules'). These negotiated commitments apply to specific service sectors and specific modes of supply. Therefore, in order to be able to schedule commitments regarding specific services and service suppliers, Members must be

Trade Negotiations Uruguay Round, Group of Negotiations on Services, 'Scheduling of Initial Commitments in Trade in Services: Explanatory Note', MTN.GNS/W/164, 3 September 1993, para 18.

[501] Pending new disciplines on domestic regulation, the obligations in Article VI:1 and 5 GATS are also subject to specific commitments.

able to identify the relevant service sector and mode of supply. As will become clear in Chapter 5, this is often a difficult exercise.

The application of the GATS to barriers to digital services trade is encumbered by the GATS' peculiar structure, with some obligations only applying where specific commitments have been made with regard to the relevant service sector and mode of supply. These commitments are scheduled on the basis of a 'positive list', which entails that they only include service sectors that are explicitly listed. A WTO Member's obligations are limited to those service sectors and modes of supply for which commitments were scheduled. Service sectors that do not fall within the existing service classification system are *by default* not subject to the market access and national treatment obligation.

Conversely, Members can also exempt measures in specific service sectors from their MFN obligation by including them in their list of Article II exemptions.[502] From a GATS perspective, it is therefore important to understand what service sectors are applicable when dealing with digital services, making the investigation into their classification worthwhile. The classification of services is seldom a straightforward exercise, as is illustrated by the disagreement on 'the services at issue' in various GATS cases.[503]

4.2 The Position of Digital Services within the GATS

No legal provision included in the GATS expressly regulates digital services. As early as 1999, the divergent views of WTO Members on how to assess digital services became clear:

> *Several delegations expressed the view that all products delivered electronically are services and that in the context of the work programme it would be useful to make clear that the GATS applies to all products delivered electronically. Other delegations said that it was not clear to them that all electronically delivered products are services and that if there were some which would not be considered services, rules other than those of the GATS would apply to them.*[504]

[502] The listing of exemptions is referred to as a 'negative list'.

[503] For a discussion of these issues, see Ruosi Zhang, 'Covered or Not Covered: That Is the Question – Services Classification and Its Implications for Specific Commitments under the GATS' (World Trade Organization 2015) WTO Staff Working Paper ERSD-2015-11, 20–22<www.wto.org/english/res_e/reser_e/ersd201511_e.htm>.

[504] WTO Work Programme on Electronic Commerce, 'Progress Report to the General Council Adopted by the Council for Trade in Services on 19 July 1999', S/L/74, 27 July 1999, para 6.

Digital trade has created new business models, which poses challenges to the existing legal framework. Additionally, with the development of the Internet, the transmission/content dichotomy has become much less clear. Content services are increasingly being supplied by the companies that perform their transmission.[505] The question therefore arises how these digital services qualify under the existing framework.[506]

Interpretative tools are available to deal with 'new' phenomena and address technological advancements. For example, the Panel in *EC – IT Products* favoured a teleological interpretation of Members' Schedules of Commitments, arguing that the list of IT products would otherwise soon be outdated.[507] Based on the teleological approach, the liberalisation objective of WTO Members embodies new products having similar functions. Even though no similar findings have been made dealing explicitly with digital services, it is clear that a teleological interpretation of Schedules is to be preferred over historical interpretations, especially considering the deadlock that multilateral negotiations are currently in.[508] In the context of the classification of electronically supplied sound recording services, the Appellate Body (AB) in the *China – Publications and Audiovisual Products* confirmed that where the terms used in GATS Schedules are sufficiently generic, what they apply to may change over time. The Appellate Body thereby adopted an evolutionary application of the terms.[509] The scope of application of commitments may thus change over time and with technological development.[510]

505 Peng, 'GATS and the Over-the-Top Services: A Legal Outlook' (n 102) 22. This kind of services has been referred to as OTT services. See *supra* Section 1.2.5. Tuthill (n 125) 361–362.

506 For a more comprehensive analysis of the qualification of these OTT services, see Peng, above n 102.

507 Panel Report, *EC – IT Products,* paras 7.596–7.602. The panel clarified in a footnote (fn 807) that it did not consider it necessary to resort to any form of evolutionary interpretation of the terms, in light of their conclusion on the ordinary meaning of the terms.

508 Weber and Burri (n 5) 15.

509 On the distinction between evolutionary application and evolutionary interpretation of terms, see Graham Cook, 'The Illusion of "Evolutionary Interpretation" in WTO Dispute Settlement' in Georges Abi-Saab and others (eds), *Evolutionary Interpretation and International Law* (Hart Publishing 2019)181–194.

510 In assessing the scope of 'sound recording distribution services', the panel considered whether electronic distribution of sound recordings was technically feasible and a commercial reality at the time of China's accession (and the negotiation of its Schedule); Panel Report, *China – Publications and Audiovisual Products,* para 7.1242; AB Report, *China – Publications and Audiovisual Products,* paras 396–397, 408.

The analysis of the application of the GATS to digital services is undertaken in three steps. First, the broad scope of the GATS is expounded upon. Second, the relevance of the different modes of supply for digital services is explored. Third, the principle of technological neutrality is explained and framed within the context of the GATS.

4.2.1 The Scope of the GATS

Article I:1 GATS clarifies the scope of the agreement as applying to '*measures by Members affecting trade in services*'. The GATS covers all services, as it applies to all measures affecting trade in services (except for those supplied in the exercise of governmental authority).[511] This entails that measures affecting the electronic delivery of services fall within the scope of the agreement.[512] Moreover, 'affecting' has been interpreted as covering measures that govern directly the supply of a service, as well as those indirectly affecting it.[513] This term is wider in scope than terms such as 'regulating' or 'governing'.[514] 'Measures by Members' covers measures by central, regional as well as local governments and non-governmental bodies that are exercising governmental powers.[515]

Every service sector covers all of its subsectors, as clarified in the definition of 'sector' in Article XXVIII(e) GATS.[516] The Appellate Body also clarified that a specific service cannot fall within the scope of two or more (sub)sectors simultaneously, considering the fact that Members' obligations regarding specific services depend on the commitments undertaken with regard to the specific service sector in which that service falls.[517] Sectors and subsectors in a Member's Schedule are mutually exclusive.

[511] Article I:3(b) GATS.

[512] WTO Council for Trade in Services, 'The Work Programme on Electronic Commerce' Note by the Secretariat, S/C/W/68, 16 November 1998, para 37.

[513] AB Report, *EC – Bananas III*, paras 217–222.

[514] AB Report, *EC – Bananas III*, para 222.

[515] Article I:3 GATS.

[516] '*"sector" of a service means, (i) with reference to a specific commitment, one or more, or all, subsectors of that service, as specified in a Member's Schedule, (ii) otherwise, the whole of that service sector, including all of its subsectors*'.

[517] AB Report, *US – Gambling*, para 180.

Article I:2 GATS confirms the broad scope of the GATS, stating that 'trade in services' entails the supply of a service through various 'modes' of supply. The GATS therefore not only covers the cross-border supply of services, but also the supply of services through the movement by either the service supplier or the consumer, as explained *supra*.[518] The Secretariat opined that it is clear that electronic delivery of digital services can fall within any of the four modes of delivery.[519] For example, a foreign bank established locally can supply its services to consumers electronically. A foreign natural person present locally may use electronic means to deliver consultancy services.

In the 1999 Progress Report to the General Council in the framework of the Work Programme on Electronic Commerce, it was set out that '*[i]t was the general view that the electronic delivery of services falls within the scope of the GATS, since the Agreement applies to all services regardless of the means by which they are delivered, and that electronic delivery can take place under any of the four modes of supply*'.[520] The electronic delivery of services therefore does not change the qualification of the service itself, which confirms that the GATS is 'technologically neutral' (see *infra*). Mattoo and Schuknecht confirm that there can be little doubt that the GATS applies to electronically delivered services.[521]

Article I:3 (b) GATS defines 'services' as including any service in any sector. Historically, two service sectors were most often discussed when discussing digitally supplied services: telecommunications services and computer and related services. These two sectors were designated as most relevant based on their function as an 'enabling service' to allow for a digital delivery. First, the telecommunications services sector encompasses telecommunications services both as distinct tradable services as well as a means of conduit for other service sectors, with many WTO Members scheduling extensive commitments. Elaborations

518 See subparagraphs (a) through (d) in Article I:2 GATS.

519 WTO Council for Trade in Services, 'The Work Programme on Electronic Commerce' Note by the Secretariat, S/C/W/68, 16 November 1998, para 3. This will be further elaborated in Section 4.2.2.

520 WTO Work Programme on Electronic Commerce, 'Progress Report to the General Council Adopted by the Council for Trade in Services on 19 July 1999', S/L/74, 27 July 1999, para 4. The Chairman of the Council for Trade in Services also reported that '*Members agreed that all services delivered electronically were covered by the GATS*'. WTO Council for Trade in Services, 'Report of the Meeting Held on 14 and 15 December 1998' Note by the Secretariat, S/C/M/32, 14 January 1999, para 16.

521 Mattoo and Schuknecht (n 72) 11.

on the GATS commitments in this service sector can be found in the Annex on Telecommunications and the Fourth Protocol on Basic Telecommunications services (or 'Agreement on Basic Telecommunications'). Second, the service sector of computer and related services encompasses data transmission services. As already discussed in the first part of this book, the transmission of data is crucial to the delivery of digital services. It is important to identify the relevant commitments here, as extensive commitments in these service sectors will allow countries to exploit the market access opportunities of the Internet.[522] Chapter 5 elaborates on the arguments that the distinction between 'transmission services' and 'content services' is outdated, which complicates the classification of digital services within the GATS framework.

4.2.2 Modes of Supply and Electronic Delivery

It has always been quite a difficult and abstract exercise to classify different means of delivery within the four modes of supply as described in Article I:2 GATS. The determination of which mode of supply applies not only determines the commitments applicable to the delivery of the service, but also indicates the applicable jurisdiction.[523] The following statements are relevant to the classification of digital services:

(i) 'the supply of a service through telecommunications or mail' is an example of cross-border supply (mode 1).[524] The Secretariat aptly observed that the '*increased feasibility and reduced costs of electronic delivery have added a new dimension to cross-border trade in services*'.[525] Mode 1 arguably also entails services that are supplied through the transmission of data over telecommunication networks;

[522] Kariyawasam, *International Economic Law and the Digital Divide: A New Silk Road?* (n 69) 70.

[523] If the delivery of digital services is determined to fall within the scope of mode 1, the regulations of the consumer's country will apply; if the delivery is determined to fall within the scope of mode 2, the applicable regulations are determined by the supplier's nationality. Here, it can also be noted that the applicability of the regulations from the supplier's country will generally have a more liberalising impact. Mattoo and Schuknecht (n 72) 18; ibid 119.

[524] WTO Council for Trade in Services, 'Guidelines for the Scheduling of Specific Commitments under the General Agreement on Trade in Services (GATS)' Adopted by the Council for Trade in Services on 23 March 2001, S/L/92, 28 March 2001, para 28.

[525] WTO Council for Trade in Services, 'Cross-Border Supply (Modes 1& 2)' Background Note by the Secretariat, S/C/W/304, 18 September 2009, para 2.

(ii) Mode 2 not only encompasses the movement of the consumer, but also of its property.[526] The question remains whether data sent by the consumer can be considered its own property and whether the consumer can thereby 'move' electronically;

(iii) Mode 3 requires commercial presence, which includes not only corporations and joint ventures but also representative offices and branches.[527] This raises the question whether the installation and maintenance of domestic servers also constitutes 'commercial presence'.

As was already stated *supra* (Section 4.2.1), all four modes of supply can be implicated in the digital trade of services.[528] Furthermore, increased digitisation and involvement of the Internet lead to different modes of supply being supplied in conjunction.[529] However, where a service transaction requires the combined use of more than one mode of supply, commitments in all relevant modes of supply are required to ensure coverage of the service at issue.[530] The modes of supply that are most often mentioned with regard to electronic delivery are modes 1 and 2. The cross-border supply of digital services is quite easily conceivable: the digital service is being supplied from a server or IP address to the consumer located in another WTO Member. The service supplier sends

[526] WTO Council for Trade in Services, 'Guidelines for the Scheduling of Specific Commitments under the General Agreement on Trade in Services (GATS)' Adopted by the Council for Trade in Services on 23 March 2001, S/L/92, 28 March 2001, para 29; ibid para 8.

[527] WTO Council for Trade in Services, 'Guidelines for the Scheduling of Specific Commitments under the General Agreement on Trade in Services (GATS)' Adopted by the Council for Trade in Services on 23 March 2001, S/L/92, 28 March 2001, para 32.

[528] See also WTO General Council, 'Possible List of Trade Principles on Electronic Commerce', part of Communication from the European Communities and their Member States, WTO Work Programme on Electronic Commerce, preparations for the 1999 Ministerial Conference, WT/GC/W/306, 9 August 1999, para 4 and WTO Work Programme on Electronic Commerce, 'Progress Report to the General Council Adopted by the Council for Trade in Services on 19 July 1999', S/L/74, 27 July 1999, para 4. It should be noted that not all WTO Members share this view. Australia, for example, has stated that only two modes of supply are relevant for e-commerce: mode 1 and mode 2. WTO Council for Trade in Services, 'Work Programme on Electronic Commerce' Communication from Australia, S/C/W/108, 18 May 1999, para 1.

[529] WTO Council for Trade in Services, 'Cross-Border Supply (Modes 1& 2)' Background Note by the Secretariat, S/C/W/304, 18 September 2009, para 4.

[530] GATT Multilateral Trade Negotiations Uruguay Round, Group of Negotiations on Services, 'Scheduling of Initial Commitments in Trade in Services: Explanatory Note', MTN.GNS/W/164, 3 September 1993, para 19.

the data from its own servers to the location of the consumers. Often, this is how digital services will be supplied. Wu even notes that '*whether or not intended by the drafters, this delivery mode formulation is nearly synonymous with "Internet-based"*'.[531]

The consumption abroad of digital services is less straightforward but still happens frequently. In 1999, the United States argued that mode 2 is the relevant mode of supply when a consumer 'visits' the website of a(n Internet) service provider in another country.[532] Another example is the supply of electronic payment services. When a consumer uses his credit card, issued by a financial service supplier whose servers are located in another country, it is the consumer that will be accessing the servers of the service supplier in another Member's territory. By using the credit card, the consumer is itself actively sending a request to the server of the supplier abroad. The digital service is thereby consumed abroad. What makes this hard to conceive is the fact that, for digital services, the consumer will not physically have to cross borders. The accessing of (foreign) servers by the consumer substitutes the physical movement.[533]

Admittedly, it will be hard to distinguish between both, as already noted by the Secretariat in 1998.[534] In situations where consumer and supplier are located in different territories but work closely together for the delivery of the service, the line between mode 1 and mode 2 becomes blurred.[535] It will be difficult to assess who is moving, the consumer or the service supplier, when electronic delivery of services does not require any physical movement, only that of data. The Secretariat cautions that Members should not focus on the wrong question. As the classification under the modes of supply is only relevant for the classification of commitments in Services Schedules, the distinction between modes 1 and 2 should be seen in this light. Scheduling 'none' in a service sector for mode 1 entails that the Member cannot restrict the ability of a foreign service supplier to supply the service from another Member's territory. Correspondingly, scheduling 'none' for mode 2 entails that Members cannot restrict the

[531] Wu (n 48) 275.

[532] WTO Work Programme on Electronic Commerce, 'Submission by the United States', WT/GC/16, G/C/2, S/C/7, IP/C/16, WT/COMTD/17, 12 February 1999, 4.

[533] As also noted in Carlos A Primo Braga, 'E-Commerce Regulation: New Game, New Rules?' (2005) 45 The Quarterly Review of Economics and Finance 541, 553.

[534] WTO Council for Trade in Services, 'The Work Programme on Electronic Commerce' Note by the Secretariat, S/C/W/68, 16 November 1998, paras 7–8.

[535] WTO Council for Trade in Services, 'Cross-Border Supply (Modes 1& 2)' Background Note by the Secretariat, S/C/W/304, 18 September 2009, para 9.

consumer from buying or consuming a service abroad.[536] This raises the question who the measure is affecting: the supplier (mode 1) or the consumer (mode 2).

This consideration touches upon another complication in the classification of digital services, namely, the difficulty of correctly identifying who the supplier of the service is. This is especially the case for services in the so-called 'sharing economy', where private individuals share assets or services with other individuals, very often facilitated by a company through a website of an application against a service fee.[537] Confusion could partly be avoided if similar commitments were made in both modes wherever possible.[538]

Even though the Secretariat has tried to clarify the distinction between mode 1 and mode 2, its statements have also turned out to be somewhat confusing. In the Scheduling Guidelines, the Secretariat clarified that '*in making this distinction between modes 1 and 2, one should focus on the delivery of the service itself, and not confuse this with the underlying flows of capital or the act of ordering or requesting the supply of a service*'.[539] However, ignoring the act of requesting a service (digitally reaching out by consumer to the servers of the supplier) would lead to a classification of almost all digital services under mode 1, as an online transaction will always be delivered across borders. The Secretariat seems to fall victim to circular reasoning as well, suggesting that '*mode 1 transactions could be defined as those that take place under the laws of the Member, while mode 2 transactions could be defined as those that take place under the laws of the foreign country from which the service is supplied*'.[540] This would entail that the mode of supply can therefore depend on the applicable jurisdiction (instead of the mode of supply dictating the applicable jurisdiction), which risks creating perverse incentives in domestic jurisdictions.

536 The essence of the second mode of supply is that the service is being delivered outside the territory of the Member making the commitment. See WTO Council for Trade in Services, 'Guidelines for the Scheduling of Specific Commitments under the General Agreement on Trade in Services (GATS)' Adopted by the Council for Trade in Services on 23 March 2001, S/L/92, 28 March 2001, para 29.

537 Well-known examples include Uber and Airbnb.

538 WTO Council for Trade in Services, 'Cross-Border Supply (Modes 1& 2)' Background Note by the Secretariat, S/C/W/304, 18 September 2009, para 10.

539 WTO Council for Trade in Services, 'Guidelines for the Scheduling of Specific Commitments under the General Agreement on Trade in Services (GATS)' Adopted by the Council for Trade in Services on 23 March 2001, S/L/92, 28 March 2001, 19.

540 ibid 20.

E-commerce interactions with foreign websites can be classified as constituting both mode 1 and mode 2, and countries wanting to liberalise digital trade are recommended to undertake commitments in both service sectors.[541] Generally, WTO Members have scheduled more commitments in their GATS Schedules under mode 2 than mode 1. Members had little incentive to limit commitments on the liberalisation of services that are being consumed abroad. The Secretariat clarified that obligations and commitments under the GATS can only relate to service and service suppliers and cannot be targeted at consumers. Members can therefore only impose restrictive measures affecting their own consumers, '*not those of other Members, on activities taking place outside its jurisdiction*'.[542]

Guidance on how to qualify digital trade within the GATS modes of supply can be found in the *US – Gambling* dispute, where the panel as well as the Appellate Body followed Antigua's claim and categorised the remote supply of gambling services as a service supplied under mode 1.[543] Even though the panel in *Mexico – Telecoms* confirmed that mode 1 supply does not require presence of the service supplier in the territory of the consumer, this issue seems far from settled.[544] In 1996, the Secretariat circulated an informal note that touched upon the difficulty of qualifying financial services within the correct mode of supply. It contemplated other criteria, including the location where the funds are borrowed, the location where the funds are delivered and the place where the service was purchased.[545] As pointed out by De Meester, these alternative criteria have so far not been used in WTO disputes.[546]

Weber and Burri note the relevance of mode 3, as commercial presence can enable the provision of a service on the domestic market by electronic means.[547] Moreover, the panel in *China – Electronic Payment Services* confirmed that mode 3 commitments also cover the delivery of electronic payment services.[548] Members, however, seem to prefer classification of

541 Weber and Burri (n 5) 51.

542 WTO Council for Trade in Services, 'Guidelines for the Scheduling of Specific Commitments under the General Agreement on Trade in Services (GATS)' Adopted by the Council for Trade in Services on 23 March 2001, S/L/92, 28 March 2001, para 30.

543 Panel Report, *US – Gambling*, paras 6.280–6.287; AB Report, *US – Gambling*, para 215.

544 Panel Report, *Mexico – Telecoms*, paras 7.28–7.45; Weber and Burri (n 5) 51.

545 WTO Committee in Financial Services, 'Technical Issues Concerning Financial Services Schedules' Note by the Secretariat, S/FIN/W/9, 29 July 1996, para 10.

546 Bart De Meester, *Liberalization of Trade in Banking Services: An International and European Perspective* (Cambridge University Press 2014) para 230.

547 Weber and Burri (n 5) 47.

548 Panel Report, *China – Electronic Payment Services*, para 7.575.

cross-border electronic transmissions as being supplied as mode 1 services or, *à la limite,* mode 2 services for reasons of convenience.[549]

Some authors have voiced the opinion that the existing list of four modes of supply is too restrictive in today's trade in (digital) services landscape.[550] Due to increasing servicification, a subset of services has been created which consists of services that are not traded separately but that are incorporated into manufactured goods. 'Mode 5 services' have been defined as production services embodied in the production process of a manufacturing good.[551] It has been argued by Cernat, the Chief Trade Economist at the European Commission, that these services fall outside the scope of the four traditional modes of supply as included in the GATS and that, due to their economic importance and the lack of proper regulation, a new mode of supply should be identified. He advocates for policymakers to take this separate mode of supply into account when negotiating new rules relating to customs valuation, rules of origin and trade facilitation.[552]

Even though the 'mode 5' theory is an interesting one and should be explored further in the context of the phenomena of servicification and digitisation of international trade, its relevance for the topic of this research is limited. The concept of trade in digital services does not depend on the mode of supply through which the service is ultimately being supplied. The WTO Secretariat opined that e-commerce can take place under any of the existing four modes of supply and it arguably also falls within the newly defined 'fifth mode of supply'. Besides, I do not share the opinion that the four modes of supply as defined in the GATS are too limitative for the purpose of regulating digital services per se.

4.2.3 The Principle of Technological Neutrality

The principle of technological neutrality entails that no distinction is made on the basis of the underlying technology.[553] In its application to

549 WTO General Council, 'Exploratory Work on Electronic Commerce – Non-paper from Brazil', JOB/GC/176, 12 April 2018, para 4.6.

550 For example, Lucian Cernat and Zornitsa Kutlina-Dimitrova, 'Thinking in a Box: A "Mode 5" Approach to Services Trade' (2014) 48 Journal of World Trade 1109.

551 ibid 7; Antimiani and Cernat (n 461) 67.

552 Cernat and Kutlina-Dimitrova (n 550) 1123–1124.

553 The EU explained technological neutrality as: '*where a rule or a specific commitment was written in a manner that did not distinguish between technologies, then that rule or specific commitment would apply for any sort of technology used*'. WTO Work Programme on Electronic Commerce, Submission from the European Communities, 'Classification Issue', WT/GC/W/497, 9 May 2003, fn 3.

the GATS, the principle causes this agreement to be applicable to all services, regardless of the technology through which they are being supplied.

The principle of technological neutrality has various implications: (i) digital services trade is not excluded from the GATS simply because of the underlying technology through which the services are supplied; (ii) a distinction must be made between the transmission and the actual service supplied. It is the latter that decides the classification; and (iii) generally, classification into service sectors is not dependent on the way in which the service is provided: the same service online and offline should have the same classification. At the same time, the application of the principle to the GATS should be nuanced, as several elements in the discourse on digital services point to a technological bias: (i) the current services classification based on the W/120 is in certain instances not technologically neutral, but refers to specific technologies;[554] (ii) the duty-free moratorium on electronic transmissions currently being maintained also points to a different treatment of certain products/services based on the way in which they are being supplied; and (iii) the chairman's note on Basic Telecommunications set out that commitments on basic telecoms *should* be technology neutral (and hence are not at this point in time?).[555] It should therefore be clarified that the principle of technological neutrality entails that the GATS applies to all services, regardless of the means (i.e. technology) of supply, but that does not necessarily mean that service sectors themselves are considered to be technologically neutral.[556]

Even though some Members have contested the existence of this principle, various supporting elements exist: the technologically neutral definitions in Article XXVIII GATS, the explicit recognition in the 1999 progress report as well as later documents and the confirmation in *US – Gambling*. The principle was confirmed and used by the Panel in the *US – Gambling* case.[557] However, the Appellate Body stated in the context of the analysis of the justifiability of the measures under Article XIV GATS that

> *[w]e see no error in the Panel's maintaining such a distinction [between remote and non-remote supply of gambling services] for purposes of*

554 Examples are provided in Wu (n 48) 271–272.

555 WTO Group on Basic Telecommunications, 'Note by the Chairman. Revision', S/GBT/W/2/rev.1, 16 January 1997, para 1(c). Mattoo and Schuknecht (n 72) 16.

556 Unlike what has been argued by Kelsey, who disagrees altogether with the consensus on the principle of technological neutrality. Kelsey (n 437).

557 Panel Report, *US – Gambling*, para 6.285.

> *analysing any discrimination in the application of the three federal statutes. Such an approach merely reflects the view that the distinctive characteristics of the remote supply of gambling services may call for distinctive regulatory methods, and that this could render a comparison between the treatment of remote and non-remote supply of gambling services inappropriate.*

This indicates that even though both (quasi-judicial) bodies recognise the principle of technical neutrality, they equally recognise that different means of supply might give rise to different concerns and may require a different regulatory approach. It can therefore be questioned whether the principle of technological neutrality equally applies in the assessment of the likeness of services supplied by different means.

Throughout various documents, Members have voiced their support for the proposition that the principle of technological neutrality applies to the GATS. In the Council for Trade in Services' Chairman's summary of informal talks held in December 1998, it was stated that '*Members agreed that the GATS applied to all services regardless of the means of technology by which they were delivered*'.[558] Moreover, the principle also applies to scheduled commitments unless specified otherwise.[559] It was noted that further study was required to assess how this principle would apply to existing commitments and to certain new services. In March 1999 it was reported that a common understanding appeared to be emerging according to which the electronic delivery of services is

[558] WTO Council for Trade in Services, 'Report of the Meeting Held on 14 and 15 December 1998' Note by the Secretariat, S/C/M/32, 14 January 1999, paras 13 and 16. See also WTO Council for Trade in Services, 'REVISED DRAFT – Work Programme on Electronic Commerce – Progress Report to the General Council', S/C/W/115/Rev.1, 20 July 1999, para 4; and the final progress report delivered to the General Council: WTO Council for Trade in Services, 'Work Programme on Electronic Commerce – Progress report to the General Council' Adopted by the Council for Trade in Services on 19 July 1999, S/L/74, 27 July 1999, para 4. The WTO Secretariat pointed back to this last document in the course of a 2013 meeting of the Working Party on Domestic Regulation and a 2015 meeting of the Committee on Specific Commitments, respectively: WTO Working Party on Domestic Regulation, 'Report of the Meeting Held on 19 June 2013' Note by the Secretariat, S/WPDR/M/58, 30 August 2013, para 1.33 and WTO Committee on Specific Commitments, 'Report of the Meeting Held on 14 October 2015' Note by the Secretariat, S/CSC/M/74, 27 November 2015, para 2.35.

[559] WTO Council for Trade in Services, 'Report of the Meeting Held on 9 and 15 February 1999' Note by the Secretariat, S/C/M/33, 15 March 1999, paras 10 and 15; WTO Council for Trade in Services, 'Work Programme on Electronic Commerce – Interim Report to the General Council', S/C/8, 31 March 1999, para 4; WTO Council for Trade in Services, 'Report of the Meeting Held on 22 and 24 June 1999', S/C/M/37, 20 July 1999, para 8.

deemed to fall within the scope of the GATS, considering the applicability of the principle of technological neutrality.[560]

However, several (developing) WTO Members have also voiced their dissatisfaction with the statements of the WTO Secretariat. One of the first instances of voiced disapproval can be found in India's statement during meetings in the Committee on Trade and Development in 2000, where it stated that it did not find in any document an agreement by Members on the technological neutrality of the GATS.[561] The MERCOSUR parties indicated that further analysis is required into '*the concept of technological neutrality of the Agreement*'.[562] India reiterated in 2001 that it did not consider that existing commitments applied to new services delivered through new technologies, thereby explicitly going against the principle of technological neutrality.[563] Saint Lucia has outright challenged the notion of technological neutrality, arguing that it could have a far-reaching impact on future commitments.[564] Cuba has pointed out that the GATS does not include a definition of technological neutrality.[565] In their response to a Swiss proposition on e-banking,[566] both Uruguay and the Philippines opined that the concept of 'technological neutrality' was not present in the GATS but was rather a legal interpretation of Switzerland.[567]

In the context of the *China – Publications and Audiovisual products* dispute, China stated that the principle of technological neutrality was still under consideration among WTO Members and that the Appellate

[560] WTO Council for Trade in Services, 'Work Programme on Electronic Commerce – Interim Report to the General Council', S/C/8, 31 March 1999, para 4.

[561] WTO Committee on Trade and Development, 'Note on the Meeting of 27 October and 8 November 2000', WT/COMTD/M/31, 14 December 2000, para 57.

[562] WTO General Council, 'Electronic Commerce – Horizontal and Sectoral Issues Which Require Further Analysis' Communication from MERCOSUR, WT/GC/W434, 7 May 2001, para 8.

[563] WTO Committee on Trade in Financial Services, 'Report of the Meeting Held on 9 May 2001' Note by the Secretariat, S/FIN/M/31, 1 June 2001, para 11.

[564] WTO Council for Trade in Services Special Session, 'Report of the Meeting Held on 9 to 12 July 2001' Note by the Secretariat, S/CSS/M/10, 21 September 2001, para 204.

[565] WTO Council for Trade in Services Special Session, 'Report of the Meeting Held on 5, 8 and 12 October 2001' Note by the Secretariat, S/CSS/M/12, 28 November 2001, para 143.

[566] WTO Committee on Trade in Financial Services, 'E-banking in Switzerland – Communication from Switzerland', S/FIN/W/26, 30 April 2003.

[567] WTO Committee on Trade in Financial Services, 'Report of the Meeting Held on 16 May 2003' Note by the Secretariat, S/FIN/M/40, 30 June 2003, paras 28 and 34. The Philippines raised this point again during a later meeting, stating that '*technological neutrality was not a basic assumption of the GATS*': WTO Committee on Trade in Financial Services, 'Report of the Meeting Held on 6 October 2003' Note by the Secretariat, S/FIN/M/42, 12 November 2003, para 16.

Body had never confirmed the statements made in its *US – Gambling* report.[568] In proposing principles in the context of the negotiations on e-commerce, Brazil pointed out that rights and obligations should be the same and apply equally online and offline.[569] However, it also cautioned that it could not agree to an interpretation/application of the principle of technological neutrality that would entail that existing commitments can be extended to cover '*new and revolutionary businesses models based on digital environment*'.[570] To avoid endless debates on this, Brazil proposed a separation between old and new commitments.[571] It's yet unclear how such a distinction would be made.

Regardless of whether there is consensus as to whether this principle applies to the GATS, the importance of the principle of technological neutrality should not be underestimated. Businesses have also signalled the need to negotiate trade agreements (discussing bilateral and regional RTAs) '*that do not just address the problems of today, but also anticipate the problems of tomorrow*'.[572] These businesses suggest crafting rules in a technologically neutral way and negotiating commitments on a negative list basis '*such that all service sectors (including yet-to-be-developed sectors) are covered unless the negotiators specifically agree to exclude them*'.[573] However, it is difficult to conceive how WTO Members would agree to the negative list approach where that entailed that 'new and yet-to-be-developed sectors' would also be covered. What did not exist at the time of scheduling could also not have been included in that list. Moreover, Zhang notes that interpreting specific commitments as covering new services would go against the positive list approach under the GATS.[574] Lastly, even a negative list approach requires a clear classification of digital services in order to function. Otherwise, Members would be unable to include any of these services in their negative list.

Even though Members have contested the applicability of this principle, I argue that the GATS incorporates the principle of technological neutrality, based on the case law, the statements within the WPEC and

568 Panel Report, *China – Publications and Audiovisual Products*, para 4.477.
569 WTO General Council, 'Exploratory Work on Electronic Commerce – Non-paper from Brazil', JOB/GC/176, 12 April 2018, para 2.1.
570 ibid para 4.4.
571 ibid.
572 National Foreign Trade Council, 'Promoting Cross-Border Data Flows: Priorities for the Business Community' (NFTC 2011) 5.
573 ibid 5.
574 Zhang (n 503) 30.

statements of the Secretariat set out above.[575] There is simply nothing in the GATS that disproves the applicability of this principle, especially considering the agreement's broad scope.

4.3 The WTO's Relationship with Digital Services Trade – A Short History of the WTO Work Programme on E-commerce

4.3.1 Origin and Scope of the WPEC

In 1998, WTO Members agreed upon a 'Declaration on Global Electronic Commerce' in which they launched the initiative to establish a Work Programme on Electronic Commerce dealing with this specific type of commerce, as well as promised a continued moratorium on customs duties on electronic transmissions.[576] This illustrates the fact that WTO Members recognised the importance of liberalising electronic commerce, including digital service trade, quite early on. Unfortunately, the positive start of the work on e-commerce did not extend to later meetings and progress achieved on clarifying the legal framework applicable to digital service trade (or e-commerce in general) is still very limited.

In its decision establishing the WPEC, the General Council defined 'electronic commerce' as '*the production, distribution, marketing, sale or delivery of goods and services by electronic means*'.[577] Therefore, digital services can be understood as part of e-commerce. The scope of the

[575] The GATS' modes of delivery have been indicated as being technologically neutral. WTO Council for Trade in Services, 'The Work Programme on Electronic Commerce' Note by the Secretariat, S/C/W/68, 16 November 1998, para 3; Farrokhnia and Richards (n 59) 806. Moreover, the text of the GATS does not distinguish between different technological means of supply. WTO General Council, 'WTO Agreements and Electronic Commerce' Note by the Secretariat, WT/GC/W/90, 14 July 1998, para 3. The principle of technological neutrality was explicitly recognised by the Panel in *US – Gambling*, stating that technological neutrality encompasses all means of delivery, including the Internet. Panel Report, *US – Gambling*, para 6.285. WTO Council for Trade in Services, 'Work Programme on Electronic Commerce – Progress to the General Council' Adopted by the Council for Trade in Services on 19 July 1999, S/L/74, 27 July 1999 ('1999 WPEC Progress Report'), para 24.

[576] WTO Ministerial Conference Geneva, 'Declaration on Global Electronic Commerce' Adopted 20 May 1998, WT/MIN(98)/DEC/2, 25 May 1998. For a brief history of the work in the context of the WPEC until 2004, see Wunsch-Vincent, 'WTO, E-Commerce, and Information Technologies – From the Uruguay Round through the Doha Development Agenda' (n 41) 8–24.

[577] WTO, 'Work Programme on Electronic Commerce – Adopted by the General Council on 25 September 1998', WT/L/274, 30 September 1998.

WPEC's work was explicitly extended to issues related to the development of e-commerce infrastructure.[578]

In this same decision, the General Council stipulates that the work of other intergovernmental organisations should be taken into account in the context of the Work Programme. Additionally, it designates four different WTO bodies that are to work on the issues of electronic commerce and that are to report to the General Council on a regular basis: (i) the Council for Trade in Service; (ii) the Council for Trade in Goods; (iii) the Council for TRIPS; and (iv) the Committee for Trade and Development.[579] Different aspects of the operations of these WTO bodies are deemed relevant for the WPEC, ranging from issues on scope, basic WTO principles (non-discrimination and transparency) and standards to rules of origin, intellectual property rights and effects on developing countries and SMEs.

The decision establishing the work programme provided for a well-mapped overview of the outstanding issues on e-commerce.[580] As early as 1998, WTO Members already identified issues that nowadays still present the principal barriers to digital services trade, as will be discussed in this book. This is especially the case for the issues regarding scope (including mode of supply: does digital supply constitute mode 1 or mode 2 delivery?) and classification (how to deal with 'new', uncommitted services?), applicability of the market access obligation, the national treatment obligation and the Annex on Telecommunications and the recognition and protection of privacy and public morals. These outstanding questions are a testimony to the non-existent progress made regarding e-commerce within the WTO/GATS framework. In this context, it should be noted that the WPEC is not mandated to conduct rulemaking, but rather to '*examine all trade-related issues relating to global electronic commerce*'.[581] It was thus never expected that the WPEC established new rules, thereby directly addressing the lacunae in the legal framework. The WPEC, however, retains an important role in clarifying the applicability of the existing legal framework and identifying the substantive lacunae, something it has only succeeded at to a limited extent. It is, however, clear that e-commerce is nothing new under the sun and that digital trade is well within the scope of WTO rules.[582]

578 ibid para 1.3.

579 ibid paras 1.1 and 2-5.

580 Wunsch-Vincent and Hold (n 497) 180.

581 OECD, UNCTAD and WTO, 'Discussion Paper on E-Commerce for the G20' (2016) 2016/TMM/12, 3.

582 As noted by Mexico, Indonesia, South-Korea, Turkey and Australia in WTO General Council, 'MIKTA E-Commerce Workshop Reflections', JOB/GC/99, 22 July 2016.

4.3.2 Progress in the WPEC throughout the Years

Progress on trade in services achieved within the context of the WPEC has been recorded in two main sources: the Ministerial Conference Declarations that were released since the WPEC's establishment and the review or progress reports issued by the Chairman of the Council for Trade in Services to the General Council.

In the Doha Ministerial Conference Declaration of 2001, Members acknowledged that the work conducted in the framework of the WPEC so far unveiled not only complex challenges but also opportunities for trade for all Members. They explicitly '*recognize the importance of creating and maintaining an environment which is favourable to the future development of electronic commerce*'.[583] They additionally affirmed the continuing duty-free moratorium on electronic transmissions.[584] The Ministerial Conference Declaration of Hong Kong (2005) noted that the examination of the issues regarding e-commerce under the Work Programme had not yet been completed. Moreover, it was agreed that reinvigoration of the work was required, indicating the very limited progress made at that point in time. Again, the duty-free moratorium on electronic transmissions was maintained.[585] At the 2013 Bali Ministerial Conference, a Ministerial Decision was adopted in the context of the WPEC. This Decision merely reiterated the importance of continued positive work in the WPEC, the importance of adhering to the WTO's basic principles in e-commerce discussions and the duty-free moratorium on electronic transmissions.[586] Similar observations on the work within the WPEC were made in the Ministerial Decision adopted at the 2015 Nairobi Ministerial Conference: limited to no progress had been made on the issues of e-commerce, but WTO Members reiterated the importance of continuing work in this regard. The duty-free moratorium on electronic transmissions continued to apply.[587] Both the Bali and

[583] WTO Ministerial Conference Doha, 'Ministerial Declaration' Adopted 14 November 2001, WT/MIN(01)/DEC/1, 20 November 2001, para 34.

[584] Using the wording: '*We declare that Members will maintain their current practice of not imposing customs duties on electronic transmissions until the Fifth Session.*'

[585] WTO Ministerial Conference Hong Kong, 'Ministerial Declaration' Adopted 18 December 2005, WT/MIN(05)/DEC, 22 December 2005, para 46.

[586] WTO Ministerial Conference Bali, 'Work Programme on Electronic Commerce – Ministerial Decision of 7 December 2013', WT/MIN(13)/32, WT/L/907, 11 December 2013.

[587] WTO, Ministerial Conference Nairobi, 'Work Programme on Electronic Commerce – Ministerial Decision of 19 December 2015', WT/MIN(15)/42, WT/L/977, 21 December 2015.

Nairobi WPEC Decisions mandated a periodic review by the General Council of the progress and recommendations made within the Work Programme.

The progress report to the General Council on the WPEC, as adopted by the CTS on 19 July 1999, summarised Members' positions regarding the various issues identified in the Decision on the Establishment of the WPEC. First, regarding the scope and classification, Members agreed that the electronic delivery of services falls within the scope of the GATS.[588] The GATS was thereby recognised as technologically neutral, comprising all services, regardless of whether they have been electronically supplied or not.[589] Members additionally recognised that electronic supply can happen under any mode of supply, and that the distinction between electronic supply under modes 1 and 2 is hard.[590] The report mentioned disagreement between the Members on whether all products delivered electronically qualify as services.[591] It was put forward by some Members that identification of new services due to digitisation should keep in mind the current way of classifying service sectors, that is, '*the existing classification structure based on the Services Sectoral Classification List (MTN.GNS/W/120) and the UN CPC*'.[592] The classification of digital services in Chapter 5 will be based upon the premise that the GATS is technologically neutral and the existing classification structure should (and can) provide the basis for a clear classification of various digital services.

Regarding the specific commitments on market access and national treatment obligations, Members agreed that the means of delivery do not alter specific commitments (it can arguably be inferred that existing commitments already apply to digital services trade, which will be confirmed *infra* (Section 4.2.1)) but that, when scheduling commitments, it is possible to explicitly exclude supply through electronic means.[593] It was also submitted by some Members that commitments in 'basic telecommunications' do not automatically entail commitment in 'Internet access services', as the latter have been explicitly included in their schedule by some

588 WTO, Council for Trade in Services, 'Work Programme on Electronic Commerce – Progress to the General Council' Adopted by the Council for Trade in Services on 19 July 1999, S/L/74, 27 July 1999 ('1999 WPEC Progress Report'), para 4.

589 ibid para 24.

590 ibid para 5.

591 ibid paras 6 and 25.

592 'UN CPC' refers to the United Nations Central Product Classification; ibid para 26.

593 ibid para 15.

Members (e.g. Vietnam). Other Members, however, disagreed with this statement.[594] Regarding the Annex on Telecommunications, the Members agreed that the Annex guarantees access to and use of public telecommunication networks for Internet providers, but also that it is unclear whether it also guarantees service suppliers access to and use of Internet networks and services.[595] In this context, it was also noted that the applicability of the Annex to Internet services (partly) turns on the question whether 'Internet related services' are 'public telecommunication transport networks', '*as the Internet is a network of networks*'.[596] *Infra* it will be argued that the Annex on Telecommunications does apply to Internet infrastructure and service suppliers based on the parallels that can be drawn between the Internet (as a network of networks) and basic telecommunications services.

The CTS reported the agreement of Members that various GATS obligations apply to services supplied electronically: the MFN obligation (Article I GATS), the transparency obligation (Article III GATS), the domestic regulation provision (Article VI GATS), the general exceptions (Article XIV GATS) and the obligations on market access (Article XVI GATS) and national treatment (Article XVII GATS).[597] Regarding the MFN, market access and national treatment obligations, Members highlighted the possible issues of likeness of products based on the means of delivery. For the MFN obligation, some Members agreed that likeness does not necessarily depend on whether or not an electronic means of delivery is used.[598] '*The likeness of "like services" for the purposes of the application of the GATS MFN and national treatment obligations does not depend on whether the services are delivered electronically or not.*'[599]

Regarding domestic regulation, some Members have suggested developing e-commerce-specific disciplines under Article VI:4 GATS (without specifying the form). Additionally, some Members have emphasised the importance of keeping regulations to a minimum as they argue that limited regulation has allowed for the expansive growth in e-commerce.[600] Related

594 ibid para 16.
595 ibid para 20.
596 ibid para 21.
597 ibid paras 7, 9, 11, 14, 15 and 17.
598 ibid para 8.
599 WTO General Council, 'Possible List of Trade Principles on Electronic Commerce', part of Communication from the European Communities and their Member States, WTO Work Programme on Electronic Commerce, preparations for the 1999 Ministerial Conference, WT/GC/W/306, 9 August 1999.
600 ibid para 11.

to regulatory cooperation, regulatory autonomy is secured by the applicability of the general exceptions as set out in Article XIV GATS, with the nuance that exceptions should be interpreted narrowly, should be applied on a case-by-case basis and that the scope of this Article is limited to the listed objectives.[601]

Lastly, the report notes disagreement as to the applicability of duties to digital products.[602] Additionally, a discord exists between the Members as to whether the duty-free moratorium on electronic transaction should be made permanent or not. It is noted in the report that it was raised that a decision on the standstill on customs duties is a political decision, which can only be taken by the General Council.[603]

Several elements of the 2016 reports are noteworthy. Firstly, Brazil, supported by other Members, proposed an update of the 1998 Secretariat note[604] '*to assist Members' examination of the treatment of electronic commerce in the GATS legal framework, in light of the significant market and regulatory developments in e-commerce since the launch of the Work Programme*'.[605] Additionally, many Members favoured suggestions on enhanced transparency and information exchange on measures concerning digital certificates, electronic signature and electronic authentication.[606] Lastly, a few Members again called for a permanent moratorium on customs duties on electronic transmissions.[607]

During the first decade of the WPEC's existence, its work was mainly driven by developed countries with a well-developed IT sector and that had integrated e-commerce into their economies. Participation of developing countries has been limited and that of least-developed countries (LDCs) practically non-existent.[608] This has been changing in recent years. A group of diverse but like-minded countries on the topic of e-commerce have

601 ibid para 14.
602 ibid para 22. This disagreement relates back to the classification of such products.
603 ibid para 23.
604 This Secretariat note addresses the relevance of GATS provisions to points raised in the context of the WPEC. WTO Council for Trade in Services, 'The Work Programme on Electronic Commerce' Note by the Secretariat, S/C/W/68, 16 November 1998.
605 WTO Council for Trade in Services, 'Work Programme on Electronic Commerce – Report by the Chairman of the Council for Trade in Services to the General Council', S/C/49, 11 July 2016, para 1.4.
606 WTO Council for Trade in Services, 'Work Programme on Electronic Commerce – Report by the Chairman of the Council for Trade in Services to the General Council', S/C/51, 2 December 2016, para 1.5.
607 ibid.
608 Wunsch-Vincent, 'WTO, E-Commerce, and Information Technologies – From the Uruguay Round through the Doha Development Agenda' (n 41) 19.

established the Friends of E-commerce for Development (FED) group. The members of this non-negotiation group are Argentina, Chile, Colombia, Costa Rica, Kenya, Mexico, Nigeria, Pakistan, Sri Lanka and Uruguay. These countries acknowledge that e-commerce is a tool to drive growth, narrow the digital divide and generate digital solutions for developing countries and LDCs.[609] In its first gathering, the FED drafted a roadmap, setting out key issues in the e-commerce debate: (i) identification of strategies for e-commerce readiness; (ii) access to ICT infrastructure and services; (iii) trade logistics and trade facilitation; (iv) e-payment solutions; (v) legal certainty and regulatory frameworks; (vi) capacity building and technical assistance; (vii) access to financing.[610] In its 2016 submission on the prospects for the 11th Ministerial Conference, China requested the WPEC to focus on facilitating and promoting cross-border trade in *goods* enabled through the Internet and of the services incidental to this form of e-commerce. This aptly illustrates China's reluctance to participate in the debate on digital services. Moreover, China noted that '*the discussions at this stage should not lead to new market access commitments including tariff reductions*'.[611]

4.3.3 *The Plurilateral Negotiations on Electronic Commerce*

At the 11th Ministerial Conference, organised in Buenos Aires in December 2017, 71 governments issued a Joint Statement on Electronic Commerce.[612] This document is the first firm statement by part of the WTO Membership on their willingness to substantively further the work on digital trade since the conception of the WPEC. These 43 WTO Members (the EU

[609] UNCTAD, 'Friends of E-commerce for Development Launch Roadmap for International Trade and Development Policy', *United Nations Conference on Trade and Development* (4 May 2017).

[610] ibid.

[611] WTO General Council, Work Programme on Electronic Commerce, 'Aiming at the 11th Ministerial Conference' Communication from the People's Republic of China, JOB/GC/110, JOB/CTG/2, JOB/SERV/243, JOB/DEV/39, 4 November 2016, 1.

[612] WTO Ministerial Conference Buenos Aires, 'Joint Statement on Electronic Commerce', WT/MIN(17)/60, 13 December 2017. The original signatories of the Joint Statement were Albania, Argentina, Australia, Bahrain, Brazil, Brunei Darussalam, Cambodia, Canada, Chile, Colombia, Costa Rica, European Union, Guatemala, Hong Kong (China), Iceland, Israel, Japan, Kazakhstan, Republic of Korea, Kuwait, Lao PDR, Liechtenstein, the former Yugoslav Republic of Macedonia, Malaysia, Mexico, Republic of Moldova, Montenegro, Myanmar, New Zealand, Nigeria, Norway, Panama, Paraguay, Peru, Qatar, Russian Federation, Singapore, Switzerland, Separate Customs Territory of Taiwan, Penghu, Kinmen and Matsu, Turkey, Ukraine, United States and Uruguay.

representing its 27 Member States) have publicly declared their intention to '*initiate exploratory work together toward future WTO negotiations on trade-related aspects of electronic commerce*'.[613] Meetings to this end have been ongoing since early 2018. The initiative is open for other Members to join, without prejudice to their positions in future negotiations. Even though the Joint Statement represents an important step in the furthering of negotiations on the position of electronic commerce within the WTO framework, it remains to be seen whether these plurilateral meetings will have any constructive outcome. As noted by Japan in its April 2018 submission: it is important that the WTO membership agrees to general and overarching international principles through negotiations at the WTO level to avoid fragmentation.[614] This should moreover be done through stocktaking of both the existing WTO obligations as well as the progress made in regional trade agreements.

An important development in the context of this plurilateral initiative happened at the World Economic Forum on 25 January 2019, where 78 WTO Members agreed to start negotiating rules on electronic commerce.[615] In their Joint Statement, the Members confirmed their intention to start WTO negotiations on trade-related aspects of electronic commerce. The negotiating Members aim to build on existing WTO agreements and will take account of '*the unique opportunities and challenges faced by Members, including developing countries and LDCs, as well as by micro, small and medium sized enterprises, in relation to electronic commerce*'. Taking account of the fact that WTO negotiations are conducted on the basis of consensus and considering the initial refusal by the African Group,[616] India and the countries in the Bolivarian Alliance to enter into negotiations on the topic of e-commerce, a breakthrough on e-commerce-related issues that can be multilateralised still seemed far off. However, more countries joined

613 WTO Ministerial Conference Buenos Aires, 'Joint Statement on Electronic Commerce', WT/MIN(17)/60, 13 December 2017.

614 WTO General Council, 'Joint Statement on Electronic Commerce Initiative – Proposal for the Exploratory Work by Japan', JOB/GC/177, 12 April 2018, para 3.1.

615 WTO, 'Joint Statement on Electronic Commerce', WT/L/1056, 25 January 2019. The signatories to the Joint Statement at the Ministerial Conference were joined by China, El Salvador, Georgia, Honduras, Mongolia, Thailand and United Arab Emirates. Cambodia and Guatemala did not sponsor the 2019 Joint Statement.

616 WTO General Council, 'Draft Ministerial Decision on Electronic Commerce' Communication for the African Group, JOB/GC/155, 21 November 2017.

the negotiations in the following months, including several sub-Saharan African countries.[617]

Whereas the WTO Membership principally calls for clarification of the legal framework, some authors have argued that there is a clear need to update the GATS. Mitchell and Mishra state that '*the WTO should focus on building consensus around high-level principles that recognize the importance of maintaining an open and free environment for digital trade flows, while simultaneously addressing consumer concerns related to trust and security of digital products*'.[618] Another option that has been raised is the drafting of a completely new 'Digital Economy Trade Agreement', which would contain horizontal disciplines for all trade-related aspects of data flows.[619] This option is currently being pursued in the plurilateral negotiations on the trade-related aspects of electronic commerce. Even though this option is hailed as more valuable in the long term, it is also considered difficult to achieve, both technically and politically. Such a new agreement would raise questions and complications as to the overlap with existing disciplines: would the 'Digital Economy Trade Agreement' qualify as *lex specialis* to the GATS? I consider that it is necessary to first take stock of the existing obligations, both at the multilateral as well as at the regional level, to assess Members' rights and obligations with regard to digital services trade for two reasons: (i) it clarifies Members' current position, pending the conclusion of the ongoing plurilateral negotiations, and (ii) negotiation of new disciplines should be based on a clear understanding of existing rules, addressing identified gaps rather than creating unnecessary overlaps.

617 Benin (29 March 2019, INF/ECOM/18), Côte d'Ivoire (15 July 2019, INF/ECOM/38), Kenya (17 July 2019, INF/ECOM/37), Indonesia (22 November 2019, INF/ECOM/47), Cameroon (4 December 2019, INF/ECOM/48), Philippines (3 February 2020, INF/ECOM/50), Burkina Faso (16 March 2020, INF/ECOM/53) and Guatemala (27 July 2020, INF/ECOM/56).

618 Mitchell and Mishra (n 307) 1124 building on; Burri, 'Designing Future-Oriented Multilateral Rules for Digital Trade' (n 96) 349.

619 Mitchell and Mishra (n 307) 1127–1129.

5

Classification of Digital Services within the GATS Framework

Following the analysis of the scope of the GATS, classification of digital services within the existing GATS framework is the subsequent step in the analysis of the legal framework applicable to digital services and the barriers with which they are presented. Weber and Burri already touch upon the complex nature of what they refer to as 'IT services', stating that this industry has grown out of a convergence of telecommunications, computer technology and software and is now being combined with content-oriented industries, such as broadcasting and publishing.[620] The inherent hybrid nature of digital services is part of the reason why they are so difficult to classify within the existing services framework. This chapter deals with this classification, explaining the basics of GATS services classification, clarifying the difference between digital infrastructure services and digitally enabled services and how these services fit within the GATS framework. In tackling the issue of the classification of digital services, the GATS acquis should be respected, which includes not changing the bargains struck within the existing GATS commitments.[621] Kelsey warns against the dangers of too expansive a reading of existing commitments, stating that '*the negative impacts will be most significant for developing countries, and especially LDCs, given the systemic asymmetries of the digital ecosystem and the often-rudimentary state of their regulatory regimes*'.[622]

Reading through the various submissions of Members and discussions in the context of the WPEC, it becomes quite clear that the classification question has become a political quarrel as much as it is a technical issue. As stated by Tuthill: '*WTO Members have proven in recent years that they do not have the collective resolve to clarify classification questions*'.[623] Moreover, Members have used the lack of clear distinctions regarding classification to

[620] Weber and Burri (n 5) 58.
[621] Kelsey (n 437) 286.
[622] ibid 287.
[623] Tuthill (n 125) 379.

justify measures that possibly violate their GATS commitments.[624] This part of the book aims to provide an answer to the technical legal question of how classification of digital services should be approached. In doing so, it takes account of the political difficulties that surround this issue, but only to the extent of avoiding proposition of politically completely unfeasible solutions. WTO Members will have to muster the political resolve to recognise that the solution to this issue is technical rather than political.

5.1 Services Classification

5.1.1 GATS Services Classification

Members' Schedules of Specific Commitments (or 'Services Schedules') contain the negotiated commitments WTO Members have undertaken on market access and the national treatment obligation on trade in services. The WTO classification of service sectors is set out in the Secretariat's note containing the Services Sectoral Classification List (or the 'W/120').[625] Almost every sector in the W/120 refers to a corresponding CPC number.[626] For clarity: any mention to the 'CPC' in this book refers to the provisional version of the CPC (or CPCprov) unless indicated differently.[627] Even though Members are not required to adopt the structure of the W/120 in their Schedules of Commitments, the Appellate Body in *US – Gambling* confirmed that a presumption exists

[624] Burri, 'The Governance of Data and Data Flows in Trade Agreements: The Pitfalls of Legal Adaptation' (n 177) 85.

[625] This list contains twelve service sectors with several sub-sectors. WTO, 'Services Sectoral Classification List' Note by the Secretariat, MTN.GNS/W/120, 10 July 1991.

[626] The explanatory notes can be found in the UN Provisional Central Product Classification, which was the CPC version that was in force at the time of drafting the Scheduling Guidelines. Even though the CPC has evolved from its provisional version in 1991 to the latest version at the time of writing (CPC 2.1, adopted in 2015), these changes have not been translated into the WTO framework. WTO Council for Trade in Services, 'Guidelines for the Scheduling of Specific Commitments under the General Agreement on Trade in Services (GATS)' Adopted by the Council for Trade in Services on 23 March 2001, S/L/92, 28 March 2001, para 23; Weber and Burri (n 5) 14.

[627] The Provisional Central Product Classification (CPCprov) was the version of the CPC in force at the time of the drafting of the W/120 document in 1991. The final draft of the CPCprov was considered and approved by the Statistical Commission at its twenty-fifth session in February 1989. The Economic and Social Council adopted resolution 1989/3 recommending Member States to make use of this classification system to allow for international comparability for data classified according to goods and services. See Official Records of the Economic and Social Council, 1972, *Supplement No./2* (E/5236), para 104 and Resolution of the Economic and Social Council 1989/3, *International economic classifications* (E/1989/85), Adopted 22 May 1989.

that, absent a clear indication to the contrary, the structure and the language of a Schedule of Commitments follow the W/120 and CPC nomenclature.[628] The Appellate Body held that the fact that the US' Schedule followed the structure of the W/120 while not including references to CPC codes did not mean that the terms in the Schedule *must* be given a different meaning.[629] Additionally, the Scheduling Guidelines note that where Members decide to deviate from the proposed classification and formulate their own definitions, they have to explicitly mention the concordance with the CPC.[630]

The GATS specific commitments are based on a positive list approach. This approach entails that whatever is not included in the list is not covered. The alternative to this approach is the negative list approach, which only lists those elements that are not covered. Everything that is not explicitly listed is therefore covered. Often, the negative list approach is considered as the next step in the liberalisation of services trade, as it automatically includes new or unforeseen services.[631] It has, however, been argued that a negative list approach is not necessary to address the problem of classification of 'new' services as the W/120 is supposed to exhaustively cover all possible service sectors.[632] Even though it is unclear whether the W/120 is exhaustive,[633] it will be shown *infra* that, in fact,

[628] AB Report, *US – Gambling*, para 204; See also Panel Report, *US – Gambling*, para 6.285. Neither the W/120 nor the Scheduling Guidelines are binding on WTO Members.

[629] Additionally, the Appellate Body disagreed with the panel by stating that the W/120 does not qualify as 'context' within the meaning of Article 31.2 VCLT, but rather constitutes a supplementary means of interpretation (Article 32 VCLT). AB Report, *US – Gambling*, paras 178, 183, 197 and 204.

[630] *'If this is not possible, it should give a sufficiently detailed definition to avoid any ambiguity as to the scope of the commitment.'* WTO Council for Trade in Services, 'Guidelines for the Scheduling of Specific Commitments under the General Agreement on Trade in Services (GATS)' Adopted by the Council for Trade in Services on 23 March 2001, S/L/92, 28 March 2001, para 24 and GATT Multilateral Trade Negotiations Uruguay Round, Group of Negotiations on Services, 'Scheduling of Initial Commitments in Trade in Services: Explanatory Note', MTN.GNS/W/164, 3 September 1993, para 16.

[631] Burri, 'Designing Future-Oriented Multilateral Rules for Digital Trade' (n 96) 356; Tuthill and Roy (n 106) 159. The negative list approach is also regularly adopted in FTAs that want to increase the level of services liberalisation, including: the US – Korea FTA (KORUS), the Comprehensive and Progressive Trans-Pacific Partnership Agreement (CPTPP) and the Comprehensive Economic and Trade Agreement between the EU and Canada (CETA).

[632] Zhang (n 503) 11.

[633] Zhang points to the statement by the Appellate Body in *US – Gambling*; however, strictly speaking the Appellate Body only confirmed that the CPC classification is exhaustive, not whether this consideration also applies to the W/120. See AB Report, *US – Gambling*, para 172.

very limited genuinely new services exist and that many 'new' digital services can be classified within the W/120. Moreover, adopting a negative list approach does not eliminate the need for clear classification as Members wishing to exclude (digital) services from the scope of the specific commitments need to be able to identify the relevant service sectors.

It has been held by the Appellate Body in the case of *China – Publications and Audiovisual Products* that the meaning attributed to the terms used in Members' Schedules of Commitments should not be limited to the meaning that they had at the time the Schedule was concluded as this '*would mean that very similar or identically worded commitments could be given different meanings, content, and coverage depending on the date of their adoption or the date of a Member's accession to the treaty*'.[634] By recognising that the GATS (and by extension all WTO Agreements) constitute continuing obligations that Members entered into for an indefinite period, the Appellate Body allowed for the evolutionary application of generic terms in Members' commitments.[635] In the context of digital services, such evolutionary application of subsectors allows for the classification of new-generation digital services within subsectors classically containing offline services, even where they were not necessarily supplied electronically at the time of scheduling. The Appellate Body did, however, clarify that the fact that the service was technically feasible or commercially viable at the time of scheduling does not necessarily entail that the commitment includes that service.[636]

The evolutionary approach nonetheless remains contested, based on the argument that Members cannot be certain of the scope of their specific commitments, considering that new services, non-existent at the time of scheduling, could also be covered. This has been said to undermine the value of GATS-specific commitments.[637] However, it should be noted that the existence of 'new digital services' is likely overrated. Many digital services are merely 'digitised' versions of already existing services, as will become apparent when the classification of several digital services

[634] AB Report, *China – Publications and Audiovisual Services*, para 397.

[635] ibid para 396.

[636] As also observed by Shin-yi Peng, 'Renegotiating the WTO Schedules of Commitments: Technological Development and Treaty Interpretation' (2012) 45 Cornell International Law Journal 403, 425. ibid paras 407–410.

[637] Panagiotis Delimatsis, 'Trade in Services and Regulatory Flexibility: 20 Years of GATS, 20 Years of Critique' in Marc Bungenberg and others (eds), *European Yearbook of International Economic Law 2016* (7th edn, Springer 2016) 163.

is discussed later on. Moreover, the fact that a commitment comprises various ways of delivering that service is already implied by the principle of technological neutrality that applies to the GATS. As noted by Peng, the Appellate Body's holding should be interpreted in light of this principle.[638] Weber and Burri refer to a teleological approach (in contrast to a historical approach) and emphasise the importance of this interpretation method '*in view of rapid technological developments*'.[639] Zhang notes that interpreting specific commitments as covering new services would go against the positive list approach under the GATS.[640] On the other hand, it should be acknowledged that the use of generic terms in service schedules seems to invite an interpretation that can adapt over time.[641]

The customary rules of interpretation of public international law (Articles 31 and 32 VCLT)[642] should be applied to interpret Members' Services Schedules and the common intent of all negotiating parties should be taken into account.[643] First, the ordinary meaning of the relevant terms in the Schedule must be determined, based on the dictionary meaning.[644] However, the Appellate Body cautioned that panels should acknowledge when multiple interpretations are possible and not solely focus on their preferred interpretation.[645] Additionally, caution should be exercised when taking into account the translation of the terms, as Services Schedules are often only authentic in one language (unlike WTO Covered Agreements).[646] In a second instance, the meaning of the terms can be informed by the relevant context. This relevant context includes: (i)

638 Peng, 'Renegotiating the WTO Schedules of Commitments: Technological Development and Treaty Interpretation' (n 636) 430.

639 Weber and Burri (n 5) 15.

640 Zhang (n 503) 30.

641 This consideration stood at the basis of the Appellate Body favouring the evolutionary approach. AB Report, *China – Publications and Audiovisual Products*, para 396.

642 In accordance with Article 3.2 Understanding on Rules and Procedures Governing the Settlement of Disputes (DSU).

643 The common intent has to be determined by applying the customary rules of treaty interpretation as set out in Articles 31 and 32 of the Vienna Convention on the Law of Treaties (VCLT): United Nations, *Vienna Convention on the Law of Treaties*, 23 May 1969, United Nations, *Treaty Series*, vol 1155, 331; AB Report, *EC – Computer Equipment*, para 84. For more on the interpretation of services schedules see Isabelle Van Damme, 'The Interpretation of Schedules of Commitments' (2007) 41 Journal of World Trade 1.

644 The Appellate Body has clarified that, in order to identify the ordinary meaning, an interpreter may start with the dictionary meaning of the terms that need to be interpreted. AB Report, *US – Gambling*, para 164.

645 AB Report, *US – Gambling*, para 167.

646 ibid para 166.

the remainder of that Member's Schedule; (ii) the substantive provisions of the GATS; (iii) the provisions of other Covered Agreements; and (iv) Services Schedules of other Members.[647] However, it does not include the W/120 Service Sectoral Classification List or the 1993 Scheduling Guidelines, as these documents do not constitute agreement between the parties.[648] The Appellate Body also took account of the object and purpose of the GATS in interpreting the US' Schedule.[649] In a third instance, Article 31 VCLT requires taking account of subsequent practice.[650]

Where the ordinary meaning of the terms, interpreted together with the context, leaves the meaning of the terms ambiguous, recourse should be had to the supplementary means of interpretation provided in Article 32 VCLT. The Appellate Body confirmed that both the W/120 and the 1993 Scheduling Guidelines, together with the cover note for the US' Schedule, constituted supplementary means of interpretation.[651] Moreover, the circumstances of the conclusion of the treaty can be taken into account as they help to discern the common intention of the parties *at the time of conclusion*.[652] The question can therefore be asked whether it was the common intention of the Members that drafted their Services Schedule in 1994 to also liberalise the provision of services through electronic means, considering that this means of supply was not very widespread at the moment of scheduling. In considering this question, it should not be forgotten that the Internet was already gaining more widespread use in 1994 and that elements of services, including sales and marketing, could already then be delivered over phone lines and 'through electronic means'.[653] Even though it is true that countries did not anticipate the extent and opportunities for scalability of digital services at the time, there is nothing in the language of either the scope of the GATS or the definition of mode 1 that would point towards a limitative interpretation of this agreement that excludes delivery through electronic transmission.

In classifying services within the GATS framework, an integrated approach should be applied, not distinguishing the production of the service

647 ibid para 178. However, it should also be noted that each Schedule has its own 'intrinsic logic'.
648 AB Report, *US – Gambling*, paras 175–176.
649 ibid para 187.
650 The Appellate Body in *US – Gambling* noted that the complainant did not identify any relevant subsequent practice that could be taken into account. ibid paras 193–194.
651 AB Report, *US – Gambling*, paras 196 and 197.
652 See AB Report, *EC – Chicken Cuts*, paras 282–309.
653 See the definition of 'supply of a service' in Article XXVIII(b) GATS.

from its distribution.[654] After all, the GATS defines the supply of a service as including production, distribution, marketing, sale and delivery of a service.[655] The panel in *China – Electronic Payment Services* clarified that the principle of mutual exclusivity of services classification is not incompatible with a combination of different services being classified under a single subsector, so called integrated services, if these services '*result in a distinct service that is supplied and consumed as such*'.[656] CPC version 2.1 also addresses integrated services, stating that 'composite services' should be classified based on the service that gives them their essential character, whereas 'bundled products' (consisting of a combination of goods and services) should be classified on the basis of their main component (value added).[657] Where classification is impossible, the service should be classified '*under the category appropriate to the services to which [it is] most akin*'.[658] Meltzer argues that the difficulty posed by an increased use of such integrated services is that they in practice reduce the relevance of CPC (sub) categories as the service will be classified within the service sector that relates most directly to the 'main component' of the integrated service.[659] Arguing that the CPCprov categories cannot adequately reflect technological developments, Meltzer considers that the CPC categories are ill-suited to be used for present-day renegotiation of the services commitments.[660]

The applicability of one specific service sector to a so-called integrated service is especially relevant from the perspective of digital services. Many digital service suppliers provide a wide range of services at the same time. Digital services have been called 'multifunctional', which entails that various services are used to supply a comprehensive product.[661] Mitchell and Mishra use this element to argue that the existing classification system is outdated and unfit to address digital services trade. They argue that the fact that service sectors in Members' Service Schedules are mutually exclusive is

[654] Panel Report, *China – Publications and Audiovisual Products*, para 7.1209; AB Report, *China – Publications and Audiovisual Products*, para 379.

[655] See Article XXVIII(b) GATS.

[656] This implies that all components of the service are required to be able to supply the service; Panel Report, *China – Electronic Payment Services*, paras 7.59 and 7.188.

[657] Central Product Classification Version 2.1, ST/ESA/STAT/SER.M/77/Ver.2.1, 2015, United Nations, New York, paras 56 and 58.

[658] ibid para 57.

[659] Meltzer, 'Supporting the Internet as a Platform for International Trade Opportunities for Small and Medium-Sized Enterprises and Developing Countries' (n 9) 23; Weber and Burri (n 5) 56.

[660] Meltzer, 'Supporting the Internet as a Platform for International Trade Opportunities for Small and Medium-Sized Enterprises and Developing Countries' (n 9) 22.

[661] Mitchell and Mishra (n 307) 1090.

incompatible with the multifunctionality of digital services.[662] However, under closer scrutiny, this argument does not hold. It is true that digital businesses seem to provide intricate services, with revenue not always deriving from what seems to be the main service. Nevertheless, this book argues that many digital services can be narrowed down to a specific service sector, whether as an integrated service or not. In doing this, it is key to distinguish *who* the service is being supplied *to*. For example, the service provided by search engines, for example Google, to consumers is in essence limited to database services. The fact that Google derives its revenue from selling the data it gathers from its users to advertisers should not distract from the service Google provides to the users of its search engine.

It should be additionally noted that GATS classification is based upon the *outputs* provided by service suppliers. This is clarified in the Scheduling Guidelines, which state that market access and national treatment commitments '*do not imply a right for the service supplier of a committed service to supply uncommitted services which are inputs to the committed service*'.[663] The GATS deals with measures affecting trade in service outputs, not the activity that generates the output. This is also reflected in the structure of the CPC and the W/120 list. The intrinsic nature of service outputs lies in the determined end-use of the service, rather than the means of delivery.[664] An additional element that points in this direction is footnote 9 to the GATS, which excludes input services from the market access obligation in Article XVI GATS. Historically, this footnote was included to allow regulation of zoning and floor space by Japan.[665] It has been argued that Members wanted to clearly separate main services and their inputs.[666] Some authors argue that this footnote provides a safeguard against unwanted

[662] ibid.

[663] WTO Council for Trade in Services, 'Guidelines for the Scheduling of Specific Commitments under the General Agreement on Trade in Services (GATS)' Adopted by the Council for Trade in Services on 23 March 2001, S/L/92, 28 March 2001, para 25 and GATT Multilateral Trade Negotiations Uruguay Round, Group of Negotiations on Services, 'Scheduling of Initial Commitments in Trade in Services: Explanatory Note', MTN.GNS/W/164, 3 September 1993, para 17.

[664] Zhang (n 503) 9.

[665] Aaditya Mattoo and Sacha Wunsch, 'Pre-Empting Protectionism in Services: The WTO and Outsourcing' (World Bank 2004) WPS3237, 15 <https://openknowledge.worldbank.org/handle/10986/14438>.

[666] ibid; Panagiotis Delimatsis and Martin Molinuevo, 'Article XVI GATS' in Rüdiger Wolfrum, Peter-Tobias Stoll and Clemens Feinäugle (eds), *WTO – Trade in Services*, vol 6 (Brill 2008) 381.

liberalisation.[667] Others have focussed on the narrowing effect the footnote has on the scope of application of the market access obligation in Article XVI(c) GATS.[668] It is unclear whether footnote 9 is interpretative, merely clarifying the language of subparagraph (c), which already refers only to outputs, or substantive, entailing a separate right for Members to maintain measures limiting services inputs.[669] This footnote has, as of yet, not been interpreted by a panel or the Appellate Body. The panel in *Mexico – Telecoms*, however, clarified that '*a supplier under the GATS is no less a supplier because elements of the services are subcontracted to another firm, or are carried out with assets owned by another firm*'.[670] The panel pointed out that what matters in the end is the service that is offered and supplied to the consumers. They pay the price for the end-to-end service regardless of the contracting out or use of other firm's assets by the service supplier.[671]

Basing classification on the service output is in accordance with the panel's finding on 'integrated services' in *China – Electronic Payment Services*. The concern that the findings on service outputs and integrated services are not compatible is ill-founded as the panel in *China – Electronic Payment Services* did not investigate whether China had scheduled commitments for all constituent services. Rather it found, in accordance with the focus on output, that the final services, as supplied to the consumer ('*considering the transaction from start to end*'), were classified within a single subsector.[672] No statement was made as to whether the services elements individually would also have been committed.[673] Zhang takes a different position, questioning how integrated services are committed and what rights/obligations are derived thereof: does a full commitment on an integrated service entail that all component services are fully liberalised or is there no commitment on the integrated service unless this is made explicit in the Schedule?[674] In assessing

667 Delimatsis and Molinuevo (n 666) 381; Karen Lapid, 'Outsourcing and Offshoring under the General Agreement on Trade in Services' (2006) 40 Journal of World Trade 341, 355; Mattoo and Wunsch (n 665) 15.

668 Nellie Munin, *Legal Guide to GATS* (Kluwer Law International 2010) 197.

669 Krajewski takes the position that this is an interpretative footnote. See Markus Krajewski, *National Regulation and Trade Liberalization in Services: The Legal Impact of the General Agreement on Trade in Services (GATS) on National Regulatory Autonomy* (Kluwer Law International 2003) 90.

670 Panel Report, *Mexico – Telecoms*, para 7.42.

671 ibid.

672 Panel Report, *China – Electronic Payment Services*, paras 7.59 and 7.204.

673 On this point I disagree with Zhang, who interprets the panel's finding as implying that all services constituting the integrated services were covered by China's commitment under 'money and transmission services'. Zhang (n 503) 23–24. ibid paras 7.186–7.188.

674 These questions were also raised in ibid 24.

whether an integrated service is liberalised, it is the commitment applicable to that integrated service (and its output) that should be assessed, not the commitments applicable to the component services.

In discussing classification of services, it should be borne in mind that classification in the context of the GATS exists for the purpose of regulating services trade and negotiating liberalisation of service sectors.[675] This purpose should be distinguished from classification for statistical reasons.[676]

5.1.2 Other Services Classification Systems and Choice for the CPC

Several other classification regimes exist, including the Joint OECD–Eurostat Trade in Services Classifications, the Manual on Statistics of International Trade in Services (MSITS), the Extended Balance of Payments Services Classifications (EBOPS), the IMF's Balance of Payments Manual (BPM, currently version 6), the System of National Accounts (SNA, currently 2008) and the United Nations International Standard Industrial Classification of all Economic Activities (ISIC).[677] However, as none of these classification regimes are used within the WTO framework, they will not be included in the classification study *infra*. These different uses of classification systems within the broader international trade law framework can make it difficult to reconcile GATS and other obligations in concrete circumstances.[678] It is clear that there is a need for a stable classification scheme, which does not change too often, to ensure predictability. Where classifications at the national and international level are not harmonised, classification problems ensue.[679]

In its preparation of the 1991 sectoral classification list (W/120), the Secretariat considered several sectoral classification systems to use as a basis. It identified three types of classification, respectively, focussed on activities (the ISIC and the SNA),[680] on products (CPC) or on international transactions (the IMF Balance of Payments [BOP]). The Secretariat

675 So far, the GATS classification system is the only services classification system for the purpose of trade negotiations; ibid 3.

676 WTO Committee on Specific Commitments, 'Computer and Related Services Overview of Classification Issues' Informal Note by the Secretariat, JOB/SERV/39, 4 March 2011, para 6.

677 Weber and Burri (n 5) 21–29.

678 ibid 14.

679 ibid 49.

680 Activities-based classification seems to include production-based classification. Weber and Burri distinguish between both types and identify production-based classification as

identified two shortcomings in the activities-based classification of ISIC: (i) because this system defines an industry as the summation of all units primarily engaged in the same or similar kinds of activities, this classification is incomplete. It will '*include services which are not characteristic of the principal kind of economic activity of the producing unit*'[681] and (ii) it is not activities but services outputs that enter international trade. The Secretariat also noted the greater degree of disaggregation of product-based classification, as there are more identifiable products than activities.[682] Neither activities- nor product-based classification provides distinct definitions of goods or services.[683] The Secretariat dismissed transaction-based classifications as a viable basis for GATS classification as it deems this type of classification ill-equipped to '*capture fully the universe of commercially-provided services*'.[684]

The Secretariat voiced its preference for the product-based classification using three arguments: (i) activities are primarily statistical constructions, and do not pertain to international transactions; (ii) product-based classification entails a higher level of disaggregation as well as the possibility to encompass factor flows and foreign provision of services; and (iii) using a product-based system achieves '*the highest degree of concordance with existing and proposed systems for recording statistics on services trade and production*'.[685] The CPC was therefore chosen as the basis for the proposed reference list of service sectors, focussing on services outputs rather than the activity generating the output.[686]

5.2 Classification Typology

Even with a classification list available, the question remains how all tradable services should be classified within the listed service sectors. This is what I refer to as 'classification methodology' throughout this book.[687]

a fourth type of classification (e.g. the North American Industry Classification System (NAICS)). See ibid 40–41.

681 GATT Multilateral Trade Negotiations Uruguay Round, Group of Negotiations on Services, 'Reference List of Sectors' Note by the Secretariat, MTN.GNS/W/50, 13 April 1989, para 2.

682 ibid para 3.

683 But the CPC does distinguish between goods, services and intangible assets. This is not the case for the ISIC. ibid.

684 ibid para 5.

685 ibid para 6.

686 Zhang (n 503) 5.

687 Put differently: the method used to identify the relevant service sector(s).

This section assesses some of these methodologies and proposes the most appropriate methodology to be used in the context of the WTO framework. No clear classification methodology is prescribed by the WTO Secretariat in its scheduling guidelines nor can the methodology be deduced from the W/120. Moreover, no statements can be found on the methodology used for the classification of services under the GATS. Neither can more information be found by looking into the '*principles used in constructing the CPC[prov]*' as it is merely stated that the classification is based on the nature of the products.[688] No specific information is provided on how the classification of services was conceived and what methodology is used.[689] However, several different methodologies can be conceived in approaching the classification problem. The classification typology identified in this section is based on a mapping of previous efforts in classifying (digital) services.[690]

Apart from the classification, another element that should be considered is the level of specificity of the scheduled commitments.[691] Should preference be given to broad sectoral commitments, or rather to commitments in specific subsectors? Whereas specific commitments might lead to more certainty and predictability in trading relations, it also leads to less leeway for the future and might cause more limited overall commitments. I argue that the level of specificity as used in the Services Sectoral Classification List (W/120) adequately balances these concerns. Members can always opt for scheduling commitments for more specific subsectors where they deem this appropriate.

5.2.1 Textual Approach

This classification method is based on the ordinary meaning of the terms used to refer to the services. Two examples can be provided, one of which arguably leads to a correct classification, whereas the other example clearly does not. First, Internet telephony services might be classified

688 CPCprov, full publication, available at <www.mauritiustrade.mu/ressources/pdf/UN_CPC_Codes.pdf>, para 25.

689 For goods, the CPCprov clarifies that '*CPC categories for transportable goods are based on the physical properties and the intrinsic nature of the products, as in the HS*'. ibid para 21.

690 Including: Henry Gao, 'Googling for the Trade-Human Rights Nexus in China: Can the WTO Help?' in Mira Burri and Thomas Cottier (eds), *Trade Governance in the Digital Age* (Cambridge University Press 2012) 247–275; Peng, 'GATS and the Over-the-Top Services: A Legal Outlook' (n 102); Tuthill and Roy (n 106); Weber and Burri (n 5); Zhang (n 503).

691 Weber and Burri (n 5) 93.

within the 'voice telephone services' subsector (W/120 – 2.C.a). Both of these services refer to telephone services in the same sense. The only distinction is the way in which the service is supplied.

Second, web publishing services arguably do not fit within the 'publishing' subsector (W/120 – 1.F.r) as this subsector deals with manufacturing of paper products. Looking into the structure of the corresponding CPCprov subclass (88442), it becomes clear that two conditions are linked to this subclass.[692] The service must be incidental to manufacturing and it must be provided on a fee or contract basis. Most web publishing services (e.g. online news websites, blogs) do not meet either of these conditions. Looking merely at the wording used, it would be expected that the 'publishing' service sector also includes printing on the web, which is not the case here. Therefore, I consider that the textual approach does not take sufficient account of the (underlying) nature of the services and will often lead to misleading classification. It can therefore not provide for a consistent classification approach. This is also reflected in the Appellate Body's statement in *US – Gambling* that the ordinary meaning of terms in Services Schedules cannot simply be assessed based on dictionary definitions, requiring a full interpretative analysis under Article 31 VCLT.[693]

5.2.2 Components-based Approach

This classification method is based on identifying the separate components of the service. This approach is often subconsciously used when addressing digital services. Digital services tend to be broken down into their different components, after which the 'main' component (or the one most easily classified) determines the classification of the service. An example includes breaking down video-on-demand (VOD) services into data processing services (necessary for the transmission), database services (the storage of the videos), circuit-switched data transmission services, advertisement services (the main source of revenue) and possibly online information and database retrieval services.

By explicitly excluding inputs from the committed service (*supra* Section 5.1.1), the WTO Secretariat seems averse to a components-based approach to classification. Inputs are not part of the commitment and should therefore not dictate the classification. A components-based

[692] Henry Gao, 'Google's China Problem: A Case Study on Trade, Technology and Human Rights under the GATS' (2011) 6 Asian Journal of WTO & International Health Law and Policy 347, 360.

[693] AB Report, *US – Gambling*, para 164.

classification approach arguably leads to unpredictable classification, based on the different inputs into the service, rather than the final service being provided. Paradoxically, for digital services the components-based approach will most often lead to a classification as a data processing or transmission service,[694] based on the fact that any and all digital services require the processing of data and cross-border data flows to be supplied and traded. The focus on the means of delivery when classifying a service, leads to an incorrect classification.[695]

Several authors have referred to the relevance of advertisement services in their classification of digital services.[696] This undue focus on the source of revenue illustrates the inadequacy of the components-based approach. The service that is supplied to consumers by search engines and social networks is not an advertisement service, regardless of the fact that this is where the service supplier derives most, if not all, of its revenue from. That of course does not mean that companies like Google or Facebook do not provide advertisement services. They do, but only in the service that they provide to the companies that buy advertisement space on their platforms. To the users of the platform, however, they do not provide advertisement services.

5.2.3 Functional or Teleological Approach

The functional or teleological approach to services classification is based on the answer to the question 'what function is achieved by the service?' Based on this assessment, the service sector that has the closest relation to the function will be deemed the correct classification.[697] Such an approach is supported by the principle of technological neutrality, as the focus on the end-use of the service does not take account of, or is at least not determined by, the means through which the service is being supplied. A functionally similar service, that can be supplied both online and offline, will thus be classified within the same service (sub)sector. This classification approach also sits comfortably with the Appellate

[694] Or, as stated by Erixon and others, 'online processing services'. Erixon, Hindley and Lee-Makiyama (n 413) 10–11. However, classifying 'most Internet services' as online processing services does not lead to a desirable or predictable classification outcome.

[695] As done in Kelsey (n 437) 287. This leads to most digital services being classified as 'computer and related services', which, as she notes as well, would lead to a *de facto* universal commitment on digital services.

[696] Weber and Burri (n 5); Sen (n 118). This is elaborated on in Section 5.4.4.

[697] Weber and Burri (n 5) 93.

Body's findings on integrated services and the focus on services outputs for classification. In its 2011 informal note, the WTO Secretariat similarly asked whether the classification should not be determined by the end service, rather than the inputs or technologies used to create or enable the service.[698]

This approach arguably provides for the most faithful method to classify services as it requires consistency with what the service actually *does* or *intends to do*.[699] This is to be contrasted with *how* the service is delivered (i.e. the means of supply). It also makes the most sense from a policy perspective: the components-based approach would lead to most digital services being classified as data transmission services, which does not allow for effective and clear scheduling or negotiations. Tuthill also clarified that it is the function of the service and the end service that is supplied to the consumer that determines its classification, not whether the service is being marketed under a new name (which is often the case for digital services).[700]

5.3 Digital Infrastructure Services

Wu identifies the problem of services classification as one of '*interpretative "technological translation"*'.[701] The WTO is being faced with the issue of applying legal texts to technologies that were not envisioned at the time of drafting. He argues that the negotiators of the GATS were insufficiently aware of the fact that every type of service would eventually be tradable via the Internet.[702] Because the negotiators saw the Internet as a service sector rather than a mode of supply, we are now confronted with an opaque classification, not only of the services that make up the functioning of the Internet, but also of any service that is supplied digitally. This section discusses digital infrastructure services in more depth and links it to the classification issues, whereas the next section will discuss the classification of digitally enabled services. The functional approach to classification will be applied to several illustrative examples.[703]

[698] WTO Committee on Specific Commitments, 'Computer and Related Services Overview of Classification Issues' Informal Note by the Secretariat, JOB/SERV/39, 4 March 2011, para 9.

[699] Similarly, the Panel in *China – Electronic Payment Services* took account of the expectations of the users of services in determining the correct classification. Panel Report, *China – Electronic Payment Services*, para 7.180.

[700] Tuthill (n 125) 379.

[701] Wu (n 48) 264.

[702] ibid 266.

[703] These examples have been chosen on the basis of them often being raised in the discussions on ('new') digital services.

In dealing with the classification of so-called new services, Zhang notes that '*some "popular" services which do not seem to figure in W/120 and the CPC are simply labelled in business or industry terminology and thus may be read or mapped into the classification by examining their nature or functions*'.[704] As early as the late 1990s, the WTO's Committee on Specific Commitments mentioned three approaches to identifying and defining new services: (i) only services not yet listed in the CPC are new and not covered by existing commitments; (ii) a service previously not technologically feasible (and therefore not available) cannot be covered by existing commitments; and (iii) any service 'unforeseen' at the time of scheduling commitments should not be covered by that commitment (even if the CPC code covered that service).[705] It should, however, be noted that this does not seem to fit with the panel's findings in *US – Gambling*, where it clarified that the scope of a commitment cannot merely depend on what a Member intended or did not intend to do at the time of negotiations.[706] In more recent discussions, it was reiterated that, in considering 'new services', Members should be mindful of the distinction between new means of delivery and genuinely new services.[707] Classification done in a technologically neutral way is based on the end-use of the product/service, which confirms the choice for the teleological approach to classification.[708]

5.3.1 *Criticising the Outdated Distinction between Basic and Value-Added Telecommunications Services . . .*

The 1998 WTO Secretariat's background note on telecommunications sets out the distinction between *use* and *supply* of telecommunications services.[709] This distinction is related to the difference

704 Zhang (n 503) 14.

705 These approaches range from narrow to far-reaching; ibid 15.

706 Panel Report, *US – Gambling*, para 6.136, referring to AB Report, *EC – Computer Equipment*, para 84. Kelsey disagrees, stating that '*progressive liberalization and request and offer bargaining over schedules clearly imply that Members are only bound by what they could foresee at the time of negotiating their commitments*'. Kelsey (n 437) 285.

707 WTO Committee on Specific Commitments, 'Report of the Meeting Held on 18 September 2014' Note by the Secretariat, S/CSC/M/71, 15 October 2014; Zhang (n 503) 16.

708 WTO Committee on Specific Commitments, 'Report of the Meeting Held on 18 September 2014' Note by the Secretariat, S/CSC/M/71, 15 October 2014, para 1.8.

709 WTO Council for Trade in Services, 'Telecommunications Services' Background Note by the Secretariat, S/C/W/74, 8 December 1998.

between basic telecommunications services and value-added telecommunications services as used to guide WTO negotiations in this service sector.[710]

Basic telecommunications services constitute those telecommunications services that are used as a means of delivery. It therefore covers the 'use' of these services in order to be able to supply other services. Or put differently, 'basic telecommunications' covers telecommunications transport networks and services.[711] The W/120 breaks the sector of telecommunications services down into fourteen subsectors. Subsectors a through g,[712] as well as some services falling within the 'other' category,[713] have been marked as basic telecommunications services,

[710] The distinction between basic and value-added telecommunications services originates from the US telecommunications law. In delineating the jurisdiction of the Federal Communications Commission the basic services were defined as 'the offering of transmission capacity for the movement of information' whereas value-added services were characterised as 'any offering over the telecommunications network which is more than a basic transmission service'. See Weber and Burri (n 5) 67, 69, referring to *Second Computer Inquiry*, Docket 20828, Final Decision, FCC 80–189, 77 FCC 2.d 384, 7 April 1980; *Third Computer Inquiry*, CC Docket 85–229, Report and Order, FCC 86–252, 104 FCC 2.d 958, 15 May 1986; See WTO Council for Trade in Services, 'Classification in the Telecommunications Sector under the WTO-GATS Framework' Communication from the United States, TN/S/W/35, S/CSC/W/45, 22 February 2005, para 6.

[711] See paragraph 1 of the Ministerial Decision on Negotiations on Basic Telecommunications. *'This definition has legal force, as the Ministerial Decision is referred to in the Fourth Protocol'.* WTO Group on Basic Telecommunications, 'Notes for Scheduling Basic Telecommunications Services – Note by the Chairman', S/GBT/W/2/Rev.1, 16 January 1997; See Paul Nihoul, 'Audio-Visual and Telecommunications Services: A Review of Definitions under WTO Law' in Damien Geradin and David Luff (eds), *The WTO and Global Convergence in Telecommunications and Audio-Visual Services* (Cambridge University Press 2004) 361.

[712] These subsectors are identified in as:

a. Voice Telephone Services
b. Packet-Switched Data Transmission Services
c. Circuit-Switched Data Transmission Services
d. Telex Services
e. Telegraph Services
f. Facsimile Services
g. Private Leased Circuit Services

[713] Analog/digital cellular/mobile telephone services; mobile data services; paging; personal communications services; satellite-based mobile services (including telephony, data, paging, and/or PCS); fixed satellite services; VSAT services; gateway earthstation services; teleconferencing; video transport; and trunked radio system services. These examples are available on the WTO webpage explaining the coverage of telecommunications services, available at <www.wto.org/english/tratop_e/serv_e/telecom_e/telecom_coverage_e.htm>.

as they *'provide real-time transmission of customer supplied information'*.[714]

The WTO bases its categories of basic telecommunications upon four distinguishing criteria: (i) geographical distance, (ii) means of technology (fixed or wireless), (iii) type of supply (facilities or non-facilities based) and (iv) type of consumers (public or non-public).[715] These criteria were used to help define the scope of commitments in basic telecommunications services.[716] That meant that any basic telecom service could be provided based on all possible outcomes of the four criteria, unless otherwise noted in the sector column.[717] Further commitments regarding basic telecommunications services were included in the 'Basic Agreement on Telecommunications' or Fourth Protocol to the GATS.[718] The Fourth Protocol consists of a series of Schedules of Specific Commitments and Lists of Exemptions from Article II GATS, annexed to the Protocol.[719] The Fourth Protocol is considered as constituting important progress in the liberalisation of this service sector.[720]

Within the context of the Fourth Protocol, a Reference Paper was adopted, setting out definitions and principles on the regulatory framework for the basic telecommunications services.[721] This Reference Paper has been incorporated into the Schedules of 82 WTO Members.[722] It sets

[714] WTO Council for Trade in Services, 'Telecommunications Services' Background Note by the Secretariat, S/C/W/74, 8 December 1998, para 7.

[715] Originally, these criteria were set out in WTO Group on Basic Telecommunications, 'Notes for Scheduling Basic Telecommunications Services' Note by the Chairman, S/GBT/W/2/Rev.1, 16 January 1997; See also ibid para 10 and WTO Council for Trade in Services, 'Telecommunications Services' Background Note by the Secretariat, S/C/W/299, 10 June 2009, para 10.

[716] Tuthill and Roy (n 106) 161.

[717] WTO Group on Basic Telecommunications, 'Notes for Scheduling Basic Telecommunications Services' Note by the Chairman, S/GBT/W/2/Rev.1, 16 January 1997; Weber and Burri (n 5) 70.

[718] In 1994 a decision was adopted to establish a Negotiation Group on Basic Telecommunications to carry out voluntary negotiations on the progressive liberalisation of these services. See *Decision on Negotiations on Basic Telecommunications* 33 ILM 144 (1994).

[719] WTO, Fourth Protocol to the General Agreement on Trade in Services, S/L/20, 30 April 1996.

[720] Ian Walden and John Angel (eds), *Telecommunications Law and Regulation* (2nd edn, Oxford University Press 2005) 493.

[721] WTO, Negotiating Group on Basic Telecommunications, *Reference Paper*, 24 April 1996, available at <www.wto.org/english/tratop_e/serv_e/telecom_e/tel23_e.htm>.

[722] Out of 99 WTO Members who have committed to extended competition in telecommunications services within the context of the Fourth Protocol. The WTO website clarifies that the Reference Paper is *'a set of regulatory principles that is legally binding for those*

out objectives for the achievement of a pro-competitive regulatory environment for telecommunications services, which, once incorporated into the Schedule, are enforceable before the DSB.[723] Interesting to note is that the Reference Paper focusses on ends rather than the means to achieve this end.[724] The obligations imposed by the Reference Paper relate to (i) enabling interconnection between transport networks and services, (ii) universal services, (iii) public availability of licensing criteria, (iv) independence of regulators and (v) allocation and use of scarce resources.[725]

Little clarification is provided on the content of the basic telecom services subsectors by the corresponding CPC codes, as all supposedly fall within the ambit of CPCprov 7521, 7522 or 7523.[726] Nihoul analyses these subsectors as follows: (a) voice telephone services consist of transmission of conversation between people; (b) packet-switched data transmission services and (c) circuit-switched data transmission services are both services that refer to transmissions of data that is not voice or audiovisual signals, using two different technologies (packet-switched entails dividing of data in packets that are sent separately to the receiver, circuit-switched entails data being sent to the receiver over a designated circuit); (d) telex services: transmission of text from sender to receiver (requires specialised equipment by both); (e) telegraph services: transmission of written messages in the form of sounds (requires human intervention); (f) facsimile services: transmission of written messages to a receiver (more complex technology, also allows transmission of services); and (g) private leased circuit services: part of network rented by the infrastructure operator to clients.[727] He groups telex, telegraph and facsimile services under the group of 'text transmission services', arguing that all of them have become redundant due to the more convenient and cheaper alternative of transmitting documents electronically, over the

WTO governments which have committed to it by appending the document, in whole or in part, to their schedules of commitments'. See, WTO, 'Telecommunications Services', available at <www.wto.org/english/tratop_e/serv_e/telecom_e/telecom_e.htm>.

723 Walden and Angel (n 720) 494.

724 It sets out control mechanisms to be set on the major suppliers' ability to restrict competition as well as 'appropriate measures' to prevent anti-competitive practices in the basic telecommunications market. It contains core competition law concepts, referring to market dominance and abuse of dominant position. See ibid 493–495; Weber and Burri (n 5) 65.

725 Respectively sections 2 through 6 of the Reference Paper.

726 These classes respectively refer to: 'public telephone services', 'business network services' and 'data and message transmission services'.

727 Nihoul (n 711) 366–368.

Internet.[728] Here it should be cautioned that the transmission of text through telex and facsimile services is no different in basic technology from the transmission of data. For these services, text is always transformed into data to allow transmission and data turned back into text to allow reading by the recipient. It is, however, true that all of these services have fallen somewhat into disuse because of the availability of the Internet.

Regarding data transmission, it should be noted that, in the context of digitalisation, everything can be converted into data and can be expressed using the same code. In that context, it can be submitted that data transmission refers to all digital transmissions, regardless of their content. Nihoul, however, submits that this meaning should not be linked to data transmission in the W/120 as that would mean that all telecommunications (including broadcasting services) are covered under this single subsector.[729] This submission indeed highlights the dangers of using a components-based approach to classification. However, as has been established *supra*, this risk can be avoided by adopting the functional or teleological approach to classification.

Value-added telecommunications services are being supplied when the services add an element of functionality (rather than mere transmission), for example, storage, forwarding, processing and/or retrieval. Examples of value-added telecommunications services are electronic mail, voice mail, online information and database retrieval, electronic data interchange, code and protocol conversion and online information and/or data processing.[730] These examples are identified in subsectors h through n in the W/120 list. These value-added telecommunications services '*are not supplied on a real-time basis or [. . .] transform the form or content of customer's information*'.[731] Tuthill notes the lack of commitments undertaken in these service subsectors as one of the main obstacles to further liberalisation of digital services.[732]

Regarding the meaning of the different subsectors of value-added telecommunications services, we are faced with the same issue as only two corresponding CPC numbers are included in the W/120.[733] Here as

728 ibid 366–367.
729 ibid 367.
730 Weber and Burri (n 5) 68.
731 WTO Council for Trade in Services, 'Telecommunications Services' Background Note by the Secretariat, S/C/W/74, 8 December 1998, para 7.
732 Tuthill (n 125) 378.
733 CPCprov 7523 ('data and message transmission services') and 843 ('data processing services').

well, I summarise Nihoul's excellent analysis.[734] In assessing value-added telecommunications services, he refers to the fact that all of them require special software and equipment to perform the services. He explains them as: (h) electronic mail: sending messages comparable to traditional letters; (k) electronic data interchange: allows for easy exchange of data in a given community; (m) code and protocol conversion: necessary when transferring data between various networks that might use different technologies; (n) online information and/or data processing: the former allowing access to information through computers that are linked to a network,[735] while the latter uses data for a specific purpose.[736]

When negotiating the GATS, Members also adopted a supplementary Telecommunications Annex, which aimed to elaborate on the provisions of the Agreement with regard to measures affecting access to and use of public telecommunications transport networks and services. It was therefore conceived to deal with the supply of basic telecoms services over public networks.[737] The Annex turned out to be most impactful on the supply of other service sectors and value-added telecom services. Because of the guarantee of access to and use of public telecommunication networks, service suppliers providing their services over telecommunication networks benefitted most.[738] However, the panel in *Mexico – Telecoms* confirmed that this does not mean that the Annex does not apply to basic telecommunications services, where commitments have been scheduled.[739] The Annex itself only excludes '*measures affecting the cable or broadcast distribution of radio or television programming*'.[740]

The Annex in itself does not impose market access or national treatment obligations in the sector of telecommunication; it '*provides notes and supplementary provisions to the Agreement*'.[741] The substantive obligations in the Telecommunications Annex can be found in paragraph 5,

[734] Nihoul (n 711) 366–367.

[735] With the World Wide Web as the classic example of an online information service. The Internet and the World Wide Web should be distinguished, as they are two distinct but related phenomena. The World Wide Web is a way of accessing information over the medium of the Internet. It is an information-sharing model that is built on top of the Internet.

[736] Nihoul (n 711) 368.

[737] Walden and Angel (n 720) 491.

[738] Weber and Burri (n 5) 62.

[739] Panel Report, *Mexico – Telecoms*, paras 7.273–7.288.

[740] See Annex on Telecommunications, para 2(b). The Annex is available at <www.wto.org/english/tratop_e/serv_e/12-tel_e.htm>.

[741] ibid paras 1 and 2(c)(i).

which ensures access to and use of public telecommunications transport networks and services for foreign services suppliers on reasonable and non-discriminatory terms and conditions.[742] These obligations are subordinate to and qualified by certain restrictions, found in paras 5(e) and (f).[743] It is noteworthy that elements relating to 'access' in GATS are covered by regulatory obligations, rather than liberalisation commitments.[744] Weber and Burri submit that the Annex remains relevant, even taking into account the further-reaching commitments found in the abovementioned Fourth Protocol and Reference Paper.[745]

Related to telecommunications services, some problems have been identified regarding the 1991 W/120 classification list as the basis for ongoing negotiations on the liberalisation of trade in services. Not only does the 'telecommunications' service sector contain very limited reference to more modern ways of transmitting information (mainly through the Internet), some of its categories are not technologically neutral and have arguably become redundant because of continued technological change.[746] The 1997 Chairman's note on the scheduling of basic telecommunication service commitments set out that all basic telecommunications services can be provided through any means of technology (including cable, wireless, satellites).[747] Could it therefore be argued that basic telecommunications services also cover communications over the Internet? Following the teleological approach to classification of services, I argue that this is the case.

Because many of the 'basic telecommunications services' are now being provided over the Internet, the distinction between basic and value-added services is increasingly softened.[748] Whereas telecommunications services used to be seen as distinct applications bundled with separate networks, they are now understood as the platform for an abundance of other

[742] On the interpretation of 'reasonable' see Panel Report, *Mexico – Telecoms*, para 7.334.

[743] Panel Report, *Mexico – Telecoms*, para 7.308.

[744] Tuthill and Roy (n 106) 163.

[745] Weber and Burri (n 5) 63–64.

[746] Telex services, for example, still exist but have been almost completely superseded by fax, email and other online messaging services. WTO Council for Trade in Services, 'Classification in the Telecom Sector under the WTO-GATS Framework' Communication from the European Communities, TN/S/W/27, S/CSC/W/44, 10 February 2005, para 9; Kariyawasam, *International Economic Law and the Digital Divide: A New Silk Road?* (n 69) 67.

[747] WTO group on basic telecommunications, 'Notes for Scheduling Basic Telecom Services Commitments' Note by the Chairman, revision, S/GBT/W/2/Rev.1, 16 January 1997, para 1.

[748] Meltzer, 'Supporting the Internet as a Platform for International Trade Opportunities for Small and Medium-Sized Enterprises and Developing Countries' (n 9) 19.

services.[749] It has been argued that due to the prevalence of integrated services, the reference to 'use of telecommunications services' has lost its purpose.[750] Others observe an increased fading of classification boundaries, not only within (sub)sectors (basic v value-added telecoms), but also across sectors due to the bundling of telecoms services with computer and audiovisual services.[751] Considering technological developments, it has been argued that the distinction between both kinds of telecommunications services is outdated and should no longer serve as a basis for future services negotiations.[752] However, the distinction does retain its relevance for identifying the applicable commitments: the Fourth Protocol and the Reference paper only apply to basic telecommunications services, whereas the Annex on Telecommunications relates to the supply of value-added services.[753] Moreover, the fact that providers of basic telecommunications services are increasingly supplying value-added telecommunications services as well does not devalue the distinction between both. Even though more and more ISPs provide both, Members might still want to distinguish between both 'kinds' of telecommunications services when liberalising parts of the services market. In its 2009 background note, the Secretariat stressed the continuing importance of the basic v value-added distinction for the implementation of certain public or universal service objectives, licensing requirements or regulatory obligations.[754]

5.3.2 . . . and Trying to Clarify the Distinction between Transmission and Content?

The United States tried to clarify the distinction between basic and value-added services in its 2003 initial services liberalisation offer, by adding a short definition to both terms in its services schedule. For basic telecommunications services, reference is made to the original US law and the focus remains on transmission without change in form or content of the information transmitted. Conversely, value-added telecoms services

749 Wu (n 48) 267.
750 See also Meltzer, 'Supporting the Internet as a Platform for International Trade Opportunities for Small and Medium-Sized Enterprises and Developing Countries' (n 9) 19.
751 Lopez-Gonzalez and Ferencz (n 6) para 98.
752 Weber and Burri (n 5) 73.
753 WTO Council for Trade in Services, 'Telecommunications Services' Background Note by the Secretariat, S/C/W/299, 10 June 2009, para 8.
754 ibid.

are grouped under the new subtitle of 'information services', defined as '*the offering of a capability for generating, acquiring, storing, transforming, processing, retrieving, utilizing, or making available information via telecommunications*'.[755] In their 2015 list of 'new issues requiring guidance in the CPC' the UN ECOSOC mentioned the distinction between transmission and content, summarising WTO Members' opinions voiced in the context of the Committee of Specific Commitments as:

> *it was understood that telecommunication transmission was the process of sending either data or voice through wired or wireless means, while audiovisual services could be provided to end-users via a telecommunication transmission service. Telecommunication carriage services, i.e. data transmission, were inputs to the supply of audiovisual services to end-users. However, some considered the carriage of video content to be a form of data transmission.*[756]

The EU tried to resolve the transmission/content dichotomy in its 2005 conditional revised services liberalisation offer. It omitted the reference to basic and value-added telecommunications services and explicitly mentioned in its Schedule that telecommunications services did not cover the economic activity consisting of the provision of content services which require telecommunications services for their transport, thereby trying to clearly distinguish between the transmission of content and content itself.[757] Adopting the teleological approach to services classification would arguably also resolve the problem of the unclear distinction between the two, as focussing on the function of the service will clarify whether it is

[755] WTO Council for Trade in Services, 'Communication from the United States – Initial Offer', TN/S/O/USA, 9 April 2003, 51 and 54. In its revised offer, the US changed its definitions for both groups of telecoms services: basic telecommunications services are '*transmission between/among points specified by the user of information of the user's choosing without change in form or content of information as sent or received*'. Enhanced telecom services are '*services over public telecoms transport services, employing computer processing applications*'. Weber and Burri (n 5) 104–105.

[756] United Nations Department of Economic and Social Affairs, Meeting of the Expert Group on International Statistical Classifications New York 19–22 May, 'New Issues Requiring Guidance in the Central Product Classification (CPC)', ESA/STAT/AC.289/20, 12 May 2015, para 1.11, referring to WTO docs JOB/SERV/73, para 12; JOB/SERV/75, para 16; JOB/SERV/82, para 4; JOB/SERV/82/Add.1, paras 3 and 10; and JOB/SERV/82/Add.2, para 5.

[757] WTO Council for Trade in Services, 'Communication from the European Communities and its Member States – Conditional Revised Offer', TN/S/O/EEC/Rev.1, 29 June 2005, 187; it did so again in its 2006 draft consolidated GATS Schedule: WTO Council for Trade in Services, 'Communication from the European Communities and its Member States – Certification Draft Consolidated GATS Schedule', S/C/W/273, 9 October 2006, 150.

a transmission (i.e. telecom) or a content service. The EU equally called for a new, functional definition of all telecommunications services as '*any service consisting of the transmission and reception of signals by any electromagnetic means*', based on the definition in the Annex itself. It argues that this would prevent regulators from discriminating between different technologies in providing services, between different content or between different business models.[758]

5.3.3 *Applicability of the Annex on Telecommunications*

Taking all of the above into account, the question arises whether such basic transmission services can be linked to the Internet. Can it be argued that something like 'basic Internet services' exist, and should access to and use of the Internet network not be safeguarded? Luff argues that the Annex on Telecommunications would benefit from making explicit that it equally applies to broadband networks and Internet services, thereby ensuring access to and use of the network (including the Internet) where relevant commitments have been made.[759] Kariyawasam suggests broadening the scope of the Reference Paper, so that it equally applies to new-generation networks (i.e. the Internet).[760] He argues that this will enhance effective competition and ensure interconnection and equal access as well as safeguard the principle of non-discrimination.[761]

In its 1999 progress report to the General Council, the Members in the context of the WPEC noted that it was unclear whether the Annex guarantees service suppliers access to and use of Internet networks and services.[762] The key question to determine applicability of the Annex to

[758] WTO Council for Trade in Services, 'Communication from the European Communities – Classification in the Telecom Sector under the WTO-GATS Framework', TN/S/W/27, S/CSC/W/44, 10 February 2005, paras 15–16.

[759] David Luff, 'Convergence: A Buzzword to Remain?' in Mira Burri and Thomas Cottier (eds), *Trade Governance in the Digital Age* (Cambridge University Press 2012) 90.

[760] It is contested whether the Reference Paper (as an existing WTO commitment) applies to Internet services. For more information see Kariyawasam, *International Economic Law and the Digital Divide: A New Silk Road?* (n 69).

[761] Rohan Kariyawasam, 'Better Regulation of Digital Markets: A New Look at the Reference Paper' in Mira Burri and Thomas Cottier (eds), *Trade Governance in the Digital Age* (Cambridge University Press 2012) 241.

[762] WTO Council for Trade in Services, 'Work Programme on Electronic Commerce – Progress report to the General Council' Adopted by the Council for Trade in Services on 19 July 1999, S/L/74, 27 July 1999, para 20.

the Internet is whether Internet-related services can be considered 'public telecommunications networks'.[763]

In 1999, Australia stated that it supported the application of the Annex on Telecommunications to the Internet (as a communication service).[764] Some months later, the EU stated that it considered the obligations of the Annex on 'access to and use of' public telecom networks to be applicable to Internet access and Internet network services. Additionally, the provisions on interconnectivity in the Reference paper apply to ISPs that supply telecom services over the Internet and supply Internet access and network services.[765] In 2000, the EU clarified that the notion of 'public networks' in the Annex '*cannot be construed restrictively to mean only networks owned by publicly-owned companies and with a universal services obligation*'.[766] This statement is in line with the broad interpretation of the scope of the Annex by the panel in *Mexico – Telecoms.*[767]

The Telecoms Annex obliges every Member to ensure that service suppliers of other Members can use public telecommunication networks and services for the movement of information across borders and for access to information in databases or stored electronically in the territory of another Member. Considering the need for data flows across borders since the transformation of international trade due to digitisation, the Annex has not lost any of its relevance in the last decade. It could even be said that the Annex is as indispensable for trade in services now as it was at the time of its conception. The Annex on Telecommunications should be considered as applying to digital infrastructure services (or digital network services), for the same reasons as originally conceived for telecom services: access to and use of public telecommunication networks (including the Internet) should be guaranteed. It will benefit the digitally enabled services, in the same way as it originally benefitted the telecommunication-enabled services.

763 ibid para 21.

764 WTO Council for Trade in Services, 'Work Programme on Electronic Commerce' Communication from Australia, S/C/W/108, 18 May 1999, 5.

765 WTO General Council, 'Possible List of Trade Principles on Electronic Commerce', part of Communication from the European Communities and their Member States, WTO Work Programme on Electronic Commerce, preparations for the 1999 Ministerial Conference, WT/GC/W/306, 9 August 1999.

766 WTO Work Programme on Electronic Commerce, 'Communication from the European Communities and their Member States', S/C/W/183, 30 November 2000, para 5.

767 Panel Report, *Mexico – Telecoms*, para 7.278.

5.3.4 *Application of the Classification Methodology*

5.3.4.1 Carrier Services, Network Management Services and Hosting and IT Infrastructure Provisioning Services

Digital infrastructure services include a range of services necessary for the provision of digital services. Services that enable access to the Internet include carrier services, network management services and hosting and IT infrastructure provisioning services. Another term used for these kinds of services are 'Internet backbone services' and 'Internet access services', falling within the more general group of 'Internet telecommunications services' in CPC2.1. This group includes '*providing access to the Internet*' and '*providing telecommunications services on the Internet and similar distributed computer networks that rely on, but are not part of, the normal telecommunications network*'.[768] Following the correspondence tables, CPC2.1 group 842 corresponds to CPCprov class 7523 ('data and message transmission services'). The W/120 list contains nine telecommunication subsectors relating to CPCprov 7523. Looking at this correspondence with CPC2.1, it can be argued that many of these service sectors contain digital infrastructure services.

Classifying these Internet telecommunication services using the teleological approach as set out above does not confirm the classification as telecommunication services in the W/120. Rather, whereas some classify as telecommunication services, other are basic computer services as they relate to IT infrastructure (which contains both hardware and software).

First, both carrier services for Internet access and network management services can be classified as 'packet-switched data transmission services' (W/120 – 2.C.b). Carrier services for Internet access support the functioning of the Internet. The purpose of network management services lies in the maintenance and provision of the network that is the Internet. As explained in Part I, the Internet is a network of computers that transmits data in packets. The services that are crucial to the functioning of the Internet can therefore be classified as packet-switched data transmission services.

Second, hosting and IT infrastructure provisioning services can be considered 'basic computer services' as they enable the provision of other services.[769] On the basis of their function, these services can be

[768] Explanatory note to group 842 in CPC2.1.

[769] Parallel to the basic and value-added distinction in telecommunications, digital infrastructure services qualify as 'basic computer services' considering that they are required for the supply of services over the Internet – thereby enabling digital services. See WTO

classified in the subsectors 'software implementation services' (W/120 – 1.B.b) and 'other' (W/120 – 1.B.e), depending on whether they relate to, respectively, software or hardware. 'Software implementation services' include provision and maintenance services of software (IT infrastructure) and 'other' computer services contain '*maintenance and repair services of [. . .] computers and related equipment*',[770] arguably stretching to all IT hardware infrastructure necessary to provide and establish Internet connections and host processes for consumers.

5.3.4.2 Cloud Computing

Cloud computing is a generic commercial term used to refer to the delivery of computing services – servers, storage, databases, networking, software, analytics and more – over the Internet. In terms of functionality, cloud computing is not something new.[771] Gasser and Palfrey refer to cloud computing as 'Internet-based computing', explaining that this phenomenon allows for tapping data and software from the Internet, rather than accessing it 'offline', via a personal computer or a local server.[772] Meltzer clarified that cloud computing turns a fixed IT cost into a variable operating cost.[773] Three general ways in which services can be supplied through the cloud have been identified: (i) software as a service (SaaS): the cloud provider hosts and manages the software application and the consumer uses the providers' application on various client devices;[774] (ii) cloud platform as a service

Council for Trade in Services, 'Understanding on the scope of coverage of CPC 84 – Computer Services' Communication from Albania, Australia, Canada, Chile, Colombia, Croatia, the European Communities, Hong Kong China, Japan, Mexico, Norway, Peru, the Separate Customs Territory of Taiwan Penghu, Kinmen and Matsu, Turkey and the United States, TN/S/W/60, S/CSC/W/51, 26 January 2007, para 1.4.

770 Explanatory note to subclass 84500 in CPCprov, which is identified as the corresponding CPC code for 'other computer and related services'.

771 Tuthill (n 125) 360.

772 They also provide a supplementary definition for cloud computing as: '*A model for enabling ubiquitous, convenient, on-demand network access to a shared pool of configurable computing resources (e.g., networks, servers, storage, applications, and services) that can be rapidly provisioned and released with minimal management effort or service provider interaction.*' This is based on the definition of 'cloud computing' that can be found in the glossary of Computer Security Resource Centre of the US National Institute of Standards and Technology (NIST). Gasser and Palfrey (n 166) 142.

773 Meltzer, 'Governing Digital Trade' (n 172) 31.

774 The service supplier manages the application and the underlying infrastructure and handles maintenance. Users generally connect to the software over the Internet, on any kind of device.

(PaaS): the consumer-producers can create and/or acquire applications developed with the programming languages and tools supported by the provider;[775] (iii) cloud infrastructure as a service (IaaS): the consumer can rely on the provider for the processing, storage, networks and other fundamental computing resources, located in the cloud.[776] This illustrates the hybrid nature of 'cloud computing' as a service. It can be provided in many different ways, for the provision of many different online services. A variety of service sectors is implied in the phenomenon of 'cloud computing'. It has been suggested by Members that cloud computing consists of data processing services, telecommunications services and other services.[777] Moreover, cloud computing is offered by a wide range of service suppliers who supply different services.[778] The Secretariat referred to cloud computing as 'an emerging commercial model'.[779]

Considering the above, it is submitted that cloud computing should not be considered as one final service output, but merely as the online equivalent of the functioning of a personal computer – through use of remote servers to store, manage and process data, rather than local servers or hard drives. Cloud computing is not a service in itself that can be supplied and consumed as such but is rather a means of providing the service.[780] The concept of cloud computing cannot be reduced to a single service sector. Both computer and related services and telecommunications services are relevant service sectors, as some 'cloud computing activities' can fall into various data-related subsectors.[781]

[775] PaaS is designed to make it easier for developers to quickly create web or mobile apps, without worrying about setting up or managing the underlying infrastructure of servers, storage, network and databases needed for development.

[776] The consumer rents IT infrastructure from a service provider on a pay-as-you-go basis.

[777] WTO Committee on Specific Commitments, 'Informal Discussion of Classification Issues on Computer and Related Services (CRS) on 10 March 2011 – Summary by the Chairperson – Addendum', JOB/SERV/44/Add.1, 27 May 2011, para 6.

[778] Tuthill (n 125) 360.

[779] WTO Council for Trade in Services, 'Computer and Related Services' Background Note by the Secretariat, S/C/W/300, 22 June 2009, para 28.

[780] In their OECD working paper, Lopez-Gonzalez and Ferencz qualify cloud computing services as 'digital inputs', which can help firms access IT services with little upfront investment. They define cloud computing as 'the storage and processing of data remotely'. Use of cloud services allows for flexibility and cost-efficiency, enabling internationalisation of SMEs. Lopez-Gonzalez and Ferencz (n 6) paras 11 and 17.

[781] Renee Berry and Matthew Reisman, 'Policy Challenges of Cross-Border Cloud Computing' (2012) Journal of International Commerce and Economics 1, 21–22.

In discussing cloud computing, the EU stressed that the fact that the service was delivered in another manner '*did not change what was provided to the final consumer and the substance remained a computer service*'.[782] Additionally, it noted that business models did not change the type of service delivered.[783] The United States takes a similar approach, equally classifying cloud computing as a computer service.[784] China, on the other hand, submitted that cloud computing is a new service.[785] Australia disagreed with China's statement and maintained that '*cloud computing fit very well within the existing classification under the GATS*', without, however, elaborating on its specific classification.[786]

It is not self-evident that all services using cloud computing amount to computer services, considering the fact that a wide range of services can be supplied by means of cloud computing. Examples include online mail services, online calendars, online back-up of files, social networks, VOD services and web-based word processors. While all of these services make use of cloud computing for the storing of and access to data, the service that is ultimately provided will not necessarily be a 'data base service' (W/120 – 1.B.d, for the remote storing of data) or 'data processing service' (W/120 – 1.B.c, for the remote managing and processing of data) but can also classify as 'electronic mail services' (W/120 – 2.C.h) or 'television transmission services' (W/120 – 2.D.d) based on the functional approach to classification. Other services provided through cloud computing (e.g. online storage of files) will, however, clearly fall within the scope of 'data base services'.

Positing that cloud computing requires a new specific service sector ignores the essence of what cloud computing is: it is impossible to capture computing over the Internet within one service sector as cloud computing is effectively a *means* of providing various services. The functionalities of cloud computing are as diverse as the functionalities of a computer.

Table 5.1 summarises the classification of the digital infrastructure services discussed.

[782] WTO Committee on Specific Commitments, 'Report of the Meeting Held on 18 September 2014' Note by the Secretariat, S/CSC/M/71, 15 October 2014, para 1.6.
[783] ibid.
[784] WTO Council for Trade in Services, 'Communication by the United States – Work Programme on Electronic Commerce', S/C/W/359, 17 December 2014, paras 5.4 – 5.11.
[785] WTO Committee on Specific Commitments, 'Report of the meeting Held on 5 October 2016', S/CSC/M/77, 21 November 2016, para 2.2.
[786] ibid para 2.4.

Table 5.1 *Classification of digital infrastructure services*

Digital infrastructure services are the 'Internet equivalent' of basic telecommunication services. Due to their ancillary function, they will likely classify as telecommunication or computer services.	
Examples:	
Carrier services	Packet-switched data transmission services
Network management services	Packet-switched data transmission services
Hosting and IT infrastructure provisioning services	Software implementation services and other computer and related services, depending on whether related to software or hardware
Cloud computing	Not a specific service sector but rather a means through which services can be supplied. Services supplied through cloud computing can classify as 'data base services', 'data processing services', 'electronic mail services', 'television transmission services' and so forth

5.4 Digitally Enabled Services

5.4.1 Digitisation and the Advent of Digitally Enabled Services

In their 2001 World Bank study, Mattoo and Schuknecht perceive a distinction between two types of digital (or electronic) services: 'trade in digitisable media products' and 'electronic services trade'. They define the former term as '*a number of products that have traditionally been delivered as goods [which] can now be sent across networks in digital form*'[787] and the latter term as '*international cross-border trade in a wide range of services, financial, legal, telecommunications, customized software, etc. [that] is carried out by electronic means*'.[788]

A 2005 study conducted for the European Parliament pointed to the fact that trade in services is a crucial aspect of the digital economy and that these services come in a variety of forms, including content and

[787] Including film, printed materials, video games and various recorded information on physical carriers.

[788] Mattoo and Schuknecht (n 72) 4–5.

communication services.[789] The study goes on to state that '*digital services include traditional electronic communication services (voice, text and video) and a whole range of newer services (social media, online shopping, games, cloud computing, searching, and navigation)*'.[790] It clarifies that most of these digital services are available on the Internet (OTT services[791]), while many of the traditional electronic communication services are often also provided in bundle with a broadband connection by an ISP. This leads to a direct competitive relationship between some OTT services and services provided by ISPs.[792]

Digitisation is considered a cause for the convergence of certain value chains, where new digital services are being added to or merged with existing services. The EP study illustrates this by referring to the fact that both telecom operators as well as cable operators are now offering VOD services.[793] The same service is now offered simultaneously through multiple ways of delivery.[794]

The service sector of computer and related services has been significantly impacted by technological evolution and the increased presence of integrated services. The Understanding on CPC 84, however, suggests that, regardless of the technological evolution, the functions that are referred to in the W/120 are largely the same as to today.[795] The same observation can be made for digital services in general: even though many services seem new, the nature of their function is not much different from services that

789 Directorate General for Internal Policies – Policy Department A: Economic and Scientific Policy, 'Challenges for Competition Policy in a Digitalised Economy' (European Parliament 2015) Study PE 542.235, 17.

790 ibid.

791 OTT services can be defined as content provision over the Internet, thereby bypassing traditional distribution networks. See Peng, 'GATS and the Over-the-Top Services: A Legal Outlook' (n 102) 22–23. In the provision of digital or OTT services, there is no control involved over the underlying network. This is different for the traditional electronic communication services, where the ISP uses its own infrastructure or rents it to deliver these services instead of over the Internet. Directorate General for Internal Policies – Policy Department A: Economic and Scientific Policy (n 789) 17.

792 Directorate General for Internal Policies – Policy Department A: Economic and Scientific Policy (n 789) 17.

793 ibid 19.

794 E.g. Voice services can be provided by telecom operators as well as through online applications. TV services can be provided by ISPs over traditional telecommunication networks as well as via an application or over a website. ibid.

795 WTO Committee on Specific Commitments, 'Computer and Related Services Overview of Classification Issues' Informal Note by the Secretariat, JOB/SERV/39, 4 March 2011, para 4.

were listed in 1991. For classification purposes it is essential to distinguish between the enabling service (i.e. digital infrastructure service) and the enabled service. Digitally enabled services are not per definition covered by CPC 84, as their classification should be based on an assessment of the final service provided to the end user.[796] This statement is in line with the functional or teleological approach as presented *supra* (Section 5.2.3). That does, however, not entail that digitally enabled services can never be covered by CPC 84 (and, by extension, basic telecommunications services).

The category of digitally enabled services contains for a large part 'traditional' services that can now be supplied electronically. Examples can be found in various submissions and statements made by Members at the WTO. As early as 1998, the EU signalled that legal services could be requested and provided across borders electronically; films could be ordered and distributed via the Internet; and banking services could be provided online.[797] In the context of the Committee on Trade in Financial Services, Switzerland discussed e-banking, stating that it was generally an extension of traditional banking, which is in line with the principle of technological neutrality under the GATS.[798] Other Members have, however, also argued that digital services are 'new services'.

5.4.2 *Are We Being Confronted with New Services? Confusion Caused by Convergence*

Telecommunications services are often used to supply other services, like computer services, audiovisual services or other telecommunication-enabled services. However, using telecommunications as a means for delivering another service does not alter the applicable commitments.

[796] WTO Committee on Specific Commitments, 'Informal Discussion of Classification Issues on Computer and Related Services (CRS) on 10 March 2011 – Summary by the Chairperson', JOB/SERV/44, 4 April 2011, para 6.

[797] WTO Council for Trade in Services, 'Work Programme on Electronic Commerce. Scope and Classification Issues' Communication from the European Communities and its Member States, S/C/W/87, 9 December 1998, para 1.

[798] The representatives of Uruguay and the Philippines contested that there was a principle of technological neutrality under the GATS. WTO Committee on Trade in Financial Services, 'Report of the Meeting Held on 16 May 2003' Note by the Secretariat, S/FIN/M/40, 30 June 2003, paras 18, 28 and 34. See for original submission by Switzerland: WTO Committee on Trade in Financial Services, 'E-banking in Switzerland' Communication from Switzerland, S/FIN/W/26, 30 April 2003.

Due to the convergence between telecommunications, broadcasting and audiovisual services and their delivery, it has become increasingly difficult to identify and apply the correct commitments. Convergence is not only an issue for the classification of services, with, for example, traditional telecom suppliers venturing beyond mere transmission of audiovisual products, but also impacts telecom regulators who now have to also regulate broadcast and other (traditionally) ICT services.[799] Apart from the fact that convergence makes distinction between different service sectors more difficult, the distinction itself might become irrelevant where companies now provide integrated services.[800]

Several WTO Members have pointed out the growing convergence between telecommunications services and computer services and audiovisual services and have proposed solutions to this classification issue.[801] Taiwan, for example, in its 2003 communication regarding computer and related services, voiced its concerns regarding what it calls 'convergence services'. It identified two types of convergence services: the 'Internet-based telecom services' and the 'multimedia content', the former being a combination between computer services and telecommunications services, whereas the latter is an integration of computer and audiovisual services.[802] Taiwan concluded that it would rather see these integrated services classified under, respectively, the telecommunications services and the audiovisual services, because of '*their great impact on the regulatory environment*'. This argumentation leads to a similar basic versus value-added (or transmission v. content) distinction being made for the computer service sector, with the conclusion that service classification is not altered by the fact that the services are Internet-enabled. Such an argument fits with the principle of technological neutrality and is helpful to Members wanting to (partially) liberalise these services.

799 Tuthill and Roy (n 106) 161.

800 Weber and Burri (n 5) 56.

801 For example, Taiwan, the EU and the US have voiced their opinion on such integrated services. Additionally, Voice over Internet Protocol (VoIP) services have been raised as a problematic example of the classification of converging services. WTO Committee on Specific Commitments, 'Informal iDscussion of Classification Issues on Telecommunications on 11 May 2011 – Summary by the Chairperson', JOB/SERV/75, 27 May 2011, para 10.

802 WTO Council for Trade in Services, 'Computer and Related Services' Communication from the Separate Customs Territory of Taiwan, Penghu, Kinmen and Matsu, TN/S/W/10, S/CSC/W/37, 8 January 2003, para 6.

5.4.2.1 Telecommunications and Computer Services

Especially relevant in the assessment of digital supply of services is the increasing convergence between computer services and telecommunications. This overlap was already recognised by the WTO Secretariat in its 1998 Background Note on computer and related services.[803] It explained that '*[t]he IT industry has grown out of a convergence of telecommunications, computer technology and software as well as more content-oriented industries such as broadcasting and publishing. The blend can yield hybrid IT services difficult to categorize into any particular sector.*'[804] This strong interlinkage makes it hard to identify the correct service sector for these services, additionally complicated by the overlap in the W/120 list as described *infra* (Section 5.4.2(i)). In its 2009 background note, the Secretariat elaborated upon this and stated that '*some computer services have become nearly impossible to distinguish from value-added telecommunications services. In addition, a commercial trend towards integrated offerings of the subsectors identified in the GATS Classification makes it increasingly difficult to distinguish among them.*'[805] This increasing overlap adds to the difficulty in classifying digital services within the correct service sector and thereby determining the specific obligations that apply to them. The Secretariat also pointed to the increased feasibility of cross-border supply of services through the Internet and the spur in technological and commercial convergence.[806]

An interesting overlap is found in the W/120 classification of telecommunication and computer services. 'Data processing services' are included in two different service sectors: 1.B.c. for computer services and 2.C.n. for telecommunications services. Both refer to the same CPCprov group code (843 – Data processing services). However, whereas the subsector of computer services refers to the whole of the CPCprov group, the reference to CPCprov in the telecommunications sector includes the double asterisk, indicating that the service specified only constitutes a part of the total

[803] Focussing specifically on the online supply of data base and data processing services. WTO Council for Trade in Services, 'Computer and Related Services' Background Note by the Secretariat, S/C/W/45, 14 July 1998, paras 2 and 8.

[804] ibid para 4.

[805] WTO Council for Trade in Services, 'Computer and Related Services' Background Note by the Secretariat, S/C/W/300, 22 June 2009, para 6.

[806] ibid para 4. See also WTO Committee on Specific Commitments, 'Computer and Related Services Overview of Classification Issues' Informal Note by the Secretariat, JOB/SERV/39, 4 March 2011, para 10, where the Secretariat noted that computer and related service suppliers can equally supply connectivity or transmission as an integral offering to the consumer.

range of activities covered by the CPC concordance. Nowhere is it specified which part of group 843 (which is further broken down into input preparation services, data processing and tabulation services, time sharing services and other data processing services) relates to both computer and telecommunications services.[807] The only conceivable difference with the text of W/120 is that the subsector under telecommunications services refers in full to '*on-line information and/or data processing (incl. transaction processing)*'. Does the reference to 'on-line' relate only to information or also to data processing? Does this mean that subsector 2.C.n. only applies to online data processing services? If that were the case, then classification would be based on the means through which the service is supplied, which would go against the principle of technological neutrality. Overall, the overlap in CPC references for data processing and the unclear language reveal flaws in the drafting of the W/120, as its service sectors are considered mutually exclusive.[808]

Another interaction between the telecommunication and computer services classification can be found in the CPCprov explanatory note corresponding to database services (subsector 1.B.d.). The note explains database services as '*all services provided from primarily structured databases through a communication network*' and then goes on to exclude data and message transmission services (CPC 7523). In the W/120, the latter are covered in nine different telecommunications subsectors.[809] This illustrates the close interlinkage between telecommunication and computer services, already acknowledged in 1991.

Another factor adding to the increased ambiguity is the historical nature of the WTO's classification system. When conceived in 1991, 'electronic data interchange' (EDI – scheduled under W/120 2.C.j) was an electronic service only used by businesses in their supply chain management.[810] Burri and Weber argue that this is no longer the case as '*everybody can be involved in a general data "interchange" and the*

[807] In the context of the Committee on Specific Commitments, it was reported that a Member '*urged that data processing (CPC 843 cited in both sectors) should be committed under computer services*'. WTO Committee on Specific Commitments, 'Informal Discussion of Classification Issues on Computer and Related Services (CRS) on 10 March 2011 – Summary by the Chairperson', JOB/SERV/44, 4 April 2011, para 10.

[808] AB Report, *US – Gambling*, para 180.

[809] Those subsectors being: packet-switched data transmission services, circuit-switched data transmission services, telex services, private leased circuit services, electronic mail, voice mail, on-line information and data base retrieval, electronic data interchange (EDI) and enhanced/value-added facsimile services, incl. store and forward, store and retrieve.

[810] Weber and Burri (n 5) 55.

direct relation to a telecommunications system can hardly be seen anymore, a classification as computer related service might make more sense'.[811] However, EDI is still almost solely used for communication in B2B commerce. Whereas the way in which the interchange is done might have evolved with technological changes, the function of EDI is still B2B communication, not a computer service.

As mentioned *supra* (Section 5.3.2), the EU proposed a new, broad and functional definition of 'telecommunications services' in 2005 in an attempt to resolve the issues surrounding the existing W/120 classification of this service sector. It proposed a simplified definition for telecommunications services, based on the definition in the Telecoms Annex: '*any service consisting of the transmission and reception of signals by any electromagnetic means*'.[812] Additionally, the EU clarified that the telecommunication service sector does not cover those services that are being provided over telecom services,[813] regardless of whether these services are being provided by the service provider of the transmission services or by another service supplier. It was thereby, rightfully so, trying to distinguish between core telecommunications services and other services (that provide another service than the transmission or reception of signals) that should be classified under their own service sector. The EU recognised the increasing overlap between the telecom and computer service sectors, especially when it comes to data processing.[814] It proposed that, when dealing with 'enhanced services provided by operators', all of the relevant commitments should apply, even if that leads to a combined application of commitments in two different service sectors.[815] It concluded by setting out the principle that '*services that provide transmission and reception of signals by electromagnetic means are covered by the telecom sector, and the rest, including any additional function that is not intrinsically linked to the transmission and reception, should find its place elsewhere, whether or not it is the same entity providing both services*'.[816] I agree with the EU's attempt to simplify these classification issues.

[811] ibid.

[812] WTO Council for Trade in Services, 'Classification in the Telecom Sector under the WTO-GATS Framework' Communication from the European Communities, TN/S/W/27, S/CSC/W/44, 10 February 2005, para 16.

[813] Examples that the EC refers to include financial services (e-banking), information services (online news provision or location-based information supply) and entertainment services (video-on-demand services). ibid para 17.

[814] ibid para 20.

[815] ibid para 21.

[816] ibid para 22.

However, the United States strongly disagreed with this proposal by the EU, stating that it creates uncertainty regarding value-added telecommunications services, excluding these from the scope of the telecommunication service sector due to the limited definition as proposed by the EU.[817] The United States submitted that value-added telecommunications services should be explicitly included within Member's Schedules, proposing a new definition: '*All services consisting of the transmission and reception of signals by any electromagnetic means, alone or in combination with enhancing, storing, forwarding, retrieving, or processing functions added to the transmission and reception of signals.*'[818]

5.4.2.2 Telecommunications/Computer Services and Audiovisual Services

Like the service sectors discussed *supra*, audiovisual services have been subject to significant technological changes in the last two decades.[819] Historically, telecom suppliers and users were a clearly distinct group from the audiovisual broadcaster and viewer.[820] These services were applied separately or were at least clearly distinguishable in their supply. This is different nowadays, where, due to the Internet, the same networks are being used regardless of the content. The convergence between both service sectors impacts the way in which they need to be addressed.

The increased bundling of telecommunications and audiovisual services also has an impact on the classification of these services within the WTO framework and the coherence of the GATS commitments regarding these services. Because of technological innovation, companies that used to solely provide telephony telecom services can now provide digitised audiovisual services (e.g. telecom providers are increasingly providing multimedia-on-demand).[821] In tackling the classification of services because of their changed provision, inspiration might be drawn from how WTO Members have addressed (or even anticipated) this convergence in their Services Schedule of Commitments. For example, the EU Schedule distinguishes between (i) telecommunications services, defined as '*transport of*

[817] WTO Council for Trade in Services, 'Classification in the Telecommunications Sector under the WTO-GATS Framework' Communication from the United States, TN/S/W/35, S/CSC/W/45, 22 February 2005, para 2.

[818] ibid para 11.

[819] Tuthill and Roy (n 106) 167.

[820] Luff, 'Convergence: A Buzzword to Remain?' (n 759) 65.

[821] Shin-yi Peng, 'Trade in Telecommunications Services: Doha and Beyond' (2007) 41 Journal of World Trade 293, 298.

electro-magnetic signals – sound, data image and any combinations thereof; (ii) broadcasting services, defined as '*uninterrupted chain of transmission for the distribution of tv and radio programme signals to the general public*'; and (iii) content provision, stating that '*commitments in this schedule do not cover the economic activity consisting of content provision which require telecommunications services for its transport. The provision of that content, transported via a telecommunications service, is subject to the specific commitments undertaken by the European Communities and their Member States in other relevant sectors.*'[822] Taking into account these EU definitions, Luff argues that where the classic television or radio broadcasting services would be categorised as audiovisual services,[823] the provision of television or radio over the Internet rather falls within the packet-switched data transmission service (under telecommunications services, subsector 2.C.b of the W/120 classification).[824] Such classification is flawed as it leads to classification discrepancies, with different commitments applying to services depending on how they are being supplied. It is difficult to envisage how directly competing services could be subject to different commitments (and therefore to different obligations).[825]

Additional confusion is caused by the fact that the classification of audiovisual services contains references to both what is being transmitted and the transmitting itself. Subsector 2.D.d in the W/120 list radio and television *transmission* services. A clear and consistent delineation between content and mode of transmission would lead to a clearer classification.[826] The mode of transmission should be neutral, not impacting classification.

This interesting anomaly in the W/120 classification does not reflect the CPC's approach. Looking at the corresponding CPC codes, it's apparent that the provisional CPC classification classified radio and television transmission services within the sector of telecommunications services. This classification in W/120 is distracting from a technologically neutral regulation of audiovisual services. For the sake of consistency, taking into account

822 WTO, Supplement 3 to the Schedule of Specific Commitments of the European Communities and their Member States, GATS/SC/31/Suppl.3, 11 April 1997. See also Luff, 'Convergence: A Buzzword to Remain?' (n 759) 78.

823 More specifically within the subsector of 'Radio and Television Transmission Services' (W/120 2.D.d).

824 David Luff, 'Telecommunications and Audio-Visual Services: Considerations for a Convergence Policy at the World Trade Organization Level' (2004) 38 Journal of World Trade 1059, 1079.

825 Luff, 'Convergence: A Buzzword to Remain?' (n 759) 79.

826 Weber and Burri (n 5) 89.

technological developments, it would make more sense to classify the transmission services related to radio and television within the sector of telecommunications services.[827] This would extend the distinction between 'content services' and 'enabling services', or put differently, the distinction between production and transmission, working towards a more straightforward classification of these convergent services.[828] Looking into the content of this subsector, it is difficult to accept Luff's argument in the preceding paragraph. The relevant service subsector for the broadcasting of TV and radio can be found under the heading 'Radio and television transmission services' (W/120 2.D.d.). The corresponding CPC code 7524 includes further subclasses 75241 'Television broadcast transmission services' and 75242 'Radio broadcast transmission services'. The explanatory note to subclass 75241 describes television broadcast transmission services as '*Network services necessary for the transmission of television signals, independently of the type of technology (network) employed*'. Considering this definition, it is not readily apparent why digital television broadcasting would be excluded from this technologically neutral definition.[829]

In clarifying this anomaly and preventing the different classification of directly competing services, inspiration might be drawn from the EU's proposed classification and definition of telecommunications services. The EU's proposed technologically neutral and functional approach to determining the scope of the telecommunication service sector excludes content (i.e. services that are provided over these telecommunications services) from the scope of the telecom sector and makes them subject to the commitments undertaken in their specific service sector (e.g. banking services, audiovisual services, information services).[830] It similarly excludes services enabled by computer services from classification under CPC 84.[831]

827 Including cable networks, satellite, radio frequencies, etc. This was proposed in Peng, 'Trade in Telecommunications Services: Doha and Beyond' (n 821) 298–299.

828 ibid 299–300.

829 Luff argues that Internet television services in the EU cannot be classified as broadcasting services since they are not supplied through an uninterrupted chain of transmission. This argument, however, does not hold for live streaming.

830 Peng, 'Trade in Telecommunications Services: Doha and Beyond' (n 821) 304–305.

831 As examples, the EU refers to accounting services, architectural services, medical services, audiovisual services and educational services. WTO Council for Trade in Services, 'Communication from the European Communities and its Member States – Certification Draft Consolidated GATS Schedule', S/C/W/273, 9 October 2006, 90.

As regards telecommunications, the EU additionally included a note to its Schedule of Commitments clarifying this distinction.[832] The EU's strong opinion on this distinction is (at least partly) prompted by its aversion to liberalising anything related to 'culture'. It does not want to liberalise digital content-related services.[833] In the same line, the EU also contended that services involving publication, production and transmission of recreational software (i.e. games) to the public classifies as audio-visual services.[834] Following the EU's line of thought, an *a contrario* reasoning would lead to the classification of business software within the sector of computer services as it lacks a recreational aspect.

5.4.3 *Are We Being Confronted with New Services? Confusion Caused by New Business Models*

As noted *supra* (Section 5.3), many of the so-called new digital services are not services that did not exist before, but are services that are being combined and converged within the context of new business models. The new business models that have been facilitated by digital platforms have been referred to as 'platform economy', 'sharing economy', 'collaborative economy', 'on-demand economy', 'peer-to-peer economy', 'gig economy', 'crowd-based capitalism' and so on.[835] Because of the development of these new business models (and especially the way in which they market themselves), the general impression grew among both consumers and policy makers that they were dealing with new services altogether.[836] A similar observation was made in the context of discussions in the Committee on Specific Commitments, where the Secretariat noted the use of new technical

[832] WTO Trade in Services, 'European Communities and their Member States – Schedule of Specific Commitments – Supplement 3', GATS/SC/31/Suppl. 3, 11 April 1997, 2. Weber and Burri (n 5) 97.

[833] ibid.

[834] ibid 98.

[835] The UNCTAD Secretariat, however, cautioned that these terms tend to be used interchangeably, thereby not adequately reflecting the right business model. For example, even though companies like Uber and Airbnb are often classified as part of the sharing economy, they rather enable e-commerce than enable sharing resources. A true sharing economy involves the sharing of assets or time. When companies are involved in the exchange of money or creation of some form of employment, they extend the market to idle resources or assets rather than share them. UNCTAD, 'Fostering Developments Gains from E-Commerce and Digital Platforms' (n 26) paras 11–12.

[836] See also Tuthill (n 125) 374–375; and Aaditya Mattoo and Joshua P Meltzer, 'International Data Flows and Privacy: The Conflict and Its Resolution' (2018) 21 Journal of International Economic Law 769, 780.

terminology and commercial names in the marketing of computer and related services. The question is raised whether classification should not be based on the nature of the service rather than the equipment or technology used to supply the service.[837] Canada observed that most services that have been declared 'new' are combinations of existing services or are existing services that are being delivered through a new medium. It stated, '*truly new services [are] very rare if they [exist] at all*'.[838]

Gao uses the example of Google as a multifunctional company (in a similar vein, the Chinese company Alibaba markets itself as a global e-commerce *ecosystem*) to illustrate the wide range of services it provides (and the different shapes it takes): 'information searching services' through the Google search engine, 'online hosting and publication services' through its ownership of several platforms (YouTube, Blogger, Instagram) and 'advertising services' through its use of AdWords (its main source of revenue).[839] All of these different services of course have their own services classification, which is not always straightforward. Whereas the classification of the advertising services within the W/120 classification is straightforward ('advertising services' 1.F.a), this is less so for online hosting and publication services. YouTube is arguably a 'video distribution service', which can fall within the audiovisual sector 2.D,[840] whereas the others might be classified as online storage and retrieval of data, falling within the scope of 'data base services' 1.B.d.[841] Search engines are also difficult to classify within the W/120's classification. Gao argues that, through an analysis of the correspondence with newer CPC versions, search engines fall within CPCprov Group 844, or W/120 subsector 'data base services' (1.

[837] WTO Committee on Specific Commitments, 'Computer and Related Services Overview of Classification Issues' Informal Note by the Secretariat, JOB/SERV/39, 4 March 2011, para 7. In its background note on Computer and Related Services the Secretariat also referenced '*the commercial trend towards integrated offerings of the subsectors identified in the GATS classification*'. WTO Council for Trade in Services, 'Computer and Related Services' Background Note by the Secretariat, S/C/W/300, 22 June 2009, para 6.

[838] WTO Committee on Specific Commitments, 'Report of the Meeting Held on 18 September 2014' Note by the Secretariat, S/CSC/M/71, 15 October 2014, para 1.3.

[839] Gao, 'Googling for the Trade-Human Rights Nexus in China: Can the WTO Help?' (n 690) 251–252.

[840] In the *China – Publications and Audiovisual Products* case, it was found by the Panel that China had inscribed 'Video distribution services' into its Schedule under the service sector 2.D 'Audiovisual Services'. See Panel Report, *China – Publications and Audiovisual Products*, paras 4.55 and 4.65.

[841] Gao, 'Googling for the Trade-Human Rights Nexus in China: Can the WTO Help?' (n 690) 252–253.

B.d).[842] My view on the classification issue will be detailed *infra* (Section 5.4.6.1).

Other services that have explicitly been identified as 'new' services include Internet telephony services such as those provided through Skype and Apple's Facetime as well as 3D printing.[843] As will be shown *infra* (Section 5.4.6.3), Internet telephony services qualify as voice telephone services. As to 3D printing, there seems to be some confusion on what service is being provided and by whom. The printing that is done by the 3D printer itself is not a service that is being provided by a service provider. For example, where a consumer has bought a 3D printer that allows it to manufacture various goods, no service is being provided to that consumer. The consumer has merely procured a good that allows it to print other goods, in the same way as a normal printer manufactures paper products. Where a service supplier owns a 3D printer and supplies the service of manufacturing goods with that printer on demand, the service supplier clearly provides services incidental to manufacturing (W/120 – 1.F.i.). However, for a 3D printer to function, it requires a computer-aided design (CAD) file, which generates the electronic blueprint.[844] The provision of the CAD file (which entails the design of the printed good) should be classified as 'other business service' (W/120 – 1.F.t., which includes 'specialty design services'[845]) if consumer goods are designed, or as 'engineering service' (W/120 – 1.A.e., which includes engineering design services) if industrial goods are designed.

To conclude on the question as to whether there are new services, it is almost impossible to answer this question without the (exhaustive) qualitative and quantitative research to back this up. To be able to safely answer that question, it would be necessary to investigate the classification of all digital services that have been claimed to be 'new'. Such research goes beyond the scope of this book, not only due to the vastness of the digital

842 ibid 257.

843 Sen (n 118) 334. Russia for example identifies '*search engines, mobile applications, cloud computing, other digital products*' as 'new' services. WTO General Council, Work Programme on Electronic Commerce, 'Ways to Move Forward' Communication from the Russian Federation, JOB/GC/131, 14 July 2017, para 3.2. The IMF identifies 'matching services' and 'cloud computing' as services that are not covered by the CPC. International Monetary Fund (n 265) 7.

844 This CAD file will often capture the majority of the value of the 3D manufacturing. Neeraj (n 95) 126.

845 See the explanatory note to CPCprov code 87903, which states: '*Services consisting in creating designs and preparing patterns for a variety of products by harmonizing aesthetic considerations with technical and other requirements. Included in this category are furniture designs, interior designs and decorations and aesthetic designs for various other consumer products.*'

economy but also because of the ever-evolving world of digital services. On top of the examples raised above, two elements point to a limited number of actual new services. First, the fact that one service supplier seems to supply various different services at the same time does not affect the classification of the individual services (unless we are dealing with integrated services). Rather, it should be accepted that a service supplier can supply various different services at the same time, to the same or different types of consumers. Second, it is incredibly important to always be clear in the identification of the service at issue and its end users. This is what will allow for a clear classification of the various services supplied by the same service supplier. For the purpose of this research, it suffices to say that many digital services that have been called 'new' are not new in the sense that they do not fit within the existing service classification system. Even though it cannot be said that not a single new service exists at this point in time or in the future, it can be noted that, applying the correct classification methodology, all of the digitally enabled services discussed in this book seemed to fit within the existing classification framework.

5.4.4 'Services Supplied on a Commercial Basis': Advertisements as Only Source of Revenue

Discussions on the classification of various digitally enabled services (including search engines, social networks and blogs) are very often tainted by references to the way in which the service suppliers of these services generate revenue: through the sale of advertisements on their website/platform.[846] The argument has been raised that the GATS only covers services that are provided on a commercial basis, thereby reasoning that any (digital) service whose main source of revenue is advertisement rather than sales to consumers might have to be classified under 'advertising services'.[847] Such an argument, however, is based on too narrow an interpretation of the term 'on a commercial basis'.

The GATS only indirectly requires services to be supplied on a commercial basis as it excludes from its scope all services 'supplied in the exercise of governmental authority'. Article I:3(c) explains that this entails the exclusion of '*any service which is supplied neither on*

[846] See for example United Nations Department of Economic and Social Affairs, Meeting of the Expert Group on International Statistical Classifications New York 19–22 May, 'New Issues Requiring Guidance in the Central Product Classification (CPC)', ESA/STAT/AC.289/20, 12 May 2015, paras 1.5 and 1.6.

[847] ibid para 1.5.

a commercial basis, nor in competition with one or more service suppliers'. Similarly, in Article XIII GATS, dealing with government procurement, it is stated that Articles II (most-favoured-nation obligation), XVI (market access obligation) and XVII (national treatment obligation) do not apply with regard to government procurement of services '*not with a view to commercial resale or with a view to use in the supply of services for commercial sale*'.

Unfortunately, the GATS does not elaborate on what is to be understood under 'commercial' or 'on a commercial basis'. Guidance on how to interpret this term can be found in case law. Panels and the Appellate Body have found that the dictionary meaning of 'commercial' refers to *inter alia* 'financial return', 'likely to make a profit' and 'as a matter of business'.[848] It was added that the fact that the actor (read: service supplier) is the government does not automatically imply that the good or service is not being supplied on commercial terms.[849] This also fits with the context provided in Article I:3(c). This subparagraph clarifies that services are only considered to be supplied in the exercise of governmental authority if they are not supplied on a commercial basis. In assessing whether something is 'commercial', it should be considered whether commercial profit is the sole or primary objective.[850] In *Canada – Renewable Energy*, the Appellate Body clarified that commercial resale requires profit-orientation, even if long term.[851]

Considering the above, it can definitely not be contended that 'supplied on a commercial basis' only comprises situations where the consumer would pay, in currency, directly for the service supplier to provide the consumer with the service. Rather, especially considering the changing business model of how services are being supplied, profit can be gained from something else that consumers 'trade' for their continued access to a platform: data. Even though 'payment in data' does not take the same form as traditional currency payment, it has turned out to be a tried-and-tested business model that is currently being used by a wide variety of service suppliers. Consumers are not required to pay to have continued access to a platform but in return (whether consumers are aware of this or not) the service suppliers gather users' data and use this data to, for example, sell

848 Panel Report, *Canada – Wheat Exports and Grain Imports*, para 6.84; AB Report, *US – Anti-Dumping and Countervailing Duties (China)*, para 478.

849 AB Report, *US – Anti-Dumping and Countervailing Duties (China)*, para 479.

850 Panel Report, *EC – Seal Products*, para 7.287.

851 AB Report, *Canada – Renewable Energy*, para 5.71. The Panel had already established that commercial resale does not always necessarily involve profit. Panel Report, *Canada – Renewable Energy*, para 7.151.

targeted advertising on its platform. The service supplied by the service supplier to the consumer is the access to its platform and not the advertising services it sells to advertisers. These are two clearly distinguishable services being supplied by the same service supplier. One should therefore be cautious when taking the source of revenue into account in the classification of digital services. It is the *function* of the service supplied that determines its classification, not the means of supply nor the source of revenue.

5.4.5 *Relation of Data Flows to Digitally Enabled Services*

Virtually all digital services are extremely data-intensive. They require enormous amounts of data flows to be supplied (intra-firm, cross-border, etc.). Considering the 'buzz-word' status of the term 'data flows', I wanted to expressly address this phenomenon and contextualise it within the research.

In this context, the finding in the panel report on *China – Electronic Payment Services* regarding integrated services is relevant. The panel held that integrated services necessarily fall within the scope of the specific (sub) sector that covers the service supplied. In the words of the panel: '*[. . .] these activities, even though they are not explicitly listed in [the relevant] subsector, are necessarily included within the scope of the definition of that subsector because they must operate together for the payment and money transmission service to be supplied*'.[852] Data flows fit within the integrated services narrative as they are inextricably linked to the provision of digital services.

Data, when traded and if considered a service, will classify as 'packet-switched data transmission services', 'circuit-switched data transmission services' or 'data processing services' depending on the function of the supplied services and the transmission technology that is required for that specific kind of data. Where data crosses borders in the context of the supply of a service, it is an input into this service. Due to the panel's finding on integrated services, data flows, as essential components for the provision of digital services, will be classified within the service sector covering the overall integrated services. For example, digital telecommunication via computer programs like Skype will require the transfer of data to function but is classified as Internet telephony, not as data transmission. This links closely to the reservations formulated to the components-based approach to classification *supra* (Section 5.2.2). For the purpose of this book, data is therefore only considered when ancillary to the supply of a service.

[852] Panel Report, *China – Electronic Payments*, para 7.180. See also Porges and Enders (n 135) 8.

5.4.6 *Application of the Classification Methodology*

Before analysing and classifying certain specific digitally enabled services, some general observations can be made regarding the issues of scheduling ambiguity in the three most often mentioned service sectors in the context of digital services: telecommunications services, computer and related services, and audiovisual services.

The W/120 isn't always consistent in its references to corresponding CPC codes, which leads to ambiguity. For example, neither the subsector 'sound recording' nor the subsector 'other' in the audiovisual service sector have a corresponding CPCprov code. This creates uncertainty as to the exact content of these service sectors, as there is hence no elaboration on what these subsectors entail. For example, do the types of services included in the sound recording subsector also encompass recordings made by smart speakers like Amazon's Alexa, Google's Assistant or Apple's Siri, or is it limited to studio recordings of professional music? The fact that governments are also allowed to schedule their own definitions, which may not always be clear to other Members, adds to the risk of ambiguous services schedules.[853] Another example of the ambiguous references to the CPC can be observed in the telecommunication sector, where no less than nine subsectors are said to cover part of CPCprov 7523. It becomes even more confusing when one takes account of the fact that both CPCprov 7521 and 7522 simultaneously correspond to two separate subsectors, but only indicate the 'partial coverage' (**) of one subsector.[854] A strict interpretation of the CPC references would entail that one of the two subsectors covers the whole of the CPC reference and therefore also encompasses the other 'partial' subsector, causing an overlap in service sectors which should be impossible.[855] Interpretation of the W/120 list on the basis of its CPC correspondences is therefore not always straightforward and should be done with some degree of caution.

Unlike the W/120, the CPC has been regularly updated by the United Nations and can therefore reflect the technological changes of the last

[853] Tuthill and Roy (n 106) 170.

[854] Subsectors 2.C.a. as well as 2.C.f correspond to 7521. Voice telephone services (a) refer to the whole CPCprov code, whereas facsimile services (f) only partially correspond to this code. The same observation can be made for respectively subsectors 2.C.e (telegraph services) and 2.C.g (private leased circuit services).

[855] AB Report, *US – Gambling*, para 180.

decades.[856] The latest version of the CPC (version 2.1) was adopted in 2013. It includes several digital trade-related service sectors: mobile data services (CPC2.1 84133), Internet telecommunications services (CPC2.1 842 – comprising Internet backbone services, Internet access services and other Internet telecommunications services), online content (CPC2.1 843 – comprising online text-based information, online audio content, online video content, software downloads and other online content, e.g. online software and web search portal content), hosting and information technology (IT) infrastructure provisioning services (CPC2.1 8315 – including website hosting services, application service provisioning and video and audio streaming services) and sales of Internet advertising space (CPC2.1 83633). For some other services, the CPC2.1 provides explicit clarification that the service can be provided over the Internet (reservation services for transportation, general medical services, and specialised medical services). It is unclear why the reference to the online provision of services is limited to these three specific services, as many other services can equally be digitally provided. It has been suggested to update the existing references to the CPCprov to the new CPC2.1, therefore allowing for a clearer classification of digital services. Tuthill warns that updating the existing references in W/120 would entail the risk of losing (whether on purpose or not) commitments negotiated and obtained in previous negotiation rounds, as it would allow Members to reassess their commitments.[857]

As explained *supra* (Section 2.4.3), the category 'digitally enabled services' covers all services that are provided through the use of the Internet. Consequently, this 'group' of services consists of a vast array of widely diverging services, some of which *seem* so new and different from services as they have traditionally been classified within the GATS classification that Members become doubtful, frustrated or even opportunistic in their ignorance on the appropriate classification of these services. I highlight a handful of digitally enabled services and classify them within the existing GATS classification. These specific services were selected as examples based on the controversy and discussions surrounding their classification. Other digitally enabled services for which classification is less contested include digitally delivered consulting services, digitally delivered legal services and online retail services. The

[856] For a more elaborate analysis of newer CPC versions in this context, see Tuthill and Roy (n 106).

[857] Tuthill (n 125) 375.

classification proposed for the examples in this Section is based on the teleological approach, thereby respecting the principle of technological neutrality.[858]

5.4.6.1 Search Engines

Search engines can most appropriately be classified as 'data base services' (W/120 – 1.B.d.). This conclusion is based on an application of the teleological classification approach: search engines use algorithms to grant access to databases containing a plethora of webpages.[859] Through the use of 'web crawlers' a search engine browses the web and indexes the information of all the pages it visits. Through the creation of this index (or database), search engines are able to display relevant results of search queries made by users of their service. The main function of the search engine service is therefore the compilation, maintenance of and allowing access to this database and thereby presenting results to search queries by consumers.

Considering the function of search engines, it becomes clear that the service they provide falls within the service sector of database services. The corresponding CPCprov subsector 844 indicates two characteristics: the service must be provided from a primarily structured database and it must be provided through a communication network. Search engines are characterised by both of these attributes. Regardless of the underlying technology used to provide this service, it is the granting of access to this database to the consumer that is the defining criterion (aim) of this service. This finding is confirmed through an analysis of more recent CPC classes. CPC2.1 explicitly includes online search engines, classified under subclass 84394. Following through the corresponding codes in earlier CPC versions, it can be concluded that CPCprov group 844 ('data base services') includes search engines.[860] The extensive classification analysis undertaken by Gao in his 2011 article also comes to the same conclusion.[861] He elaborates upon why search engine services do not classify as publishing services (because they are neither incidental to manufacturing, nor on a fee or contract basis) or data processing services (Google does not provide computer calculating services

[858] For several of these services, it is also indicated why a components-based approach would not lead to suitable classification.

[859] It should be noted that search engines themselves do not contain any content per se, but display links to locations where the requested information can be found. Erixon, Hindley and Lee-Makiyama (n 413) 5.

[860] Gao, 'Googling for the Trade-Human Rights Nexus in China: Can the WTO Help?' (n 690) 257.

[861] Gao, 'Google's China Problem: A Case Study on Trade, Technology and Human Rights under the GATS' (n 692) 359–365.

nor rental of computer time). Moreover, as noted *supra* (Section 5.4.4), the fact that search engine service suppliers only generate their revenue through the posting of advertisements does not alter this classification.[862]

5.4.6.2 Social Networks

China contends that social network services constitute new services that '*[can]not be captured properly by any service sector in the provisional CPC, nor [can] they fit neatly in the current WTO classification system*'.[863] Weber and Burri describe social networks as platforms structured around interactions between persons and entities, which technically amount to online storage and data retrieval services.[864] In trying to classify 'social networks' into the correct service sectors, Weber and Burri make reference to computer and related services (including data processing services (CPC 843), online information and/or data processing (CPC 843) and database services (CPC 844)), telecommunications services (including online information and data base retrieval (CPC 7523)) as well as other services (CPC 845 – maintenance and repair services of computers and CPC 849 – other computer services).[865]

Weber and Burri point to several possible service sectors that come to mind when categorising social media services. Firstly, social networks derive most of their revenue from selling advertisement space on their platforms. This part of their functionality can quite easily be classified under 'advertising services' (W/120 1.F.a (CPC 871)). However, as this is not the defining feature of social networks, this is not the ultimate service being supplied to its users (*supra* Section 5.4.4). Other elements of these platforms need to be studied as well. Social networks provide online hosting and publication services.[866] Such publication services do not fit within the subsector of 'printing, publishing' within 'Other Business Services' (W/120 1.F.r), as this service sector is concerned with publishing and printing on paper (*supra* Section 5.2.1). Two subsectors from the telecommunication

[862] As suggested in: United Nations Department of Economic and Social Affairs, Meeting of the Expert Group on International Statistical Classifications New York 19–22 May, 'New Issues Requiring Guidance in the Central Product Classification (CPC)', ESA/STAT/AC.289/20, 12 May 2015, para 1.5.

[863] WTO Committee on Specific Commitments, 'Report of the meeting Held on 5 October 2016', S/CSC/M/77, 21 November 2016, para 2.2. Interestingly, even though some Members refuted China's statement as to cloud computing being a new service, they did not do so for social networking services.

[864] Weber and Burri (n 5) 115.

[865] ibid 115–118.

[866] ibid 116.

service sector come to mind when discussing online hosting and publication services: 'on-line information and database retrieval' (W/120 2.C.j (CPC 7523)) and 'on-line information and/or data processing' (W/120 2.C.n (CPC 843)). However, Weber and Burri admit that neither of these subsectors cover social networks because the former is focussed on necessary network services for data transmission, while the latter only covers the conversion of disorganised raw data into useful information.[867] Two subsectors from the computer and related services sector seem relevant to the discussion on classification of social networks as well. First, 'data processing services' (W/120 1.B.c (CPC 843)) and second, 'data base services' (W/120 1.B.d. (CPC 844)). The data processing services under the computer services heading deal with the same issue of limited scope as discussed in the preceding paragraph. As data processing is limited to the active processing of disorganised data, it does not encompass the services supplied by social networks. This is different for database services. These are '*all services provided from primarily structured databases through a communications network*'.[868] They submit that the services provided by social networks can appropriately be classified under the database retrieval heading.[869] However, this classification seems to focus on a components-based approach, considering not the output of the service, but rather its technical function. Because of the reasons mentioned *supra* (Section 5.2.3), I deem a teleological approach to classification more appropriate.

Therefore, considering the function of social networks, that is, enabling the interaction between users through the sharing of text, image and/or video, the arguably correct classification based on the CPCprov would be 'electronic message and information services' (CPCprov 75232). Social network services enable electronic interaction and allow access to and manipulation of information in databases (arguably whatever is posted or 'shared' by social network users is included in the online database of that social network). Due to the unclear correspondence between the telecommunications services sector in W/120 and the CPC for the 7523 code, it is more difficult to link social networks to a specific subsector as listed in W/120.

Two subsectors appear relevant to the service provided through social networks: first, packet-switched data transmission services (W/120 – 2.C.

867 For a more elaborate analysis, see ibid 117–118.

868 See the explanatory note to subclass 84000 of the CPCprov classification.

869 They come to this conclusion based on a process of elimination, deeming none of the other proposed service sectors as being appropriate. For a full analysis, see Weber and Burri (n 5) 118.

b) as the function of social networks is the *sharing* of information. However, packet-switched data transmission services have traditionally been classified as a basic telecommunications service, thereby not altering the underlying information. This goes against the definition provided in the CPC, which categorises electronic message and information services as value-added network services. The second arguably relevant service sector is 'on-line information and data base retrieval services' (W/120 – 2. C.j). This last service sector seems a more appropriate classification as the function of social networks inherently deals with access to online information that consumers share with one another. This example illustrates the fact that a components-based approach can sometimes lead to the same classification as the teleological approach to services classification.

5.4.6.3 Internet Telephony

To assess the classification of Internet telephony (or 'Voice over Internet Protocol'), the similarities and differences with regular telephony services should be considered. Even though the underlying technology of Internet telephony is different from 'offline' telephony, the function is exactly the same: both enable one-to-one direct voice communication.[870]

Weber and Burri break down Internet telephony into three distinct elements: (i) existence of an Internet-enabled network; (ii) software; (iii) the actual performance of the services, transforming voice into digital data.[871] Based on these components, they point out two considerations. First, a classification under telecommunications services, specifically online information and/or data processing, can be argued based on the likeness between both services. Secondly, Internet telephony could fall within the service sector of computer and related services, particularly data processing services, considering the importance of data processing in the supply/functioning of Internet telephony. They consider classifying Internet telephony under data processing services,[872] arguing that this is the most relevant element in the broken-down functioning of Internet telephony.[873] 'Data processing services' as included in the W/120

[870] Whereas traditional telephony transmits electric current, varying in frequency and amplitude, to produce audio output, Internet telephony converts analogue voice signals into digital signals, transmits them in 'data packets' and converts them back to analogue voice signals upon delivery.

[871] Weber and Burri (n 5) 119.

[872] Either under telecommunications services (W/120 – 2.C.n) or computer and related services (W/120 – 1.B.c).

[873] Weber and Burri (n 5) 120–121.

classification are primarily focussed on '*converting disorganised raw data into useful information arranged and presented in a systematic format*'.[874] They submit that, whereas analogue telephony and Internet telephony can be considered 'like services' in the context of the GATS (these services are arguably in a direct competitive relationship), a different classification might be warranted because of their different functioning.

Based on the teleological approach, I argue that the above reasoning cannot be applied to the classification of Internet telephony. Even though the analogue voice signals need to be converted into digital data packets, the primary service that suppliers of Internet telephony supply to consumers is not this data processing, but rather the transmission of audio and the enabling of voice communication. Based on the function of Internet telephony, the more appropriate classification would be 'voice telephone services' (2.C.a – CPC 7523).[875] The corresponding CPC code refers *inter alia* to 'data network services', which is understood as '*network services necessary to transmit data between equipment using the same or different protocols*', which is what Internet telephony boils down to.

5.4.6.4 Video-On-Demand Services

It has been submitted that emerging ways of supplying films to consumers, including online viewing, do not clearly fit within the service subsectors of audiovisual services.[876] VOD services are defined as audiovisual content that can be selected and watched on demand, to be contrasted with classic television broadcast, which is provided as simultaneous viewing of programs on the basis of a program schedule.[877] This distinction is expressly set out in the EU's Audiovisual Media Service Directive (AVMS), which distinguishes between television broadcasts or linear services and on-demand or non-linear services based on two criteria: choice and control of the consumer and impact on society (whether the broadcasts are being 'pushed' nation/worldwide or 'pulled' individually).[878]

[874] ibid 118.

[875] As also proposed by Weber and Burri: ibid 121; This classification is also supported by an analysis of the CPC2.1 classification of online telephony (CPC2.1 84290) which corresponds to CPCprov 7523.

[876] Tuthill and Roy (n 106) 172.

[877] Weber and Burri (n 5) 121–122.

[878] See Article 1(e) and (g) of Directive 2010/13/EU of the European Parliament and of the Council of 10 March 2010 on the coordination of certain provisions laid down by law, regulation or administrative action in Member States concerning the provision of

The CPC 2.1 redraft suggests a classification within the telecommunications service sector. A new subclass 'online content' (CPC2.1 843) is created as part of the telecommunications services sector.[879] Though, interestingly, whereas streamed video content falls within the ambit of 'online content', video and audio streaming services are classified under the subclass 83159 'Other hosting and IT infrastructure provisioning services' under general IT services. The CPC2.1 thereby clearly distinguishes between content and transmission.

Continuing the distinction between 'online content' and 'streaming services', tracking through the CPC correspondences, streamed video (online) content links back to CPCprov 844000, 'data base services' (W/120 1.B.d) and streaming services link back to CPCprov subclass 843, 'data processing' (W/120 1.B.c). It is unclear how online video-content services would fall within database services, which are explained as '*All services provided from primarily structured databases through a communication network*'. This service sector represents the *way* in which online content services are supplied, rather than their *function*. This example clearly shows that reference to CPC classifications does not always resolve classification issues. Moreover, the distinction made by CPC2.1 between services on the basis of the means of supply (it categorises 'online content' differently than offline content) prevents a clear classification on the basis of the teleological approach.

Applying the teleological approach, I consider that VOD services should be classified differently. VOD services are services that allow for the (online) streaming of video content. These services should thus be distinguished from the content that is being streamed (online video content).

VOD services, or online streaming services, fall within the subsector 'radio and television transmission services' (W/120 2.D.d), which relates to '*network services necessary for the transmission of television signals, independently of the type of technology (network) employed*'.[880] A functional approach would indeed classify VOD services as those

audiovisual media services (Audiovisual Media Services Directive), OJ L 95, 15 April 2010, 1.

[879] Weber and Burri argue that this subclass includes VOD services (CPC2.1 84331 and 84332). Weber and Burri (n 5) 123.

[880] Depending on the definition of 'television signals' the explicit technological neutrality of this definition might indicate the relevance of this service subsector. It is, however, contested whether 'television signals' also include the conversion into data (allowing transmission over the Internet). I would argue that this is the case.

services that allow for online viewing of video content, regardless of the way in which this service is provided.

The service of providing online video content rather classifies under 'radio and television services' (W/120 – 2.D.c).[881] This subclass covers the *production* of television programmes '*whether live, or on tape or other recording medium for subsequent broadcast*'.[882] The explanatory note explicitly excludes '*Transmission services for television programmes produced by others*'. This, however, also entails that when the VOD provider also produces its own content (as does e.g. Netflix), that part of its services will be classified as 'Radio and Television Services' (W/120–2. D.c) as the corresponding CPC code also covers 'combined programme making and broadcasting services' (CPC 96133).

For the sake of completeness, I briefly address why the other two audiovisual subsectors dealing with videos and motion pictures are not applicable to VOD services. The subsector of 'Motion picture and video tape production and distribution services' (W/120 – 2.D.a) covers the sale or rental of movies or tapes to other industries. This only covers the right to use the films and not the sale of film on physical carriers.[883] 'Motion picture projection service' (W/120 – 2.D.b.) only covers '*Motion picture projection services in cinemas or in the open air and in private screening rooms or other projection facilities*'. Neither seems to cover the online viewing of films or television.

5.4.6.5 E-payment Services

On the basis of their function, e-payment services, such as those supplied by PayPal, should be classified as 'payment and money transmission services' (W/120 – 7.B.d). The panel in *China – Electronic Payment Services* interpreted 'all payment and money transmission services' comprehensively, covering the entire spectrum of payment and money transmission services. This includes services that manage, facilitate or enable the act of paying or transmitting money.[884] It is the nature of the service, facilitating online payment, that determines its classification. The nature of the service supplier, which for e-payment services are often companies instead of banks, is irrelevant for the sake of the service's classification.[885] Because the function

[881] As proposed in Weber and Burri (n 5) 123.
[882] See the explanatory note to CPC 96132.
[883] Sale of film on physical carriers is classified under distribution services (W/120 – 4).
[884] Panel Report, *China – Electronic Payment Services*, para 7.100.
[885] Juan Marchetti, 'Addressing E-Payment Challenges in Global E-Commerce' (World Economic Forum 2018) White Paper 9 <www.weforum.org/whitepapers/addressing-e-payment-challenges-in-global-e-commerce>.

of e-payment services is the enabling or facilitating of payment and money transmission, a classification under this service subsector is straightforward for online payment processing services as supplied by PayPal.

5.4.6.6 Blogs

The Oxford English Dictionary defines blogs, or weblogs, as '*[a] frequently updated website, typically run by a single person and consisting of personal observations arranged in chronological order, excerpts from other sources, hyperlinks to other sites, etc.; an online journal or diary*'.[886] The EU opined in the context of the CTS that 'blog' services essentially involved two computer-related services: database services (hosting messages, documents and comments) and data processing services (computing the number of visitors of a blog).[887] Here, it is important to distinguish between two distinct services related to the phenomenon of a 'blog': the hosting and maintaining of blogs on a particular website and the writing of blogs. These services are most often supplied by different service suppliers and to different consumers. The classification based on the two components identified by the EU only pertains to this first service but does not apply to the second service. Several companies like WordPress, Tumblr or Blogger supply a blog-hosting service. These blog-hosting services boil down to the hosting of the webpage of the blog on their servers and the maintenance of the platform on which the blogs are created. Considering this function, it can indeed be argued that the service provided by these companies is a database service (W/120 – 1.B.(d)). The corresponding CPC code (CPCprov 844) pertains to all services that are provided from primarily structured databases through a telecommunication network. As the service supplied by these service suppliers amounts to hosting these blogs and their content on dedicated servers, it is clear that they provide a database service. The service provided can also include the development and implementation of software (W/120 – 1.B.(b)), but this is arguably ancillary to the main function of storing and allowing access to the online database of blogs.[888]

[886] Oxford English Dictionary, 'Blog', available at <https://en.oxforddictionaries.com/definition/blog>.

[887] WTO Council for Trade in Services, 'Classification in the Telecom Sector under the WTO-GATS Framework' Communication from the European Communities, TN/S/W/27, S/CSC/W/44, 10 February 2005, para 6.

[888] The software written by the blog hosting platform allows for an easy creation and maintenance of uniform webpages.

Considering the classification of the service provided by the 'blog owner' or the writers (i.e. blogging services), the function the blog performs for its consumers should be considered. Blogs exist in a wide variety of forms, but the most prevalent form is that of blogs existing for entertainment purposes. Generally, blogs contain personal observations or the author's musings about any possible topic, often written in conversational style. Considering this function, blogs are considerably more like services provided by authors than the maintenance of an online database. Based on the functional approach, it therefore seems most appropriate to classify blogging services as author services under 'entertainment services' (W/120 – 10.A, CPC 96192).[889]

Table 5.2 summarises the classification of the digitally enabled services discussed.

Table 5.2 *Classification of digitally enabled services*

Digitally enabled services encompass a wide range of services that can be supplied electronically. Based on their diverse functions, their classification is not limited to certain specific service sectors.	
Examples:	
Search engines	Database services
Social networks	Online information and database retrieval services
Internet telephony	Voice telephone services
Video-on-demand services	Online streaming services: radio and television transmission services
	Online video content services: radio and television services
E-payment services	Payment and money transmission services
Blogs	Blog hosting services: database services
	Blogging services: entertainment services

[889] The CPCprov does not elaborate on this subsector and merely refers to the title 'services provided by authors, composers, sculptors, entertainers and other individual artists'.

5.5 Recommendations for Scheduling Digital Services

Based on the above study, it has become clear that digital services can very often be classified within the existing classification framework. However, that does not mean that the issues surrounding the applicability of the GATS legal framework to digital services have been resolved. Members should be aware of several important elements that have been established throughout this chapter. As the principle of technological neutrality applies to the GATS, Members should depart from the presumption that any commitment that is technologically neutral in its wording will apply to the delivery of that service through electronic means. Where Members want to exclude the digital supply of services that cannot (yet) be supplied digitally, they could schedule 'Unbound*' with the asterisk referring to a footnote that states '*unbound due to lack of technical feasibility*'. This entails that when the mode of supply that is thought to be technically impossible becomes possible in the future, the entry should be read as unbound, which implies that the Member did not liberalise the supply of that service through the specific mode of supply.[890]

However, when interpreting existing commitments, Members should not overestimate the 'technological unfeasibility' of supplying these services through electronic transmissions. If one considers the definition of 'supply of a service', which includes the production, distribution, marketing, sale and delivery of a service, it becomes clear that for *all services* it was already possible in 1994 to deliver certain aspects of these services through electronic transmission.[891] It cannot be contended that the marketing and the sale of any kind of service was not already possible through electronic means. That does not mean that these services were necessarily already marketed through the use of the Internet, but it was definitely possible. Therefore, at least certain aspects of any service could be delivered digitally at the time of scheduling.

The ambiguity in the liberalisation of digital services is not only caused by the lack of clarity on services classification. The lack of comprehensive

[890] As was already established in the 1993 Scheduling Guidelines: GATT Multilateral Trade Negotiations Uruguay Round, Group of Negotiations on Services, 'Scheduling of Initial Commitments in Trade in Services: Explanatory Note', MTN.GNS/W/164, 3 September 1993, para 28.

[891] Article XXVIII(b) GATS. See also WTO Trade in Services, 'Guidelines for the Scheduling of Specific Commitments under the General Agreement on Trade in Services (GATS)' Adopted by the Council for Trade in Services on 23 March 2001, S/L/92, 28 March 2001, para 47.

commitments undertaken by most Members in service sectors that are particularly relevant to digital services (including the audiovisual service sector) provide WTO Members with a wide regulatory margin.[892] In order to ensure market access and national treatment for digital services and to unlock the potential for developing countries as well as MSMEs worldwide, Members should focus on both clarifying services classification and engaging in deeper commitments at the multilateral level. In doing so, Members should keep in mind that, for service sectors that are so far not liberalised, they retain the right to schedule limitations to the effect of excluding digital supply of certain services. For example, Members could schedule limitations to specific service sectors excluding supply through electronic transmission or subjecting it to domestic requirements on security and personal data protection. Examples of such limitations include 'for supply of the service through electronic transmission or the Internet: unbound', 'supply of the service through electronic transmission is subject to relevant licensing procedures', 'supply of the service through electronic transmission is subject to compliance with domestic regulation on privacy and personal data protection'. Because digital trade impacts several modes of supply, these limitations should primarily be inscribed for mode 1, 2 and 3. A horizontal limitation excluding the electronic supply of any type of service would lower the overall level of commitment (as committed service sectors already include digital supply) and should therefore not be permitted. Generally, Members should refrain from including horizontal limitations on 'new services' as such inclusions raise more questions than they solve. Some WTO Members have included such limitations in their regional trade agreements.[893]

5.6 Summary

Part II has clarified that, even though the GATS does not refer to digital services, the WTO's framework agreement on services trade clearly applies to digital services. The principle of technological neutrality causes the GATS to apply to all services, regardless of the underlying technology required for

[892] As pointed out by Trachtman: '*[The GATS] served more as an instrument of standstill than as an instrument of active liberalization, at least in connection with regulatory barriers to trade*'. Joel P Trachtman, 'Addressing Regulatory Divergence through International Standards: Financial Services' in Aaditya Mattoo and Pierre Sauvé (eds), *Domestic Regulation & Service Trade Liberalization* (World Bank Publications 2003) 30.

[893] See *infra* Section 9.2.

their supply. Even though digital trade is surrounded by ambiguous and/or unclarified terms such as digital products, digital content and data, the interpretation of these terms does not affect the applicability of the GATS to services that are being supplied through electronic means. It will be up to the WTO Membership to clarify the delineation between digital products and digital content and what type of commodity data qualifies as.

Because some of the GATS obligations are subject to commitments undertaken by Members, it is indispensable to assess the classification of digital services within the classification system that has been used to schedule GATS commitments. For the sake of classification, I distinguished two groups of digital services: digital infrastructure services and digitally enabled services. Whereas the former group will consist of those services that constitute and support digital infrastructure, generally classified as telecommunication and computer and related services, the latter consists of all services that are delivered through electronic means/digitally. The services in this second group can be classified within any service sector, depending on the function of the service. I therefore take a functional or teleological approach to the classification of (digital) services, as this approach sits most comfortably with the aim of services classifications, the focus on end use and the Appellate Body's findings on integrated services. The functional approach was applied to various examples of (contested) digital services.

Some Members have argued that some digital services are new services. This grants political leeway and allows them to reassess whether they want to liberalise the digital supply of these services. However, it should be considered whether such leeway is desirable and in line with the aim and purpose of the GATS, as it provides Members with a great deal of freedom to circumvent obligations that were negotiated in good faith. This would arguably go against other Members' reasonable expectations with regard to the commitments that were scheduled. That being said, the historical circumstances of the negotiations of an agreement should not be disregarded. However, I argue that many of these services are not new, but rather supplied through a new means of supply. Nothing in the GATS indicates that such services would not be included in the existing classification system.

Even after the issue of classification has been clarified, it remains to be determined what commitments apply to the different WTO Members. Where Members have not committed to certain service sectors, neither the online nor offline service will be subject to the market access or national treatment obligation. However, where commitments have been scheduled, Members must respect these when enacting regulation affecting trade in digital services. Digital services trade is subject to numerous barriers that take various forms. Chapter 3 identified and discussed two specific barriers in depth: restrictions on cross-border data transfer and web filtering. Both of these barriers are prompted by policy concerns related to the rise of electronic commerce and can considerably hinder trade in digital services. Four additional barriers and obstacles to digital services trade are mentioned and briefly explained, illustrating the divergent forms that such barriers can take. The WTO consistency of several examples of these barriers is assessed in Chapter 7 of this book.

PART III

Addressing Barriers at the WTO Level

It has been argued that WTO rules do not deal adequately with the issues surrounding digital services trade.[894] Some argue that because digital trade did not exist in the same sense at the time of the negotiation process as it does now, the current rules are not fit to deal with recent digital trade issues.[895] At the same time, other authors point to the undeniable relevance of specific WTO agreements to the digital economy.[896] WTO Members themselves are clearly divided on the issue of whether the existing framework sufficiently deals with the issues surrounding digital trade.[897]

Even if it was found that the existing framework cannot adequately address the concerns related to digital trade, it should nonetheless be kept in mind that existing WTO disciplines remain crucial as long as new rules are not agreed upon.[898] This part addresses this issue in two steps. Chapter 6 first analyses the relevance of existing WTO instruments to digital services trade. It clarifies how existing obligations can be

[894] See for example Burri, 'Designing Future-Oriented Multilateral Rules for Digital Trade' (n 96) 335.

[895] ICTSD, 'Updating the Multilateral Rule Book on E-Commerce' (ICTSD 2018) Policy brief 2 <https://ictsd.iisd.org/themes/services-and-digital-economy/research/updating-the-multilateral-rule-book-on-e-commerce>.

[896] '*Specific WTO Agreements (including GATS) include rules that matter for the digital economy – either by endorsing or detailing the application of the non-discrimination principles or by specifically addressing certain issues (e.g. interconnection and abuse of dominant position in the telecoms services sector).*' Burri, 'The Governance of Data and Data Flows in Trade Agreements: The Pitfalls of Legal Adaptation' (n 177) 75.

[897] This divide was described by Japan in its 2017 submission to the General Council where it encouraged the Members to evaluate whether clarification or strengthening of the existing WTO rules is necessary. WTO General Council, 'Possible Way Forward on Electronic Commerce' Communication from Japan, JOB/GC/130, 14 July 2017, para 2.2.

[898] Crosby (n 337) 1.

applied to electronically supplied services. Chapter 7 then applies these obligations to four case studies that are illustrative of the barriers and obstacles to digital services trade that were identified in Chapter 3: Russia's amended Law on Personal Data, the EU's GDPR, China's Great Firewall and the US' Restoring Internet Freedom Order.

6

WTO Instruments Applicable to Digital Services Trade

This chapter conducts an analysis of the GATS disciplines and their applicability to digital services trade. The panel in the *US – Gambling* dispute made clear that the WTO rules, and the GATS specifically, are applicable to electronically supplied services.[899] Only a brief summary is provided of the GATS obligations themselves as in-depth analyses of these obligations can be found elsewhere.[900] The focus is rather on their relevance and applicability to digital services trade.

6.1 GATS Obligations Applicable to Digital Services Trade

As already argued in Chapter 4, the GATS is applicable to digital services trade. The broad scope of this Agreement is set out in Article I GATS and confirmed by the principle of technological neutrality. It is therefore impossible to claim the inapplicability of the GATS to this extensive group of services. The applicability of the GATS to all measures affecting the supply of digital services (or services delivered through electronic means) entails that Members will be subject to the GATS' obligations when they are enacting measures to regulate these services, or the Internet more generally.

[899] Thereby confirming the GATS to be technologically neutral; Panel Report, *US – Gambling*, paras 6.287 and 6.290; See also WTO, 'Special Session of the Council for Trade in Services – Report by the Chairman to the Trade Negotiations Committee', TN/S/23, 28 November 2005, 14.

[900] See, for example, Kern Alexander and Mads Andenas (eds), *The World Trade Organization and Trade in Services* (Martinus Nijhoff 2008); Nicolas F Diebold, *Non-Discrimination in International Trade in Services – 'Likeness' in WTO/GATS* (Cambridge University Press 2010); Krajewski, *National Regulation and Trade Liberalization in Services: The Legal Impact of the General Agreement on Trade in Services (GATS) on National Regulatory Autonomy* (n 669); Munin (n 668); Pierre Sauve and Martin Roy (eds), *Research Handbook on Trade in Services* (Edward Elgar Publishing 2016); Rüdiger Wolfrum, Peter-Tobias Stoll and Clemens Feinäugle (eds), *WTO – Trade in Services*, vol 6 (Martinus Nijhoff 2008).

The GATS is a peculiar Agreement, containing both generally applicable obligations and obligations subject to specific commitments. Some obligations apply to all services supplied by service suppliers of any Member, regardless of their undertaken commitments. This is the case for the most-favoured-nation (MFN) treatment obligation as contained in Article II GATS and the transparency obligations in Article III GATS. Members have, however, been left the (one time) option of scheduling MFN-inconsistent measures that they want to maintain in the Annex on Article II exemptions.[901] Other obligations are subject to specific commitments undertaken by Members on the market access or the national treatment obligations. These include the substantive obligations on domestic regulation (Article VI:5 GATS), the prohibition on abuse of monopoly position (Article VIII:2 GATS), the market access obligation (Article XVI GATS) and the national treatment obligation (Article XVII GATS).

Members' specific commitments are inscribed in their Schedule of Specific Commitments. These Schedules contain three separate columns to schedule market access commitments, national treatment commitments and additional commitments.[902] Every Member has inscribed its commitments for each specific service sector and mode of supply. GATS commitments are scheduled on the basis of a 'positive list'. Members only commit to those service sectors that are explicitly listed. This entails that service sectors that do not fall within the existing sectoral classification are *a priori* not subject to the market access and national treatment obligations. Through the listing of commitments, the GATS provides Members with a high degree of autonomy in deciding their level of openness in every specific service sector. It is therefore important to clarify the relevant service sectors when dealing with digital services, as was done in Chapter 5.

This chapter discusses the GATS obligations relevant to digital services trade. When it comes to barriers to digital services trade, several of the GATS' obligations can be applicable. For each obligation its relevance to digital trade will be set out, as well as how it has been perceived in the context of the WPEC.[903]

901 Provided in Article II.2 GATS.

902 Article XVIII clarifies that Members can also schedule specific commitments for measures that are not subject to scheduling under XVI and XVII.

903 The WTO's Secretariat in its 1998 Note on the WPEC discussed various GATS obligations and their relevance to electronically supplied services. WTO Council for Trade in

In the meeting held in the context of the CTS on 14 and 15 December 1998, the EU stated that the GATS applies to all the various elements of electronic commerce transactions.[904] In April 2018, Russia circulated a preliminary list of e-commerce issues, indicating the matters that fall within the WTO legal framework but that need further clarification and those matters that are not covered by the existing WTO rules. Russia qualified *inter alia* the application of different specific commitments under the GATS, as well as separate services related to e-commerce as part of the former, while it identifies e-signatures, e-payments, privacy, personal data protection, secure data flows and consumer protection principles as part of the latter.[905] Even though Members and scholars alike argue that WTO rules do not adequately deal with the issues surrounding digital services trade, I show in the analysis in this part of the book that many barriers to digital services can already be addressed under the GATS.

6.1.1 General Obligations

6.1.1.1 Most-favoured-nation Treatment (Article II GATS)

Article II GATS requires WTO Members not to discriminate between each other in the treatment they accord to services and service suppliers. Under Article II, Members shall immediately and unconditionally accord no less favourable treatment to services and service suppliers of any Member than they accord to like services and service suppliers of other Members. This obligation applies to all measures affecting trade in services.[906] In the context of the WPEC, it was noted that Members share the general view that the MFN obligation is applicable to the supply of services through electronic means.[907]

An analysis of consistency with the MFN obligation consists of three elements: (i) whether the services and service suppliers at issue are like; (ii) whether no less favourable treatment is accorded to other Members'

Services, 'The Work Programme on Electronic Commerce' Note by the Secretariat, S/C/W/68, 16 November 1998.

904 WTO Council for Trade in Services, 'Report of the Meeting Held on 14 and 15 December 1998' Note by the Secretariat, S/C/M/32, 14 January 1999, para 9.

905 WTO General Council, 'Joint Statement on Electronic Commerce Initiative – Communication from the Russian Federation', JOB/GC/181, 16 April 2018, para 1.6.

906 Falling within the scope as set out in Article I GATS.

907 WTO Council for Trade in Services, 'Work Programme on Electronic Commerce – Progress Report to the General Council' Adopted by the Council for Trade in Services on 19 July 1999, S/L/74, 27 July 1999.

services or services suppliers; and (iii) whether this is done immediately and unconditionally.

(i) Likeness The assessment of whether services and service suppliers are 'like' will be based on a study of their nature and characteristics.[908] The Appellate Body clarified that 'like' refers to sharing a number of identical or similar characteristics or qualities.[909] Most importantly, the focus of a likeness analysis in the context of Article II GATS should be on the competitive relationship of services and service suppliers at issue.[910] However, it also cautioned that any likeness assessment must be conducted on a case-by-case basis, thereby rendering blanket statements on the likeness of certain services impossible.[911] In assessing the particular features of the competitive relationship, considerations relating to both the services and the service providers are relevant and should be accorded due weight.[912] The question that should be answered is '*are the services and service suppliers at issue in a competitive relationship?*'[913] The panel in *China – Electronic Payment Services* used the wording 'essentially the same in competitive terms'.[914] The assessment of this competitive relationship requires a market-based analysis.[915]

Moreover, there is a presumption of likeness when the measure distinguishes between products solely on the basis of origin.[916] The scope of this presumption is more limited under the GATS than it is under the GATT and the presumption involves greater complexity because (i) the determination of likeness involves consideration of both service and service supplier; (ii) there is more complexity in determining origin and whether the distinction is exclusively based on origin; and (iii) there is more complexity because of the existence of different modes of supply.[917] Yet, these added complexities do not render the presumption inapplicable to the GATS.[918]

[908] Panel Report, *EC – Bananas III*, para 7.322.

[909] AB Report, *EC – Asbestos*, para 91.

[910] AB Report, *Argentina – Financial Services*, para 6.25. On the controversy on the Appellate Body's analysis in this case, see Panagiotis Delimatsis and Bernard Hoekman, 'National Tax Regulation, Voluntary International Standards, and the GATS: Argentina – Financial Services' (2018) 17 World Trade Review 265.

[911] AB Report, *Argentina – Financial Services*, para 6.26.

[912] ibid para 6.29.

[913] ibid para 6.34.

[914] Panel Report, *China – Electronic Payment Services*, para 7.704.

[915] AB Report, *Argentina – Financial Services*, para 6.26.

[916] Panel Report, *China – Publications and Audiovisual Products*, para 7.975.

[917] AB Report, *Argentina – Financial Services*, paras 6.38–6.40.

[918] ibid.

The main issue in the application of the MFN obligation to digital trade is the question of how different means of delivery impact the likeness of the services: can an online service be considered 'like' an offline service? Members, rightly, seem to be hesitant to make blanket statements on this issue. It has been noted that '*within the limits of individual sectors and modes of supply, it should be possible to agree that likeness would not depend on whether a service was delivered electronically or otherwise*'.[919] The Appellate Body in *Argentina – Financial Services* cautioned that the likeness analysis may require additional considerations of how it is affected by the mode of service supply.[920] This has also been stated by the Secretariat, which pointed out that likeness depends on attributes of 'product or supplier' rather than on the means by which the product is delivered.[921] It can be argued that, due to the principle of technological neutrality in the GATS, there is nothing in the agreement that leads to an inherent unlikeness due to the different means of delivery.[922] Assessment of whether offline and digital services are 'like' should turn on an analysis of their competitive relationship, on a case-by-case basis.[923] It is easily conceivable how online and offline services could have a strong competitive relationship. Examples include the text messaging services provided by traditional telecom companies and the online direct messaging provided through digital applications.[924] It can thus not be maintained that online and offline services will never be considered 'like', which confirms the relevance of Article II GATS to measures affecting trade in digital services. An example by the WTO Secretariat

[919] WTO Council for Trade in Services, 'Work Programme on Electronic Commerce – Progress Report to the General Council' Adopted by the Council for Trade in Services on 19 July 1999, S/L/74, 27 July 1999, para 8.

[920] AB Report, *Argentina – Financial Services,* para 6.33 and Panel Report, *China – Electronic Payment Services*, para 7.706.

[921] The Secretariat notes that inter-modal distinctions by Members in their Schedule are possible. But intra-modal distinctions based on the technique on delivery are in principle open to challenge. WTO Council for Trade in Services, 'The Work Programme on Electronic Commerce' Note by the Secretariat, S/C/W/68, 16 November 1998, para 10 and fn 5. Australia agreed with the Secretariat in WTO Council for Trade in Services, 'Work Programme on Electronic Commerce' Communication from Australia, S/C/W/108, 18 May 1999, para 5.

[922] As was also noted by the CTS' Chairman in WTO Council for Trade in Services, 'Report of the Meeting Held on 18 May 1999' Note by the Secretariat, S/C/M/36, 15 June 1999, para 11.

[923] AB Report, *Argentina – Financial Services*, para 6.24.

[924] However, the Appellate Body has cautioned that the assessment of likeness will always have to be done on a case-by-case basis, taking into account the specific circumstances of the particular case. ibid para 6.26.

illustrates this issue: if a country imposes a higher tax on legal advice delivered electronically (mainly coming from country X) than on the same legal advice delivered by post, this could amount to less favourable treatment accorded to like products coming from different countries.[925]

(ii) No Less Favourable Treatment The Appellate Body has clarified that Article II GATS focuses on whether a measure modifies the conditions of competition.[926] Assessing less favourable treatment therefore requires an investigation into whether the measure discriminates on a *de jure* or a *de facto* basis.[927] This does not entail '*an inquiry into the regulatory objective of, or the regulatory concerns underling, the contested measure*' as such considerations are most appropriately addressed under the GATS' relevant exceptions.[928] The 'aims and effects' of a measure are not deemed relevant for an analysis of less favourable treatment in the context of the GATS.[929]

Regarding digital services, it is therefore important to keep in mind that the regulatory objectives of the measures that form barriers to digital trade should not and cannot be taken into account when assessing their consistency with the MFN obligation. Even though most, if not all, measures regulating digital services aim to protect privacy, public security, consumers, etc., the regulatory reasons for enacting discriminatory measures will only be assessed at the moment of possible justification of the measures and cannot exempt these measures from an MFN violation.

(iii) Accorded Immediately and Unconditionally Members are not prevented from attaching any conditions to the granting of an 'advantage' in the sense of Article II GATS, but they are not allowed to impose conditions that have a detrimental impact on the competitive opportunities for like products from another Member.[930] 'Conditionally' therefore has a broader meaning than simply not requiring compensation, but rather requires advantages to be accorded not limited by or subject to conditions that modify conditions of competition.[931] The interpretation

[925] WTO Council for Trade in Services, 'The Work Programme on Electronic Commerce' Note by the Secretariat, S/C/W/68, 16 November 1998, para 10.

[926] AB Report, *Argentina – Financial Services*, para 6.106.

[927] AB Report, *EC – Bananas III*, para 231.

[928] AB Report, *Argentina – Financial Services*, paras 6.106 and 6.115.

[929] AB Report, *EC – Bananas III*, para 241.

[930] AB Report, *EC – Seal Products*, para 5.88. Even though the above findings were made in relation to Article I GATT, they are equally applicable to the MFN obligation on trade in services.

[931] Panel Report, *EC – Tariff Preferences*, para 7.59.

of 'immediately' is more straightforward, having been interpreted as 'without delay', 'at once' and 'instantly'.[932]

Members are, however, allowed to maintain discriminatory measures if such measures are listed in, and meet the conditions of, the Annex on Article II exemptions.[933]

6.1.1.2 Transparency (Article III GATS)

The transparency obligation included in the GATS is a 'general obligation' that applies across the board, to all measures affecting trade in services. Article III GATS entails three separate obligations, requiring Members to (i) publish all relevant measures of general application relevant to trade in services; (ii) notify new or changed laws, regulations or administrative guidelines that significantly affect trade in services; and (iii) establish national enquiry points to provide specific information to other Members. It was generally understood by the Members that the obligations of Article III apply to all laws and regulations affecting the supply of a service through electronic means.[934] The WTO Secretariat noted in 1998 that '*the field of electronic commerce is in general lightly regulated at present, but any existing regulations, or any which might be adopted in future would need to be notified under Article III*'.[935] Members have also recognised that measures affecting electronic commerce (or rather 'affecting digital services') should be notified pursuant to Article III GATS.[936]

6.1.1.3 Monopolies and Exclusive Service Suppliers (Article VIII GATS) and Business Practices (Article XI GATS)

The GATS contains two relevant provisions dealing with anti-competitive practices, Article VIII ('Monopolies and Exclusive Service Suppliers') and Article XI ('Business Practices') GATS. Interestingly, the 1999 Progress Report noted on the one hand that the expansion of electronic commerce could help reduce restrictive business practices,[937]

[932] AB Report, *US – Tuna II (Mexico)*, para 7.412.

[933] Article II:2 GATS.

[934] WTO Work Programme on Electronic Commerce, 'Progress Report to the General Council Adopted by the Council for Trade in Services on 19 July 1999', S/L/74, 27 July 1999, para 9.

[935] WTO Council for Trade in Services, 'The Work Programme on Electronic Commerce' Note by the Secretariat, S/C/W/68, 16 November 1998, para 11.

[936] For example, Australia in WTO Council for Trade in Services, 'Work Programme on Electronic Commerce' Communication from Australia, S/C/W/108, 18 May 1999, para 5.

[937] Through the facilitation of market entry for smaller service suppliers.

and on the other hand that monopolies and restrictive business practices might pose obstacles to electronic commerce.[938]

The scope of Article VIII GATS is narrower than the equivalent provision in the GATT, because it only applies to monopoly suppliers and exclusive service suppliers.[939] Article XXVIII(h) elaborates on the concept of 'monopoly supplier' stating that the service supplier needs to be '*authorized or established formally or in effect by that Member as the sole supplier of that service*', thereby requiring some direct government involvement. The panel in *China – Electronic Payment Services* explained the concept of 'exclusive services supplier' as '*one of a small number of suppliers in a situation where a Member authorizes or establishes a small number of service suppliers, either formally or in effect, and that Member substantially prevents competition among those suppliers*'.[940] The Article only provides that these service suppliers cannot act in a manner inconsistent with a Member's obligation under Article II (the MFN obligation) and its specific commitments. Because the national treatment obligation under the GATS is limited to those sectors where a Member has undertaken commitments,[941] monopoly suppliers will often be able to disregard this obligation in sensitive sectors.[942] The GATS does not prohibit state monopolies as such, but only prohibits the abuse of a monopoly position. It is, however, hard to assess the efficiency of this Article as it has not yet been brought before the WTO dispute settlement mechanism (DSM).

Article IX GATS sets out that Members '*recognize that certain business practices of services suppliers, other than those falling under Article VIII, may restrain competition and thereby restrict trade in services*'.[943] The Article continues by imposing an obligation upon Members to cooperate in eliminating such anti-competitive practices, '*upon the request of another Member*'.[944] The wide scope of this provision could

938 WTO Council for Trade in Services, 'Work Programme on Electronic Commerce – Progress Report to the General Council', S/L/74, 27 July 1999, paras 12, 13.

939 Unlike Article XVII GATT, this Article does not apply to 'state trading enterprises'. The first interpretative note to Article XVII defines a state trading enterprise as a '*state enterprise, wherever located, and any enterprise that has been granted, formally or in effect, exclusive or special privileges, including marketing boards and import monopolies*'.

940 Panel Report, *China – Electronic Payment Services*, para 7.587.

941 See Article XVII GATS.

942 Ines Willemyns, 'Disciplines on State-Owned Enterprises in International Economic Law: Are We Moving in the Right Direction?' (2016) 19 Journal of International Economic Law 657, 667.

943 Article IX:1 GATS.

944 Article IX:2 GATS.

allow for taking action against more anti-competitive practices than those covered by the very limited scope of Article VIII, were it not that Article IX has weaker disciplines, only containing an obligation on consultation and transparency. Therefore, Article IX of the GATS does not adequately remedy the limited scope of Article VIII.

In its 1998 note, the WTO Secretariat cited the dual relevance of Article VIII GATS to electronic commerce.[945] First, Members are required to ensure that monopolies of basic telecommunications services do not discriminate against rival Internet access providers (for which market access has been granted). Second, exclusive suppliers of Internet services cannot frustrate commitments made on other services that are supplied over the Internet. Members have been reported to share the general view that electronic commerce facilitates market entry for small services suppliers, which could help reduce the extent of restrictive business practices.[946] However, monopolies and restrictive business practices have also arisen in the context of electronic commerce itself, which is why it is important that competitive safeguards apply to digital services.[947] The importance of the Reference Paper on Telecommunications was also noted (analysis *infra* Section 6.1.3.3). Australia explicitly voiced the desirability of applying Article VIII GATS to electronic commerce as well.[948]

6.1.2 Obligations Subject to Specific Commitments

The GATS requires each WTO Member to maintain a Schedule of Specific Commitments which contains its commitments on the market access and national treatment obligations.[949] Members are, however, not obliged to schedule commitments.[950] Members undertake service sector-

945 WTO Council for Trade in Services, 'The Work Programme on Electronic Commerce' Note by the Secretariat, S/C/W/68, 16 November 1998, para 19.

946 WTO Council for Trade in Services, 'Work Programme on Electronic Commerce – Progress Report to the General Council' Adopted by the Council for Trade in Services on 19 July 1999, S/L/74, 27 July 1999, para 12.

947 ibid para 13.

948 WTO Council for Trade in Services, 'Work Programme on Electronic Commerce' Communication from Australia, S/C/W/108, 18 May 1999, para 7.

949 Additional commitments can also be scheduled pursuant to Article XVIII GATS. These include undertakings (not limitations) with respect to qualifications, technical standards, licensing requirements or procedures and other domestic regulations. GATT Multilateral Trade Negotiations Uruguay Round, Group of Negotiations on Services, 'Scheduling of Initial Commitments in Trade in Services: Explanatory Note', MTN.GNS/W/164, 3 September 1993, para 12.

950 Panel Report, *US – Gambling*, para 6.316.

specific commitments and can differentiate based on the mode through which the service is being supplied. Schedules contain both a horizontal section and sectoral sections.[951] The commitments undertaken in the sectoral sections only apply to those specific service sectors but entail commitment of the *whole* sector, including subsectors.[952] Additionally, where commitments have been made for one or more modes of supply, all means of supply within that specific mode are committed, unless specified.[953] Commitments undertaken or limitations scheduled in the horizontal sections of Member's Schedules apply to all service sectors, but often limit themselves to a specific mode of supply.

Article XX:2 GATS tries to simplify scheduling and avoid contradictory inscriptions in the market access and national treatment columns for the same service sector. This paragraph clarifies that, for a measure inconsistent with both the market access and national treatment obligation, Members are only required to make a single inscription of the measure under the market access column, which then provides an implicit limitation under national treatment as well.[954] Not only does the scope of Articles XVI and XVII overlap (see *infra* Section 6.1.2.4), this paragraph recognises a possible simultaneous violation. It thereby also indicates that measures falling within any of the subparagraphs of Article XVI:2 can have discriminatory aspects.[955] In *China – Electronic Payment Services*, China had scheduled 'Unbound' in the market access column, which entitled it to maintain any measure falling within the ambit of Article XVI:2, regardless of whether it is also discriminatory in the sense of Article XVII.[956] In other words, if a Member schedules national

[951] The horizontal section, as a separate section at the beginning of the schedule, allows Members to inscribe market access and national treatment limitations that apply to all scheduled sectors. Panel Report, *China – Publications and Audiovisual Products*, para 7.920.

[952] It was also confirmed that the description of service sectors does not need to enumerate every activity that is included within the scope of that service. AB Report, *US – Gambling*, para 180; Panel Report, *China – Publications and Audiovisual Products*, paras 7.968 and 7.1014; Panel Report, *China – Electronic Payment Services*, para 7.719.

[953] For example, mode 1 under the GATS encompasses all possible means of supplying services from the territory of one Member into the territory of another Member. Panel Report, *US – Gambling*, para 6.285.

[954] The text of Article XX:2 GATS reads: '*Measures inconsistent with both Articles XVI and XVII shall be inscribed in the column relating to Article XVI. In this case the inscription will be considered to provide a condition or qualification to Article XVII as well.*' Moreover, the Scheduling Guidelines confirm such a reading of Article XX. Panel Report, *China – Electronic Payment Services*, paras 7.654 and 7.658.

[955] Panel Report, *China – Electronic Payment Services*, para 7.654.

[956] ibid.

treatment commitments but refrains from scheduling market access commitments, it will only be prevented from imposing discriminatory measures that are not quantitative in nature.[957]

Several Members, including the EU and Australia, have recognised that the GATS' obligations subject to specific commitments also apply to digital services where relevant commitments have been made.[958] Part II of this book has shown that many digital services can be classified within the existing classification system. Therefore, where Members have undertaken commitments in relevant service sectors, measures that inhibit trade in digital services could possibly violate their market access or national treatment obligation. In the 1993 Scheduling Guidelines, the possibility of modes of supply becoming applicable or feasible in the future was already foreseen.[959]

One of the main challenges for the liberalisation of digital services trade is, however, the lack of specific commitments that have been undertaken in a wide variety of relevant service sectors.[960] Whereas the negotiations on Basic Telecommunications services have led to high levels of commitments on basic telecommunications services, this is not the case for value-added telecommunications services. Even though these value-added telecoms services are increasingly being traded across borders due to digitalisation, commitments are so far limited.[961] Even more limited are the commitments undertaken in the audiovisual service sector.[962] In contrast, commitments in computer and related services (another service sector crucial to the digital trade age) are relatively high. In 2009, the Secretariat reported that 83 GATS Schedules include

957 ibid para 7.663.

958 See for the EU: WTO Council for Trade in Services, 'Work Programme on Electronic Commerce, Scope and Classification Issues' Communication from the European Communities and its Member States, S/C/W/87, 9 December 1998, para 5; and Australia: WTO Council for Trade in Services, 'Work Programme on Electronic Commerce' Communication from Australia, S/C/W/108, 18 May 1999, paras 16 and 18.

959 It was clarified that a scheduled 'unbound*', which means 'unbound due to lack of technical feasibility', should be read as simply 'unbound' as soon as that mode of supply becomes applicable. GATT Multilateral Trade Negotiations Uruguay Round, Group of Negotiations on Services, 'Scheduling of Initial Commitments in Trade in Services: Explanatory Note', MTN.GNS/W/164, 3 September 1993, para 28.

960 Burri, 'Designing Future-Oriented Multilateral Rules for Digital Trade' (n 96).

961 Tuthill (n 125) 378.

962 At the same time, this service sector also has the most MFN exemptions listed, which are often justified on the basis of 'cultural policy purposes'. WTO Council for Trade in Services, 'Audiovisual Services' Background Note by the Secretariat, S/C/W/310, 12 January 2010, paras 63 and 69.

commitments in this service sector, with high incidence of full commitments.[963]

6.1.2.1 Market Access (Article XVI GATS)

The general market access obligation can be found in Article XVI GATS, which prohibits the adoption of a limitative[964] list of six quantitative (-like) limitations. The obligation only applies to Members that have undertaken market access commitments with regard to the relevant service sector. Article XVI GATS sets out a minimum standard of non-discriminatory treatment, allowing Members to maintain a market access regime that is less restrictive than what is set out in their Schedule.[965] The quantitative restrictions listed in XVI:2 refer to maximum limitations.[966] As explained *supra* (Section 6.1.2), liberalisation of a certain service sector or mode of supply implies liberalisation of all subsectors or means of delivery, unless otherwise specified. Therefore, where a Member has scheduled an unlimited market access commitment, every means of delivery, including remote supply, must be allowed.[967]

The first paragraph of Article XVI GATS obliges members to accord services and service suppliers of other Members '*no less favourable treatment than that provided for under the terms, limitations and conditions agreed and specified in its Schedule*'.[968] To find a violation of the market access obligation, a twofold test must be met. It must be shown that (i) the Member has undertaken a relevant commitment and (ii) the measures at issue constitute an impermissible limitation in the sense of Article XVI:2.[969] The purpose of the second paragraph of Article XVI is to define the measures Members cannot adopt or maintain for those

963 WTO Council for Trade in Services, 'Computer and Related Services' Background Note by the Secretariat, S/C/W/300, 22 June 2009, paras 20–21.

964 Panel Report, *US – Gambling*, paras 6.292–6.298.

965 Panel Report, *China – Publications and Audiovisual Products*, para 7.1353.

966 Minimum requirements do not fall within the scope of Article XVI. Where such requirements are discriminatory, they fall within the scope of Article XVII, where they are not, they are subject to Article VI:5 GATS. GATT Multilateral Trade Negotiations Uruguay Round, Group of Negotiations on Services, 'Scheduling of Initial Commitments in Trade in Services: Explanatory Note', MTN.GNS/W/164, 3 September 1993, para 5.

967 Panel Report, *US – Gambling*, 6.287. This finding was not appealed by the United States. The Appellate Body stated that it had not been asked to revisit these findings and therefore upheld them. AB Report, *US – Gambling*, para 239.

968 AB Report, *US – Gambling*, para 214; Panel Report, *US – Gambling*, para 6.265; Panel Report, *China – Publications and Audiovisual Products*, para 7.1353.

969 AB Report, *US – Gambling*, para 143.

service sectors where commitments have been made.[970] Whereas the first four subparagraphs concern quantitative limitations on market access, the fifth and sixth subparagraphs, respectively, cover measures that require specific types of legal entities and limitations on participation of foreign capital.[971] Only the fifth and sixth subparagraphs expressly include discriminatory limitations. Whether the first four subparagraphs also extend to discriminatory measures is not indicated by their text. The panel in *China – Electronic Payment Services*, however, concluded that measures falling within any of the subparagraphs can have discriminatory aspects, which could entail an overlapping scope of Articles XVI:2 and XVII.[972]

The *US – Gambling* dispute made clear that Article XVI GATS is relevant to measures that inhibit digital services trade. The question before the panel and the Appellate Body was whether the US' prohibition on the remote supply of gambling services violated its market access commitments. The United States had scheduled a commitment on 'other recreational services (except sporting)' for the first mode of supply, which was found to include gambling services.[973] In assessing whether prohibiting gambling services over telephone lines or the Internet violated the US' mode 1 commitment, the panel decided that the principle of technological neutrality applied to the GATS.[974] The GATS does not technologically limit the means of delivery under mode 1, which also includes delivery

[970] ibid para 233; Panel Report, *China – Publications and Audiovisual Products*, para 7.1353.

[971] AB Report, *US – Gambling*, para 214; Panel Report, *Argentina – Financial Services*, paras 7.416 and 7.417. The panel in *Mexico – Telecoms* simplified the six categories as follows:

> The categories differ depending on whether they place limitations on:
>
> (a) *the number of service suppliers;*
> (b) *the value of services transactions or assets;*
> (c) *the number of service operations or quantity of service output;*
> (d) *the number of natural persons that may be employed;*
> (e) *the forms of legal entity; or*
> (f) *the participation of foreign capital.*

Panel Report, *Mexico – Telecoms*, para 7.77.

[972] Panel Report, *China – Electronic Payment Services*, paras 7.653–7.656. This is elaborated upon *infra* Section 6.1.2.4.

[973] See AB Report, *US – Gambling*, paras 158–213.

[974] The panel cited the 1999 WPEC Progress Report in deciding that this principle has been recognised by the Membership and that it therefore applies to the GATS. The finding on the applicability of the principle of technological neutrality was not appealed by either party. Panel Report, *US – Gambling*, para 2.685.

through the Internet.[975] A prohibition on the remote supply of services, even if their 'non-remote' delivery is allowed, will amount to a violation of Article XVI GATS where commitments have been undertaken. The panel concluded that a full market access commitment on the first mode of supply entailed other Members' right to supply the service into the territory of the committed Member through the Internet.[976]

The quantitative limitations prohibited by Article XVI:2(a) and (c) have been interpreted by panels and the Appellate Body as being quantitative *in nature*. This entails that the thrust of these subparagraphs is not on the form of the limitations but rather on their nature. A numerical quota, as prohibited by subparagraph (a), can be interpreted as a '*quantitative limit on the number of service suppliers*'.[977] Both the panel and the Appellate Body in *US – Gambling* found zero to be numerical and concluded that a total prohibition on a means of supply amounts to a zero quota, which is a limitation that is quantitative in nature.[978] Not only does the prohibition on the supply of gambling services through remote means amount to a limitation on the number of service suppliers in the form of a numerical quota in the sense of Article XVI:2(a), it also amounts to a limitation on the number of service operation or the total quantity of service output in the form of quotas in the sense of Article XVI:2(c) GATS.[979] It is clear that the *a priori* exclusion of services supplied through a specific means of supply will violate the market access obligation if commitments have been undertaken.[980]

A relevant example of the limitations that can be scheduled in Members' Services Schedules can be found in Mexico's Schedule. The

975 Panel Report, *US – Gambling*, paras 6.281 and 6.285.

976 ibid para 6.285.

977 AB Report, *US – Gambling*, para 227.

978 ibid para 238. The Appellate Body additionally pointed to the 1993 Scheduling Guidelines to confirm that zero quota are covered by Article XVI:2 GATS. GATT Multilateral Trade Negotiations Uruguay Round, Group of Negotiations on Services, 'Scheduling of Initial Commitments in Trade in Services: Explanatory Note', MTN.GNS/W/164, 3 September 1993, para 6.

979 Panel Report, *US – Gambling*, paras 6.330 and 6.355.

980 Non-quantitative limitations on digital supply would, however, not be actionable under Article XVI itself. Yet the WTO Secretariat noted that such a measure could be the subject of a 'non-violation' complaint under Article XXIII:3 GATS as it could be argued that such a measure nullifies or impairs the benefits which other Members could reasonably have expected to accrue from market access commitments. WTO Council for Trade in Services, 'The Work Programme on Electronic Commerce' Note by the Secretariat, S/C/W/68, 16 November 1998, para 32. That being said, such a restriction on technical means could also amount to a violation of Article VI or XVII GATS.

panel in *Mexico – Telecoms* studied the routing restriction that Mexico had scheduled in its market access column and assessed whether it fell within one the six categories of measures that restrict market access according to Article XVI GATS. Members can only schedule limitations falling within one of these categories in their Services Schedule.[981] For telecommunications services, Mexico has taken a sectoral approach, scheduling the same limitation for various subsectors. It did, however, limit its commitments to telecommunications services that are supplied by a facilities-based public telecommunications network (thereby excluding these services supplied by resale or leased capacity).[982] Mexico's routing restriction required international traffic to be routed through the facilities of an enterprise that has a concession.[983] After assessing three main elements ('international traffic', 'routed through facilities' and 'enterprise that has a concession') of the limitation, the panel concluded that this limitation prohibits market access for the supply of telecommunications services on a non-facilities basis in Mexico, but does allow full access for those services on a facilities basis, subject to the routing restriction. Whereas the elements of 'international traffic'[984] and 'enterprise with a concession'[985] do not fall within one of the measures listed in Article XVI:2 GATS, the element of 'routed through facilities' does constitute a zero quota in the sense of Article XVI:2(a), (b) and (c) for the terminating segment of cross-border supply not supplied on a facilities basis.[986] To conclude, based on this scheduled market access

[981] Article XVI:2 GATS exhaustively enumerates the limitations to market access that Members are prohibited from maintaining or enacting, unless scheduled. Members should therefore only schedule limitations that fall within the scope of Article XVI GATS, as other market access limitations are not prohibited by Article XVI.

[982] Panel Report, *Mexico – Telecoms*, para 7.71.

[983] WTO Trade in Services, 'Mexico – Schedule of Specific Commitments' Supplement 2, GATS/SC/56/Suppl.2, 11 April 1997, 2.

[984] Where telecoms services are supplied cross-border, they will always constitute international traffic. This element therefore did not impose a market access limitation. Panel Report, *Mexico – Telecoms*, para 7.79.

[985] In order to qualify for a concession, the enterprise must be established in conformity with Mexican Law and not have more than 49 per cent foreign ownership. These nationality and commercial presence requirements applicable to the concessionaire (the entity routing international calls transferred by foreign service suppliers at the border) did *not* amount to nationality or commercial presence requirements for the cross-border supplier. Panel Report, *Mexico – Telecoms*, para 7.90.

[986] 'Routing through facilities' is to be understood as requiring that calls be terminated through use of facilities of a (in this case Mexican) concessionaire and not through leased capacity. Panel Report, *Mexico – Telecoms*, paras 7.84 and 7.85. The OECD defines 'facilities-based service supplier' as *'a telecommunications service provider owning, as*

limitation, Mexico was allowed to require foreign telecoms service suppliers to route international telecoms traffic through local routers. Members that made a full commitment for the supply of telecommunications services through mode 1 but that require international traffic to be routed through local facilities would violate their market access obligation. With some imagination, it is perceivable that such a requirement is similar to data localisation requirements as discussed *supra* (Section 3.2.1).

Of specific relevance to regulations dealing with consumer and privacy protection is the finding by the panel in *US – Gambling* that various US measures did not violate Article XVI GATS because they targeted consumers. This decision was motivated by the panel on the basis that regulations applying to consumers and not to 'services suppliers' (Article XVI:2(a)) or to 'service operations' and 'service output' (Article XVI:2(c)) do not fall within the scope of these respective Articles.[987] If such a statement survives scrutiny by a panel or the Appellate Body in future proceedings,[988] this would mean that regulations targeting consumers do not fall within the scope of the market access obligation of Article XVI GATS, generally or at least regarding the specific paragraphs (a) and (c). This gives considerable leeway to governments that want to protect consumer interest through regulation of *consumer* behaviour. Only limitations on service suppliers, service operations or services outputs could potentially constitute a violation of the market access obligation.[989] This is especially important for digital trade, considering that a practical means to implement controls on cross-border trade is precisely through measures directed at the consumer.[990]

opposed to leasing, networks used to provide telecommunications services'. OECD Glossary of Statistical Terms, 'Facilities-based service supplier (or operator)', available at <https://stats.oecd.org/glossary/detail.asp?ID=4962>.

[987] Panel Report, *US – Gambling*, paras 6.382–6.383, 6.397–6.398, 6.401–6.402, 6.405–6.406.

[988] The Appellate Body in *US – Gambling* declined to rule on this issue as it deemed that the Panel was not entitled to make findings on the eight state laws under scrutiny, including the four state laws targeting consumers, as no *prima facie* case of inconsistency had been made by the complainants. See AB Report, *US – Gambling*, para 254.

[989] It has been nuanced that it should not *a priori* matter whether a measure with a quantitative thrust is directed at consumers or service suppliers, but that it could influence the analysis of that measure's quantitative thrust. Bregt Natens, *Regulatory Autonomy and International Trade in Services: The EU under GATS and RTAs* (Edward Elgar Publishing 2016) 191.

[990] WTO Council for Trade in Services, 'Cross-Border Supply (Modes 1& 2)' Background Note by the Secretariat, S/C/W/304, 18 September 2009, para 40.

6.1.2.2 National Treatment (Article XVII GATS)

The national treatment obligation can be found in Article XVII GATS and prohibits Members from according (*de jure* or *de facto*)[991] less favourable treatment to services and service suppliers of other Members than it accords to its own like services and service suppliers.[992] The relevance of this obligation to digital services is confirmed by Members' recognition that commitments on national treatment also cover services that are supplied through electronic means.[993]

To substantiate a claim of violation of Article XVII GATS, a complainant must show that (i) a national treatment obligation was undertaken in the relevant sector and mode of supply; (ii) the measure at issue affects the supply of services; and (iii) the measure accords to services or service suppliers of another Member treatment less favourable than that accorded to the Member's own like services and service suppliers.[994] Hence, once a commitment on the national treatment obligation is ascertained, three elements have to be established: (i) whether the measure affects the supply of services; (ii) whether the service or service suppliers at issue are like; and (iii) whether those of the complaining party are being treated less favourably than those of domestic origin.[995] In the assessment of whether a Member's national treatment commitment has been violated, the 'aims and effects' of a measure are not considered in any way relevant.[996] Whether a legitimate policy is being pursued and whether the measure is inherently discriminatory in design or effect is therefore not something that is taken into account in the assessment of Article XVII GATS.[997]

991 Panel Report, *EC – Bananas III*, para 6.106. Formally identical treatment is not required; GATT Multilateral Trade Negotiations Uruguay Round, Group of Negotiations on Services, 'Scheduling of Initial Commitments in Trade in Services: Explanatory Note', MTN.GNS/W/164, 3 September 1993, para 7.

992 Unlike the GATT, Article XVII GATS does not distinguish between taxes and regulatory measures. Krajewski, *National Regulation and Trade Liberalization in Services: The Legal Impact of the General Agreement on Trade in Services (GATS) on National Regulatory Autonomy* (n 669) 96.

993 WTO Council for Trade in Services, 'Work Programme on Electronic Commerce – Progress report to the General Council' Adopted by the Council for Trade in Services on 19 July 1999, S/L/74, 27 July 1999, para 17.

994 Panel Report, *China – Publications and Audiovisual Products*, para 7.944; Panel Report, *China – Electronic Payment Services*, para 7.641; Panel Report, *Argentina – Financial Services*, para 7.448.

995 Panel Report, *EC – Bananas III*, para 6.94.

996 AB Report, *EC – Bananas III*, para 241.

997 '*[The legal standard of "treatment no less favourable"] does not contemplate a separate step of analysis regarding whether the "regulatory aspects" relating to service suppliers*

(i) Likeness The likeness considerations under the national treatment obligations are somewhat different than those under the MFN obligation.[998] Due to the nature of the national treatment obligation, the groups of services and service suppliers compared to assess a violation will automatically pitch foreign service suppliers against domestic service suppliers. Because the four modes of supply as defined in the GATS only apply to trade with a cross-border element, domestic service suppliers strictly speaking do not supply their services under any of the modes of the GATS.[999] In relation to e-commerce, the question can therefore be asked whether there is likeness between services supplied through foreign electronic supply (mode 1 or 2) and services supplied through domestic non-electronic supply. Diebold highlights that this issue was raised in the context of the WPEC but so far remains unresolved. However, he opines that the principle of technological neutrality, as explained *supra* (Section 4.2.3), also applies to the issue of likeness.[1000]

Likeness is not an inherent issue for digital services. Whether online and offline services are like should be assessed on a case-by-case basis, taking into account the competitive relationship between the services and service suppliers at issue. The different method of supply is only relevant if consumers perceive them as affecting substitutability.[1001] This question does not arise if the companies in competition are a foreign and a domestic online service supplier. In that case, the method of supply is the same and should not per definition impact the likeness assessment.

could "convert []" the measure's detrimental impact on the conditions of competition into "treatment no less favourable"'. Where evidence relating to the regulatory aspects has a bearing on the conditions of competition, it can be taken into account, but only as an integral part of the analysis of whether the measure at issue modifies the conditions of competition to the detriment of like services or service suppliers. Assessing whether the detrimental impact of the measures stems exclusively from a legitimate regulatory distinction is not part of the correct legal standard of 'treatment no less favourable'. AB Report, *Argentina – Financial Services*, paras 6.111, 6.127, 6.136 and 6.137.

998 Of course, the concept of 'likeness' in Articles II and XVII GATS is the same and concerns itself with the competitive relationship of services and service suppliers. Any statements as to the likeness criterion in Article II GATS equally apply to likeness in Article XVII GATS. See AB Report, *Argentina – Financial Services*, para. 6.22.

999 Diebold (n 900) 222–223.

1000 Based on WTO Council for Trade in Services, 'Work Programme on Electronic Commerce – Interim Report to the General Council', S/C/8, 31 March 1999, 8 and WTO Council for Trade in Services, 'The Work Programme on Electronic Commerce' Note by the Secretariat, S/C/W/68, 16 November 1998, paras 10 and 33. ibid 225–226.

1001 ibid 227.

(ii) No Less Favourable Treatment The object and purpose of paragraph 1 of Article XVII GATS is to prohibit discrimination against foreign services or service suppliers. It thereby wants to secure other Members' competitive opportunities for like services and service suppliers.[1002] Whether less favourable treatment is being accorded to like services and service suppliers will depend on whether the measure modifies the conditions of competition to the detriment of foreign service or service suppliers.[1003] The third paragraph of Article XVII GATS clarifies the concept of 'less favourable' along these lines. However, ensuring equal competitive conditions (which is required by Article XVII GATS) does not entail guaranteeing that one group of services or service suppliers does not have any competitive advantages over another group, nor does it require identical treatment, as clarified by Article XVII:2.[1004] Rather, Members must guarantee equality of opportunities to compete in the marketplace.[1005] The Appellate Body clarified that while Article XVII:3 GATS refers to modifications of competition in favour of domestic services or service suppliers, the legal test requires an examination of whether the measure modifies the conditions of competition to the detriment of services or service suppliers of another Member.[1006] Footnote 10 clarifies that the analysis of less favourable treatment must be based on the impact on conditions of competition that result from the measure.[1007]

Examples of how the 'no less favourable treatment' element of the national treatment obligation in Article XVII GATS is applied can be found in *China – Electronic Payment Services*. In that case, the panel found that the conditions of competition were modified in favour of the Chinese supplier (CUP) by a series of Chinese requirements on suppliers of EPSs: (i) the requirement for bank cards to bear the UnionPay logo considerably raised CUPs profile;[1008] (ii) the interoperability requirements guaranteed that all commercial banks

1002 AB Report, *Argentina – Financial Services*, para 6.22.

1003 See *inter alia* AB Report, *EC – Bananas III*, para 243 and ibid para 6.106.

1004 Panel Report, *China – Publications and Audiovisual Products*, para 7.1130.

1005 Or, as stated by the Panel in *Korea – Various Measures on Beef*, '*[Article XVII:3 of the GATS] is concerned with the effective equality of opportunities in the application of laws, regulations and requirements*'. Panel Report, *Korea – Various Measures on Beef*, para 624. See also AB Report, *Argentina – Financial Services*, para 6.144.

1006 These are flip-sides of the same coin. AB Report, *Argentina – Financial Services*, para 6.103.

1007 AB Report, *Argentina – Financial Services*, para 6.104.

1008 Panel Report, *China – Electronic Payment Services*, para 7.712.

become members of CUP without any time or effort expended by CUP;[1009] (iii) the terminal equipment requirements guaranteed that terminals in China accept bank cards bearing the UnionPay logo, without any time or effort expended by CUP;[1010] and (iv) the interoperability requirements on acquirers guaranteed that they join CUP's network, without any time or effort expended by CUP.[1011] In the panel's assessment, all of these requirements resulted in EPS suppliers from other Members being treated less favourably than the domestic EPS supplier (CUP). This conclusion was founded on the observation that most of the competitive advantages that were accorded to CUP through the measures at issue were only available to EPS suppliers from other Members through expenditure of considerable time and effort. This put EPS suppliers from other Members at a competitive disadvantage.

The WTO Secretariat clarified that it is possible to schedule national treatment limitations that expressly discriminate against electronic supply by foreign service suppliers.[1012] Examples of such limitations include the requirement of local presence to provide cross-border digital services or the requirement to store data locally in order to supply cross-border services electronically. However, no such explicit limitations have been included so far.

In the context of the national treatment obligation, the Secretariat also discussed customs duties, which, as border measures, are relevant to cross-border supply of digital services (regardless of whether mode 1 or mode 2).[1013] For example, taxes on the electronic supply of services surpassing the commitment undertaken for that service would violate that Member's national treatment commitment. It is therefore important to assess whether Members have scheduled a national treatment commitment, ruling out recourse to discriminatory taxes.[1014]

6.1.2.3 Domestic Regulation (Articles VI and VII GATS)

Trade in services is generally less hampered by tariffs (contrary to trade in goods), and more by non-tariff barriers (NTBs), often in the form of

[1009] ibid para 7.714.
[1010] ibid para 7.725.
[1011] ibid para 7.737.
[1012] WTO Council for Trade in Services, 'The Work Programme on Electronic Commerce' Note by the Secretariat, S/C/W/68, 16 November 1998, para 33.
[1013] ibid para 35.
[1014] Whereas the GATT national treatment obligation does not apply to border measures (e.g. tariffs and quotas), the GATS national treatment obligation applies to *all* measures affecting the supply of services, including taxes.

domestic regulation.[1015] Several GATS provisions deal to a larger or smaller extent with domestic regulation. Domestic regulation that discriminates between WTO Members falls within the scope of the most-favoured-nation treatment obligation (Article II GATS) or the national treatment obligation (Article XVII GATS). Where domestic regulation amounts to a market access barrier within the ambit of Article XVI GATS, it will equally be prohibited if commitments have been undertaken. Domestic regulation that does not discriminate or present a market access barrier in the sense of Article XVI GATS should still be scrutinised under Article VI GATS.

Not only does Article VI GATS not enact enforceable disciplines on unnecessary regulatory trade barriers, it also currently limits its scope to sectors where specific commitments have been undertaken. The Article does, however, leave room for the 'development of any necessary disciplines' aiming to ensure that domestic regulation is based on objective and transparent criteria and are not more burdensome than necessary.[1016] Such disciplines have so far not been developed at the multilateral level, which in part explains why countries have turned to bilateral and plurilateral initiatives to deal with these trade barriers.

Non-quantitative measures affecting trade in services that are not discriminatory do not violate the market access or national treatment obligation in the GATS. However, such measures can still seriously impede trade in services. Differences in (non-discriminatory) regulation can be a considerable barrier to trade. A foreign service supplier must redesign its product or restructure its business model to meet the requirements of the host country.[1017] Article VI GATS' main obligation requires Members to administer measures of general application in a reasonable, objective and impartial manner.[1018] This requirement is limited in three ways: it only applies (i) where countries have undertaken sector-specific commitments, (ii) to measures generally applied affecting trade in services and (iii) as to the way in which the measures are administered.

[1015] Henk Kox and Arjan Lejour, 'Regulatory Heterogeneity as Obstacle for International Services Trade' (CPB Netherlands Bureau for Economic Policy Analysis 2005) 4.

[1016] Article VI:4 GATS.

[1017] Hildegunn Kyvik Nordas, 'Domestic Regulation: What Are the Costs and Benefits for International Trade in Services?' in Aik Hoe Lim and Bart De Meester (eds), *WTO Domestic Regulation and Services Trade: Putting Principles into Practice* (Cambridge University Press 2014) 51.

[1018] Article VI:1 GATS.

(i) **Article VI GATS: Procedural Requirements** The procedural requirements of Article VI GATS can be found in paragraphs 1–3 and 6. These paragraphs only influence the procedural side of the law and do not impose any substantive obligations.[1019] Article VI:1 GATS requires Members to apply measures of general application in a reasonable, objective and impartial manner. This paragraph articulates a fundamental standard of rule of law and of good governance.[1020] The scope of this obligation is limited to service sectors where specific commitments have been undertaken. Paragraph 2 of Article VI GATS contains the obligation for WTO Members to ensure review of administrative decisions affecting trade in services. This shall be done through the maintenance or institution of judicial arbitral or administrative tribunals or procedures unless this would be inconsistent with a WTO Member's constitutional structure.[1021] This obligation applies to all measures affecting trade in services. Article VI:3 GATS contains the transparency requirement, demanding Members to inform applicants about the decisions and the status of their application within reasonable time. This paragraph thereby recognises that application procedures can create impediments to services trade, but at the same time limits this obligation to service sectors where specific commitments have been undertaken.[1022] Upon closer analysis, this paragraph contains three obligations: (i) applicants must be informed of the status of their application without undue delay; (ii) service suppliers must be informed of the decision within reasonable time; which implies that (iii) administrations are required to take decisions on applications within reasonable time. Lastly, paragraph 6 of Article VI GATS requires Members who have undertaken specific commitments in professional services (service sector 1A of the W/120) to provide for adequate procedures to verify the competence of professionals of other Members. The paragraph thereby wishes to ensure that Members cannot devalue their market access commitments by not instituting relevant verification procedures.[1023]

1019 Krajewski, *National Regulation and Trade Liberalization in Services: The Legal Impact of the General Agreement on Trade in Services (GATS) on National Regulatory Autonomy* (n 669) 140–141.

1020 Markus Krajewski, 'Article VI GATS' in Rüdiger Wolfrum, Peter-Tobias Stoll and Clemens Feinäugle (eds), *WTO – Trade in Services*, vol 6 (Martinus Nijhoff 2008) 168.

1021 Subparagraph (b) contains a 'constitutional safeguard clause'.

1022 Krajewski, 'Article VI GATS' (n 1020) 176.

1023 Panagiotis Delimatsis, 'Due Process and "Good" Regulation Embedded in the GATS – Disciplining Regulatory Behaviour in Services through Article VI of the GATS' (2007) 10 Journal of International Economic Law 13, 47.

This also clarifies that Members do have a right to subject market access conditions to a verification of the service suppliers' competences.[1024]

(ii) Article VI GATS: Substantive Obligations Article VI:4 GATS requires the Council for Trade in Services to develop necessary disciplines to ensure that measures relating to qualification requirements and procedures, technical standards and licensing requirements do not constitute unnecessary barriers to trade in services.[1025] As noted by the WTO Secretariat, measures that fall within the scope of this paragraph are intended to serve regulatory or other public policy objectives and are not intended to restrict trade.[1026] These disciplines must ensure that where measures under Article VI:4 GATS do restrict trade, their requirements are based on objective and transparent criteria (e.g. competence and ability to supply the service) and are not more burdensome than necessary to ensure quality of the service. The necessity test included in this paragraph is an important indication of the balance that needs to be struck between preserving Members' regulatory autonomy and discouraging Members from abusing this freedom. The exact scope of future disciplines under Article VI:4 GATS remains a contentious issue: should preference be given to horizontal or sectoral disciplines and should disciplines apply to all sectors or only sectors where specific commitments have been taken? Since the successful conclusion of the Uruguay Negotiation Round in 1995, the WTO has not succeeded in achieving new, considerable liberalisation of trade in services.[1027]

Binding disciplines have not yet been enacted by the CTS, thereby so far failing to fulfil the potential of this paragraph. Article VI:5 GATS

1024 Krajewski, 'Article VI GATS' (n 1020) 177.

1025 The definition of 'qualification requirements', 'qualification procedures', 'licensing requirements', 'licensing procedures' and 'technical standards' can be found in WTO Working Party on Professional Services, 'The Relevance of the Disciplines of the Agreements on Technical Barriers to Trade (TBT) and on Import Licensing Procedures to Article VI:4 of the General Agreement on Trade in Services' Note by the Secretariat, S/WPPS/W/9, 11 September 1996, para 4.

1026 Measures that intend to restrict trade should be dealt with under Article II, XVI or XVII GATS. ibid para 3.

1027 Countries liberalised trade in services by scheduling specific commitments in their Schedule of Specific Commitments, thereby liberalising per service sector. The extent of services liberalization differs considerably between countries and most adopted a cautious approach to services liberalisation. Article XIX of the GATS mandated successive rounds of trade in services liberalisation, but these were never realised. Rafael Leal-Arcas, 'The GATS in the Doha Round: A European Perspective' in Kern Alexander and Mads Andenas (eds), *The World Trade Organization and Trade in Services* (Martinus Nijhoff 2008) 45–54.

applies pending the entry into force of these disciplines, prohibiting Members from applying licensing and qualification requirements and technical standards that nullify or impair their specific commitments. Like other parts of Article VI, this paragraph is limited to those sectors for which countries have undertaken specific commitments. Moreover, measures which reasonably could have been expected at the time the specific commitments were made are exempted from application of paragraph 5.[1028] Additionally, this paragraph requires taking into account international standards when assessing a Member's conformity with regard to the above obligation.[1029] The scope and impact of Article VI:5 GATS are even further limited by the requirement of nullification or impairment of specific commitments. Based on its wording, it seems like a mere violation of the obligations in Article VI:5 cannot be used as a basis for a claim. The complainant will have to show that a specific commitment is nullified or impaired through a national regulation that does not comply with the requirements of Article VI:4 GATS.[1030]

The Accountancy Disciplines are so far the only set of disciplines that have been developed under Article VI:4.[1031] Several authors have documented the tough negotiations and disagreement between Members on the best approach regarding new disciplines.[1032] In its most significant paragraph, the Accountancy Disciplines mandate a necessity test, linking it to a non-exhaustive list of legitimate objectives. This obligation only applies to measures not subject to scheduling under Article XVI or XVII GATS, thereby explicitly excluding possible overlap between different obligations (see Section 6.1.2.4 *infra*). Other paragraphs contain obligations regarding transparency and specific types of regulation. However, the strength of language used varies widely. It should be taken into

[1028] See Articles VI:5(a) and 5(a)(ii) GATS.

[1029] Article VI:5(b) GATS.

[1030] Krajewski, *National Regulation and Trade Liberalization in Services: The Legal Impact of the General Agreement on Trade in Services (GATS) on National Regulatory Autonomy* (n 669) 153.

[1031] WTO Council for Trade in Services, 'Disciplines on Domestic Regulation in the Accountancy Sector', S/L/64, 17 December 1998.

[1032] Delimatsis, 'Due Process and "Good" Regulation Embedded in the GATS – Disciplining Regulatory Behaviour in Services through Article VI of the GATS' (n 1023) 38–39; Krajewski, *National Regulation and Trade Liberalization in Services: The Legal Impact of the General Agreement on Trade in Services (GATS) on National Regulatory Autonomy* (n 669) 132, 134–138; Jan Wouters and Dominic Coppens, 'GATS and Domestic Regulation: Balancing the Right to Regulate and Trade Liberalization' in Kern Alexander and Mads Andenas (eds), *The World Trade Organization and Trade in Services* (Martinus Nijhoff 2008) 220–225.

account that the Accountancy Disciplines do not have the same legal status as the GATS and are not yet legally binding.[1033] One of the main achievements of these Accountancy Disciplines is that they clearly set out a necessity test based on the regulations '*not [being] more trade-restrictive than necessary*'. This stipulates more clearly what is actually expected from the necessity test, than what can be found in Article VI:4(b) GATS, which requires regulations to '*not [be] more burdensome than necessary*'.[1034] Only when Article VI:4(b) is interpreted in the light of the chapeau of that paragraph, it becomes clear that 'burdensome' refers to unnecessary barriers to trade, that is, trade restrictiveness.[1035] Moreover, the Accountancy Disciplines also include an indicative list of legitimate objectives, whereas Article VI:4 only references '*the quality of the service*'.[1036]

(iii) Article VII GATS: Recognition A second provision in the GATS relevant to domestic regulation is Article VII. This Article does not require but authorises recognition of education or experience obtained, requirements met, or licenses or certifications granted in a particular country.[1037] It also requires that, where Members enact mutual recognition agreements (MRAs), room and possibility must be left for other Members to become party to this arrangement or they should be granted

[1033] The original plan was to formally integrate these disciplines into the GATS by 2005, but this has not been achieved so far. Krajewski, 'Article VI GATS' (n 1020) para 39.

[1034] A distinction should be made between the necessity test as found in exception clauses (e.g. Articles XIV GATS and XX GATT) and in obligation provisions (e.g. Articles VI:5 GATS, 2.2 TBT Agreement and 2.2 SPS Agreement). Whereas the former often contain a closed list of policy objectives, the latter usually refer to an illustrative list. The burden of proof also differs. Whereas the burden of proof is on the respondent to show that a measure is necessary to achieve a specific policy objective (exception), the complainant bears the burden of showing that the measure is not necessary for the obligation. WTO Working Party on Domestic Regulation, '"Necessity Tests" in the WTO' Note by the Secretariat, S/WPDR/W/27/Add.1, 18 January 2011, para. 6. Natens (n 989) 223.

[1035] Krajewski, *National Regulation and Trade Liberalization in Services: The Legal Impact of the General Agreement on Trade in Services (GATS) on National Regulatory Autonomy* (n 669) 142. Not everyone agrees with this interpretation. Looking into the ordinary meaning of 'burdensome', situations can be envisaged where regulation is more burdensome than necessary but not necessarily trade-restrictive. Natens (n 989) 225.

[1036] Compare Article VI:4(b) GATS and para 2 Accountancy Disciplines (including the protection of consumers, the quality of the service, professional competence and the integrity of the profession).

[1037] Joel P Trachtman, 'Mutual Recognition of Services Regulation at the WTO' in Aik Hoe Lim and Bart De Meester (eds), *WTO Domestic Regulation and Services Trade: Putting Principles into Practice* (Cambridge University Press 2014) 110–126.

the possibility to negotiate similar ones with the original parties. Additionally, Members should be accorded adequate opportunity to demonstrate their eligibility for autonomous recognition.[1038] Lastly, the obligation of non-discrimination applies, and it is set out that '*wherever appropriate, recognition should be based on multilaterally agreed criteria*'.[1039] In 1997, the CTS drafted (non-binding) guidelines for MRAs or arrangements in the accountancy sector, thereby providing practical guidance regarding both procedure of negotiation and the substantive elements that should be part of such agreements.[1040] No such guidelines have been drafted for service sectors that are specifically relevant to digital services trade. However, WTO Members themselves have turned to MRAs in the context of cross-border data flows. A prominent example was the (recently invalidated) EU–US Privacy Shield under which US companies guaranteed that they would protect EU citizens' data in accordance with the Privacy Shield Principles.[1041]

It can be concluded that only limited substantive provisions have been included in the GATS to deal with the barriers to trade created by domestic regulation, not only specifically related to digital services, but more generally for all services. The limited scope of existing provisions and the lack of appropriate disciplines enacted within the GATS leads to regulatory barriers to trade in services being inadequately addressed at the multilateral level. Currently, the lack of scrutiny of whether existing regulatory barriers are unnecessarily burdensome leads to the maintenance of considerable trade barriers, causing inefficient trade in services. Of course, the call for more efficient services trade should be balanced against Members' regulatory autonomy.

Members share the general view that the obligations on domestic regulation apply to electronic commerce.[1042] For example, Australia requested a clarification of how Article VI GATS relates to electronic commerce, but at the same time implied the applicability of this Article to

1038 Article VII:2 GATS.

1039 Articles VII:3 and 5 GATS.

1040 WTO Council for Trade in Services, 'Guidelines for Mutual Recognition Agreements or Arrangements in the Accountancy Sector', S/L/38, 28 May 1997.

1041 Mattoo and Meltzer (n 836) 787. The Court of Justice of the European Union invalidated the Privacy Shield on the basis of it not providing an essentially equivalent level of protection. Judgment of the Court of 16 July 2020, *Data Protection Commissioner v Facebook Ireland Limited and Maximillian Schrems*, C-311/18, EU:C:2020:559.

1042 WTO Council for Trade in Services, 'Work Programme on Electronic Commerce – Progress report to the General Council' Adopted by the Council for Trade in Services on 19 July 1999, S/L/74, 27 July 1999, para 11.

electronic commerce.[1043] Additionally, the applicability of Article VI GATS to services that are electronically supplied was implicitly confirmed by the panel in *US – Gambling*, where it assessed the consistency of the US' measures with paragraphs 1 and 3 of Article VI GATS.[1044] In that dispute, Antigua and Barbados challenged the overall and cumulative effect of various US federal and state laws that prohibited the remote supply of gambling services. 'Remote supply' was explained by the United States as constituting supply of gambling services where the service supplier and consumer are not physically together, where the gambling services is offered through '*some means of distance communication*'.[1045] This effectively amounted to a prohibition on the supply of gambling services over the Internet.

The WTO Secretariat noted that '*the question of standards is likely to be particularly important, since one of the basic characteristics of the Internet itself is the use of common frameworks and standards for interconnectivity and interoperability in order to maintain "universal" communication*'.[1046] However, so far the standards supporting the Internet have been developed by private (non-profit) organisations with little to no interference of governments.[1047] Members seem to disagree as to the role of regulation in the digital world. Whereas some attribute the high pace of technological development to the lack of regulation, others emphasise the importance of developing disciplines under Article VI:4 GATS.[1048] Hoekman and Mavroidis argue that Members should focus on increasing their understanding of what necessity could mean in practice in the ongoing domestic regulation negotiations.[1049] They recommend using

[1043] WTO Council for Trade in Services, 'Work Programme on Electronic Commerce' Communication from Australia, S/C/W/108, 18 May 1999, paras 5 and 6.

[1044] Panel Report, *US – Gambling*, paras 6.430–6.437. This issue was not appealed.

[1045] Panel Report, *US – Gambling*, paras 6.156 and 6.164.

[1046] WTO Council for Trade in Services, 'The Work Programme on Electronic Commerce' Note by the Secretariat, S/C/W/68, 16 November 1998, para 16.

[1047] An important example of such an organisation is the Internet Corporation for Assigned Names and Numbers (ICANN), which is a non-profit organisation that was founded in 1998. It coordinates the unique identifiers that are assigned to all devices connected to the Internet (IP addresses) and maintains the domain name system (DNS – which is required to make the Internet accessible to humans). For more information see ICANN, 'What Does ICANN Do?', *Internet Corporation for Assigned Names and Numbers*, available at <www.icann.org/resources/pages/what-2012-02-25-en>.

[1048] WTO Council for Trade in Services, 'Work Programme on Electronic Commerce – Progress report to the General Council' Adopted by the Council for Trade in Services on 19 July 1999, S/L/74, 27 July 1999, para 11.

[1049] Bernard Hoekman and Petros C Mavroidis, 'A Technical Barriers to Trade Agreements for Services?' (European University Institute – Robert Schuman Centre for Advanced Studies 2015) RSCAS 2015/25 14 <https://cadmus.eui.eu/handle/1814/35419>.

existing GATS structure to focus attention on gaining a better understanding of the areas where regulation unnecessarily restricts trade.

6.1.2.4 Relationship between Market Access and National Treatment and Domestic Regulation

There seems to be confusion on the exact delineation between the obligations in Article VI:5, XVI and XVII GATS. Even though this issue, referred to as '*the thorniest systemic issue in GATS today*',[1050] is not crucial to the research conducted in this book, it is addressed briefly as the measures will be considered under the various GATS obligations in Chapter 7. In doing so, a pragmatic approach will be taken, assessing any possible violation, regardless of the compatibility of these different possible violations. This approach is based on the presumption that, were these measures brought before the WTO DSM, the complaining party would allege any possible violation, leaving it up to the panel in question, and possibly the AB, to rule on what provision(s) of the GATS has/have been violated.[1051]

In discussing the overlap between the various GATS obligations, it is important to distinguish between the scope of application and the violation of the various measures.[1052] As regards their scope of application, several overlaps exist between the three obligations. The national treatment obligation, to start with, has a very wide scope of application, applying to 'all measures affecting supply of services' (Article XVII:1 GATS). The scope of the market access obligation is more limited, as it only applies to the six specific market access restrictions as enumerated in Article XVI:2 GATS. An additional distinction between both obligations is that Article XVI sets negative criteria, prohibiting the use of certain types of measures, whereas Article XVII provides normative criteria that Members must follow when enacting regulations.[1053] The scope of application of Article VI:5 GATS is equally limited as it only applies to licensing and qualification requirements and technical standards. It also distinguishes itself from Article XVI, as Article VI imposes

[1050] Panagiotis Delimatsis, 'Don't Gamble with GATS – The Interaction between Articles VI, XVI, XVII and XVIII GATS in the Light of the US – Gambling Case' (2006) 40 Journal of World Trade 1059, 1061.

[1051] Thereby probably also exercising judicial economy when deemed appropriate.

[1052] As noted in Natens (n 989) 232.

[1053] Gilles Muller, 'Troubled Relationships under the GATS: Tensions between Market Access (Article XVI), National Treatment (Article XVII), and Domestic Regulation (Article VI)' (2017) 16 World Trade Review 449, 453.

minimum limitations (relating to the quality of services) whereas the market access obligation imposes maximum limitations.[1054]

It is, however, the possibility of simultaneous violations that raises important systemic issues. According to standing case law, a measure cannot violate both Article VI:5 and Articles XVI and XVII simultaneously.[1055] The main distinction between the national treatment obligation and the other two obligations is that the former deals with any discriminatory measure, whereas the latter two can be violated by measures that are non-discriminatory. Here we observe a first overlap (between market access and national treatment), as it was found by the panel in *China – Electronic Payment Services*: any of the subparagraphs of Article XVI can be discriminatory.[1056] The panel concluded that the scopes of Article XVI and XVII are therefore not mutually exclusive. It additionally gave precedence to Article XVI GATS, analysing the discriminatory measures listed in Article XVI:2 GATS in terms of Article XVI. Other discriminatory measures are assessed under Article XVII GATS.[1057]

The distinction between the market access obligation and the obligation applying to domestic regulation is twofold: whereas Article XVI deals with quantitative restrictions, Article VI:5 deals with qualitative requirements. In other words, the market access obligation imposes quantitative maximum limitations while the domestic regulation obligation imposes qualitative minimum requirements.[1058] Article XVI and VI:5 GATS address origin-neutral domestic regulations that affect trade in services, but because of the double distinction, it has been argued that a measure cannot simultaneously violate Article XVI and VI:5 GATS.[1059]

[1054] ibid 458.

[1055] Panel Report, *US – Gambling*, para 6.305. As noted by Natens, this case law does not seem to have a sufficient textual basis but should be followed nonetheless due to a lack of alternative authoritative guidance. Natens (n 989) 230–231. Muller argues that the Appellate Body seemed to distance itself from this finding but concludes that the case law does not provide a clear demarcation between these Articles. AB Report, *US – Gambling*, para 250. Muller (n 1053) 457.

[1056] Panel Report, *China – Electronic Payment Services*, para 7.654.

[1057] Muller (n 1053) 455.

[1058] GATT Multilateral Trade Negotiations Uruguay Round, Group of Negotiations on Services, 'Scheduling of Initial Commitments in Trade in Services: Explanatory Note' MTN.GNS/W/164, 3 September 1993, para 5; WTO Council for Trade in Services, 'Guidelines for the Scheduling of Specific Commitments under the General Agreement on Trade in Services (GATS)' Adopted by the Council for Trade in Services on 23 March 2001, S/L/92, 28 March 2001, para 11.

[1059] Natens (n 989) 229–233. Muller, however, cautions that the interpretation of 'quantitative restriction' in the *US – Gambling* dispute raises concerns that the broad

As Article XVII also covers *de facto* discrimination, it can be contended that both Article XVII and Article VI deal with measures that are origin neutral. Muller argues that Article XVII should take precedence over Article VI, if the scope of the prohibition of *de facto* discrimination in Article XVII is interpreted narrowly.[1060]

Less immediately applicable, but nonetheless interesting to consider as well, is the overlap with Article VI:4 GATS. The fourth paragraph of the provision on domestic regulation has a broader scope of application, applying to qualification requirements and procedures, technical standards and licensing requirements in any service sector. In practice, it is perceivable that there might be an overlap in scope of application of Article VI:4 GATS and Articles XVI and XVII GATS. Krajewski argues that it might be useful to agree the mutual exclusiveness of Article VI:4 disciplines and the scheduling requirements of Articles XVI and XVII. This is because, under Articles XVI and XVII, Members have the right to schedule commitments and therefore exclude some measures from the application of these Articles. This right would be limited if these (non-scheduled) measures could still be disciplined on the basis of domestic regulation.[1061]

6.1.3 Annexes and Protocols

6.1.3.1 GATS Annex on Telecommunications

The GATS Annex on Telecommunications (Telecoms Annex) was enacted by WTO Members to elaborate on the provisions of the GATS with respect to measures that affect access to and use of 'public telecommunications transport networks and services'. It was felt that the Telecoms Annex was necessary due to the specificities of the telecommunications sector, especially considering the dual role of telecom services as a distinct sector of economic activity and also an underlying means of transportation for other economic activities (*supra* Section 5.3.1). Some authors have argued that the Telecoms Annex requires WTO Members

interpretation of Article XVI GATS affects WTO Members' regulatory autonomy. Muller (n 1053) 462.

1060 Muller (n 1053) 472. However, he admits that even though the Appellate Body ruled out considerations of regulatory purpose in the assessment of less favourable treatment in Article XVII GATS, it failed to clarify the scope of the prohibition, thereby leaving the demarcation between Article XVII and Article VI undefined.

1061 Krajewski, *National Regulation and Trade Liberalization in Services: The Legal Impact of the General Agreement on Trade in Services (GATS) on National Regulatory Autonomy* (n 669) 139–140.

to impose access obligations on suppliers of telecom services.[1062] The WTO Secretariat simplified the aim of this Annex to '*a response to the central role of telecommunications as a medium of transporting services*'.[1063]

The Telecoms Annex has a very broad scope: it applies to all measures that affect access to or use of public telecommunications transport networks and services with regard to all service sectors for which Members have undertaken commitments.[1064] Members are thus not required to authorise the supply of a service for which no commitments were undertaken.[1065] The substantive obligations in Section 5 apply to measures ensuring access to and use of public telecommunications transport networks and services for the supply of services, not only on a cross-border level but also through commercial presence.[1066]

It is important to note that the Telecoms Annex in effect did not cause the liberalisation of telecommunications services, but rather opened up opportunities for cross-border trade of other service sectors that require access to and use of communication networks and services to be supplied. The Telecoms Annex thereby substantially facilitates market access for committed services and avoids that access to telecommunications becomes a *de facto* barrier to trade.[1067] Its aim is to '*ensure that [other commitments] are not frustrated through the lack of access to and use of telecoms services*'.[1068]

The main substantive obligation of the Telecoms Annex can be found in Section 5, which requires access to and use of public telecommunications transport networks and services on a non-discriminatory basis.[1069] This obligation thereby aims at facilitating the exploitation of scheduled commitments.[1070] The structure of

1062 ibid 169.

1063 WTO Council for Trade in Services, 'The Work Programme on Electronic Commerce' Note by the Secretariat, S/C/W/68, 16 November 1998, para 20.

1064 Section 2(c)(i) of the GATS Annex on Telecommunications and the interpretation in Panel Report, *Mexico – Telecoms*, para 7.278.

1065 In the case of *Mexico – Telecoms* the service at issue was a basic telecommunications transport service. Panel Report, *Mexico – Telecoms*, para 7.291.

1066 Panel Report, *Mexico – Telecoms*, paras 7.281, 7.380–7.381.

1067 Weber and Burri (n 5) 63.

1068 Krajewski, *National Regulation and Trade Liberalization in Services: The Legal Impact of the General Agreement on Trade in Services (GATS) on National Regulatory Autonomy* (n 669) 167.

1069 Footnote 2 to the GATS Annex on Telecommunications clarifies that 'non-discriminatory' includes both the most-favoured-nation obligation and the national treatment obligation.

1070 Panel Report, *Mexico – Telecoms*, para 7.293.

Section 5[1071] is quite peculiar, with paragraph (a) both informing and being informed by the elements of paragraphs (b) through (f) and paragraph (b) being subordinate to (i.e. qualified by) paragraphs (a) and (e).[1072] Paragraph (a) requires Members to ensure access to and use of public telecoms transport networks and services to any supplier of any other Member for the supply of a service that is included in that Member's Schedule.[1073] Such access must be provided on reasonable terms and necessary conditions, which implies that the terms should be non-discriminatory towards foreign service suppliers, should be cost-based and not limiting competition.[1074] Paragraph (e) prohibits conditions to access and use of public telecommunications services, unless necessary to achieve a limited number of public policy objectives. Whether the conditions are necessary is assessed based on the illustrative list that can be found in paragraph (f).[1075] In *Mexico – Telecoms*, the panel clarified that necessity in paragraph (e) relates more to 'making a contribution' to a policy goal than to being 'indispensable'.

Section 5(b) of the Telecoms Annex requires Members to ensure access to and use of private leased circuits[1076] and to allow service suppliers to interconnect these circuits.[1077] As mentioned *supra*, the obligations formulated in paragraph (b) are qualified by certain (regulatory) conditions, which can only be imposed where necessary: (i) to safeguard public service responsibilities of public service suppliers; (ii) to protect technical integrity of the public networks; (iii) to ensure that service suppliers of other Members do not supply services that are not liberalised in the Member's Schedule.[1078]

1071 *5. Access to and use of Public Telecommunications Transport Networks and Services*

(a) Each Member shall ensure that any service supplier of any other Member is accorded access to and use of public telecommunications transport networks and services on reasonable and non-discriminatory terms and conditions, for the supply of a service included in its Schedule. This obligation shall be applied, inter alia, through paragraphs (b) through (f).

1072 Panel Report, *Mexico – Telecoms*, para 7.309.

1073 ibid paras 7.314 and 7.317.

1074 ibid paras 7.324–7.343.

1075 ibid para 7.326.

1076 Private leased circuits are privately owned circuits (often fibre-optic lines) which access is provided to for a monthly rent. Private leased circuits can be used for Internet access, but also business data exchange and other forms of telecommunication.

1077 Panel Report, *Mexico – Telecoms*, paras 7.379–7.384.

1078 Sections 5(e) and (f) of the GATS Annex on Telecommunications.

Section 5(d) provides Members with a ground to justify limitations that are necessary to ensure security and confidentiality of messages. It even includes a chapeau-like requirement of no arbitrary or unjustifiable discrimination or disguised restriction on trade. Finally, Section 5(g) recognises the right for developing Members to schedule limitations for certain objectives: strengthening domestic telecommunications infrastructure and service capacity and increasing its participation in international trade in telecommunications services. However, it does not allow that Member to impose conditions that are inconsistent with its specific commitments.[1079] Section 5(g) therefore does not function as a justification.

Section 5(c) requires Members to ensure that foreign service suppliers can use public telecommunications transport networks and services for the movement of information within and across borders. This obligation is thus especially relevant from the digital trade perspective, as data flows are necessary to allow any digital service to be supplied. Tuthill argues that the explicit reference and applicability of the Telecoms Annex to 'movement of information' shows that movement of data was already a concern during the negotiation of the Telecoms Annex in the 1990s.[1080] The reference to access to information and databases in Section 5(c) does indeed show that WTO Members were aware, already at the conception of the GATS, that free movement of data is required for the supply of many services. Even though Members are allowed to take measures necessary to ensure security and confidentiality of messages, they must ensure that these measures are not applied in a manner that would constitute arbitrary or unjustifiable discrimination or a disguised restriction on trade in services.[1081]

To assess whether the Telecoms Annex is applicable to the Internet, thereby facilitating market access for committed services that are digitally supplied, it will be necessary to show that the Internet is a public telecommunications transport network. First, the Internet is a telecommunications transport service. The Internet is equivalent to other basic telecommunications services which are a means of conduit for the cross-border supply of services. As the network of networks that has enabled global cross-border supply of a vast group of services, the Internet is the prototype of a telecommunication transport network.

1079 Panel Report, *Mexico – Telecoms*, para 7.388.
1080 Tuthill (n 125) 367.
1081 Section 5(d) of the GATS Annex on Telecommunications.

Second, the reference to 'public' telecoms transport networks and services does not relate to the ownership structure (the networks and services can be either public or private) but rather implies an assigned universal service or public service requirement.[1082] There is often such a requirement on ISPs, with access to the Internet increasingly recognised as a public service. However, in many countries, submarine cable consortia and satellite systems are not considered to be public.[1083] Does this entail the inapplicability of the Telecoms Annex to this infrastructure that is necessary for the supply of Internet services? No. Even though certain constitutive elements of the infrastructure that is necessary to provide access to the Internet are not publicly owned, it is the Internet itself that constitutes a public telecommunications transport network and Internet access constitutes a public telecommunications transport service. Due to its vital importance to everyday life, it has been recognised as subject to a universal service obligation.[1084] The 2030 United Nations Sustainable Development Goals include the need for increased access to information and communications technology and strive to provide universal and affordable access to the Internet in LDCs by 2020.[1085]

The EU as early as 1998 clarified its opinion on the Annex on Telecom's applicability to electronically supplied services, stating that

[1082] See para 3(a) of the GATS Annex on Telecommunications: '"*public telecommunications transport service" means any telecommunications transport service require, explicitly or in effect, by a Member to be offered to the public generally*'. Henry Gao, 'Annex on Telecommunications' in Rüdiger Wolfrum, Peter-Tobias Stoll and Clemens Feinäugle (eds), *WTO – Trade in Services*, vol 6 (Martinus Nijhoff 2008) 692.

[1083] Lee Tuthill and Laura Sherman, 'Telecommunications: Can Trade Agreements Keep up with Technology?' in Juan Marchetti and Martin Roy (eds), *Opening Markets for Trade in Services: Countries and Sectors in Bilateral and WTO Negotiations* (Cambridge University Press 2009) 177.

[1084] The European Union required its member states to ensure availability of universal service of electronic communications networks: Directive 2002/22/EC of the European Parliament and of the Council of 7 March 2002 on universal service and users' rights relating to electronic communications networks and services (Universal Service Directive) 2002 OJ L 108, 24 April 2002, 51. This Directive was amended by the Regulation (EU) 2015/2120 of the European Parliament and of the Council of 25 November 2015 laying down measures concerning open Internet access OJ L 310, 26 November 2015, 1, which defines 'Internet access service' as a publicly available electronic communications service (Article 2(1)). Countries like India, Indonesia and Mexico have universal service frameworks applicable to Internet access. See OECD, 'OECD Communications Outlook 2013' (OECD Publishing 2013).

[1085] Target 9.c of the United Nations Sustainable Development Goals. See United Nations G. A. Res. 70/1, U.N. Doc. A/RES/70/1, 25 September 2015, 21.

> the Telecoms Annex guarantees that whenever a WTO Member has specific market access and national treatment commitments for a particular service sector/sub-sector, the commitments apply also to those services sectors/subsectors when delivered in electronic form. This is regardless of whether the WTO Member in question has bound GATS commitments on telecommunications services or not. We share the view that the rules applying to content services should be those relating to the content itself, not those relating to the means of transmission.[1086]

Australia supported the applicability of the Telecoms Annex to the Internet (as a communications service).[1087] In a later submission, the EU stated that it considered the obligations of the Annex on 'access to and use of' public telecom networks to be applicable to Internet access and Internet network services.[1088] A handful of WTO Members recently opined that the Telecoms Annex is a cornerstone of Members' regulatory framework for e-commerce.[1089] The EU also suggested that the notion of 'public networks' in the Annex '*cannot be construed restrictively to mean only networks owned by publicly-owned companies and with a universal services obligation*'.[1090] Looking at the broad interpretation the panel in *Mexico – Telecoms* gave to the scope of the Annex, this statement does not seem too far-fetched.[1091] The United States has even alleged the inconsistency of China's 2016 Cybersecurity Law with Section 5 of the Annex, arguing that VPNs and leased lines fall within the ambit of public

[1086] WTO Council for Trade in Services, 'Work Programme on Electronic Commerce, Scope and Classification Issues' Communication from the European Communities and its Member States, S/C/W/87, 9 December 1998, para 5.

[1087] '*Australia considers that the Internet is a packet-switched data service in the context of telecommunications commitments*'. WTO Council for Trade in Services, 'Work Programme on Electronic Commerce' Communication from Australia, S/C/W/108, 18 May 1999, para 18.

[1088] WTO Work Programme on Electronic Commerce, 'Communication from the European Communities and their Member States', S/C/W/183, 30 November 2000, para 6.

[1089] WTO General Council, 'Work Programme on Electronic Commerce – Trade Policy, the WTO, and the Digital Economy' Communication from Canada, Chile, Colombia, Côte d'Ivoire, the European Union, the Republic of Korea, Mexico, Montenegro, Paraguay, Singapore and Turkey, JOB/GC/116, 13 January 2017, 4.

[1090] WTO Work Programme on Electronic Commerce, 'Communication from the European Communities and their Member States', S/C/W/183, 30 November 2000, para 5.

[1091] Panel Report, *Mexico – Telecoms*, para 7.278. See also the statement of the chairman of the Group on Basic Telecommunications, stating that basic telecoms can be provided through *any means of technology*. WTO Group on Basic Telecommunications, 'Notes for Scheduling Basic Telecommunications services – Note by the Chairman', S/GBT/W/2/Rev.1, 16 January 1997.

telecommunications services.[1092] However, not all Members share this view, with some stating that it is unclear whether the Annex guarantees service suppliers access to and use of Internet networks and services.[1093]

To conclude, as the Internet constitutes a public telecoms transport network, Internet access suppliers qualify as suppliers of public telecommunication transport networks or services. The applicability of the Telecoms Annex to the Internet entails that Members are required to ensure that service suppliers from other WTO Members are granted access to and use of (domestic gateways of) the Internet on reasonable and non-discriminatory terms.[1094] Members must ensure access to the Internet for the movement of information across borders and for access to information in databases or stored electronically in the territory of another Member.[1095] Since the transformation of international trade due to digitalisation, there is an increased need for data flows across borders. The Telecoms Annex has thus not lost any of its relevance in the last decade. It could even be said that the Telecoms Annex is as indispensable to trade in services now as it was at the time of its conception.[1096] The scope of the Annex is sufficiently broad to also cover Internet access and network services, for the same reasons as originally conceived for telecom services: access to and use of public telecommunication transport networks should be guaranteed.[1097] It will benefit the digitally enabled services, in the same way as it originally benefitted the telecommunication-enabled

[1092] WTO Council for Trade in Services, WTO Council for Trade in Services, 'Measures Adopted and under Development by China Relating to its Cybersecurity Law' Communication from the United States, S/C/W/376, 23 February 2018, para 7.

[1093] WTO Council for Trade in Services, 'Work Programme on Electronic Commerce – Progress Report to the General Council' Adopted by the Council for Trade in Services on 19 July 1999, S/L/74, 27 July 1999, para 20. However, as pointed out by the European Communities, there is arguably a flaw in the Members' reasoning as they argue that it is unclear whether the Internet is a public telecommunications transport network because *'the Internet is a network of networks, which includes public and private networks'*. Whether networks are public or private is not the determining criterion. Rather, a public telecoms transport network is characterised by its assigned public service obligation.

[1094] See paragraph 5(c) of the GATS Annex on Telecommunications.

[1095] Porges and Enders (n 135) 8.

[1096] For an analysis of the Annex on Telecommunications in this context see *inter alia*: Luff (n 759); Porges and Enders (n 135); Weber and Burri (n 5); WTO General Council, 'Possible List of Trade Principles on Electronic Commerce', part of Communication from the European Communities and their Member States, WTO Work Programme on Electronic Commerce, preparations for the 1999 Ministerial Conference, WT/GC/W/306, 9 August 1999.

[1097] WTO Work Programme on Electronic Commerce, 'Communication from the European Communities and their Member States', S/C/W/183, 30 November 2000, 2.

services, which is key to enabling digital services trade and e-commerce in general.

Admittedly, other authors do not seem to interpret the Telecoms Annex in a similar broad fashion. Luff argues that the Telecoms Annex would benefit from making explicit that it equally applies to broadband networks and Internet services.[1098]

6.1.3.2 Fourth Protocol to the Trade in Services Agreement

The Annex on Negotiations of Basic Telecommunications was attached to the GATS to ensure that all Members undertook commitments with regard to basic telecommunications services.[1099] Pending further commitments, the Annex suspended MFN obligations and Article II exemptions for basic telecommunications. This suspension was terminated on 15 February 1997 when the Fourth Protocol to the Trade in Services Agreement or 'Agreement on Basic Telecommunications' was adopted. The Fourth Protocol contained the results of the basic telecommunications negotiations, with new commitments undertaken by 69 governments and nine new Article II exemptions.[1100]

The Fourth Protocol significantly liberalised trade in basic telecommunications through a series of Schedules of Specific Commitments concerning these services.[1101] The new commitments supplemented or modified existing Schedules, overriding the procedure for modification of Schedules in Articles II and XXI GATS.[1102] The Agreement led to the adoption of the 'Reference Paper'.[1103]

6.1.3.3 Reference Paper on Basic Telecommunications

The Reference Paper on Basic Telecommunications spells out the guiding principles for WTO Members on the regulatory framework for basic

1098 Luff (n 759) 90.

1099 Henry Gao, 'Annex on Negotiations on Basic Telecommunications' in Rüdiger Wolfrum, Peter-Tobias Stoll and Clemens Feinäugle (eds), *WTO – Trade in Services*, vol 6 (Martinus Nijhoff 2008) 713.

1100 Henry Gao, 'Fourth Protocol to That General Agreement on Trade in Services' in Rüdiger Wolfrum, Peter-Tobias Stoll and Clemens Feinäugle (eds), *WTO – Trade in Services*, vol 6 (Martinus Nijhoff 2008) 716.

1101 The Protocol is an integral part of the GATS (see Article XX:3 GATS) and entered into force on 5 February 1998.

1102 Gao, 'Fourth Protocol to That General Agreement on Trade in Services' (n 1100) 716–717.

1103 WTO Negotiation Group on Basic Telecommunications, 'Reference Paper on Basic Telecommunications', 24 April 1996.

telecommunications services.[1104] More specifically, it contains principles on competition safeguards, interconnection guarantees, transparent licensing processes and the independence of regulators.[1105] It should be noted that the Reference Paper provides a regulatory framework, it does not include ready-made regulatory proposals.

Unlike the Annex on Telecommunications, the Reference Paper does not apply to all Members and all sectors in which commitments have been undertaken.[1106] The scope of the Reference Paper is limited to basic telecommunications services and only for those Members that have included the Reference Paper in their Schedule.[1107] It is therefore Members' commitments that form the basis for, for example, the interconnection requirement in the Reference Paper.[1108] Another important difference between both documents lies in the targeted operators. Whereas the Annex applies to all operators of public telecommunications transport networks and services, regardless of their competitive situation, the principles in the Reference Paper only apply to 'major suppliers'.[1109] Finally, while the Annex deals with the broader 'access to and use of', the Reference Paper only focusses on competitive safeguards and interconnection guarantees. Despite these differences, there is a possible overlap between the Annex and the Reference Paper: '*to the extent that the Reference Paper requires cost-oriented interconnection on reasonable terms and conditions, it supplements Annex* Section 5, *requiring additional obligations as regards "major suppliers"*'.[1110] In its 2019

[1104] The Reference Paper does not apply to value-added telecommunications services.

[1105] Tuthill and Sherman (n 1083) 159.

[1106] Panel Report, *Mexico – Telecoms*, para 7.331.

[1107] For a discussion on the distinction between basic telecommunications services and value-added telecommunications services, see *supra* Section 4.3.1. The Reference Paper is generally added as an annex to existing Service Schedules and commitments based on the Reference Paper are scheduled as 'additional commitments' in accordance with Article XVIII. The following Members have adopted the Reference Paper: Antigua and Barbados, Argentina, Australia, Bangladesh, Belize, Bolivia, Brazil, Brunei, Canada, Chile, China, Colombia, Cote d'Ivoire, Dominican Republic, Ecuador, El Salvador, European Union (and its member states), Ghana, Grenada, Guatemala, Hong Kong, Iceland, India, Indonesia, Israel, Jamaica, Japan, Jordan, Korea, Kyrgyz Republic, Malaysia, Mauritius, Mexico, Morocco, New Zealand, Norway, Pakistan, Papua New Guinea, Peru, Philippines, Senegal, Separate Customs Territory of Taiwan, Penghu, Kinmen and Matsu, Singapore, South Africa, Sri Lanka, Switzerland, Thailand, Trinidad and Tobago, Tunisia, Turkey, US and Venezuela.

[1108] Panel Report, *Mexico – Telecoms*, para 7.95.

[1109] ibid para 7.331.

[1110] WTO Analytical Index, 'GATS – Annex on Telecommunications (Jurisprudence)', 9 January 2018, available at <www.wto.org/english/res_e/publications_e/ai17_e/gats_anntelecommunications_jur.pdf>.

proposal in the context of the plurilateral negotiations on electronic commerce at the WTO, the EU proposed a revision of the Reference Paper, replacing references to 'basic telecommunications services' with 'public telecoms transport services', thereby drawing a clear link between the scope of the Annex and the Reference Paper.[1111] The scope of the latter, however, still remains limited to telecoms service supplied by major suppliers.

The first Section of the Reference Paper requires Members to maintain appropriate measures to prevent major suppliers from engaging in anti-competitive practices. The panel in *Mexico – Telecoms* defined those as '*actions that lessen rivalry or competition in the market*'.[1112] The focus of this section is on a major supplier's ability to materially affect the terms of participation.[1113] Examples of such practices include anti-competitive cross-subsidisation, misusing information obtained from competitors and withholding technical information about essential facilities and commercially relevant information necessary for other service suppliers to provide services.[1114] Horizontal price-fixing and market-sharing agreements by suppliers have been added as additional examples in disputes.[1115] The fact that the practice is required under national law does not erode this obligation.[1116] The panel in *Mexico – Telecoms*, however, recognised that Section 1 contains a voluntary, additional commitment[1117] to maintain certain 'appropriate' measures, which provides Members with some flexibility in accepting and implementing this commitment.[1118] Appropriate measures are not expected to forestall every occurrence of anti-competitive practices by major suppliers, but they should logically be appropriate in preventing this behaviour.[1119]

Section 2 of the Reference Paper requires Members to ensure that interconnection with major suppliers is ensured '*at any technically*

1111 WTO, Joint Statement on Electronic Commerce, 'EU Proposal for WTO Disciplines and Commitments Relating to Electronic Commerce – Communication from the European Union', INF/ECOM/22, 26 April 2019.

1112 Panel Report, *Mexico – Telecoms*, para 7.230.

1113 ibid para 7.234.

1114 Section 1.2 of the Reference Paper on Basic Telecommunications.

1115 Panel Report, *Mexico – Telecoms*, para 7.237.

1116 To the contrary, the Reference Paper was adopted to limit WTO Members' regulatory power when it comes to anti-competitive practices on basic telecoms. ibid para 7.244.

1117 The Reference Paper is an additional commitment in the sense of Article XVIII GATS.

1118 Panel Report, *Mexico – Telecoms*, para 7.267.

1119 ibid para 7.266.

feasible point in the network'.[1120] The purpose of the interconnection obligation is to prevent basic telecom service suppliers from being restricted by unduly onerous interconnection terms, conditions and rates.[1121] The right to interconnect applies to any service sector where conditions on market access and national treatment have been undertaken.[1122] The panel in *Mexico – Telecoms* clarified that this obligation does not distinguish between domestic and international interconnection.[1123] Therefore, regardless of whether we are dealing with cross-border traffic or traffic provided through commercial presence, the interconnection obligation applies. Interconnection should be provided under non-discriminatory terms, conditions and rates, of a quality at a national treatment standard and in a timely fashion and on terms, conditions and cost-oriented rates[1124] that are transparent and reasonable.[1125]

Further sections of the Reference Paper elaborate on (i) Members' right to define universal service obligations in whatever way they want, so long as they are administered in a transparent, non-discriminatory and competitively neutral manner and are not more burdensome than necessary; (ii) the requirement to make licensing criteria publicly available together with the period of time needed to come to a decision as well as the terms and conditions of individual licenses; (iii) the requirement that regulatory bodies are independent from and not accountable to suppliers of basic telecoms services; and (iv) the requirement to ensure that procedures for allocation and use of scarce resources is done in an objective, timely and non-discriminatory manner.[1126]

As early as 1998, the Secretariat clarified that the Reference Paper could help in the creation of efficient infrastructure for electronic

[1120] Section 2.2 of the Reference Paper on Basic Telecommunications.

[1121] Panel Report, *Mexico – Telecoms*, para 7.94.

[1122] ibid para 7.94.

[1123] The object and purpose of the GATS support the inclusion of international interconnection. Section 2 of the Reference Paper does not exclude foreign service suppliers from its scope. ibid paras 7.105, 7.117 and 7.121.

[1124] Cost-oriented rates were interpreted as those rates brought into a defined relation to known costs or cost principles. They do not need to equate costs, but they need to be founded on the costs incurred in providing the service. Panel Report, *Mexico Telecoms*, paras 7.168 and 7.174.

[1125] Section 2.2(a) and (b) of the Reference Paper on Basic Telecommunications. The Panel in *Mexico – Telecoms* found that the interconnection rates charged by Telmex were not cost oriented (as they were substantially higher than the costs incurred), which violated Section 2.2 of the Reference Paper. Panel Report, *Mexico – Telecoms*, para 7.216.

[1126] Respectively Sections 3, 4, 5 and 6 of the Reference Paper on Basic Telecommunications.

commerce.[1127] In the 1999 progress report of the WPEC, it was noted that monopolies and restrictive business practices might equally pose problems for service suppliers of digital services.[1128] Members raised that the Reference Paper might be applicable to digital services where Internet access providers qualify as major suppliers of basic telecommunications.[1129] The European Union opined that the principles of the Reference Paper are applicable to Internet access and Internet network services.[1130] Mexico, Indonesia, Korea, Turkey and Australia proposed an update to the Reference Paper 'to support digital competition'.[1131] Brazil called for a reassessment of the Reference Paper, to ensure an open and free environment for the development of e-commerce.[1132]

It can be argued that Internet access qualifies as a basic telecommunication service. More specifically, it generally classifies as a packet-switched data transmission service (W/120 – 2.C.b).[1133] As a basic telecommunication service, there is no reason why the Reference Paper should not apply to the Internet access services. Some scholars, however, have a different take on the existing scope of the Reference Paper. For example, Kariyawasam suggests broadening the scope of the Reference Paper, so that it equally applies to new-generation networks.[1134] He argues that this will enhance effective competition, ensure interconnection and equal access, and safeguard the principle of non-discrimination.[1135] Other scholars have

1127 WTO Council for Trade in Services, 'The Work Programme on Electronic Commerce' Note by the Secretariat, S/C/W/68, 16 November 1998, para 24.

1128 WTO Council for Trade in Services, 'Work Programme on Electronic Commerce – Progress Report to the General Council' Adopted by the Council for Trade in Services on 19 July 1999, S/L/74, 27 July 1999, para 13.

1129 ibid.

1130 WTO Work Programme on Electronic Commerce, 'Communication from the European Communities and their Member States', S/C/W/183, 30 November 2000, para 6.

1131 WTO General Council, 'MIKTA E-Commerce Workshop Reflections', JOB/GC/99, 22 July 2016, 1.

1132 WTO General Council, 'Exploratory Work on Electronic Commerce – Non-paper from Brazil', JOB/GC/176, 12 April 2018, para 4.3.

1133 Data transmission over the Internet happens in packets. Packet-switched data transmission services include 'data network services' (CPCprov 75231), which are explained as 'network services necessary to transmit data between equipment using the same or different protocols'.

1134 Not everyone agrees that the Reference Paper (as an existing WTO commitment) applies to Internet services. See the discussion in Kariyawasam, *International Economic Law and the Digital Divide: A New Silk Road?* (n 69).

1135 Kariyawasam, 'Better Regulation of Digital Markets: A New Look at the Reference Paper' (n 761) 241.

raised the proposal to also draft a Reference Paper on digital trade, thereby ensuring that Members combat anti-competitive practices in the area of digital trade.[1136]

6.1.3.4 The Understanding on Commitments in Financial Services

Some WTO Members have made commitments in accordance with the Understanding on Commitments in Financial Services.[1137] This Understanding provided Members with an optional and alternative approach to making specific commitments on financial services. It provides a 'formula approach' to scheduling commitments under Articles XVI and XVII GATS with regard to financial services for Members that choose to adopt it.[1138] Two provisions of the Understanding are particularly relevant to digital services supply.

Section B.7, entitled 'New Financial Services', requires Members to permit financial service suppliers of any other Member established in their territory to offer in their territory any new financial service. This provision seems to anticipate the development of 'new financial services' and encourages Members to allow the supply of such new services. The commitment, however, seems limited to provisions supplied through mode 3 ('established in its territory'). Additionally, it is unclear what qualifies as a 'new financial service' and whether establishment is a precondition.

Section B.8, entitled 'Transfers of Information and Processing of Information', provides that Members shall not

> prevent transfers of information or the processing of financial information, including transfers of data by electronic means [. . .] where such transfers of information [or] processing of financial information [. . .] are necessary for the conduct of the ordinary business of a financial service supplier. Nothing in this paragraph restricts the right of a Member to protect personal data, personal privacy and the confidentiality of individual records and accounts so long as such right is not used to circumvent the provisions of the Agreement.

[1136] For example: Burri, 'The International Economic Law Framework for Digital Trade' (n 71) 46; Mitchell and Mishra (n 307) 1127. Brazil has made a similar proposal: WTO General Council, 'Exploratory Work on Electronic Commerce – Non-paper from Brazil', JOB/GC/176, 12 April 2018, para 1.2.

[1137] The Understanding is not a part of the GATS but was appended to the Final Act of the Uruguay Round.

[1138] WTO Committee on Specific Commitments, 'Additional Commitments under Article XVIII of the GATS' Note by the Secretariat, S/CSC/W/34, 16 July 2002, para 72.

With this provision, Members recognised the importance of data flows in the provision of financial services while at the same time indicating the importance of balancing free flow of data and protection of personal data and privacy.

6.1.4 *Exceptions*

The GATS attempts to strike a balance between Member's obligations under the Agreement and their right to pursue national policy objectives.[1139] The exceptions contained in the GATS are one way in which Members' right to pursue certain objectives is ensured. These exceptions can be found throughout the Agreement. The general exceptions are listed in Article XIV GATS and the security exceptions are listed in Article XIV *bis* GATS. These two categories of exceptions are most relevant in our assessment of justifiability of barriers to digital services trade as they contain the policy objectives most often mentioned by digital trade regulators. However, both Article XII GATS and Section 2.1 of the Annex on Financial Services[1140] also contain exceptions applicable to safeguard measures and prudential measures, respectively.[1141]

6.1.4.1 General Exceptions (Article XIV GATS)

As early as 1998, the Secretariat noted the obvious relevance of the general exceptions in article XIV GATS to electronic commerce.[1142] The GATS' provision on general exceptions allows WTO Members to justify restrictions to services trade on the basis of various objectives: the protection of public morals; the maintenance of public order; compliance with laws relating to deceptive and fraudulent practices; the protection of privacy and safety; equitable or effective imposition or collection of direct taxes and avoidance of double taxation. This Article thereby ensures that WTO Members retain regulatory autonomy on issues that are deemed pertinent. It has been argued that Article XIV GATS does not address all

1139 This is recognised in the third and fourth recital of the GATS' preamble. AB Report, *Argentina – Financial Services*, para 6.114.

1140 Paragraph 2(a) can be invoked to justify inconsistencies with all of a Member's obligation under the GATS, as long as all of its requirements have been met. AB Report, *Argentina – Financial Services*, para 6.255.

1141 GATT Multilateral Trade Negotiations Uruguay Round, Group of Negotiations on Services, 'Scheduling of Initial Commitments in Trade in Services: Explanatory Note', MTN.GNS/W/164, 3 September 1993, para 13.

1142 WTO Council for Trade in Services, 'The Work Programme on Electronic Commerce' Note by the Secretariat, S/C/W/68, 16 November 1998, para 26.

policy objectives related to digital trade, such as online consumer protection and cybersecurity.[1143] However, the explicit reference to 'public morals', 'privacy', 'safety' and 'deceptive and fraudulent practices' combined with the relatively broad formulation of Article XIV's subparagraphs seems to create sufficient policy space for Members to enact measures necessary to address certain Internet policy concerns.

Some authors point out the relevance of the Appellate Body's finding in *US – Gambling* that the gambling laws, restricting remote supply of gambling services, fell within the public morals exception of Article XIV GATS, to digital services trade in the WTO framework.[1144] Based on this finding, it might be envisaged that some market access barriers to digital services trade generally, or to cross-border data supply more specifically, could find a ground for justification under the listed objectives in the general exceptions clause of the GATS.[1145] This would arguably preserve Members' regulatory autonomy when regulating access to or supply of (sensitive) digital services for reasons of *inter alia* national security or privacy protection.

Article XIV GATS, like Article XX GATT,[1146] contains a two-tier test. First, it must be assessed whether the challenged measure falls within the scope of one of the Article's subparagraphs. This is done through an assessment of whether the measure addresses the specific concern listed in that subparagraph and whether there is a sufficient nexus between the measure and the objective listed. Second, the chapeau of Article XIV GATS requires that the application of the contested measure does not constitute an arbitrary or unjustifiable discrimination between countries where like conditions prevail or a disguised restriction on trade.[1147]

(i) Preliminary Justifiability under the Subparagraphs Article XIV(a) GATS allows Members to enact measures necessary to protect public morals or to maintain public order. The Appellate Body in *US – Gambling* clarified public morals to be understood as '*standards of right and wrong conduct maintained by or on behalf of a community or*

1143 Mitchell and Mishra (n 307) 1095–1096.

1144 Burri, 'Designing Future-Oriented Multilateral Rules for Digital Trade' (n 96) 338; Wunsch-Vincent, 'Trade Rules for the Digital Age' (n 283) 8.

1145 More specifically those under subparagraphs (a) and (c): public morals/public order and securing compliance with privacy laws and regulations.

1146 Previous findings under Article XX GATT have been found relevant for the analysis of Article XIV GATS. AB Report, *US – Gambling*, para 291.

1147 AB Report, *US – Gambling*, para 292.

nation'.[1148] 'Public order' on the other hand refers to '*the preservation of the fundamental interests of society, as reflected in public policy and law*'.[1149] The content of these concepts can vary in space and time, and Members have the right to determine the level of protection that they deem appropriate.[1150] The invocation of the public order exception should take account of footnote 5 to Article XIV GATS, which limits this exception to situations where there is a genuine and sufficiently serious threat posed to one of the fundamental interests in society. This will be difficult for any WTO panel or the Appellate Body to assess.[1151]

In the more recent case of *Colombia – Textiles*, the panel and Appellate Body further elaborated on the concept of 'public morals'. Looking at the panel's analysis of public morals it becomes clear that it applies a non-intrusive standard of review. Panels and the Appellate Body look to national authorities for their assessment.[1152] Deference makes sense, especially considering that an international court lacks the democratic legitimacy to determine the content of 'public morals' in a specific country.[1153] Panels and the Appellate Body should take account of a WTO Member's right to regulate, which is an abstract and inherent right and allows WTO Members to regulate in accordance with national policies as long as this does not discriminate between like services and service suppliers.[1154] Even though Members do not require international consensus on public morals to justify their measure on this basis, they often refer to international instruments or practices in their defence.[1155] In the context of digital services, Members could refer to the OECD Privacy Principles or the General Accepted Privacy Principles as formulated by the International Association of Privacy Professionals.

For a measure to be preliminarily justifiable under Article XIV(c) GATS, it must be shown that the measure is designed to secure compliance with laws or regulations that are not inconsistent with the GATS and

[1148] ibid para 296.
[1149] ibid para 296.
[1150] Panel Report, *US – Gambling*, para 6.461.
[1151] Wu (n 48) 284.
[1152] Panel Report, *Colombia – Textiles*, paras 7.334–7.338.
[1153] Silvia Nuzzo, 'Tackling Diversity Inside WTO: GATT Moral Clause after Colombia – Textiles' (2017) 10 European Journal of Legal Studies 267, 275.
[1154] AB Report, *China – Publications and Audiovisual Products*, para 222; ibid 278.
[1155] This is done in the cases *US – Gambling, China – Publications and Audiovisual Products* and *EC – Seal Products*. ibid 279–280.

that the measure is necessary to ensure such compliance.[1156] Subparagraph (c) contains a non-exhaustive list of laws or regulations which are deemed not inconsistent with the GATS' substantive obligations. This list includes measures 'for the protection of privacy of individuals in relation to the processing and dissemination of personal data', which are very relevant to digital services trade.

The first element of the test requires an initial examination of the relationship between the inconsistent measure and relevant laws and regulations. This analysis is done through scrutinising the design of the measure, including its content and expected operation, to assess whether the measure is capable of securing compliance (it does not have to guarantee any result).[1157] The prevailing circumstances at the time of implementing the measures can be taken into account.[1158] The more precisely the respondent can indicate the specific rules, obligations or requirements that flow from the GATS-consistent laws or regulations, the easier it will be to assess the contribution of the contested measures towards these rules, obligations or requirements.[1159] The second element requires an in-depth analysis of the relationship between the inconsistent measures and the relevant laws and regulations: is the measure necessary to secure compliance? The necessity test requires various steps to be proven.

(ii) Necessity Article XIV GATS requires that measures that are enacted to protect public morals or to maintain public order (subparagraph a) or to secure compliance with laws or regulations that protect individuals' privacy (subparagraph c) are necessary.[1160] The Appellate Body has set out the standard for analysis of the necessity of the measure in *Korea – Various Measures on Beef*. Three factors must be 'weighed

[1156] This legal test was set out (with regard to Article XX(d)) in AB Report, *Korea – Various Measures on Beef*, para 157.

[1157] AB Report, *Mexico – Taxes on Soft Drinks*, paras 72–74. See also AB Report, *Argentina – Financial Services*, para 6.203.

[1158] Panel Report, *Argentina – Financial Services*, para 7.649, referring to Panel Reports, *Korea – Various Measures on Beef*, paras 655–658; *China – Auto Parts*, paras 7.309–7.312; and *Colombia – Ports of Entry*, paras 7.542 and 7.543.

[1159] AB Report, *Argentina – Financial Services*, para 6.227. Moreover, if the complainant does not contest the relationship between the envisaged objective and the measures at issue, it will more easily be considered under the relevant subparagraphs. See Panel Report, *China – Publications and Audiovisual Products*, para 7.763.

[1160] It is the measure that is sought to be justified that needs to be necessary to achieve the objective. AB Report, *US – Gasoline*, 20.

and balanced': (i) the importance of the issues and values protected;[1161] (ii) the contribution of the measure to the objective[1162] and (iii) the trade restrictiveness of the measure.[1163] It has been noted that additional factors may be relevant in specific cases.[1164] This part of the analysis will yield a preliminary conclusion as to the measure's necessity.[1165]

The preliminary conclusion on the measure's necessity must be confirmed by an analysis of whether a less trade-restrictive alternative is reasonably available. A panel must assess whether the responding party could reasonably be expected to employ an alternative measure, consistent (or less inconsistent) with the covered agreements, that would achieve the objectives pursued by the measure at issue.[1166] An alternative will not be reasonably available when it is merely theoretical, impossible to enact by the respondent or imposes an undue burden on the respondent (either financial or technical).[1167] The assessment of a possible alternative allows for a compromise between trade restrictiveness and the right to regulate.[1168] For example, selective filtering of webpages as an alternative to blocking could be considered a less trade-restrictive alternative that would still allow the Member to achieve its desired level of protection, but it might be technically very difficult or even unfeasible.[1169] The necessity test is not based on absolute requirements, but rather a weighing and balancing of all factors in the analysis to come to a conclusion on the contested measure's necessity.[1170] It is, however, an objective standard, that can take account of a Member's characterisation of the measure and the

[1161] For this part of the test, the level of protection that is being further by the responding Member will be assessed based on the measures at issue. Panel Report, *China – Publications and Audiovisual Products*, para 7.819.

[1162] Assessing the extent of contribution in a quantitative or qualitative manner, rather than whether there is a contribution or not. AB Report, *Argentina – Financial Services*, para 6.234.

[1163] AB Report, *Korea – Various Measures on Beef*, para 164.

[1164] AB Report, *China – Publications and Audiovisual Products*, para 240.

[1165] AB Report, *Brazil – Retreated Tyres*, para 178.

[1166] AB Report, *China – Publications and Audiovisual Products*, para 318.

[1167] AB Report, *US – Gambling*, para 308.

[1168] Nuzzo (n 1153) 288–289.

[1169] Liu (n 420) 1232.

[1170] Panel Report, *Argentina – Financial Services*, paras 7.662–7.740. AB Report, *Argentina – Financial Services*, para 6.234.

effectiveness of its regulatory approach, but can also find guidance in the structure and operation of the measure.[1171]

(iii) Chapeau The important final hurdle to benefit from the justifications in Article XIV GATS is the consistency with the requirements of the chapeau. The aim of the chapeau is to ensure that the rights accorded to the Members by the substantive obligations of the GATS are not frustrated.[1172] How a particular measure is being applied can be discerned from the design, the architecture and the revealing structure of the measure.[1173] In *Argentina – Financial Services*, the Panel found that there was an absence of relationship between the measures and the objectives, which indicated an arbitrary of unjustifiable discrimination. A measure will fail the test of the chapeau when it is applied in a manner that is counterproductive to the objective.[1174] Liu noted that where Members unequally apply their (blocking) measures to domestic and foreign service suppliers, this could amount to a disguised restriction on trade in services.[1175]

The applicability of the GATS also entails the availability of the general exceptions to Members to justify measures that entail barriers to digital services trade.[1176] Especially the inclusion of the objectives of protection of public morals, public order and the protection of privacy seem to provide Members with regulatory leeway to enact measures to protect these values in the digital context, even where they constitute discrimination or create barriers to digital services trade.

6.1.4.2 Security Exceptions (Article XIV *bis* GATS)

Article XVI *bis* GATS contains the security exceptions which allow Members to take '*any action which it considers necessary for the protection of its essential security interests*'. In addition, Members

1171 AB Report, *US – Gambling*, para 304.

1172 ibid para 339.

1173 Panel Report, *Argentina – Financial Services*, para 7.748, referring to AB Report, *EC – Seal Products*, para 5.302.

1174 Panel Report, *Argentina – Financial Services*, para 7.761.

1175 Liu (n 420) 1233.

1176 The 1999 WPEC progress report also referred to Article XIV GATS, recognising the protection of privacy and public morals and the prevention of fraud as policies protected. This implies recognition of the relevance of these policies for electronic commerce. WTO Council for Trade in Services, 'Work Programme on Electronic Commerce – Progress Report to the General Council' Adopted by the Council for Trade in Services on 19 July 1999, S/L/74, 27 July 1999, para 14.

cannot be required to supply information that they consider contrary to their essential security interests and Members cannot be prevented from taking action in pursuance of their obligations under the UN Charter. The language of Article XIV *bis* is virtually identical to the security exception provision of the GATT. Due to the textual similarity of both provisions, findings on Article XXI GATT will also be relevant to the interpretation of Article XIV *bis*. Existing research on the security exceptions so far mainly presumed precedence of the national security concerns over free trade concerns.[1177]

So far, guidance on the interpretation of these provisions is quite limited. Some GATT disputes as well as the 1982 Decision Concerning Article XXI of the General Agreement shine some light on these provisions. In the 1982 Decision, the contracting parties noted the risk of trade disruption and uncertainty for international trade linked to the invocation of Article XXI GATT.[1178] Moreover, the interests of third parties may be affected by the measures justified under Article XXI GATT. Two elements contribute to the considerable policy space provided by Article XIV *bis*(b) GATS. First, the provision does not contain a chapeau, which prevents abuse and misuse of the exceptions.[1179] Second, the use of the terms 'its essential security interests' evokes an inherent subjectivity in assessing the public policy concern underlying the measure. This very broad discretion is, however, not unbridled, and a certain degree of judicial review should be maintained.[1180] The panel in *Russia – Traffic in Transit* set clear limits to the subjectivity in the assessment of Article XXI(b) GATT (and thereby its GATS equivalent). The existence of an emergency in international relations is an

[1177] As noted in Ji Yeong Yoo and Dukgeun Ahn, 'Security Exceptions in the WTO System: Bridge or Bottle-Neck for Trade and Security' (2016) 19 Journal of International Economic Law 417, 418.

[1178] General Agreement on Tariffs and Trade, *Decision Concerning Article XXI of the General Agreement*, Decision of 30 November 1982, L/5426, 2 December 1982.

[1179] GATT Panel Report, *United States – Export Restrictions (Czechoslovakia)*, 8 June 1949, BISD II/28, GATT/CP.3/SR.22, Corr.1. Van den Bossche and Zdouc (n 291) 620. Yoo and Ahn argue that the lack of a substantive chapeau *'clearly implies that the subjected provisions are aimed to be all-encompassing and strong in nature'*. Yoo and Ahn (n 1177) 422.

[1180] GATT Panel Report, *United States – Trade Measures Affecting Nicaragua*, 13 October 1986, unadopted, L/6053; see also Shin-yi Peng, 'Cybersecurity Threats and the WTO National Security Exceptions' (2015) 18 Journal of International Economic Law 449, 459.

objective state of affairs, subject to an objective determination.[1181] The subparagraphs XXI(b) GATT and XIV *bis*(b) GATS are therefore not totally '*self-judging*'.[1182]

Considering the limited guidance on the interpretation of Article XIV *bis* GATS, it is difficult to assess this provision's relevance to barriers to digital services trade. Members often justify their restrictions to cross-border data flows on the basis of national security reasons.[1183] This could hint at an attempt to justify cross-border data flow limitations under the security exception. It is important to sound a note of caution considering the risk of abuse of this exception if this exception is not subjected to a sufficient degree of judicial review. Members should not be able to qualify any trade barrier as related to the protection of their national security without due consideration. The use of the term 'essential' security interest indicates a higher standard of security interest that will have to be met by the Member invoking the provision.[1184] It has been argued that Members are allowed to exercise, in good faith, a right to be cautious, as part of their sovereign right to protect national security.[1185] Moreover, it is important to establish what 'emergency in international relations' entails. The panel in *Russia – Traffic in Transit* determined that this required evidence that the relations between the WTO Members had deteriorated to such a degree that they were a matter of concern to the international community.[1186] To meet the requirement of the chapeau of Article XIV *bis* (b), the panel must review whether the measures are so remote from or

[1181] The adjective clause 'which it considers' in the chapeau of Article XXI(b) does not qualify the determination of the circumstances in subparagraph (iii). Panel Report, *Russia – Traffic in Transit*, paras 7.77 and 7.82. This was also confirmed in Panel Report, *Saudi Arabia – Protection of IPRs*, para 7.244, in which the Panel ascertained whether the actions taken by Saudi Arabia were justified under the security exception in Article 73(b)(iii) of the TRIPS Agreement.

[1182] Panel Report, *Russia – Traffic in Transit*, para 7.102.

[1183] Tuthill (n 125) 374.

[1184] Hannes L Schloemann and Stefan Ohlhoff, '"Constitutionalization" and Dispute Settlement in the WTO: National Security as an Issue of Competence' (1999) 93 American Journal of International Law 424, 446. The Panel confirmed that 'essential security interests' is evidently a narrower concept than 'security interests': Panel Report, *Saudi Arabia – Protection of IPRs*, para 7.249.

[1185] Such good faith is however subject to judicial review. ibid 446–447.

[1186] The panel noted that it is not relevant to this determination which actor or actors bear international responsibility for the existence of the situation. Nor is it necessary for the Panel to characterise the situation under international law in general. Panel Report, *Russia – Traffic in Transit*, paras 7.121 and 7.122.

unrelated to the emergency that it is implausible that the Member implemented the measure for the protection of its essential security interest arising out of the emergency.[1187]

Peng investigated how cybersecurity threats, the avoidance of which is an often-cited policy objective related to digital services, are to be assessed under the national security exceptions.[1188] She concludes that various key questions related to the security exceptions remain unanswered. At the same time, she clarifies that a balance must be struck between free trade and the responding Member's security interests. This balancing should be informed by the principle of good faith and WTO panels play an important role in fact finding and '*seeking information from other governments or nongovernmental bodies [and] evaluating and weighing the evidence*'.[1189] The burden of proof should rest on the party invoking the security exception. Considering the requirement to establish the presence of an 'emergency in international relations' it seems unlikely that the general objective of cybersecurity would fall within the ambit of Article XIV *bis* GATS.

6.1.5 The GATS Obligations Are Applicable to Digital Services

Based on the analysis in this chapter, I conclude that none of the obligations in the GATS or its Annexes are *a priori* not applicable to digital services trade. Due to the broad scope of the GATS and the applicability of the principle of technological neutrality, Members cannot argue that digital services fall outside of the GATS' scope. However, not all of the GATS obligations apply unconditionally. For example, the market access and national treatment obligations are subject to Members having undertaken commitments in the relevant service sectors and mode of supply. The obligations on domestic regulation are equally subject to Members' commitments. However, as established in Chapter 5 of this book, digitally enabled services can be classified in a wide variety of service sectors, depending on their specific function. It is therefore highly likely that Members will have committed to at least some digitally enabled services. Of course, such an analysis must be performed on a case-by-case basis. Whether any of the GATS obligations are violated by measures

1187 Panel Report, *Russia – Traffic in Transit*, para 7.139.

1188 Peng, 'Cybersecurity Threats and the WTO National Security Exceptions' (n 1180).

1189 ibid 478. Article 13.1 DSU mandates panels to play a relatively active role in fact finding.

that restrict trade in digital services will depend on whether these measures meet all of the requirements in the respective legal tests as set out in this Section.

The GATS Annex on Telecommunications and the Reference Paper on Basic Telecommunication services both also apply to digital services. I argue that the Internet, as a network of networks, qualifies as a public telecommunications transport network, subjecting Members to the Annex's obligations on access to and use of these networks and relevant services. The applicability of the Annex ensures that foreign service suppliers have access to the Internet to supply their services to domestic consumers (but only if that Member has undertaken commitments with regard to the supplied service). The Reference Paper moreover requires major suppliers of basic telecoms services (which also include certain aspects of Internet access services) to be subject to competitive safeguards and obligations on interconnection. Both of these instruments can help ensure that the lack of access to the network or anticompetitive behaviour by ISPs does not inhibit delivery of services through electronic supply.

Not only the obligations contained in the GATS, but also its exceptions apply to digital services trade. Members can therefore try to justify their measures based on the policy objectives that have been listed in Articles XIV and XIV *bis* GATS, which include public morals, public order and privacy. Members will, however, have to establish that their measures are necessary and that the application of the measures does not constitute a means of arbitrary or unjustifiable discrimination or a disguised restriction on trade. Measures with (hidden) protectionist intent will arguably fail the requirements in these exception provisions.

6.2 The Information Technology Agreement

Even though this book focusses on trade in digital services, for which the applicable provisions can be found in the GATS, one other WTO instrument is worth mentioning in the context of digital (services) trade: the Information Technology Agreement (ITA). Strictly speaking, this Agreement goes beyond the scope of this book as it does not apply to digital services. But it is still worthwhile discussing the potential it holds to possibly address certain barriers to digital services trade.

The ITA was concluded by twenty-nine participants at the Singapore Ministerial Conference in 1996 and committed its parties to eliminate tariffs on the IT products covered by the Agreement.[1190] Its conclusion was hailed as the most significant trade liberalisation that has taken place since the WTO's creation in 1995, especially considering the scale of trade volumes liberated.[1191] The conclusion of the ITA owes much to the involvement of the ICT industry, which, due to its sourcing needs for components and specialised competences, is one of the most globalised industries.[1192] Moreover, the MFN liberalisation was ground-breaking and added much to its success.[1193] At the Nairobi Ministerial Conference in 2015, fifty-four Members agreed to the expansion of the ITA, which entailed that parties lowered or eliminated tariffs on an additional list of 201 IT products. Additionally, parties agreed to '*intensify consultations concerning non-tariff barriers in the information technology sector*'.[1194]

A wide range of information technology products are covered, including telecommunication satellites, telephones for cellular networks or for other wireless networks, other apparatus for the transmission or reception of voice, images or other data, LED Backlights modules for LCDs, DVDs, 'smart cards',[1195] transmission apparatus for radio broadcasting or television, radar apparatus, electronic assemblies for incorporation into automatic data-processing machines, multi-component integrated circuits, machinery for production of IT goods and semiconductors, multichips, machinery tools for manufacture of printed circuits of semiconductors, and other IT products. All of these products, however, seem to qualify as goods and not services. The impact of their liberalisation for trade in digital services is therefore limited to the benefits that digital

1190 This group of participants has already grown to 82. WTO Committee of Participants on the Expansion of Trade in Information Technology Products, 'Status of Implementation' Note by the Secretariat, Revision, G/IT/1/Rev.58, 10 October 2018.

1191 Lee-Makiyama (n 254) 3.

1192 ibid.

1193 MFN liberalisation within a plurilateral agreement entails that the parties to the plurilateral agreement agree to liberalise on an MFN basis, thereby also benefitting those WTO Members that are not party to the plurilateral agreement.

1194 WTO General Council, 'Ministerial Declaration on the Expansion of Trade in Information Technology Products – Communication from the European Union', WT/L/956, 25 July 2015, para 10.

1195 Cards with a built-in microprocessor, often used to perform financial transactions.

service suppliers gain from having access to IT products at lower import tariffs.[1196]

It is even stated in Attachment B to the ITA expansion that '*nothing [. . .] shall affect a member's market access rights and obligations on trade in services or prevent a Member from regulating its services markets*'.[1197] It has been proposed to extend this agreement in various ways: (i) a negative list approach with tariff classification at the four-digit level (rather than the now applied six- or eight-digit level) automatically including new products under the broader classification[1198] and (ii) to cover also NTBs and services trade.[1199]

[1196] This also includes improved access to the necessary infrastructure, thereby contributing towards battling the digital divide.

[1197] WTO General Council, 'Ministerial Declaration on the Expansion of Trade in Information Technology Products – Communication from the European Union', WT/L/956, 25 July 2015, 9.

[1198] Iana Dreyer and Brian Hindley, 'Trade in Information Technology Goods: Adapting the ITA to 21st Century Technological Change' (ECIPE 2008) 6, ECIPE Working Paper 06/ 2008 <https://ecipe.org/publications/trade-in-information-technology-goods-adapting -the-itata-to-21st-century-technological-change/>; Meltzer, 'Supporting the Internet as a Platform for International Trade Opportunities for Small and Medium-Sized Enterprises and Developing Countries' (n 9) 24.

[1199] Burri, 'The International Economic Law Framework for Digital Trade' (n 71) 48.

7

GATS Consistency of Barriers to Digital Services Trade

An analysis of measures' consistency with the GATS follows a specific sequence. First, the applicability of the GATS is assessed. The general applicability of the GATS to digital services has been established *supra* (Section 4.2) and will therefore not be revisited for the case studies in this chapter. After establishing that the GATS applies to the measures at issue, a distinction must be made between obligations that apply generally to all services and those that only apply to service sectors for which Members have undertaken commitments. Whereas general obligations can immediately be applied to the measures at issue, obligations subject to specific commitments first necessitate an enquiry into that Member's specific commitments.[1200] Assessing whether a Member has undertaken commitments for the service sector at issue involves a two-step analysis. First, the relevant service sector and mode of supply must be identified; second, the Member's commitments in that service sector and mode of supply are to be interpreted. Each of these elements will be assessed in the analysis of the measures *infra*.

When dealing with barriers to cross-border data flows and Internet access, some authors seem to focus on the wrong service sector. When assessing the GATS consistency of a measure, it is not the service sector that is being targeted by the measure that is relevant, but rather the service sector that is being affected. For example, when assessing the GATS consistency of barriers to cross-border data flows, we do not look into whether commitments have been made with respect to data transmission services but rather whether the Member has liberalised an affected service (like search engines, Internet telephony or e-payment services). Even though data flows are a necessary input into the supply of a service, they are very often not the final service that is being provided. For example, if a Member has undertaken commitments for the cross-

[1200] Moreover, the classification question is equally relevant for the interpretation of MFN exemptions.

border supply of e-payment services, the requirement to localise all (payment-related) data within that Member's territory hinders service suppliers' ability to provide that service across borders.

This chapter analyses the GATS consistency of illustrative examples of the barriers identified in Chapter 3. Even though the barriers as discussed in this book can take a wide variety of forms, the case studies have been chosen on the basis that they aptly illustrate the disruptive effects these barriers can have on international trade in services.

7.1 Restrictions on Cross-border Data Transfer

The GATS was enacted before Members generally took recourse to cross-border data transfer barriers. During the Uruguay Round, WTO Members did not discuss the possible trade-distorting nature of limitations to cross-border data flows.[1201] Thus, the GATS does not contain any specific references to or disciplines on data localisation requirements, data transfer restrictions or access restrictions to content. That does not mean that the GATS does not apply to such barriers. To the contrary, several GATS obligations are relevant in the assessment of cross-border data transfer barriers.

In the years following the conclusion of the Uruguay Round, the importance of cross-border data flows to services trade was recognised in three instances: the Telecoms Annex;[1202] the Understanding on Commitments in Financial Services;[1203] and the moratorium on customs duties on electronic transmission in the context of the WPEC.[1204] As DLRs are the textbook example of cross-border data transfer barriers, this section will discuss this type of barrier more elaborately.

Not everyone agrees on the applicability of the GATS to data flows. Lee-Makiyama argues that the GATS never intended to liberalise data transfers, but merely dealt with the liberalisation of voice communication. He posits that even though the GATS is theoretically applicable to restrictions on cross-border data, the nature of the legal commitments

1201 The Uruguay Round laid the groundwork for what would become the WTO. It is also in this context that the GATS was negotiated. Negotiations lasted from 1986 until 1994. Aaronson and Leblond (n 116) 246.

1202 See paragraphs 5(c) and 5(d) of the Annex on Telecommunications.

1203 See paragraphs 3(c) and 8 of the Understanding on Commitments in Financial Services.

1204 Mitchell and Mishra (n 307) 1091–1092.

applicable remains uncertain.[1205] In the context of the WPEC, Brazil argued that GATS mode 1 already covers data flows and that any new obligations should only be enacted for issues that cannot be addressed within the existing framework.[1206]

When assessing the GATS consistency of DLRs, several considerations should be taken into account. The first consideration relates to the relevant modes of supply. Does the requirement of storing and/or processing data locally constitute a local presence requirement? Does the requirement of local presence as a condition for cross-border supply of a service imply interlinkage between mode 1 and mode 3? If commercial presence is scheduled as the condition for the cross-border supply of a service, it would render any market access commitments under mode 1 meaningless and completely subject to whether commitments have been undertaken with regard to the third mode of supply.[1207] The local presence requirement contained in DLRs generally does not require 'commercial presence' in the sense of Article I:2(c) GATS. Looking at the definition of 'commercial presence' as found in Article XXVIII(d) GATS, it becomes clear that mode 3 does not cover every type of local presence, but requires business or professional establishment through juridical persons, branches or representative offices.[1208] The mere requirement of storing data on local servers (and possibly also processing them there) does not necessarily oblige a company to establish commercial presence locally. Rather, the DLR can be met through the local maintenance of company servers or by outsourcing the storing (and processing) of the company's data to a local data processing company. Therefore, in assessing the legality of DLRs, it is important to analyse the requirements and establish whether they necessitate commercial presence in the sense of mode 3 supply or merely any kind of local presence (which would not negate mode 1 commitments).

The second consideration relates to the obligations that would be relevant in an assessment of the GATS consistency of DLRs. Several

[1205] Hosuk Lee-Makiyama, 'Cross-Border Data Flows in the Post Bali Agenda' in Simon Evenett and Alejandro Jara (eds), *Building on Bali: A Work Programme for the WTO* (CEPR 2013) 164.

[1206] WTO Work Programme on Electronic Commerce, 'Non-Paper from Brazil', JOB/GC/98, 20 July 2016.

[1207] Peng, 'GATS and the Over-the-Top Services: A Legal Outlook' (n 102) 43.

[1208] The definition states '"*commercial presence" means any type of business or professional establishment, including through (i) the constitution, acquisition or maintenance of a juridical person, or (ii) the creation or maintenance of a branch or a representative office, within the territory of a Member for the purpose of supplying a service*'.

WTO Members, scholars and Secretariat members have provided their opinion on what obligations are most relevant when discussing DLRs.

In its communication in the context of the negotiations on the Agreement on Trade Facilitation in Services, India mentioned that it understood regulatory requirements for localisation to be a national treatment limitation of services provided through mode 1.[1209] Australia questioned this characterisation as a national treatment obligation, enquiring what the difference was with economic needs tests under Article XVI GATS (market access obligation).[1210] Peng argues that localisation requirements by their nature should be considered as falling within the ambit of the national treatment obligation, as they amount to a de facto violation of this obligation by discriminating against foreign services suppliers.[1211] Chung notes that the requirement of data localisation, which formally applies equally to domestic and foreign services and service suppliers, in practice results in less favourable treatment of the latter, which entails a violation of Article XVII GATS.[1212] It has additionally been argued that if the DLR requires the localisation of computer servers, the measures might amount to local content requirements, which would constitute a violation of the national treatment obligation.[1213] Because of the possible discriminatory effects of DLRs, the national treatment obligation is an obvious choice to challenge the GATS consistency of such measures.

Whereas the national treatment obligation is relatively uncontested in the context of DLRs, the market access obligation is not. In its 2018 communication, the United States alleged that China's limitation of cross-border data flows through leased networks and VPNs presents a barrier to market access.[1214] Chung considers it likely that DLRs would be recognised as a limitation on the number of service suppliers, operators or total quantity of service outputs, which would lead to

[1209] WTO Council for Trade in Services, special session, 'India's Responses to Issues Raised by WTO Members on the Indian Proposal on the Draft Agreement on Trade Facilitation in Services' Communication from India, RD/SERV/139, 4 May 2017, 5.

[1210] WTO Council for Trade in Services, 'Report of the Meeting Held on 16 June 2017' Note by the Secretariat, S/C/M/132, 28 August 2017, para 4.29.

[1211] Peng, 'GATS and the Over-the-Top Services: A Legal Outlook' (n 102) 43.

[1212] Chung (n 327) 197.

[1213] Tuthill (n 125) 371–372.

[1214] WTO Council for Trade in Services, WTO Council for Trade in Services, 'Measures Adopted and Under Development by China Relating to its Cybersecurity Law' Communication from the United States, S/C/W/376, 23 February 2018.

a violation of Article XVI GATS.[1215] Peng, on the other hand, explicitly excludes consideration of Article XVI GATS when assessing GATS consistency of localisation requirements as such requirements are typically non-numerical in nature.[1216] Tuthill argues that, where a Member enacts a DLR that imposes a commercial presence requirement, it will violate that Member's market access commitments. However, as explained *supra* (Section 7.1), DLRs generally do not require commercial presence but rather require local storage or processing. This does not require Members to locally set up a type of business or professional establishment.

In considering the applicability of Article XVI GATS, it will have to be established that the DLR in question is quantitative in nature (i.e. amounts to a 'zero quota').[1217] Whether this is the case will arguably depend on the services at issue. Where the services at issue constitute data processing services, it is easily conceivable how the requirement to localise data (and its processing) amounts to a zero quota on the cross-border supply of this service. Foreign companies that provide data processing services cannot provide their service through mode 1 into countries that do not allow data to be stored or processed abroad. However, where the measure at issue is any kind of digitally enabled service which does not provide data processing services to its consumers, but relies on data processing to be able to provide its service (as an input, e.g. social networks, VoIP services, e-payment services and video-on-demand services), the qualification of the DLR as a measure with a quantitative nature is much less straightforward because the requirement does not prevent the provision of these services into the Member maintaining DLRs.

In several instances, the provision on domestic regulation is mentioned in the context of DLRs. Peng argues that localisation requirements could qualify as regulatory measures and should therefore be addressed under Article VI GATS. Other scholars have mentioned that where DLRs are not administered in a reasonable, objective and impartial manner or do not contribute to the attainment of the object and purpose of the regulation, such a measure might violate Article VI GATS.[1218]

[1215] Chung (n 327) 196.
[1216] Peng, 'GATS and the Over-the-Top Services: A Legal Outlook' (n 102) 44.
[1217] A zero quota is a general prohibition to supply the service. This term was first referred to by the panel and Appellate Body in *US – Gambling*.
[1218] Chung (n 327) 196; Tuthill (n 125) 372.

The United States alleged that China's Cybersecurity Law not only constitutes a violation of the market access obligation but also that it might constitute a violation of Section 5(c) of the Telecoms Annex.[1219] As explained *supra*, Section 5(c) of the Annex requires Members to ensure unencumbered movement of data within and across borders. Similar to the Telecoms Annex, the Understanding on Commitments in Financial Services allows[1220] Members to include the commitment that they will refrain from enacting measures that prevent transfer of information or the processing of financial information where that transfer or processing is '*necessary for the conduct of the ordinary business of a financial service supplier*'.[1221]

Other GATS obligations have also been mentioned in the context of DLRs. It could be argued that DLRs constitute a violation of the MFN treatment obligation in Article II GATS if they apply data localisation measures to service suppliers from some Members but not to others (e.g. Members which have been recognised as providing an adequate level of protection). It has also been argued that some barriers to cross-border data flows take the form of domestic content requirements in government procurement.[1222] Here, we are, however, confronted with the limits of the GATS. Article XIII GATS stipulates that government procurement policies are not presently covered by the GATS.

For all of these violations, the general exceptions as set out in Article XIV GATS might provide for a justification. This will, however, only be the case if it can be shown that a sufficient nexus exists between the measure and the interest protected,[1223] that the measure meets the necessity requirement[1224] and that its application does not result in arbitrary or unjustifiable discrimination.[1225] Many different reasons have been raised for the enactment of DLRs, as mentioned *supra*

1219 WTO Council for Trade in Services, WTO Council for Trade in Services, 'Measures Adopted and Under Development by China Relating to its Cybersecurity Law' Communication from the United States, S/C/W/376, 23 February 2018.

1220 The Understanding on commitments in financial services contains commitments on which Members can base themselves when scheduling financial services. The Understanding only applies insofar its obligations have been included in a Member's Schedule.

1221 Understanding on Commitments in Financial Services, 1867 U.N.T.S. 117 (1994), para B.8.

1222 Porges and Enders (n 135) 5.

1223 AB Report, *US – Gambling*, para 292.

1224 The necessity requirement is part of the legal test for justifications under subparagraphs (a), (b) and (c) of Article XIV GATS.

1225 This requirement can be found in the chapeau of Article XIV GATS.

(Section 3.2.1). It is therefore perceivable that Members will try to justify their DLRs under the GATS' general or security exceptions in case of an alleged violation of their GATS obligations. Chung states that personal data protection is a recognised rationale under Article XIV GATS and equally sees room for a possible justification under Article XIV *bis*, considering recent events that imply state security (e.g. the Snowden revelations).[1226] Even when the objectives raised by countries to justify their restrictions on cross-border data flows are recognised under Article XIV GATS, the significant trade-restrictive effects of these measures raise questions as to whether the DLRs are necessary to meet the stated objective. Are less trade-restrictive alternatives reasonably available?[1227]

Section 5(d) of the Telecoms Annex contains a specific exception to the obligation on Members to allow movement of data across borders, permitting Members to enact measures necessary to ensure the security and confidentiality of messages. This right is subject to a chapeau-like requirement: the measure may not constitute a means of arbitrary or unjustifiable discrimination or a disguised restriction on trade. Similarly, the Understanding on Commitments in Financial Services stipulates Members' right to protect privacy, as long as this right is not used to 'circumvent' their commitment not to prevent transfer or processing of data. Balancing free movement of data with privacy protection is an important acknowledgement of the fact that free movement of data should not be the ultimate goal.

Experts have argued that the issue of cross-border data flows should be addressed at the horizontal level, rather than sector by sector.[1228] Tuthill, however, warns that negotiating binding principles on data flows might be a futile effort if no additional commitments in relevant service sectors are undertaken at the multilateral level.[1229] She additionally points out that a useful blueprint for a data flow principle can be found in footnote 8 to Article XVI GATS.[1230] This footnote states:

> *If a Member undertakes a market-access commitment in relation to the supply of a service through the mode of supply referred to in subparagraph 2 (a) of Article I and if the cross-border movement of capital is an essential part of the service itself, that Member is thereby committed to allow such movement of capital. If a Member undertakes a market-access commitment*

1226 Chung (n 327) 197–198.
1227 Ferracane (n 334) 6.
1228 Mitchell and Mishra (n 307) 1121.
1229 Tuthill (n 125) 378.
1230 ibid 380.

> *in relation to the supply of a service through the mode of supply referred to in subparagraph 2(c) of Article I, it is thereby committed to allow related transfers of capital into its territory.*[1231]

Replacing the term 'capital' with 'data' would clarify the relationship between the flow of data and the provision of the service. Data is a necessary input into many (digital) services and a commitment on these services should entail a commitment to allow for the free flow of data necessary to supply the service.

7.1.1 *Case Study: Russia's Amended Law on Personal Data*

7.1.1.1 The Measure

In July 2014, the Russian Duma adopted an amendment to its 2006 Law on Personal Data. The amendment requires operators[1232] to use databases within the territory of the Russian Federation to record, systematise, accumulate, store, clarify and retrieve personal data of Russian citizens.[1233] Moreover, operators of these databases must disclose the physical locations of datacentres.[1234] Online websites that violate the prohibition could be placed on the *Roscomnadzor*'s (Federal Communications Supervisory Service's) blacklist of websites, generally reserved for those promoting drugs and child pornography.[1235] The Russian law does, however, not impose a blanket prohibition on the

[1231] Interestingly, this provision is replicated in footnote 13 to the China – Korea RTA (2015), which is studied in more depth in Part IV of this book. None of the other RTAs analysed in Chapter 9 contained this footnote.

[1232] Operators are defined as 'a state body, a municipal body, a legal entity, or a natural individual organizing and (or) carrying out personal data processing as well as determining the purposes and the content of personal data processing'. Article 3, 2 of Federal Law dated 27 July 2006 No. 152-FZ on Personal Data.

[1233] Article 2, para 1 of Federal Law No. 242-FZ of July 21, 2014 on Amending Some Legislative Acts of the Russian Federation in as Much as It Concerns Updating the Procedure for Personal Data Processing in Information-Telecommunication Networks. Federal Law No. 242-FZ amended clauses in three different Acts: Article 1 amends Article 15 and 16 of Federal Law No. 149-FZ on Information, Information Technology and Information Security of 27 July 2006, Article 2 amends Articles 18, 22 and 23 of Federal Law dated 27 July 2006 No. 152-FZ on Personal Data and Article 3 amends Article 1 of Federal Law dated 26 December 2008 No. 294-FZ on the Protection of Rights of Legal Entities and Individual Entrepreneurs During Governmental Control (Supervision) and Municipal Control.

[1234] Article 2, para 2 of Federal Law No. 242-FZ.

[1235] Article 1 of Federal Law No. 242-FZ. This Article introduces an automated IT system, called The Register of Infringers of the Rights of Personal Data Subjects, which restricts access to webpages and network addresses that breach Russian personal data laws.

transfer and storing of the same data outside of the country, as it allows copies of data to be transferred to countries with an adequate level of protection.

The stated purpose of the law is to ensure '*protection of the rights and freedoms of a human being and a citizen in the course of processing of his personal data including protection of the rights to inviolability of private life, personal and family secret*'.[1236] The law's self-declared aim is to protect the privacy of Russian citizens. Interestingly, the law itself stipulates that international treaty rules take precedence over the Law on Personal Data.[1237]

This amendment is a clear example of a data localisation requirement, mandating service suppliers to store and process personal data collected in Russia on Russian territory.[1238] Foreign service suppliers are thereby effectively required to build/maintain/hire servers within Russia. This is an example of a broad data localisation law, as its application is not limited to specific data (related to health, finance, etc.) but applies to all personal data.[1239] Another aggravating element is the limited exceptions to the requirement to localise data processing. Most importantly, express consent by the data subject is not recognised as an exception to the requirement of localisation. Rather, only processing done for the purpose of performing a contract (one of whose parties is the data subject), for scientific purposes (if the data is depersonalised), for the protection of life, health or other vital interests (if it is impossible to obtain the data subject's consent) and for the purpose of professional activities of a journalist or legitimate activities of a mass medium or for the purposes of scientific, literary or other creative activity (if this does not violate the rights and freedoms of the data subject) are recognised as exceptions to the requirement of localisation.[1240]

1236 Article 2 of amended Federal Law No. 152-FZ.

1237 Article 4, para 4 of amended Federal Law No. 152-FZ.

1238 Article 3, 3) of amended Federal Law No. 152-FZ defines 'personal data processing' as '*actions with personal data including personal data gathering, systematizing, accumulation, storage, refinement (updating, changing), use, distribution (including transmission), depersonalization, blocking, destruction*'. Article 2 of Federal law No. 242-FZ requires several of these actions to be done through the use of servers located in Russia.

1239 Personal data is defined as '*any information pertaining to a particular or identifiable, on the basis of such information, natural individual (the personal data subject)*'. Article 3, 1 of Federal Law No. 152-FZ.

1240 Clauses 2, 3, 4 and 8 of Article 6, para 1 of Federal Law No. 152-FZ.

7.1.1.2 GATS Consistency

To allow for an in-depth assessment of the GATS consistency of Russia's data localisation requirements, I assess how they impact both data processing services as well as search engine services (as an example of a digitally enabled service). Data processing will very often be an input into (digital) services, be it performed by the service supplier itself or by an external entity to which it has outsourced this task. The range of activities that rely on data processing as an input is enormous. Therefore, this analysis wants to take a look at how DLRs affect both data processing as an end service (provided to consumers or other companies) and as an input into any other kind of service. For the latter, search engine services will be used as an example of a service that does not qualify as a data processing service but that requires significant data processing to be delivered. In distinguishing inputs from end services, the case law on 'integrated services', as explained *supra* (Section 5.1.1), should be taken into account.

(i) GATS Commitments Undertaken As regards data processing services, Russia undertook full commitments in its Services Schedule for both market access and national treatment. Russia committed to cross-border supply of all computer and related services (including data processing).[1241] As regards cross-border (mode 1) telecommunications services (including data processing), Russia only scheduled a limitation on radio communication services (including satellite communication).[1242] For commercial presence, one limitation still in force is stipulated: commercial presence must be in the form of a juridical person of the Russian Federation. None of these limitations seem to allow for barriers to the cross-border supply of data.

On search engines, Russia undertook commitments in the relevant service sector: database services (W/120 – 1.B.d as subsector of computer and related services).[1243] Russia scheduled no limitation to the market access obligation for any computer service supplied through mode 1 or 3. Regarding the national treatment obligation, Russia only scheduled a limitation to mode 3, which clarifies that it reserves the right to provide subsidies and state support on national culture or identity. It can be

[1241] WTO Trade in Services, 'Russian Federation – Schedule of Specific Commitments', GATS/SC/149, 5 November 2012, 15.

[1242] ibid 25–26.

[1243] ibid 15.

concluded that Russia is bound to provide market access and national treatment for search engine services supplied through mode 1 and mode 3.

(ii) Market Access Obligation As set out *supra* (Section 6.1.2.1), a possible violation of the market access obligation in Article XVI GATS will turn on whether the measure at issue constitutes a limitation that is quantitative in nature and falls within the ambit of one of the subparagraphs of Article XVI. If we consider the services at issue to constitute 'data processing services', it can be argued that Russia's law amounts to a zero quota in the sense of *US – Gambling*. Russia's data localisation requirement effectively prohibits the cross-border supply of data processing services in a similar way as the US gambling laws prevented the cross-border supply of gambling services. A foreign data processing service supplier will no longer be able to supply its services across borders as it is required to perform the data processing (of Russian citizen's data) within the Russian territory.

Where a specific means of supply is completely prevented by a measure, it can be argued that supply of that service through a specific mode is subject to a zero quota.[1244] Because a limitation on one, several or all means of delivery cross-border is a limitation on the number of service suppliers in the form of a numerical quota,[1245] the *de facto* prohibition of the Federal Law No. 252-FZ to supply data processing services across borders (by requiring the processing of data to happen within the territory of Russia) amounts to a violation of Article XVI:2(a) GATS. Due to the measure, the only way in which a foreign data processing service supplier can supply its services within the Russian territory is to establish locally (or at least move its core business activity to Russia). The prohibition on the supply of a service through a specific mode of supply has also been found to be inconsistent with Article XVI:2 (c) GATS, which sets out that where Members have undertaken commitments, they are not allowed to maintain limitations on the total number of service operations or on the total quantity of service output.[1246] It can therefore be concluded that Russia's DLR measure possibly amounts to a violation of Article XVI:1 and XVI:2(a) and (c) of the GATS where it affects trade in data processing services.

1244 The Appellate Body found that zero is quantitative in nature, thereby falling within the ambit of Article XVI:2(a) GATS. AB Report, *US – Gambling*, para 229.

1245 AB Report, *US – Gambling*, para 239 and Panel Report, *US – Gambling*, para 6.338.

1246 AB Report, *US – Gambling*, para 251 and Panel Report, *US – Gambling*, para 6.355.

This conclusion should, however, be nuanced. Looking at the DLR from the perspective of other (digital) services that require data processing as an input into their end service, it would be difficult to allege a violation of the market access obligation. Even though DLRs will probably hamper market access for digital services suppliers as it presents them with an additional burden to enter into or remain active in, in this case, the Russian market, the requirements do not numerically limit the number of service suppliers or service output by service suppliers that do not supply data processing services. It is conceivable that multinational digital service suppliers, like Facebook and Google, incur limited problems in meeting the DLRs, which for them do not constitute prohibitive market access barriers. This is of course different for MSMEs that want to provide their services in the territory of the Russian Federation. Nevertheless, such *de facto* possible hindrance does not constitute a violation of the market access obligation in Article XVI GATS.

(iii) National Treatment Obligation Regardless of what the services at issue are, it is clear that Russia's DLR raises crucial questions under the national treatment obligation. As argued by WTO Members and other authors alike, DLRs will highly likely constitute a violation of the national treatment obligation where commitments have been made for data processing services. In considering how the measure affects service suppliers of data processing services, the likeness of services and service suppliers will be presumed as the distinction between the compared services is solely based on the origin of the service suppliers.[1247] The *de facto* prohibition to supply data processing services across borders modifies the conditions of competition to the detriment of foreign suppliers of these services.[1248] After all, domestic service suppliers will not be affected by the measure as they already generally use domestic servers to provide their services.

The same analysis applies when assessing the impact of Russia's DLR on suppliers of other (digital) services. Continuing with the example of the search engine services, the likeness between the services at issue can be presumed as well. The measure only distinguishes based on the origin

[1247] See *supra* Section 6.1.1.1(i). Panel Report, *China – Publications and Audiovisual Products*, para 7.975.

[1248] Several other articles have pointed out the disproportionate burden of DLRs on foreign companies: Chander (n 95) 15; Meltzer, 'Governing Digital Trade' (n 172) 25; Robert Wolfe, 'Learning about Digital Trade: Privacy and E-Commerce in CETA and TPP' (2019) 18 World Trade Review 63, 80.

of the service supplier (*supra* Section 6.1.1.1(i)). By requiring the local storage and processing of personal data for all services supplied over the Internet, the conditions of competition are modified to the detriment of foreign service suppliers who will have to incur significant costs to meet these requirements. Domestic like service suppliers are provided with more favourable treatment as they will already have the capacity to store and process personal data in Russia. For example, Google, as a US company providing its services in Russia through mode 1 is treated less favourably than the Russian like service supplier Yandex, as Google will be required to establish servers locally or to outsource its data processing to a locally established company. It can therefore be argued that Russia's requirement on suppliers of search engine services to store and process data locally violates its national treatment commitments.

(iv) Section 5(c) of the Telecoms Annex The question arises whether Russia's amendment to the Law on Personal Data violates its obligation under Section 5(c) of the Telecoms Annex as the law requires foreign service suppliers to locate the databases used to collect, record, systematise, accumulate, store, clarify and retrieve personal data of Russian citizens within Russian territory.[1249] Where this requirement prevents foreign service suppliers from moving information across borders and from accessing information stored in databases in any Member, Russia violates its obligations under the Telecoms Annex. However, it is unclear how broad Section 5(c) should be interpreted. Does it only capture *de jure* prohibitions from moving data across borders or does it also prohibit Members from *de facto* limiting the possibility of transferring data across borders? Russia arguably does not impose a *de jure* prohibition on the movement of data, as it requires local collection, storing and processing but does not prevent the transfer of copies of the data. This could, however, amount to a *de facto* violation of Section 5(c) of the Telecoms Annex. Due to a lack of guidance on this issue in WTO case law, it remains to be seen how a panel would interpret the scope of Section 5(c) of the Telecoms Annex and whether a DLR such as the one maintained by Russia would be found to violate this obligation.

(v) Justification Russia would most likely try to justify its DLR arguing that it is necessary to secure compliance with laws that are not inconsistent with the GATS and that relate to the protection of the

[1249] Article 18, para 5 of Federal Law No. 152-FZ.

privacy of individuals in relation to the processing and the dissemination of personal data (Article XIV(c)(ii)).[1250] As noted *supra*, the main policy objective of the Law on Personal Data is the protection of Russian citizens' privacy. The fact that consent of the data subject is required to process his personal data arguably contributes to this objective.[1251] 'Special categories of personal data', which contain sensitive information on race, nationality, political opinions, religious or philosophical commitments, health condition and intimacies, are per definition excluded from processing unless: written consent has been provided; the personal data is public; processing is necessary for health protection; processing is done by a public association or religious organisations or for the effectuation of justice.

A first hurdle in an attempt to justify the amended Law on Personal Data under Article XIV(c) GATS is that Russia must be able to point to a measure that was enacted to protect the privacy of its citizens that is not inconsistent with the GATS (*supra* Section 6.1.4.1(i)). At first sight, the amended Law on Personal Data does not seem to have been enacted to secure compliance with privacy protection laws. Second, it will be difficult to establish that the DLR in the Federal Law is necessary to ensure compliance with a privacy protection law. Even though panels and the Appellate Body will not question the importance of privacy protection as a policy objective, the contribution of the measure to privacy protection is not straightforward.[1252] Technical evidence disproves the efficiency of DLRs: they do not reduce network vulnerabilities, do not increase government access and cause engineering inefficiencies.[1253] The fact that DLRs can undermine the goal of strengthening cybersecurity and privacy disproves that they are not necessary to achieve these aims.[1254] Moreover, the measure's ineffectiveness, combined with its considerable trade restrictiveness will make it difficult to establish that the measure is necessary to secure compliance with privacy laws.[1255] Moreover, less

[1250] As argued by Mishra: considering the fact that privacy protection is a significant contemporary policy concern, Article XIV(c)(ii) should be interpreted to include domestic laws that address this concern in the online context. Mishra (n 356).

[1251] Article 9 of Federal Law No. 242-FZ.

[1252] As set out *supra* (Section 6.1.4.1(ii)), the necessity test requires a weighing and balancing of three factors: the importance of the values pursued, the contribution of the measure to those values and the trade-restrictiveness of the measure.

[1253] Mishra (n 356).

[1254] Meltzer, 'Governing Digital Trade' (n 172) 40.

[1255] Even though the direct economic impact of DLRs is difficult to assess, it is a fact that compliance with them is costly, that companies might be unwilling to move servers to

trade-restrictive and reasonably available alternatives can be imagined: instead of requiring local processing of data, Russia could safeguard the privacy of its citizens through (strict) requirements as to how the processing should be performed.[1256]

The chapeau of Article XIV GATS poses additional problems, as Russia will have to show that it is not applying the measure in a way that constitutes a means of arbitrary or unjustifiable discrimination or a disguised restriction on trade in services (*supra* Section 6.1.4.1(iii)). Here, it might be questioned why Russia is adamant on the processing of the data happening within the Russian territory but does not prevent copies of (sensitive) personal data from being transferred to countries which have an 'adequate level of protection'. How will Russia be able to justify the distinction between transfer of copies and processing? Why is the recognition of other countries having an adequate level of protection not sufficient for processing data abroad? The unlikely justifiability under the chapeau also entails that it will be unlikely that Russia would be able to justify a breach under Section 5(d) of the Telecoms Annex.[1257]

Justification under the security exceptions in Article XIV *bis* GATS does not seem to be a viable option. Russia will not be able to claim that domestic data processing is necessary for its essential security interests relating to the provisioning of a military establishment or to a situation of war or other emergency in international relations (*supra* Section 6.1.4.2).

7.1.2 Case Study: EU's General Data Protection Regulation

7.1.2.1 The Measure

The European Union's General Data Protection Regulation (GDPR) contains a conditional data flow regime, as it puts stringent conditions on the transfer of personal data to third countries. To understand the importance of the comprehensive data protection regime, the EU's view on the right to privacy should be taken into account. The EU values highly the right to privacy (and data protection) as a fundamental human

countries with inadequate regulatory and physical infrastructure and that the costs of compliance might be prohibitive for MSMEs. Mishra (n 356).

1256 Mishra, however, cautions that due to the lack of international standards on data privacy and cybersecurity, it will be difficult for a panel to assess whether alternative measures achieve the desired level of protection (which a WTO Member is allowed to set itself). ibid.

1257 This justification clause also requires measures not to be applied in a manner which would constitute a means of arbitrary or unjustifiable discrimination or a disguised restriction on trade in services.

right, contained in various instruments.[1258] The GDPR references this background, stating that its goal is to protect fundamental rights and freedoms of natural persons, especially the right to protection of personal data.[1259]

The GDPR has a very broad scope, both materially and geographically. It applies to '*the processing of personal data wholly or partly by automated means and to the processing other than by automated means of personal data which form part of a filing system*', which is done in the context of the activities of a controller or processor which is established in the EU, regardless of whether the processing is happening within the EU's territory or not.[1260] The GDPR's geographical scope even stretches to the processing of personal data of EU citizens by controllers or processors that are not established in the Union but that offer their goods or services to EU consumers or that monitor citizens within the EU.[1261] In addition, the GDPR defines several key terms broadly: 'personal data' is '*any information relating to an identified or identifiable natural person*' and 'processing' is understood as operations performed on personal data including '*collection, recording, organisation, structuring, storage, adaptation or alteration, retrieval, consultation, use, disclosure by transmission, dissemination or otherwise making available, alignment or combination, restriction, erasure or destruction*'.[1262]

The GDPR sets out a general principle for the transfer of personal data that is undergoing processing or is intended for processing to third countries. It only allows such transfers if all the conditions in chapter V of the GDPR are complied with by both the controller and the

[1258] See Article 8(a) European Union, *Charter of Fundamental Rights of the European Union*, 26 October 2012, 2012/C 326/02 (Charter of Fundamental Rights), Article 8 Council of Europe, *European Convention for the Protection of Human Rights and Fundamental Freedoms, as amended by Protocols Nos. 11 and 14*, 4 November 1950, ETS 5 (European Convention of Human Rights) and various member states' constitutions. Mattoo and Meltzer (n 836) 772.

[1259] Article 1.2 of the Regulation (EU) 2016/679 of the European Parliament and of the Council of 27 April 2016 on the protection of natural persons with regard to the processing of personal data and on the free movement of such data, and repealing Directive 95/46/EC (General Data Protection Regulation) OJ L 119, 4 May 2016, 1–88 (GDPR).

[1260] See Articles 2 and 3 GDPR. The controller is the person (natural or legal) which determines the purposes and means of the processing of personal data, whereas the processor is the person that processes personal data on behalf of the controller.

[1261] Article 3(2) GDPR. Recitals 23 and 24 offer some additional explanation of what is understood under 'offering for sale' and 'monitoring'.

[1262] Article 4(1) and (2) GDPR.

processor.[1263] Two general grounds for the transfer of personal data are provided: either on the basis of an adequacy decision or on the basis of appropriate safeguards. Adequacy decisions are made by the European Commission, which ensures that the third country guarantees an adequate level of protection taking into account *inter alia* respect for the rule of law, human rights and fundamental freedoms, the relevant legislation, the presence of independent supervisory authorities and relevant international commitments.[1264] The CJEU clarified that an adequacy decision requires that the privacy regime under scrutiny is essentially equivalent to that of the EU.[1265]

Alternatively, controllers or processors may transfer personal data to a third country if they provide appropriate safeguards and enforceable rights and remedies are available.[1266] The regulation provides various grounds which substantiate the appropriate safeguards, including a legally binding and enforceable instrument between public authorities, binding corporate rules, use of the Commission's standard data protection clauses and so forth.

Without an adequacy decision or appropriate safeguards, personal data can still be transferred if one of the following conditions has been met: explicit consent of fully informed data subject, transfer is necessary for the performance of a contract between data subject and controller, transfer is necessary for conclusion or performance of contract in the interest of data subject, transfer is necessary for important reasons of public interest, necessary for legal claims, necessary to protect vital interests of data subject or transfer is done from a public register.[1267]

1263 This is also required for any subsequent transfer to other third countries or international organisations. Article 44 GDPR.

1264 Article 45 GDPR. So far, Andorra, Argentina, Canada (commercial organisations), Faroe Islands, Guernsey, Israel, Isle of Man, Jersey, New Zealand, Switzerland and Uruguay have received a national adequacy finding. Disregarding the self-governing islands part of EU member states and two states on the European continent with which the EU maintains very close economic ties, the list looks very limited, with only 5 adequacy findings of third countries. The EU, however, reports ongoing adequacy talks with South Korea and a pending adoption procedure of the adequacy decision concerning Japan. European Commission, 'Adequacy of the protection of personal data in non-EU countries', available at <https://ec.europa.eu/info/law/law-topic/data-protection/data-transfers-outside-eu/adequacy-protection-personal-data-non-eu-countries_en>.

1265 Case C-362/14, *Maximilian Schrems v Data Protection Commissioner*, Judgement of the Court (Grand Chamber) of 6 October 2015, EU:C:2015:650, paras 73–74.

1266 Article 46 GDPR.

1267 Article 49(1) GDPR.

Even in the absence of these derogations, transfer of personal data to third countries is still allowed if the transfer is not repetitive, concerns only a limited number of data subjects, is necessary for the purposes of compelling legitimate interests pursued by the controller and if the controller has assessed all circumstances surrounding the data transfer and has provided suitable safeguards with regard to the protection of the personal data.[1268]

Mattoo and Meltzer argue that none of these derogations are suitable for businesses collecting and transferring personal data outside the EU.[1269] To illustrate the difficulty developing countries face in complying with the strict requirements of the GDPR, they studied the regulation's impact on India. They conclude that developing countries are confronted with the impossible decision to either adopt 'GDPR adequate' privacy regulation and thereby gain access to the important EU market or not to adopt prematurely stringent privacy laws, to avoid hurting efficiency and development of important (digital) domestic markets.[1270] In particular, they point out the requirement of physical presence in the EU in order to use binding corporate rules or standard contractual clauses as a prohibitive barrier to many service suppliers from developing countries.[1271]

Through the GDPR, the EU imposes considerable restraints on the cross-border flows of personal data. It is quite easily conceivable how the strict requirements on transfers to non-EU member states as contained in chapter V GDPR limit companies' ability to transfer data, thereby hampering the provision of digital services. Even though the GDPR does not contain a *de jure* data localisation requirement, there is an outstanding question as to whether the strict transfer requirements amount to a *de facto* data localisation requirement. As seen in Part II of this book, data localisation requirements have been defined very broadly, basically encompassing any measure that limits the ability of data to move globally.[1272] It can therefore be concluded that the GDPR effectively imposes a *de facto* DLR. Moreover, due to the GDPR's very broad scope of application (covering all personal data and any company with [intended] activities in the EU), these requirements constitute broad

[1268] The controller is additionally required to inform the supervisory authority and the data subject of the transfer. Article 49(1) GDPR.
[1269] Mattoo and Meltzer (n 836) 777.
[1270] ibid 778 and 788.
[1271] ibid 779.
[1272] See *supra* Section 5.1. Meltzer, 'A New Digital Trade Agenda' (n 292) 5.

DLRs. However, as data localisation requirements in and of themselves are not prohibited, it is worthwhile looking into whether the GDPR incurs any GATS inconsistency.

7.1.2.2 GATS Consistency

(i) MFN Obligation Sen argues that the GDPR's 'adequacy' test might violate the EU's MFN obligation.[1273] Depending on how the European Commission applies Article 45 GDPR and reaches its adequacy decisions, a violation of the MFN obligation could be found if like[1274] service suppliers from countries with similar or identical levels of protection of data are not both accorded an adequacy decision by the European Commission. The WTO Member which adequately protects data, but for which the Commission does not recognise its adequate level of protection, will be treated less favourably than any other Member with a like level of protection that *is* accorded an adequacy decision. Here, it should be cautioned that the autonomy of the Commission in its decision-making is limited by the listed elements that have to be taken into account when assessing the adequacy of the level of protection.[1275] Where these (neutral) criteria are applied in a non-discriminatory manner, it will be difficult to allege less favourable treatment of like service suppliers from different Members.

(ii) Market Access Obligation Mattoo and Meltzer argue that a GDPR ban on cross-border data transfer can be deemed a zero quota, inconsistent with the EU's market access commitments.[1276] Other authors disagree based on the many derogations the GDPR foresees and the fact that there has never been a full ban on data transfer.[1277] Irion, Yakovelva and Bartl conclude that there is no risk of a market access violation, as the rules on transfer of personal data to third

1273 Sen (n 118) 335.

1274 Whether the services affected by the GDPR are like will have to be determined on a case-by-case basis. The most pertinent likeness factor to take into account will be consumer preference, as this will likely be impacted to some extent by the level of privacy protection. Kristina Irion, Svetlana Yakovleva and Marija Bartl, 'Trade and Privacy: Complicated Bedfellows? How to Achieve Data Protection-Proof Free Trade Agreements' (Institute for Information Law, University of Amsterdam 2016) 30 <www.ivir.nl/projects/trade-and-privacy-complicated-bedfellows-how-to-achieve-data-protection-proof-free-trade-agreements/>.

1275 Article 45(2) GDPR.

1276 Mattoo and Meltzer (n 836) 780.

1277 Irion, Yakovleva and Bartl (n 1276) 31–32.

countries apply indiscriminately to both domestic and foreign controllers.[1278] This argument does, however, not hold as the market access obligation does not contain a non-discrimination obligation.

I consider it difficult to argue a violation of the market access obligation, as the GDPR does not (*de jure* or *de facto*) prevent data processing from taking place outside of the territory of the EU (which would arguably constitute a zero quota on data processing services through mode 1). The regulation only puts certain (stringent but not impossible) requirements on the transfer of data across borders. However, none of these requirements are quantitative in nature in the sense of Article XVI:2 GATS. Especially taking into account the various derogatory grounds for transfer in Article 49 GDPR, it can hardly be maintained that the GDPR contains a quantitative limitation on the number of cross-border service suppliers (of data processing services).

(iii) National Treatment Obligation Irion, Yakovelva and Bartl conclude that a violation of the national treatment obligation is possible considering that the GDPR '*exacerbate[s] the duplication of regulatory requirements for third countries' services and service suppliers*', thereby according less favourable treatment to foreign service suppliers.[1279]

On their face, the requirements for cross-border transfer of data to third countries apply to all controllers or processors that supply their services to EU citizens, regardless of the nationality of the service provider. Whereas paragraph 1 of Article 3 states that the regulation applies to the processing of personal data in the context of the activities of an establishment of a controller or a processor in the Union, paragraph 2 widens the scope of the regulation by including processing of personal data of EU citizens by controllers or processors not established in the Union. It is, however, the nature of the data localisation requirements that is inherently discriminatory. Whereas data can be moved, stored and processed freely within the territory of the EU, strict requirements apply to data that is moved across borders with the intention of processing it in a third country (or to data that is already being processed). It goes without saying that EU companies, which process all of their data in the EU, will be much less constrained by the requirements of the GDPR than foreign companies that provide their services in the EU but that need to move personal data of EU citizens outside of the EU for

[1278] ibid 31.
[1279] ibid 33.

processing. In that sense, it could be argued that the GDPR leads to *de facto* less favourable treatment of like foreign services and service suppliers. Others have identified the failure to extend the 'one-stop shop' mechanism to all data processors and controllers, both domestic and foreign, as a possible violation of the national treatment obligation.[1280]

(iv) Justification Here as well, it should be cautioned that the trade restrictiveness of the requirements of the GDPR is much more limited than that of other DLRs. Because of the number of different grounds on which cross-border transfer of data is allowed under the GDPR, it could be argued that the restrictive impact on trade by foreign service suppliers is limited. The level of trade restrictiveness is an important element to take into account in the necessity test that forms part of a justification under Article XIV GATS. If the GATS consistency of the GDPR would be challenged before the WTO dispute settlement mechanism, the EU would argue the (relatively) low level of trade restrictiveness of the measure. Arguably, the GDPR is necessary to protect public morals (considering how highly privacy is valued within the EU[1281]) in the sense of Article XIV(a), or to ensure compliance with a law relating to the protection of privacy of individuals (Article XIV(c)).[1282] Additionally, it may well be found that the GDPR does not violate the chapeau, as its many grounds on which controllers and processors may base their appropriate safeguards and the derogations that allow for cross-border transfer of data will make it difficult to argue that the GDPR is applied in such a way that constitutes arbitrary or unjustifiable discrimination or a disguised restriction on trade. Based on the importance of privacy as a human right to the EU, it has been deemed likely that a WTO panel would accept the GDPR as necessary to protect public morals.[1283] Therefore, even if the GDPR would be found to violate the MFN or national treatment obligations for its restriction on cross-border data flows, it would not seem impossible for such a violation to be justified under Article XIV GATS.

[1280] Mattoo and Meltzer (n 836) 780–781.

[1281] Mira Burri and Rahel Schär, 'The Reform of the EU Data Protection Framework: Outlining Key Changes and Assessing Their Fitness for a Data-Driven Economy' (2016) 6 Journal of Information Policy 479, 481; Mattoo and Meltzer (n 836) 771.

[1282] The latter could for example be Article 8 of the EU Charter on Fundamental Rights, which establishes everyone's right to the protection of personal data concerning him or her.

[1283] Mattoo and Meltzer (n 836) 781.

7.2 Web Filtering and Content Control

Web filtering and content control impede trade in digital services. They create significant obstacles for service suppliers to access consumers in a specific market, provide consumers with sufficient information and market them successfully. Because government control determines what content is available to its citizens, companies are powerless in their attempt to access new markets or remain operative in markets that are faced with increased web filtering.

Various GATS obligations can be considered relevant in the context of web filtering as a barrier to trade. First of all, the MFN treatment obligation could be violated where governments discriminate between WTO Members trying to supply their services across borders. This is the case when governments consistently block websites of service suppliers from the other side of the world, while they are more lenient when it comes to filtering Internet traffic with (geographically and/or politically) neighbouring countries. Another general obligation that risks being violated is the transparency obligation as found in Article III GATS. The practices of web filtering and content control are inherently opaque, with very limited information available to foreign service suppliers on how to comply with the (invisible) requirements that determine whether access to their website is granted or not.

Three obligations subject to the commitments undertaken by Members are at risk of being breached by web filtering of content control. Where web filtering or content control qualifies as a qualitative minimum requirement, it might violate the provisions on domestic regulation as set out in Article VI:5 GATS. Where the measure establishing the web filtering or content control is found to be discriminatory and/or quantitative in nature, the national treatment and market access obligations apply. It is these three obligations that will be applied to the example of China's Great Firewall.

7.2.1 Case Study: China's Great Firewall – The Measure(s)

The Chinese Central Government has been maintaining a system of limiting access to foreign websites since the 1990s. This practice has been referred to as the 'Great Firewall'.[1284] Ferracane and Lee-

[1284] Three regulations form the basis for China's Internet censorship policy: The Computer Information System Security Protection Regulations of the People's Republic of China (Peoples Republic of State Council Decree No. 147) of 18 February 1994 and the

Makiyama define it as a '*system based on centralised control over international gateways, filtering online content or blocking access entirely to some of the most common websites on the public Internet*'.[1285] Currently, the Great Firewall blocks access to a high number of foreign websites and slows down cross-border Internet traffic '*necessary to maintain social stability and national security*'.[1286] Blocking websites or 'web filtering' is thus justified on several bases, including preventing cybercrime (which since 2015 also encompasses network service providers' failure to perform network security obligations[1287]), ensuring network security and preserving cyberspace sovereignty, national security and the societal public interest.[1288]

Blocking or filtering websites can be done in a variety of ways. Ferracane and Lee-Makiyama identify three of them: tampering with domain name systems, http-request filtering or the blocking of virtual private networks.[1289] Liu clarifies that in China, Internet connections are controlled by a handful of state-run operations that maintain advanced international gateways.[1290] At these gateways, 'packets' of electronic information are passed through Chinese government-owned Internet routers, who then either 'lose' the information and return an error page or redirect the users to websites that have been deemed safe or politically correct.[1291] To identify how to handle electronic information, the government maintains a(n unpublished) list of banned sites ('access control list').[1292]

There is no specific legal basis for or official admission of the existence of the 'Great Firewall'. A patchwork of different laws and regulations

Computer Information Network and Internet Security, Protection and Management Regulation of 11 December 1997 and the Administrative Measures on Internet Information Services of 20 September 2000.

1285 Ferracane and Lee-Makiyama (n 296) 7.

1286 An updated list of blocked websites is available on the website of the non-profit organisation Greatfire: <https://en.greatfire.org/search/alexa-top-1000-domains>.

1287 Article 285 of Standing Committee of the National People's Congress, *Amendment IX of the Criminal Law of the People's Republic of China*, Order No. 30 of the President of the People's Republic of China, 29 August 2015.

1288 Article 1 of China's 2016 Cybersecurity Law.

1289 Since 2017 the Chinese government requires VPNs to be approved for sale in China, which leads to more blocking of VPNs. Aaronson and Leblond (n 116) 266; Ferracane and Lee-Makiyama (n 296) 7.

1290 Liu (n 420) 1207.

1291 ibid 1208.

1292 New services are automatically added to this list of blocked websites. ibid 1208, 1229; Ferracane and Lee-Makiyama (n 296) 7.

enables the Chinese government to keep a close eye on all Internet traffic coming into the country. The 1993 State Security Law gave Chinese security institutions access to 'any information or data held by an entity in China' whenever necessary.[1293] Regulation no. 291 imposes an *ex ante* licensing regime: to operate any website in China, an 'Internet Content Provider License' is required.[1294] The 2016 Cybersecurity Law provided the Chinese government with even more power to block (foreign) websites.[1295] This law, implemented in June 2017, includes an obligation of national security review of 'critical information infrastructure operators', extensive accountability for information published by users on their platform as well as the dissemination of this information online and strict data localisation requirements.[1296] Web filtering was then further embedded into China's legal framework through the inclusion of the closing down of websites and cancellation of operation permits and business licenses as sanctions, and by the right reserved for the government to restrict network communications in particular regions to protect national security and social public order.[1297] Additionally, cloud services can only be supplied by a foreign supplier in a joint venture in which the Chinese company has the majority stake.[1298] Since June 2017, providers of online news and information services need to obtain an 'Internet news information services licence' to provide their services through websites, apps, messaging services and so forth.[1299] The State Security Law was updated in 2016 and now requires digital service and content providers to monitor their users' behaviour to ensure public safety. These obligations are imposed under penalty of fines, revocation of licenses or criminal

[1293] Articles 11 and 18 of Standing Committee of the National People's Congress, *State Security Law of the People's Republic of China*, Order No. 68 of the President of the People's Republic of China, 22 February 1993.

[1294] In order to qualify for such a license, companies must submit to Chinese jurisdiction, establish themselves locally and prevent inappropriate content. Telecommunications Regulations of the People's Republic of China. Decree of the State Council of the People's Republic of China No. 291, 25 September 2000; Ferracane and Lee-Makiyama (n 296) 7; Liu (n 420) 1210.

[1295] It should be noted that the 2016 Cybersecurity Law applies to (and affects) both domestic and foreign companies. It, however, adds to the phenomenon of the Great Firewall, which only targets foreign companies.

[1296] Respectively Articles 35, 46–48 and 37 of China's 2016 Cybersecurity Law. An unofficial translation of this law was consulted at <www.chinalawtranslate.com>.

[1297] Additionally, the vague obligations and definitions included in the law make it hard for foreign firms to assess and comply with their obligations.

[1298] Aaronson and Leblond (n 116) 266.

[1299] Article 5 of the Internet News Information Service Management Regulations, which entered into force on 1 June 2017.

prosecution. This increases self-censorship by foreign service suppliers.[1300]

The control exercised over the Internet by the Chinese government is almost endless, with the government delegating and outsourcing censorship and surveillance to ISPs, Internet content providers (ICPs) and even cybercafé owners.[1301] Delegation is enforced through the threat of sanctions: revocation of business licenses or complete shutdown of operations in China. Moreover, Chinese computer producers and users have access to the software program 'Green Dam', which was supposed to protect children from pornography but actually allows the software company to gather information on user activity and censor religious and political content.[1302]

The presence of only state-owned enterprises (SOEs) in the telecommunications sector is another contributing factor to the absolute control of the Chinese government on the Internet. An incumbent SOE dominates the telecoms market for each specific telecom product.[1303] Even though foreign participation in the telecoms market is not restricted *de jure*, foreign competition is *de facto* impossible since all available licenses are in use.[1304] An example can be found in VoIP services: these services qualify as 'value-added telecom services', which requires a specific license. Moreover, to interconnect the VoIP services with the public switched telecoms network, an additional traditional operator license is required.[1305] Such licenses are (or can) often not (be) granted, leading to *de facto* impossibility to provide services in China. Other 'value-added telecom services' include online database storing and searching, online data and transactions processing, domestic multiparty communication service, cloud computing, data centre services, electronic data exchange, IP-VPN, ISP and ICP services, video teleconferencing and call centre services. None of these can be supplied by wholly owned foreign subsidiaries.[1306]

1300 Aaronson and Leblond (n 116) 266.

1301 Liu (n 420) 1209.

1302 ibid 1210.

1303 Ferracane and Lee-Makiyama (n 296) 9–10.

1304 The licensing requirements for basic telecommunications services and value-added telecommunications services can be found in Articles 10–13 of the Telecommunications Regulations of the People's Republic of China, Decree of the State Council of the People's Republic of China No. 291, 25 September 2000. A basic telecommunication service provider (which provides 'basic facilities of public networks, public data transmission and basic speech communication') is required to be at least 51 per cent state owned. ibid 10.

1305 ibid.

1306 Of all value-added telecoms services, only e-commerce has been opened up. ibid.

Of course, various different regulatory objectives are mentioned by China. The 2016 Counterterrorism Law is justified on the basis of 'public safety', considering that it requires companies, telecom suppliers and ISPs to monitor users.[1307] Another (yet implicit) objective is the implementation of national industrial policies.[1308] China fosters its domestic champions through limiting foreign participation in the domestic market and by enacting export contingent policies.[1309]

In practice, the Great Firewall limits or impedes access to foreign information sources, blocks foreign Internet tools (e.g. Google search, Facebook) and mobile apps (e.g. WhatsApp), and requires foreign companies to adapt to domestic regulations, as was done by Google from 2006 until 2010.[1310] It has been claimed that this web filtering has nurtured domestic companies (Tencent and Alibaba) at the expense of foreign competitors.[1311] Erixon et al. substantiate this alleged economic damage by comparing Google's market share in China and Japan and contrasting it with the growth of its Chinese competitor.[1312] It should, however, be recognised that whereas domestic companies are indeed not subject to the Great Firewall, they are required to comply with local laws, under penalty of being shut down at the source rather than being blocked.[1313]

7.2.2 Case Study: China's Great Firewall – GATS Consistency

It will be assessed whether China's filtering of an extensive number of foreign websites constitutes a violation of its market access and/or its national treatment obligations. To show how the Great Firewall, and more specifically the 2016 Cybersecurity Law, are applied, the analysis

1307 ibid 8.

1308 In this, China differs considerably from other Asian developing countries: whereas other countries have tended to phase out national industrial policy as domestic industry got more competitive, this is not the case for China. ibid 3–6.

1309 Through preferable corporate tax regimes, no possibility for foreign firms to apply for ICT accreditation, 'buy Chinese' policies in government procurement, etc.

1310 The Economist, 'Google and China: Searching questions', 22 March 2010, available at <www.economist.com/business/2010/03/22/searching-questions>.

1311 The Economist, 'China adopts a tough cyber-security law', 10 November 2016, available at <www.economist.com/china/2016/11/10/china-adopts-a-tough-cyber-security-law >. See also Aaronson and Leblond (n 116) 264 referring to number provided by the United States Chamber of Commerce and the European Chamber of Commerce.

1312 In 2008, Google's market share had dropped to less than 19 per cent in China, to the benefit of Baidu (its Chinese competitor). In Japan, Google's market share was more than 90 per cent at that time. Erixon, Hindley and Lee-Makiyama (n 413) 5–6.

1313 ibid 5.

will build on two examples. Because the Great Firewall blocks a myriad of websites, I use the blocking of Google's electronic mail services ('Gmail') and its video distribution service ('YouTube') as examples.

(i) GATS Commitments Undertaken As a preliminary point it should be mentioned that some authors have argued that, due to the fact that at the time of China's accession to the WTO the CPC1.0 was in force, those CPC codes should be taken into account.[1314] However, this argumentation does not hold under closer scrutiny. The W/120 was drafted on the basis of the CPCprov, and China, in the working party report on its accession, clearly stated that services classification is done based on the W/120 document.[1315] The impact of such argument can be illustrated by considering the example of classifying 'search engine' services. If CPC1.0 would be used for the classification of search engine services, it would classify as a data processing service (CPC1.0 843 'on-line information provision services', which explicitly includes search engines), for which China has undertaken full market access and national treatment commitments. Rather, based on a teleological interpretation as furthered in Part II of this book, and using the CPCprov as a basis, search engine services classify as database services (for which China did not undertake any commitments).

The service Google is trying to supply through 'Gmail' in China via cross-border supply (mode 1) is that of 'electronic mail', a subsector of telecommunications services. For that subsector and mode of supply, China has scheduled a limited commitment on market access, but no limitation (i.e. full commitment) on national treatment. However, as clarified by Article XX:2 GATS, a limitation inscribed in the market access column will also provide a limitation to the national treatment obligation. It is therefore crucial to further interpret China's scheduled commitments. For electronic mail supplied through mode 1, reference is made to mode 3 (the limitation included merely states 'see mode 3'). For mode 3, the scheduled limitation states that '*Foreign service suppliers will*

1314 Wu (n 48) 282; Erixon, Hindley and Lee-Makiyama (n 413) 10–12; References found in Gao, 'Googling for the Trade-Human Rights Nexus in China: Can the WTO Help?' (n 690) 258.

1315 WTO, 'Report of the Working Party on the Accession of China', WT/ACC/CHN/49, 1 October 2001, 138. Moreover, nothing in China's Accession Protocol alters its trade in services commitments as contained in its Schedule of Commitments. WTO, 'Accession of the People's Republic of China' Decision of 10 November 2001, WT/L/432, 23 November 2001.

be permitted to establish joint venture value-added telecommunication enterprises, without quantitative restrictions [. . .]. Within two years after China's accession, there will be no geographic restriction and foreign investment shall be no more than 50 per cent.'[1316] Does this imply that supply of electronic mail through mode 1 can only be provided by foreign companies if they are a minority part of a joint venture?[1317] If China's service schedule must be interpreted this way, the cross-border supply of value-added telecommunications services is conditioned on the local presence of foreign service suppliers.[1318] This entails that under China's Schedule of Commitments, Google does not have the right to provide its services cross-border into China. The blocking of Gmail does therefore not constitute a violation of China's market access or national treatment obligation.

Considering the blocking of Google's video distribution service YouTube as the second example, it has to be assessed whether China has undertaken commitments on audiovisual services regarding the first mode of supply. More specifically, whether Chinas has undertaken commitments with regard to television transmission services (W/120 – 2.D.d) as it was established in Chapter 5 that this is the correct classification for video-on-demand services. Looking into China's Services Schedule, it becomes clear that it did not undertake commitments for all audiovisual subsectors. Moreover, China does not seem to have followed the W/120 structure, as it only refers to the subsectors 'videos, including entertainment software and (CPC 83202), distribution services', 'sound recording distribution services' and 'cinema theatre services'. None of these subsectors can be found in the W/120. It must therefore be assessed whether

1316 WTO Trade in Services, 'The People's Republic of China – Schedule of Specific Commitments', GATS/SC/135, 14 February 2002, 17. Interestingly, footnote 3 to the Schedule also states '*All international telecommunications services shall go through gateways established with the approval of China's telecommunications authorities, which will act as an independent regulatory authority in accordance with the principles of paragraph 5 of the Reference Paper*'.

1317 The Secretariat also signalled the ambiguity of scheduling commercial presence requirements as a limitation for mode 1, as it is often unclear whether cross-border supply is not allowed at all or whether cross-border supply is allowed as long as some type of commercial presence is maintained. WTO Council for Trade in Services, 'Cross-Border Supply (Modes 1& 2)' Background Note by the Secretariat, S/C/W/304, 18 September 2009, para 31.

1318 Admittedly, this negates the use of a mode 1 commitment, as a company does not supply its services across borders if it has commercial presence in that Member. However, it is seemingly impossible to interpret the reference to mode 3 in a different way.

'video distribution services' as included in China's Schedule encompass 'television transmission services'. Unfortunately, China did not include a reference to corresponding CPC categories, which makes analysis of the meaning of the subsector harder. Even though there seems to be a textual link to the existing CPC subsector 'motion picture and video tape production and distribution services' (W/120 – 2.D.a), the conscious omission of the reference to 'tape' and the included reference to 'entertainment software' leads to the consideration that 'video distribution services' in China's Schedule does include the transmission of videos in whatever format. This consideration is supported by the fact that the wording used for the subsector scheduled by China is demonstrably more technologically neutral than that found in the CPC.

If we consider that the services supplied by YouTube classify as 'video distribution services' in China's Schedule, China would be committed to provide both market access and national treatment to these service suppliers, as it did not schedule any limitations to either obligation.[1319] Should it be found that YouTube's services do not fall within the ambit of 'video distribution services', it can only be concluded that China did not undertake commitments for these service sectors and that its measures cannot be found inconsistent with Article XVI or XVII GATS.

(ii) Market Access Obligation Members and scholars alike have voiced their opinion on how web filtering might constitute a violation of the market access obligation. In its non-paper to the WPEC, Chinese Taipei argued that '*the overall blockage of a foreign website, either for its failure to comply with data localization requirements or for any other reasons, may be considered a "limitation on the number of service suppliers" under Article XVI:2(a) of GATS given its equivalent effect of zero quota*'. At the same time, Chinese Taipei noted that it failed to see how Internet filtering would violate Article XVI:2(c) GATS, as it does not consider Internet filtering to limit the total quantity of service output in the form of quotas or an economic needs test.[1320] In a similar line, the

[1319] WTO Trade in Services, 'The People's Republic of China – Schedule of Specific Commitments', GATS/SC/135, 14 February 2002, 21.

[1320] WTO General Council, Work Programme on Electronic Commerce, 'Removing Cyberspace Trade Barriers: Towards a Digital Environment with Reciprocally Equal Access – Non-Paper from the Separate Customs Territory of Taiwan, Penghu, Kinmen and Matsu', JOB/GC/170, 16 February 2018, para 3.4.

USTR labelled China's Internet censorship as a barrier to trade in its 2016 National Trade Estimate Report.[1321] Gao has already partially discussed the issue of whether Internet filtering constitutes a trade barrier. He states that the total blocking of a website probably constitutes a zero quota, which, as established in the *US – Gambling* case, amounts to a violation of the market access obligation in Article XVI GATS.[1322] However, selective filtering of, for example, search results in a search engine is not quantitative but rather qualitative, and therefore would not violate Article XVI GATS.[1323]

Once it is established that relevant commitments have been undertaken, it should be assessed whether the measure constitutes an impermissible quantitative limitation as found in the subparagraphs of Article XVI:2 GATS. The most relevant limitations for the measure at issue are those described in paragraphs (a) and (c) of Article XVI:2: limitations on the number of service suppliers and limitations on the total number of service operations or on the total quantity of service output, respectively. Even though the blocking of the service supplier YouTube clearly prevents market access for its mother company, Google, the 2016 Cybersecurity Law is not quantitative in nature.[1324] It does not quantitatively limit the number of service suppliers (paragraph a) nor does it quantitatively limit the total output of the service supplied (paragraph c). Only in the particular circumstance where all service suppliers of a particular service sector would be blocked in China can the measure be considered to constitute a *de facto* zero quota on cross-border supply of that service in the sense of the *US – Gambling* case (where a whole means of delivery was excluded by the United States; *supra* Section 6.1.2.1).

As the web filtering done by China is intermittent, changeable and very opaque, it is difficult to contend that it will definitely violate China's market access obligations in the sense of Article XVI GATS. However, an aggravating circumstance is the fact that all new services are automatically put on the list of blocked websites before they can be considered for access by Chinese citizens. This element rather tips the balance towards

1321 United States Trade Representative, *The 2016 National Trade Estimate Report* (Washington DC: USTR, 2016) 91.

1322 Gao, 'Googling for the Trade-Human Rights Nexus in China: Can the WTO Help?' (n 690); Wu (n 48) 283.

1323 Gao, 'Googling for the Trade-Human Rights Nexus in China: Can the WTO Help?' (n 690) 261–262.

1324 See *inter alia* AB Report, *US – Gambling*, para 227.

a finding that China's web filtering practice amounts to a zero quota. A definitive assessment of the GATS consistency of the Great Firewall with the market access obligation will have to be made on a case-by-case basis and will depend on whether all service suppliers within the affected service sector see their websites (and access to the market) blocked.

(iii) National Treatment Obligation As explained *supra* (Section 6.1.2.2), the assessment of the national treatment obligation under Article XVII GATS requires looking into whether like foreign services and service suppliers are accorded less favourable treatment. Building on the YouTube example, it has to be assessed whether the services supplied by YouTube are like those supplied by Youku Tudou (a domestic video distribution service to which Chinese consumers have access). It is quite clear that YouTube and Youku Tudou are in a competitive relationship with one another, or at least that they would be if YouTube were granted access to the Chinese market.[1325] Moreover, likeness is presumed where the distinction between services and service suppliers is solely based on origin (*supra* Section 6.1.1.1(i)). Considering that China's Great Firewall only applies to foreign service suppliers, it arguably mainly, if not solely, bases its distinction on the origin of the service supplier. Finally, none of the other factors that are generally taken into account when assessing likeness (product characteristics, consumer preferences, end use and service classification) suggest that these services and service suppliers are not like.

The next step in this analysis considers whether the measure at issue, the 2016 Cybersecurity Law, accords less favourable treatment to foreign services and service suppliers. Considering the fact that the application of the Great Firewall is limited to foreign service suppliers, it can preliminarily be concluded that the conditions of competition are *de facto* modified to the detriment of foreign services suppliers (*supra* Section 6.1.2.2 (ii)). This is the case because all foreign service suppliers are subject to the scrutiny of the Chinese government as to whether they can provide their services across the border into the Chinese market, which is not the case for domestic service suppliers (or at least not in the same way). Even though it does not necessarily affect all foreign service suppliers to the same extent (not all foreign websites are blocked), it can be contended that foreign service suppliers that require the Internet to supply their

[1325] See Panel Report, *China – Electronic Payment Services*, para 7.700.

services in China are not subject to equal opportunities to compete in the Chinese market as their domestic counterparts.

Even though the Chinese Cybersecurity Law on its face applies equally to foreign and domestic service suppliers, its implications for the functioning of the Great Firewall arguably constitute a *de facto* discrimination. The difficulty in arguing a GATS inconsistency of the Great Firewall lies in the fact that China did not enact any laws or regulations that established this system of web filtering. Gao cautions that similar (or sometimes even stricter) *de facto* restrictions apply to domestic websites, which are often required to self-censor. He therefore argues that there is no demonstrable less favourable treatment of foreign service suppliers.[1326] The success of this argument will depend on whether these restrictions are sufficiently similar to rule out a finding of modification of conditions of competition. Due to the opaque nature of Chinese regulation of domestic conduct, this is an assessment which cannot be completed at this point in time. For now, I would cautiously argue that the existence of the Chinese firewall modifies the condition of competition to the detriment of foreign service suppliers, of which Google's YouTube is but one telling example.

(iv) Section 5(a) of the Telecoms Annex The Great Firewall prevents the provision of specific services over the Internet. Therefore, it should be analysed whether it is consistent with the obligations contained in the Annex on Telecommunications. The scope of this agreement is broad and applies to all measures that affect access to and use of public telecommunication transport networks (which I argue includes the Internet), with regard to all service sectors where commitments have been undertaken (*supra* Section 6.1.3.1).[1327] It can be argued that China's Great Firewall negatively affects access to and use of public telecommunication transport networks and services by foreign service suppliers. As discussed *supra*, China has undertaken commitments in various service sectors that are affected by its Great Firewall. This entails that, for the committed service sectors, China must ensure access to the Internet to foreign service suppliers on reasonable and non-discriminatory terms.

As explained *supra* (Section 6.1.3.1), Section 5(a) requires Members to ensure that foreign service suppliers have access to and can make use of

1326 Gao, 'Googling for the Trade-Human Rights Nexus in China: Can the WTO Help?' (n 690) 263; Gao, 'Google's China Problem: A Case Study on Trade, Technology and Human Rights under the GATS' (n 692) 370.

1327 Panel Report, *Mexico – Telecoms*, para 7.278.

the Member's public telecommunications transport network and services, on reasonable and non-discriminatory terms. The legal test of paragraph 5 therefore consists of two main steps: (i) Does the measure ensure access to and use of public telecommunications transport networks and services? and (ii) Does it ensure reasonable and non-discriminatory terms and conditions? Through the filtering (and consequent blocking) of website access requests by consumers to the service suppliers' website, it can be argued that service suppliers are not accorded use of public telecommunications transport services, in this case 'China's part of the Internet'.[1328] As their websites cannot be reached by consumers that use China's public telecommunications transport network (or rather, the Internet), China fails to ensure that foreign service suppliers have access to and can make use of these networks and services on reasonable and non-discriminatory terms. Thus, China's Great Firewall arguably violates Section 5(a) of the Annex on Telecommunications. Moreover, because the Great Firewall only applies to foreign service suppliers, it can hardly be maintained that access to and use of the networks and services are ensured on non-discriminatory terms and conditions.

(v) **Obligations on Domestic Regulation** If China's practice of web filtering is not considered to constitute a border measure, but rather a domestic regulation which applies to all services supplied domestically, the legality under Article VI GATS may be called into question. A possible violation of Article VI GATS will only become relevant once it has been found that the measure does not violate either the market access or the national treatment obligation (see *supra* Section 6.1.2.4). A critical part of the assessment under Article VI GATS turns on how much control contributes to legitimate domestic regulation and at what point control becomes so overbearing that it creates a barrier to trade and thereby breaches WTO commitments.[1329]

To establish a violation of Article VI GATS, it will have to be shown that China's web filtering is not administered in a reasonable, objective and impartial manner.[1330] Gao argues that, as the Chinese online censorship regime can hardly be considered reasonable, objective and impartial,

1328 Even though, technically speaking, the Internet cannot be divided into geographical areas, China's full control over its domestic ISPs leads to an unprecedented national control over the Internet.

1329 Wu (n 48) 287.

1330 Gao, 'Googling for the Trade-Human Rights Nexus in China: Can the WTO Help?' (n 690) 264.

it could be found that it violates Article VI:1 GATS.[1331] However, as pointed out by the panel in *US – Gambling*, the first paragraph of Article VI only contains disciplines of a procedural nature, which is of limited use to address the Great Firewall.[1332] A violation of the interim substantive obligation in Article VI.5 GATS would be difficult to establish as China's Internet censorship existed even before its WTO accession. In this light, it would be challenging to show that China's measures '*could not reasonably have been expected of that Member at the time the specific commitments in those sectors were made*'.[1333] Therefore, even where it can be established that the criteria used by China to perform its web filtering are neither objective nor transparent and that they are more burdensome than necessary,[1334] it is unlikely that a violation of the obligations on domestic regulation will be found.

(vi) Justification Should a case be brought against China's Great Firewall, China will try to justify the web filtering system either under the general exceptions or under the security exceptions. Under Article XIV GATS, China would likely argue that the Great Firewall protects public morals and public order, considering that it quite effectively shields Chinese citizens from Internet content which the government deems go against Chinese morals or the fundamental interests of the Chinese society. It will, however, be difficult to balance the trade-restrictiveness of the Great Firewall with its contribution to the policy objectives (*supra* Section 6.1.4.1(ii)).[1335] The necessity analysis will probably not yield a preliminary finding of justifiability considering how trade restrictive the measure is, even taking account of the importance of the objective pursued. Moreover, there are arguable less trade-restrictive alternatives available. Gao is even more pessimistic as to the justifiability of China's practices, arguing that the Chinese example of web filtering would not qualify as protecting public morals, because the standard of

1331 This argument is based on the arbitrary nature of the filtering and the fact that no objective criteria seem to be used and, should they exist at all, that such criteria are anyway not made public. Gao, 'Google's China Problem: A Case Study on Trade, Technology and Human Rights under the GATS' (n 692) 371–374.

1332 Panel Report, *US – Gambling*, para 6.432.

1333 Thereby not meeting the requirement of Article VI:5(a)(ii) GATS. For this analysis, see Gao, 'Googling for the Trade-Human Rights Nexus in China: Can the WTO Help?' (n 690) 264–266.

1334 Thereby violating Article VI:5(i) GATS.

1335 This analysis will be done in the context of the necessity test that is required under Article XIV(a) GATS.

right and wrong is dictated by the government instead of the 'community or nation'.[1336] Neither does China's Internet filtering serve to protect fundamental interests of society, as the filtering goes directly against the Chinese Constitution, which is supposed to reflect these fundamental interests.[1337]

Even if China's web filtering practice were considered necessary to protect public morals or to ensure privacy protection, it would be difficult for China to deny a disguised restriction on trade or an unjustifiable discrimination in the application of the Chinese Firewall. It is especially the uneven treatment of similar websites in different languages and based in different countries that could constitute an arbitrary or unjustifiable discrimination in the application of the measures at issue.[1338]

As mentioned *supra* (Section 6.1.4.2), justifying barriers to digital services trade on the basis of the security exceptions in Article XIV *bis* GATS is challenging. Where it might be possible for China to argue that it maintains the Chinese Firewall because it is necessary for the protection of its essential security interests (because it effectively controls all Internet traffic that enters the Chinese territory), it will not be able to argue that this relates to the provisioning of military establishment, relates to fissionable and fusionable materials, or is taken in time of war or other emergency in international relations.[1339] Considering that the Great Firewall has been in place since the early 1990s, there is a clear lack of sense of 'emergency'. In conclusion, it will be difficult for China to justify its measures under Article XIV GATS and probably impossible to justify the Great Firewall under Article XIV *bis* GATS.

7.3 Other Barriers and Obstacles to Digital Services Trade

7.3.1 Lack of Access to Infrastructure

With the increased importance of digital trade, building digital infrastructure and ensuring low-cost broadband access is becoming indispensable.[1340] As developing countries have many advantages to gain from increased digital trade (because of the low costs and reduced

[1336] Gao, 'Googling for the Trade-Human Rights Nexus in China: Can the WTO Help?' (n 690) 268–269.

[1337] ibid 270.

[1338] Gao, 'Google's China Problem: A Case Study on Trade, Technology and Human Rights under the GATS' (n 692) 380.

[1339] See the requirements as set out in Article XIV*bis*:1(b) GATS.

[1340] Lund and Manyika (n 7) 9.

need for elaborate infrastructure, enabling MSMEs), it is especially important that they are able to invest in such digital infrastructure, thereby closing the digital divide.

With regard to access to vital infrastructure, the main obligation can be found in Section 5 of the Annex on Telecommunications. Obligations related to anti-competitive practices can be found in Article VIII GATS, Article XI GATS and the Reference Paper on Telecommunications as discussed in Chapter 6.

An important aspect of removing this obstacle to digital services trade is the improvement of trade logistics. This is already (partially) being dealt with in the WTO Trade Facilitation Agreement (TFA). This Agreement desires to '*clarify and improve relevant aspects of Articles V, VIII and X of the GATT 1994 with a view to further expediting the movement, release and clearance of goods, including goods in transit*'.[1341] The TFA contains provisions that further transparency and accountability in customs procedures.[1342] Lastly, it should also be noted that the MFN liberalisation of trade in ICT products through the ITA contributes to the development of infrastructure in developing countries.

7.3.1.1 Case Study: The US' Restoring Internet Freedom Order – The Measure

In December 2017, the rules on network neutrality that had been enacted by President Obama in 2015[1343] were repealed by the US' Federal Communications Commission (FCC), with expiry of these rules on 11 June 2018. The net neutrality rules barred ISPs from interfering in the information that they transmit to consumers, thereby treating all uses of the network interchangeably. ISPs could not block or slow down access to specific content or charge consumers more for specific content. These rules also prevented ISPs from favouring their own products over those of other service suppliers, requiring them to treat all data equally.

The 'Restoring Internet Freedom' Order implemented three changes.[1344] First, it restored broadband access services to a Title I information service classification, rather than a classification as public

[1341] Preamble to the WTO Agreement on Trade Facilitation.

[1342] Meltzer, 'Supporting the Internet as a Platform for International Trade Opportunities for Small and Medium-Sized Enterprises and Developing Countries' (n 9) 27.

[1343] WC Docket No. 14–28, Report and Order on Remand, Declaratory Ruling, and Order, 30 FCC Rcd 5601 (2015) (*Title II Order*).

[1344] WC Docket No. 17–108, Declaratory Ruling, Order, Report, and Order, 33 FCC Rcd 311 (1) (2017) (*Restoring Internet Freedom Order*).

utility (Title II). This entailed the removal of common carrier requirements to Internet traffic exchange and certain interconnection requirements (which effectively abolished network neutrality).[1345] Second, it incorporated an obligation of transparency, requiring ISPs to inform consumers of when they are blocking or slowing down content and whether 'fast lane' Internet is available.[1346] Third, it eliminated the FCC's Internet Conduct Standard, referring issues of unfair and deceptive practices and antitrust to the Federal Trade Commission.[1347]

In considering the Restoring Internet Freedom Order, the peculiarity of the US' Internet access market should be taken into account. In the United States, many local or regional ISP monopolies exist, with limited to no competition between ISPs (and no possibility for consumers to switch providers). The abolishment of the network neutrality rules will highly likely have a significant impact on the market, as the existing ISPs can abuse their oligopoly position. If network neutrality rules are abandoned, ISPs can charge extra to visit certain websites, demand fees from websites or consumers to enjoy full-speed Internet and privilege their own services over those of competitors.

Considering that the United States' measure affects access to infrastructure for the trade in digitally enabled services and might impact the competitive relationship of basic telecommunication suppliers, it should be analysed whether it is consistent with the obligations contained in the Annex and the Reference Paper.

7.3.1.2 Case Study: The US' Restoring Internet Freedom Order – GATS Consistency

(i) Section 5(a) and (c) of the Telecoms Annex Before considering a possible GATS violation, it should first be acknowledged that challenging the Restoring Internet Freedom Order would be based on an 'as such' claim. An 'as such' claim challenges legislation as such, independently from the application of that measure in specific circumstances.[1348] It can apply to measures with general and prospective application that have not (yet) been applied.[1349] Because of the lack of illustrative application, finding measures 'as such' to be in violation of WTO provisions

1345 Restoring Internet Freedom Order, paras 166–167.

1346 However, it also eliminates certain reporting requirements that it considers '*unnecessary and unduly burdensome*'. ibid para 3.

1347 Restoring Internet Freedom Order, para 248.

1348 AB Report, *US – 1916 Act*, para 60.

1349 AB Report, *EU – Biodiesel (Argentina)*, para 6.226.

has more far-reaching implications than the classic 'as applied' claims.[1350] WTO disciplines were enacted not only to protect existing trade, but also to ensure security and predictability for future trade.[1351] As the Restoring Internet Freedom Order had only entered into force a few months before this chapter was written, its application had not yet become completely clear: it was unclear how US ISPs would handle their freedom to privilege specific data. It is nonetheless worthwhile considering the GATS consistency of this order, as it could have considerable consequences for foreign digital service suppliers that require access to the Internet in the United States in order to supply their services.

Several GATT panels had already dealt with the question of their jurisdiction on 'as such' claims.[1352] It was established that Article XXIII:1(a) of the GATT 1947 allowed contracting parties to bring 'as such' claims, but only with regard to legislation that mandated GATS-inconsistent behaviour. This position was later nuanced by the Appellate Body, finding that for an 'as such' claim to succeed, the measure need not be mandatory. It considered that the appropriateness of the mandatory/discretionary distinction should be assessed on a case-by-case basis and cautioned '*against application of this distinction in a mechanistic fashion*'.[1353] Rather, in assessing an 'as such' claim, several questions can be considered, including: Does the measure restrict suppliers from acting WTO consistent?;[1354] Is the measure's conduct necessarily inconsistent with its WTO obligations?;[1355] or more nuanced: Does the action in defined circumstances necessarily lead to WTO inconsistency?[1356] For a complainant to succeed in an 'as such' claim, it must prove the systemic implications of the rule. The Appellate Body pointed out that what is required to establish such claims will depend on the circumstances of

[1350] AB Report, *US – Oil Country Tubular Goods Sunset Reviews*, para 172.

[1351] AB Report, *US – Corrosion-Resistant Steel Sunset Review*, para 82.

[1352] AB Report, *US – 1916 Act*, fn 34 provides examples: GATT Panel Report, *United States – Superfund*, BISD 34S/136; GATT Panel Report, *United States – Section 337 of the Tariff Act of 1930*, BISD 36S/345; GATT Panel Report, *Thailand – Cigarettes*, BISD 37S/200; GATT Panel Report, *United States – Malt Beverages*, BISD 39S/206; and GATT Panel Report, *United States – Tobacco*, BISD 41S/131. See also GATT Panel Report, *United States – Wine and Grape Products*, BISD 39S/436, examining this issue in the context of a claim brought under the Tokyo Round *Agreement on Interpretation and Application of Articles VI, XVI and XXIII of the General Agreement on Tariffs and Trade.*

AB Report, *EU – Biodiesel (Argentina)*, para 6.226.

[1353] AB Report, *US – Corrosion-Resistant Steel Sunset Review,* para 93.

[1354] For an example of this consideration see AB Report, *US – Carbon Steel*, para 162.

[1355] AB Report, *US – Oil Country Tubular Goods Sunset Reviews*, para 172.

[1356] AB Report, *China – Raw Materials*, para 170.

each case, including the nature of the measure and the WTO obligations at issue.[1357]

Even though it cannot be contended that the Restoring Internet Freedom Order will necessarily lead to WTO-inconsistent behaviour by US ISPs, the peculiarity of the US' Internet access market, as explained *supra*, together with the nature of the obligation contained in Section 5 of the Telecommunications Annex does raise questions as to the GATS consistency of this measure (or at least its likely implications). After all, the Annex contains positive rights and obligations, requiring action from Members to *ensure* that foreign suppliers have access to their public telecommunications transport network and services. It can be argued that such a positive obligation imposes a heavier burden on Members to ensure that their domestic service suppliers act in line with their GATS obligations. An 'as such' claim should therefore be available in the absence of appropriate regulation by the responding Member. Assuming a successful 'as such' claim, this section proceeds with an analysis of the legality of the Restoring Internet Access Order. Nothing excludes the possibility of a future claim based on the GATS-inconsistent application of the Order, should foreign digital service suppliers be confronted with discriminatory treatment in their access to the Internet.

As mentioned *supra* (Section 6.1.3.1), the scope of the Telecoms Annex is broad, as it applies to all measures that affect access to and use of public telecommunication transport networks (including the Internet) and with regard to all service sectors where commitments have been undertaken.[1358] That entails that the United States must ensure that for all service sectors for which it has undertaken commitments, (foreign) service suppliers have access to the Internet to supply their services on reasonable and non-discriminatory terms. Guaranteed access to the Internet must *inter alia* be provided to service suppliers of legal services, computer and related services, advertising services, telecommunications services and audiovisual services.

Two paragraphs of Section 5 are arguably violated by the Restoring Internet Freedom Order: paragraphs (a) and (c). On its face, the Order does not prevent access to and use of public telecommunications transport networks. Nevertheless, it fails to ensure reasonable and non-discriminatory terms and conditions. The gist of the claim would thus lie in the second part of the test of Section 5(a) (*supra* Section 6.1.3.1). The

[1357] AB Report, *US – Carbon Steel*, para 157.

[1358] Panel Report, *Mexico – Telecoms*, para 7.278.

panel in *Mexico – Telecoms* understood the term 'reasonable' as referring to '*something that is "not irrational; absurd or ridiculous" [or] something of such amount, size, number, etc. as is judged to be appropriate or suitable to the circumstances or purpose*'.[1359] It additionally considered 'reasonable' to imply '*a degree of flexibility that involves consideration of the circumstances of a particular case*' and to relate to the notions of 'balance' and 'flexibility'.[1360] Footnote 2 to the Annex elaborates on the term 'non-discriminatory', referring to the MFN and national treatment obligations, stating that the terms and conditions cannot be '*less favourable than those accorded to any other user of like public telecommunications transport networks or services under like circumstances*'. This effectively means that the service suppliers (either foreign or domestic) need not be like, but that a foreign service supplier is accorded less favourable treatment in its access to or use of like networks or services (e.g. the Internet) under like circumstances.

Section 5(c) of the Annex requires Members to ensure that foreign service suppliers can use public telecommunications transport networks and services for the movement of information (read: data) within and across borders and for access to information in databases (*supra* Section 6.1.3.1). It requires Members to notify new or amended measures that significantly affect such use. Looking into its text and considering that paragraph (c) is informed by paragraph (a), the former could be interpreted as an application of the main obligation imposed by the latter. Members must thus ensure flow of data over the Internet under reasonable and non-discriminatory conditions.

Both of these obligations are arguably violated where US ISPs have the liberty to privilege the large (domestic) digital service suppliers such as Google, Facebook and Netflix to the detriment of smaller (foreign) digital service suppliers. For example, ISPs could condition data transfer by competing digital service suppliers on the payment of a higher contribution (as the Restoring Internet Freedom Order provides them with considerable leeway to do so). If such contributions turn out either not to be reasonable, because they do not reflect costs incurred,[1361] or to

[1359] ibid para 7.182.

[1360] ibid para 7.328.

[1361] See for example Panel Report, *Mexico – Telecoms*, where it was found that rates for access to and use of public telecommunications services can be examined under Section 5 to assess whether they constitute reasonable terms. In that dispute, it was clarified that rates can still be reasonable even if they are generally higher than the cost-oriented rates for interconnection. However, where they exceed cost-oriented rates by a substantial

provide less favourable treatment to foreign users of public telecommunications transport networks under like circumstances, Section 5(a) will be violated.[1362] Alternatively, a seemingly non-discriminatory general fee could be payable to allow for transfer of data by digital service suppliers. However, where such fees amount to prohibitive obstacles for (small) foreign service suppliers it could be argued that this *de facto* violates the non-discrimination obligation in Section 5(a) and (c), as it will put the foreign users of public telecoms transport networks at a competitive disadvantage, providing them with less favourable treatment. Based on these two examples, it could be argued that the removal of net neutrality rules leads to an 'as such' violation of the GATS Annex on Telecommunications.

(ii) Reference Paper The scope of the Reference Paper is limited to basic telecommunications services (*supra* Section 6.1.3.3). It requires Members to prevent major suppliers from engaging in anti-competitive practices in the basic telecommunications market.[1363] The Restoring Internet Freedom Order will most likely not violate the Reference Paper as the anti-competitive behaviour occurs downstream, in the ISP's treatment of the service suppliers that make use of their services rather than in their treatment of competing ISPs (which provide basic telecommunications services). Suppliers of digitally enabled services (e.g. Facebook, Google and Netflix) do not supply basic telecommunications services but a myriad of value-added telecommunication and other services. The abolishment of the net neutrality rules will therefore fall outside of the scope of the Reference Paper on Basic Telecommunications.

(iii) Justification First, the Annex itself provides for an exception to the obligation in paragraph (c) in Section 5(d), which allows Members to take measures necessary to ensure security and confidentiality of messages (*supra* Section 6.1.3.1). The Order does not seem to fall within the ambit of this exception as it was not enacted with the aim of protecting these values.

Considering that the Annex is part of the GATS legal framework, responding Members also have access to the exceptions of the GATS, found in Article XIV and XIV *bis*. However, the Order does not seem to

margin and where price competition is excluded, the rates will not qualify as 'on reasonable terms' in the sense of Section 5(a) of the Annex. See paras 7.331–7.335.

1362 Provided that the conditions have not been imposed to meet one of the policy objectives that are listed in paragraph (e).

1363 See the definition of 'major supplier' in the Reference Paper.

have been enacted in the pursuance of one of the listed policy objectives in either the general exceptions or security exceptions provisions. Quite to the contrary, the measure has been enacted with the aim of spurring investment, innovation and competition as well as to increase transparency and protect consumers. On their face, none of these objectives fall within the scope of public morals, public order or human, animal or plant life or health. Neither does it seem like the Order was enacted to secure compliance with laws or regulations that prevent deceptive or fraudulent practices or protect privacy. Finally, this measure was clearly not taken to protect the US' essential security interests. At first sight, it therefore seems like a possible finding of violation could not be justified under any of the available exceptions.

7.3.2 Ban on Cross-border Supply through Electronic Means

Vietnam issued its Decree No. 181/2013/ND-CP (Decree 181) on 4 November 2013. The Decree, which applies Vietnam's Law on Advertising to foreign websites that provide advertisements to Vietnamese users, entered into force on 1 January 2014. The most relevant provision of the Decree for the purpose of this section is the obligation on foreign websites to use a locally licensed advertiser to conduct advertising of goods and services of local organisations and businesses.[1364] Through this obligation, Decree 181 effectively prohibits the cross-border supply of advertising services when promoting local goods and services.

Such a straightforward limitation on the supply of advertising services through a specific means of supply is very similar to the limitations maintained by the United States in the *US – Gambling* dispute. Like Vietnam does for advertising services, the United States prohibited the cross-border supply of gambling and betting services. In that case, the panel and the Appellate Body found that the total prohibition on cross-border supply amounted to a zero quota, thereby violating the US' market access obligations.[1365]

Because of the obvious parallels between both cases, this analysis will be limited to an assessment of whether Vietnam has undertaken relevant commitments. Once it is established that relevant commitments have

[1364] Article 13, para 1 of the Decree on Elaboration of Some Articles of the Law on Advertising, No. 181/2013/ND-CP, 14 November 2013 (Decree 181).

[1365] AB Report, *US – Gambling*, para 265 and Panel Report, *US – Gambling*, para 6.421. The panel exercised judicial economy with regard to the Article XVII GATS claim.

been made, any further analysis under Article XVI GATS likely leads to the conclusion that Decree 181 amounts to a quantitative restriction in the sense of Article XVI:2 GATS, thereby violating Vietnam's obligations under this Article. Vietnam has scheduled a full market access and national treatment commitment on cross-border supply of advertising services, except for advertising for cigarettes.[1366] It can thus be concluded that Vietnam's prohibition on the cross-border supply of advertising services violates its market access obligations.

In addition, Decree 181 will likely violate Vietnam's national treatment obligation. It contains a *de jure* discrimination: it only prohibits foreign advertising service suppliers to supply their services within Vietnam for the promotion of domestic goods and services. Therefore, on its face, the measure modifies the conditions of competition between domestic advertising service suppliers and foreign advertising service suppliers (*supra* Section 6.1.2.2(ii)). It clearly treats foreign service suppliers less favourably, as they are prevented from providing certain of their advertising services to Vietnamese consumers. This results in a violation of Article XVII GATS.

It is difficult to conceive how Vietnam might try to justify this measure. It does not seem to have been enacted to protect public morals, human health or citizens' privacy. A preliminary justification under any of the subparagraphs of Article XIV GATS does not seem possible. Justification under the chapeau would be equally difficult, considering the fact that the measure is very broad, as it applies to the advertising of any domestic good or service. Therefore, the application of Decree 181 likely amounts to arbitrary or unjustifiable discrimination.

7.3.3 Digital Services Taxes

Following its Section 301 investigation into France's Digital Services Tax, the USTR considered that the tax was discriminatory and unfairly targeted US companies.[1367] France's Digital Services Tax also raises some

[1366] WTO Council for Trade in Services, 'Viet Nam – Schedule of Specific Commitments', GATS/SC/142, 19 March 2007, 16. The only limitation that has been added in the 'additional commitments' column states '*the advertising for wines and spirits shall be subject to State regulations, which are applied on a non-discriminatory basis*'.

[1367] Office of the United States Trade Representative, 'Report on France's Digital Services Tax Prepared in the Investigation under Section 301 of the Trade Act of 1974', 2 December 2019 <www.ustr.gov/issue-areas/enforcement/section-301-investigations/section-301-frances-digital-services-tax>.

questions under the GATS, more specifically under Articles II (MFN obligation) and XVII GATS (national treatment obligation).[1368] The consistency of the tax with the moratorium on electronic transmissions is also assessed.

For France's Digital Services Tax to violate its MFN obligation, it must first be assessed whether the services and service suppliers at issue are like. The likeness of digital advertising and offline advertising is relatively straightforward. These two services are clearly in a competitive relationship.[1369] The likeness analysis of digital interfaces is less straightforward in the abstract but can be illustrated by two targeted examples. While Uber is covered by the Digital Services Tax, a taxi company that operates an app would not be covered (as the latter company is selling its own service, which excludes it from the scope of the Digital Services Tax).[1370] While an SME that sells its products through Amazon's platform is covered, Amazon selling its own products through its platform is not covered by the tax. These services are clearly in a competitive relationship and can therefore be considered like. Second, the tax must treat certain foreign services or service suppliers less favourably than other services or service suppliers. In this assessment, the double threshold of France's Digital Services Tax is determinative for the *de facto* discrimination. Only companies whose taxable revenue exceeds €750 million worldwide and €25 million in France are subject to the tax. It has been predicted that, due to these thresholds, most of the affected companies will be US multinational companies. If the tax disproportionally targets US companies compared to other foreign services and service suppliers, it is possible for an MFN violation to be found.[1371]

France will only be bound by the national treatment obligation if it has undertaken commitments in relevant service sectors. France (as part of

[1368] The GATT Secretariat also noted the applicability of the GATS to tax measures that affect service suppliers. It indicated that the two relevant obligations are the national treatment obligation (Article XVII) and the MFN treatment obligation (Article II). GATT Multilateral Trade Negotiations Uruguay Round, Group of Negotiations on Services, 'The applicability of the GATS to tax measures' Note by the Secretariat, MTN. GNS/W/210, 1 December 1993.

[1369] For example, traditional media have seen their advertising income decrease with the rise of online platforms. Appellate Body Report, *Argentina – Financial Services*, para 6.25.

[1370] See also Office of the United States Trade Representative, 'Report on France's Digital Services Tax Prepared in the Investigation under Section 301 of the Trade Act of 1974', 2 December 2019, 14.

[1371] In France, the Digital Services Tax Law is also referred to as the 'taxe GAFA', which refers to Google, Apple, Facebook and Amazon.

the EU) has undertaken national treatment commitments on advertising services, telecommunications services and computer and related services for modes 1, 2 and 3.[1372] Therefore, France has committed to provide national treatment with regard to at least part of the services affected by the Digital Services Tax. For the same reasons as set out for the MFN violation above, it is likely that France's Digital Services Tax, which is origin neutral on its face, will be found to provide less favourable treatment to US services and service suppliers compared to French services and service suppliers.

Whether the Digital Services Tax can be justified under any of the general exceptions in Article XIV GATS is unclear. It seems unlikely that the measure would be considered necessary to protect public morals or to maintain public order.[1373] It would also be difficult for France to argue that the Digital Services Tax is necessary to secure compliance with certain laws or regulations, considering that the tax was adopted to address tax avoidance in general.[1374] Article XIV(d) is arguably most relevant to a justification of the Digital Services Tax, which amounts to a direct tax.[1375] This paragraph justifies difference in treatment aimed at ensuring the equitable or effective imposition or collection of direct taxes. Paragraph (d), however, only justifies inconsistencies with the national treatment obligation. It would not be able to justify any inconsistency with the MFN obligation. Where it would be found that the tax is preliminarily justifiable under any of the subparagraphs of Article XIV, the measure would need to meet the requirements of the chapeau of Article XIV in order to be justified. This requires that the tax is not applied in a manner that constitutes arbitrary or unjustifiable discrimination, which still remains to be seen, as the tax had not yet been applied at the moment of analysis.

France's Digital Services Tax does not violate the moratorium on electronic transmissions. First, the moratorium is a political agreement

1372 WTO, Trade in Services, 'European Union – Schedule of Specific Commitments', GATS/SC/157, 7 May 2019.

1373 Even though this concept has been interpreted broadly, as noted in Petros C Mavroidis, 'And You Put the Load Right on Me: Digital Taxes, Tax Discrimination and Trade in Services' (2020) 12 Trade, Law and Development 75, 98.

1374 See similarly Andrew D Mitchell, Tania Voon and Jarrod Hepburn, 'Taxing Tech: Risks of an Australian Digital Services Tax under International Economic Law' (2019) 20 Melbourne Journal of International Law 88, 105.

1375 Article XXVIII(o) GATS defines direct taxes as '*all taxes on total income, on total capital or on elements of income or of capital, including taxes on gains from the alienation of property, taxes on estates, inheritances and gifts, and taxes on the total amounts of wages or salaries paid by enterprises, as well as taxes on capital appreciation*'.

that does not create binding obligations on Members. Second, the Digital Services Tax is a direct tax, not a customs duty. The moratorium on electronic transmissions, which consisted of WTO Members agreeing not to impose customs duties on electronic transmissions, arguably does not apply to direct taxes.

7.3.4 Restrictions on Intellectual Property Rights

Many of the barriers that digital service trade is confronted with relate to the protection or abuse of IPRs. For plenty of digital products, which essentially constitute 'content', their value lies in the IPRs that are connected to them,[1376] recognising their originality, innovativeness and so forth. This is especially the case for software, online videos, streamed music and so forth. Digitisation allowed for unprecedented dissemination of copyrighted works to anywhere in the world. The work done in the context of the WPEC at the Council for Trade-Related Aspects of Intellectual Property Rights suggests that the challenges that are posed to the protection and use of IPRs by the growth and technological development of electronic commerce could be addressed within the international framework on IP law.[1377]

The WTO Agreement on Trade-Related Intellectual Property Rights (TRIPS) sets out minimum IP standards, to be respected by all WTO Members. Whereas the TRIPS was an important breakthrough for the global protection of IP, it does not address the contemporary challenges of IP protection in digital trade. For example, Meltzer notes that the TRIPS fails to address the issue of 'cybersquatting', as this problem did not yet exist at the time the Agreement was drafted.[1378] However, the TRIPS does contain provisions that address barriers created by the

[1376] See also WTO Council for Trade-Related Aspects of Intellectual Property Rights, 'Work Programme on Electronic Commerce' Progress Report to the General Council, IP/C/18, 30 July 1999, para 4.

[1377] ibid para 4. The report to the Council also points out the Secretariat background note dealing with issues arising out of electronic commerce in connection with copyrights and the use of trademarks on the Internet. WTO Council for Trade-Related Aspects of Intellectual Property Rights, 'The Work Programme on Electronic Commerce' Background Note by the Secretariat, IP/C/W/128, 11 February 1999.

[1378] Meltzer, 'Supporting the Internet as a Platform for International Trade Opportunities for Small and Medium-Sized Enterprises and Developing Countries' (n 9) 26. This issue is also discussed in the Secretariat Background Note: WTO Council for Trade-Related Aspects of Intellectual Property Rights, 'The Work Programme on Electronic Commerce' Background Note by the Secretariat, IP/C/W/128, 11 February 1999, para 60.

protection of IPRs. A strong example can be found in Article 3 TRIPS, which contains the national treatment obligation and requires Members to provide equal protection of IPRs to both foreign and domestic companies. In their recent cases against China's measures that mandate forced technology transfer, both the EU and the United States claim a violation of *inter alia* Article 3 TRIPS due to the less favourable treatment that is being accorded to foreign IPR holders as the same requirements do not apply to domestic IPR holders.[1379] Also relevant for digital trade is the specific coverage of computer programs.[1380] Article 10 TRIPS clarifies that computer programs, whether in source or object code, are granted the same IPR protection as literary works under the Berne Convention. Additionally, the second paragraph of this Article covers '*compilations of data or other material, whether in machine readable or other form*', which shall be protected as intellectual creations if prompted by the selection or arrangement of their contents.[1381] As data takes on an increasingly important (and economically valuable) role in digital trade, its protection through IPRs should not be overlooked.

The GATS, however, also remains relevant when considering barriers to trade in services created by IP regulation. Lack of information on copyright licenses as well as obscure information on IPR liability of (foreign) service suppliers could arguably violate Members' transparency obligations as contained in Article III GATS. It could additionally be argued that a forced disclosure of source code as a requirement for market access might violate Article III *bis* GATS, which prohibits Members from requiring disclosure of confidential information which would prejudice legitimate commercial interests of particular enterprises, public or private.

Even though some of the barriers related to the protection of IPRs hinder market access to the domestic market, it will be difficult to argue a market access violation in the sense of the GATS. As Article XVI GATS only prohibits quantitative limitations, encumbered market access due to the obligation to transfer IPRs, technology or source code falls outside of

1379 WTO Dispute Settlement Body, *China – Certain Measures Concerning the Protection of Intellectual Property Rights*, Request for Consultations by the United States, and WTO Dispute Settlement Body, *China – Certain Measures on the Transfer of Technology*, Request for Consultations by the European Union.

1380 Lopez-Gonzalez and Ferencz (n 6) para 40. Recall the ongoing debate about whether software qualifies as a good or a service, *supra* Section 1.2.1.

1381 It is, however, clarified that this protection does not extend to the data or material itself, only to its specific selection or arrangement.

this Article's scope. Members could, however, argue a violation of the national treatment obligation in Article XVII GATS where it can be shown that less favourable treatment is being provided to foreign service suppliers (in relation to IPR protection) than to domestic service suppliers. This will often be the case if requirements of transfer only apply to foreign service suppliers.

In its submission to the General Council, Brazil highlighted the inaptitude of current rules to protect copyright in the digital environment. According to Brazil, Members need to have a common understanding on three elements to adequately adapt national copyright systems to the digital environment.[1382] First, Members need to agree on increased transparency on the remuneration of copyright and other IPRs in the digital environment. Due to the increased tradability of copyrighted materials and the increased convergence of various services, it becomes difficult to identify the right holders. Second, Members should assert that exceptions and limitations are equally available in the digital environment. Third, Members should reaffirm that the principle of territoriality of copyright also applies in the digital environment.

The Secretariat background note on copyright highlights the issue of the liability of service providers in respect of the transmission and storage of material initiated by others. The main question related to this issue is to what extent service providers, who merely act as intermediaries transmitting or storing potentially infringing content, can and should be held liable.[1383] The Secretariat points to the remedies available in Article 44 (injunctions) and Article 45 (damages). However, the question remains whether such activities are covered by the substantive standards of protection under TRIPS. Even though the imposition of liability for the protection of IPRs on platforms and intermediary service suppliers can be highly burdensome, it would be difficult to challenge such measures under the GATS due to their domestic nature.[1384]

1382 WTO General Council and Council for Trade-Related Aspects of Intellectual Property Rights, 'Electronic Commerce and Copyright', JOB/GC/113, JOB/IP/19, 15 December 2016.

1383 WTO Council for Trade-Related Aspects of Intellectual Property Rights, 'The Work Programme on Electronic Commerce' Background Note by the Secretariat, IP/C/W/128, 11 February 1999, para 73.

1384 Arguments of a violation of the GATS would probably be limited to Article VI:5(a)(i), on the basis that the domestic regulation is more burdensome than necessary to ensure the quality of the service.

7.4 Summary

Various GATS obligations have proven to be specifically relevant to barriers to digital services trade. This part of the book has shown that both the GATS' general obligations as well as its obligations subject to specific commitments can be applied to barriers to digital services trade. Especially the market access and the national treatment obligation have turned out to be adequate tools in dealing with the specific barriers to digital services trade as discussed in Chapter 7.

Because of the broad scope of the GATS, the application of its general obligations to digital trade should be evident. There can be no doubt that Members are bound by their MFN and transparency obligations when it comes to digital services. The application of the GATS' obligations subject to specific commitments (e.g. market access and national treatment) to digital services is less self-evident. As these obligations only apply to the extent that Members have undertaken specific commitments in the relevant service sectors, they require the identification of the correct classification of the digital services at issue. Building on Part II of this book, where it has been shown that most digital services fit within the existing services classification framework, the case studies in Chapter 7 have started out with an assessment of whether relevant commitments have been undertaken. Important to add is the consideration that regulatory objectives (such as public morals/order and privacy protection) could justify barriers to digital services trade. However, as indicated *supra*, any justification will have to be assessed on a case-by-case basis. Moreover, Article XIV GATS will not allow for broad exceptions taking into account the requirement of compliance with the necessity test, the less trade-restrictive reasonably available alternative and the requirements of the chapeau.

Some WTO Members as well as scholars have argued that the GATS framework does not adequately deal with the currently existing barriers to digital services trade. They argue that the general principles found in the GATS leave much uncertainty as to the applicable rights and obligations, to a significant extent caused by unclear classification. However, being the multilateral forum for trade matters, it might be argued that the issues surrounding digital services *should* be resolved at the WTO. One of the suggestions already raised, not requiring immediate extensive renegotiation of the GATS, is to draft a Reference Paper on digital trade, encouraging Members to undertake additional commitments in their Services Schedules.[1385] Another suggestion is to draft a specific Annex to the GATS on Electronic Commerce setting out binding disciplines on e-commerce.[1386] To resolve existing obscurity as to the specific classification of digital services, an explanatory note by the Secretariat might guide Members in their negotiation of future e-commerce provisions. A more comprehensive solution that has been suggested is the renegotiation of the GATS, to incorporate substantive rules on regulatory cooperation as well as specific provisions prohibiting the imposition of duties on digital products and dealing with barriers to cross-border digital services, including data localisation, local content and source code requirements. Mitchell and Mishra note that even though the WTO is not fit to solve all digital-era issues, it can support the creation of a more suitable regulatory environment at the international level.[1387]

Based on the findings in this part of the book, the assertion that the GATS framework leaves significant gaps in how it addresses digital services trade simply does not hold. Through the application of the GATS obligations to four specific cases studies, it has been shown that several specific barriers to digital services trade, including restrictions on cross-border data flows and web filtering, *can* be addressed within the GATS framework. It has been clarified that the national treatment and market access obligations of the GATS will apply to such requirement as long as Members have undertaken commitments in the relevant service sectors. WTO Members should therefore be aware of the obligations that are applicable to them, even when regulating services that are supplied in a way that was not necessarily envisaged (but theoretically possible) when they negotiated their GATS obligations.

[1385] Based upon the Reference Paper on Basic Telecommunications Services; Burri, 'The International Economic Law Framework for Digital Trade' (n 71) 46.

[1386] Mitchell and Mishra (n 307) 1127.

[1387] ibid 1122.

PART IV

Addressing Barriers at the RTA Level

Following the classification of digital services and the assessment of how to address the barriers to digital services trade, this part of the book addresses the same questions from the perspective of the regional and bilateral level. Chapter 8 maps how the use of e-commerce-related provisions has evolved in regional trade agreements (RTAs) over the years. This chapter will set out some general trends on how WTO Members have included provisions that relate to e-commerce in their regional liberalisation agreements. To allow for the broadest possible study, all RTAs that contain e-commerce-related provisions are analysed using the technique of term-frequency analysis. The evolutions mapped in this chapter provide a broadscale introduction into the topic of e-commerce provisions in RTAs.

Chapter 9 examines the e-commerce-related provisions in six extensive e-commerce RTAs. These six RTAs cover various countries, including China, the EU and the United States, and include two comprehensive regional agreements. This provides an insight into how the largest trading nations have addressed the questions related to digital service trade while these have remained outstanding at the WTO level. The comparison of the six RTAs is done in three steps: (i) comparison of their definition, approach to technological neutrality and 'new services'; (ii) comparison of their architectural features and scope; and (iii) comparison of how they address three barriers to digital services trade that have been identified and discussed in Chapters 3 and 7.

8

Evolution of E-commerce-Related Provisions in RTAs

To add to the (limited) existing scholarship on this topic and to identify gaps, this chapter first summarises existing research before complementing it with the results of the original text analysis. The aim of this chapter is to provide an extensive picture on the evolutions and tendencies of e-commerce-related provisions in RTAs. So far, no other study has applied the text-mining approach to RTAs in order to map the various types of e-commerce-related provisions that have been included throughout the years. This book therefore adds to existing research through its unique methodology and attempt at comprehensive mapping of relevant provisions over time.

8.1 E-commerce Provisions at the Regional Level

To allow for a consistent discourse on the various trade agreements that are discussed in this part of the book, the term 'regional trade agreement' will be used to refer to all trade agreements that are discussed. Various terms are associated with economic integration. The WTO itself uses the term 'RTAs' to refer to the plethora of reciprocal trade agreements that liberalise trade between two or more parties, which do not necessarily have to belong to the same region. This chapter maps 'e-commerce-related provisions' in RTAs. This group of provisions is interpreted broadly and encompasses all provisions that are related to electronic commerce. This ranges from provisions setting out the definitions of terms used in e-commerce chapters and provisions on the scope of such chapters to any type of obligation that is related to electronic commerce. 'E-commerce-related provisions' therefore include provisions on data flows, non-discrimination obligations on electronic transmissions, cooperation obligations or endeavours on e-commerce-related issues and any provisions related to the facilitation of e-commerce.

8.1.1 The Regional Level of International Trade Agreements as Gap-Filler for the Multilateral Level

At the multilateral level, further liberalisation of trade in goods and services has proven difficult to negotiate. The Doha Negotiation Round, which was launched in 2001, is currently in a deadlock.[1388] Further liberalisation of trade in services at the multilateral level has not been possible for a plethora of reasons, including diverging interests of the Members, limitations of the 'single undertaking' principle[1389] and halt of the global liberalisation momentum. The lack of progress in the WPEC as explained *supra* (Section 4.3.2) also fits within this multilateral negotiation deadlock. So far, Members have been unable to agree multilaterally on liberalisation or further disciplines on electronic commerce. Additionally, it has been claimed that the existing WTO framework is not sufficient, as it is not keeping up with current changes, either through negotiation or development of case law.[1390]

Members are, however, increasingly aware of the economic impact of barriers to digital services trade and have progressively been addressing such issues at a regional or bilateral level. More and more RTAs include a dedicated chapter with disciplines on e-commerce. This chapter assesses where liberalisation at the regional or bilateral level goes further than what can be found at the multilateral level and will answer several related questions: (i) what types of provisions relevant to e-commerce are contained in all RTAs currently in force?; (ii) what kind of evolutions can be perceived over time, for different regions and at different income levels?; (iii) do these provisions go substantively further than what can be found in the GATS?; and (iv) are the different disciplines in different RTAs similar or do we see a wide divergence in how they tackle issues surrounding digital trade? Whereas the first two questions will be answered in Chapter 8, the second two questions will be addressed from the angle of the barriers to digital services trade in Chapter 9.

[1388] Even though negotiations in the context of the Doha Development Round are still underway, there is little prospect of a conclusion of the Doha Development Agenda. Van den Bossche and Zdouc (n 291) 100.

[1389] The application of the single undertaking principle in the Doha round entails that every item of the Doha negotiations is part of a whole and indivisible package and cannot be agreed separately.

[1390] Burri, 'The Governance of Data and Data Flows in Trade Agreements: The Pitfalls of Legal Adaptation' (n 177) 97–98.

It has been argued that e-commerce provisions in RTAs could provide useful guidance for the negotiations at the multilateral level.[1391] Multilateralisation of progress made at the regional level would minimise the costs of trade diversion and maximise the creation gains. It would reduce divergent provisions, simplify rules, create regulatory coherence and advance the development of WTO obligations.[1392] Whether the e-commerce provisions in RTAs successfully address the barriers that digital services trade is confronted with will be assessed in Chapter 10.

Herman distinguishes between bottom-up and top-down multilateralisation of e-commerce provisions in RTAs. Whereas the former boils down to extending existing RTA rules to new parties, regional convergence[1393] and inclusion of third-party MFN clauses, the latter refers to adoption of the 'deep' (or WTO+) RTA provisions at the WTO level, multilateralisation of existing commitments in RTAs and an increased transparency on the applied regimes. In 2010, Herman deemed bottom-up multilateralisation of e-commerce provisions politically feasible considering that '*the number of e-commerce provisions in existing RTAs is relatively small*'.[1394] In 2020, this statement arguably no longer holds true, considering the steady increase of RTAs that include e-commerce-related chapters and the increased complexity and length of such chapters. The analysis in this chapter will confirm that there is quite some divergence in the e-commerce provisions in RTAs. Whether top-down multilateralisation is still a feasible option is inherently a political question and therefore best left to those involved in ongoing negotiations. However, the lack of significant agreement reached in the context of the WPEC attests to the historically difficult negotiation climate surrounding e-commerce issues.

Regardless of the exact obligations or commitments applicable to electronic commerce that have been included in RTAs, these regional agreements can generally be said to further liberalisation of digital services trade. This because at the very least, RTAs elevate the level of commitment undertaken by Members which will impact the liberalisation of all services, including digital services.[1395] For example, any RTA that includes a negative list

1391 Lior Herman, 'Multilateralising Regionalism: The Case of E-Commerce' (OECD Publishing 2010) 99, 6 <www.oecd-ilibrary.org/trade/multilateralising-regionalism_5kmbjx6gw69x-en>.

1392 ibid 17.

1393 I.e. the convergence of several RTAs into a single regional RTA, applying the same provisions to various regional trade partners (rather than different rules bilaterally).

1394 Herman (n 1393) 19, 22.

1395 Sébastien Miroudot, 'The Value of Market Access and National Treatment Commitments in Services Trade Agreements' (OECD 2018) Working Party of the

approach to services commitments will considerably liberalise digital services as the parties to the RTA commit to more liberalisation of services, many of which can of course also be delivered digitally.[1396] Figure 8.1 illustrates the increased use of negative lists or hybrid lists in RTAs over time.[1397]

Several RTAs *do*, however, explicitly go beyond what can be found at the multilateral level, especially in their specific targeting of electronic commerce. As set out in Part III, all of the GATS disciplines in principle apply to digital services trade. Yet, due to the fact that the GATS does not

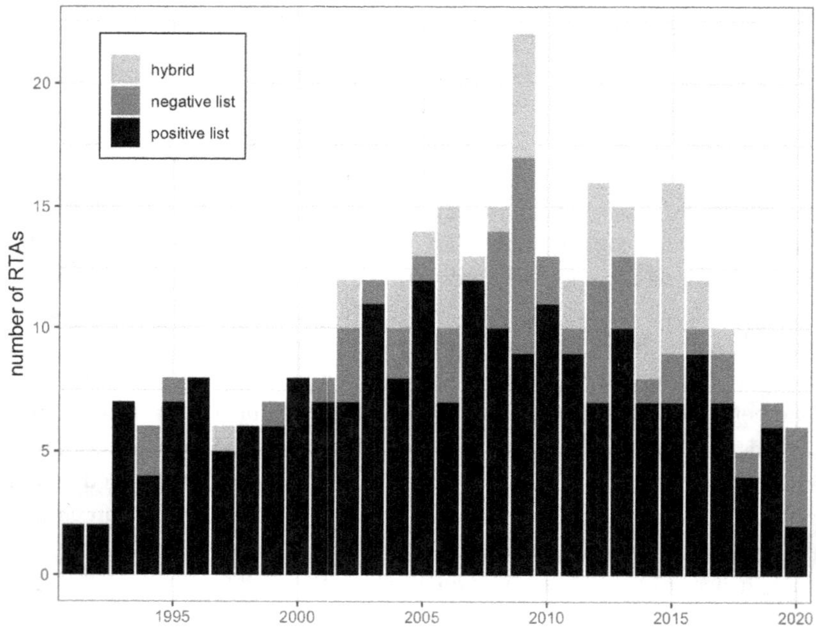

Figure 8.1 Services lists used in all RTAs that entered into force between 1990 and 2020

Trade Committee TAD/TC/WP(2016)22/FINAL <www.oecd-ilibrary.org/trade/the-value-of-market-access-and-national-treatment-commitments-in-services-trade-agreements_d8bfc8d8-en>.

1396 As also noted in the context of telecommunications in Tuthill and Sherman (n 1083) 163.

1397 Hybrid lists contain elements of both positive and negative lists, depending on the obligation. For a comparison between the types of lists used in all RTAs compared to e-commerce RTAs, see Ines Willemyns, 'Addressing Digital Services in PTAs: Only Convergence in the 11th Hour?' in Rhea Tamara Hoffmann and Markus Krajewski (eds), *Coherence and Divergence in Services Trade Law* (Springer 2020) 130.

mention digital services anywhere and because of the classification issues highlighted in Part II, not all WTO Members share this view. This obscurity is addressed in most recent RTAs, which include specific e-commerce chapters and/or provisions that explicitly mention digital trade or e-commerce. Moreover, RTAs allow countries to transpose their domestic regulatory approaches to their trading partners.[1398] Many RTAs address some of the unresolved issues as raised in the WPEC, explicitly foster regulatory cooperation, protect vital digital assets of companies (prohibiting mandated technology or source code transfer and protection of trade secrets) and encourage technical assistance and knowledge sharing.[1399]

UNCTAD highlights five strengths of RTAs when it comes to regulating international data flows. Not only do RTAs increase the potential to engage more countries in the discussion, they generally allow for a higher level of binding and further interoperability between the parties. They additionally have the potential to address the balance between data flows and privacy protection, to address new technologies and to manage cross-border data flows.[1400]

A bell of caution should be rung as to the risk of fragmentation and disruption of the global framework when RTAs go further than what can be found at the multilateral level and do so in a diverging way.[1401] This is especially the case when both multilateral and regional dispute settlement systems are used, with potentially contradictory outcomes. The issue of growing numbers of FTAs and their potentially negative impact on trade flows due to their diverging rules has been termed the 'spaghetti bowl effect'. This issue was already identified in 1995, long before the number of trade agreements rose to what they are now.[1402] Baldwin added to this debate by asserting that RTAs could serve either as building or stumbling blocks for multilateral liberalisation.[1403]

1398 Mitchell and Mishra (n 307) 1097.

1399 ibid 1103.

1400 UNCTAD, 'Data Protection Regulations and International Data Flows: Implications for Trade and Development' (United Nations Publications 2016) UNCTAD/WEB/DTL/STICT/2016/1/iPub, 37–38.

1401 Mitchell and Mishra refer to the various new provisions in the CPTPP and warn about risks of fragmentation. Mitchell and Mishra (n 307) 1097.

1402 Jagdish Bhagwati, 'US Trade Policy: The Infatuation with FTAs' in Jagdish Bhagwati and Anna O Krueger (eds), *The Dangerous Drift tot Preferential Trade Agreements* (AEI Press 1995) <https://academiccommons.columbia.edu/doi/10.7916/D8CN7BFM>.

1403 Richard Baldwin, 'Stepping Stones or Building Blocs? Regional and Multilateral Integration' (2004) Paper prepared for G-20 workshop on 'Regional Economic Integration in a Global Framework'.

There are also various advantages to dealing with the broad issue of digital trade at the multilateral level. Burri points out that the law of the WTO is intrinsically flexible but at the same time provides a stable basis of substantive and procedural rules, complemented with an effective dispute settlement system ('*that fosters legal evolution*').[1404] Moreover, the multilateral level is the more suitable fit for policy in an area that requires fluid interoperability to work.[1405] Multilateral negotiations additionally have the largest trade creation effects and (almost) zero trade diversion effects.[1406] Contrastingly, RTAs are generally better suited to reconcile diverging interest and are thereby in a better position to address new-generation trade barriers.[1407] Wu argues that, regardless of this potential, many RTAs continue to skirt around the shortcomings he identified in existing WTO obligations.[1408] It might therefore be questioned whether RTAs that do not (or only partly) fulfil their liberalisation potential have much to add to the international legal framework applicable to digital (services) trade.

8.1.2 Categorisation of E-commerce-Related Provisions

The digital trade issues dealt with differ considerably between RTAs and different authors have used different ways to categorise e-commerce-related provisions. Table 8.1, *infra*, schematises the (implicit) classification of e-commerce-related provisions that can be found in the literature that was considered for this chapter. The table clearly shows the disparity in how different authors have tackled this issue. This is of course due to the fact that there is no such thing as an agreed-upon classification of the issues surrounding e-commerce. Therefore, authors have resorted to individual listings of issues, to varying degrees of specificity. Whereas authors like Monteiro and Teh have taken a very detailed approach, listing all of the issues that they could identify in e-commerce-related provisions in the RTAs that they studied, Herman has taken a more

1404 Burri, 'The Governance of Data and Data Flows in Trade Agreements: The Pitfalls of Legal Adaptation' (n 177) 93–95.

1405 ibid 128.

1406 Herman (n 1393) 11.

1407 Burri, 'The Governance of Data and Data Flows in Trade Agreements: The Pitfalls of Legal Adaptation' (n 177) 127.

1408 The shortcomings he identifies are related to the definition of digital trade/products, classification of digital services, lack of market access liberalisation, lack of provisions on cross-border data flows, consumer-related regulatory measures, security-related regulatory measures and trade facilitation. Wu (n 298) 5.

generic approach to the classification, grouping some specific issues (which other authors do indicate as separate categories) under three general headings: 'trade rules', 'domestic regulation' and 'other provisions'.[1409]

According to Lopez-Gonzalez and Ferencz, the provisions most commonly found in e-commerce chapters (i) confirm the applicability of trade rules to e-commerce; (ii) confirm application of the MFN and national treatment obligation;[1410] (iii) confirm and extend the customs duties moratorium indefinitely; (iv) prohibit discrimination on grounds of technology (thereby applying the principle of technological neutrality); and (v) aim at minimising regulatory burdens related to e-commerce.[1411] Mitchell and Mishra add disciplines on: (vi) cross-border data flows;[1412] (vii) privacy and data protection;[1413] (viii) so-called consumer confidence-enhancing measures;[1414] and (ix) cybersecurity and spam control.

The detailed approach taken by Monteiro and Teh illustrates the large amount of different provisions in RTAs that are related to electronic commerce. Through the identification of thirty-two separate types of provisions, the authors aptly drive home their point on the wide divergence of e-commerce-related provisions.[1415]

[1409] See respectively José-Antonio Monteiro and Robert Teh, 'Provisions on Electronic Commerce in Regional Trade Agreements' (World Trade Organization, Economic Research and Statistics Division 2017) ERSD-2017-11 <www.wto.org/english/res_e/reser_e/ersd201711_e.htm>; Herman (n 1393).

[1410] This, however, often includes a (long) list of non-conforming measures.

[1411] Lopez-Gonzalez and Ferencz (n 6) para 45.

[1412] Mitchell and Mishra (n 307) 1099.

[1413] Either through a general obligation to protect the personal information of digital users (e.g. ASEAN Australia New Zealand RTA and China – Korea RTA), through international standards of data protection (e.g. KOREU, referring to OECD standards) or through adopting a legal framework of protection of personal info (e.g. CPTPP and Japan-Mongolia RTA). ibid 1100.

[1414] Includes provisions on electronic signatures, electronic authentication, consumer protection and paperless trading. Either through regulatory cooperation between parties (e.g. KORUS, KOREU and Japan-Mongolia RTA) or through international standards (e.g. CPTPP, CHAFTA). ibid 1101.

[1415] The 'main types of e-commerce provisions' identified are: objectives of the chapter on e-commerce; scope of the e-commerce chapter; definitions of e-commerce; limitations of e-commerce chapter's scope; nature of electronic transmissions; no obligation to deliver products electronically; relation to the other chapters of the RTA; application of other chapters; application of general exceptions; relationship to other chapters in case of inconsistency with them; application of dispute settlement; applicability of WTO Rules; promotion of e-commerce; customs duties; barriers to trade; non-discrimination; regulatory framework; technological neutrality; electronic authentication and signatures; online consumer protection; cross-border transfer of information; personal

Wu notes that even though plenty of e-commerce chapters contain definitions, parties take a very disparate approach to the choice of terms that are defined.[1416] Monteiro and Teh remark on the fact that even though fifty-six of the seventy-five RTAs studied include definitions related to e-commerce, only four of them define e-commerce and none of them use the same definition as used by the WTO.[1417]

The scope of e-commerce chapters has been deemed of specific interest by several authors. The scope of many e-commerce chapters is limited, explicitly exempting, for example, government procurement, subsidies, taxation measures or measures affecting broadcasting.[1418] Whereas many RTAs include the national treatment and MFN treatment obligations in relation to electronic commerce, these are often limited in scope.[1419] Not only do many RTAs include a list of non-conforming measures, which also exempt these measures from e-commerce chapters, the RTAs' dispute settlement mechanism sometimes does not apply to the e-commerce provisions.[1420] Wu, however, rightfully points out that the soft language used in many e-commerce-related provisions in RTAs probably obviates the need for explicit carve-outs from the dispute settlement chapter.[1421]

Wu observes that one of the most common obligations (and sometimes even the only substantive obligation) that can be found requires parties not to impose customs duties on digital products.[1422] The wording of provisions addressing the WTO moratorium on electronic transmissions differ, considerably. Some confirm the applicability of the moratorium to the content that is being transmitted.[1423] Many RTAs

information protection; unsolicited commercial electronic messages; paperless trading administration; access to and use of Internet; use and location of computing facilities; software source code; liability of intermediary service providers; private sector participation; transparency; cooperation and technical assistance; institutional arrangements. Some of these types have been regrouped (i.e. considered to fall within a broader category because they are interlinked) in Table 8.1.

1416 Most often these include: digital products (with the caveat that this does not prejudice the goods v services debate), electronic authentication, electronic transmission and unsolicited commercial electronic messages. Wu (n 298) 9.

1417 Monteiro and Teh (n 1411) 17.

1418 ibid 18.

1419 Wu (n 298) 10.

1420 Examples include Australia – China RTA, ASEAN – Australia – New Zealand RTA, China – Korea RTA, Hong Kong, China – New Zealand RTA, New Zealand – Taiwan RTA. Herman (n 1393) 17; Wu (n 298) 26.

1421 Wu (n 298) 26.

1422 ibid 11, 13.

1423 See also Monteiro and Teh (n 1411) 28.

still ban the imposition of duties on the means of delivery, without mentioning the content or the underlying product itself.[1424] Most often this obligation extends to all digital products on an MFN basis, but some RTAs limit it to digital products coming from RTA partners.[1425] US RTAs are specific in this regard, as they distinguish between customs duties on digital products that are delivered electronically (prohibited) and customs duties on digital products delivered through physical transmission (customs value limited to the value of the carrier medium).[1426] Some RTAs limit themselves to a mere confirmation of the WPEC practice.[1427] Others explicitly allow for internal taxes.[1428]

Several authors focus on the prominent role of regulatory cooperation provisions in e-commerce chapters. Herman identifies several areas that are relevant for regulatory cooperation in e-commerce, including increased market access, removing obstacles for MSMEs, consumer protection and confidence, privacy and data protection, provision of financial services by electronic means, cybersecurity, IPRs, development of private sector self-regulation, e-government and paperless trade, and authentication and e-signatures.[1429] Monteiro and Teh observe several topics in provisions related to the regulatory framework on e-commerce: the aim of minimising the regulatory burden; the focus on transparency and predictability; information exchange; and interoperability, innovation and competition.[1430] Moreover, they identify thirteen specific areas of e-commerce cooperation, adding also an 'other areas' category.[1431] Wu observes that it is mainly the EU and EFTA RTAs that focus on cooperation provisions related to e-commerce, often listing policy areas that are considered important.[1432] Especially

[1424] Similar to the moratorium formulated at the WTO.

[1425] E.g. Korea – Singapore RTA. Wu (n 298) 11.

[1426] See also Chile – Colombia RTA, GCC – Singapore RTA and Colombia – Northern Triangle RTA. ibid 12.

[1427] EFTA – Central America RTA and Japan – Switzerland RTA. ibid.

[1428] E.g. CPTPP, Canada – Honduras RTA, Colombia – Northern Triangle RTA, Costa Rica – Singapore RTA and Pacific Alliance.

[1429] Herman (n 1393) 15.

[1430] Monteiro and Teh (n 1411) 38.

[1431] E-commerce promotion, regulatory framework, consumer protection, electronic signature/authentication, paperless trading/e-government, personal data protection, private sector/MSME participation, cybersecurity, consumer confidence, intellectual property, cross-border information transfer, unsolicited commercial electronic messages and liability of intermediary service providers. ibid 67.

[1432] Wu (n 298) 26.

Asia-Pacific RTAs contain cooperation provisions that relate to facilitating trade for MSMEs and the collaboration with the private sector.[1433]

The principle of technological neutrality takes many forms in RTAs. Certain RTAs (especially Japanese RTAs) contain an explicit recognition of the principle of technological neutrality. Others prohibit discrimination between different forms of technology, thereby implying technological neutrality. Such implicit recognition can be found in various provisions throughout RTAs, including the requirement of non-discriminatory treatment of digital trade, the requirement of equivalent protection of consumers and the recognition of electronic trade documents.[1434]

Monteiro and Teh argue that the provisions on the nature of electronic transmission show the historical disagreement between WTO Members on whether this constitutes the provision of services or goods.[1435] Whereas some, mainly EU, RTAs explicitly recognise electronic transmission as the provision of services, other RTAs clarify that the inclusion of the e-commerce provisions do not prejudge whether electronic transmission qualifies as a good or a service. Others state that the inclusion of a definition of 'digital product' in the RTA does not affect ongoing discussion at the WTO or the domestic qualification of such products.[1436]

Several provisions require parties to mutually recognise one another's technologies, authentication procedures, etc. This is the case for provisions on electronic authentication, as well as for electronic certification and electronic signatures.[1437] Provisions on electronic authentication and signatures are found in approximately half of the studied RTAs[1438] but they take very different forms, ranging from establishing technological neutrality in recognition of certificates and technologies, focussing on the importance of interoperability to the requirement of mutual recognition.[1439] Governments often explicitly maintain their right to establish performance requirements for authentication technologies or to require specific electronic certifications.[1440]

One of the most commonly found obligations when it comes to e-commerce-related provisions are those on paperless trade.[1441] Such

1433 ibid 25.
1434 Monteiro and Teh (n 1411) 40–42.
1435 *Supra* Section 1.2.1.
1436 Monteiro and Teh (n 1411) 19.
1437 Herman (n 1393) 16.
1438 But thereby also conspicuously absent from RTAs among high income countries.
1439 Wu (n 298) 15–17.
1440 ibid 16.
1441 These are sometimes the only e-commerce provisions in RTAs. E.g. China – Peru RTA, Japan – Thailand RTA and Japan – Singapore RTA. ibid 18–19. Provisions on paperless

provisions were among the first e-commerce-related provisions to be included in RTAs. These provisions focus on facilitating e-commerce as they require RTA parties to make trade administration documents electronically available and, importantly, to recognise electronic documents as legally equivalent to their paper version.[1442] They often take the form of commitments from governments to make electronic versions of trade documents publicly available and/or to accept electronically submitted documents as equivalent (sometimes with certain exceptions).[1443]

Provisions on the protection of users of e-commerce take equally diverging forms. Provisions on consumer protection are found in most e-commerce chapters. Whereas most parties settle for a simple recognition of the importance of consumer protection, a small number of RTAs go considerably further by requiring parties to adopt binding consumer protection laws.[1444] Some RTAs stipulate that e-commerce consumers should receive protection equal to that of offline consumers and most call for cooperation on these issues. Provisions on the protection of personal information are less frequently included, as it seems that some important RTA parties still need to figure out their domestic stance on how to balance data flows and privacy.[1445] Due to the APEC Privacy Framework, many APEC countries have included provisions on the protection of personal information in their RTAs.[1446] Generally, these provisions recognise the need for protection, refer to relevant international standards or require parties to adopt or maintain a legal framework on the protection of personal information.[1447]

trade are the most consistently included e-commerce provisions in Korean RTAs. Evan Y Kim, 'E-Commerce in South Korean FTAs: Policy Priorities and Provisional Inconsistencies' (2019) 18 World Trade Review 85, 94.

1442 Herman (n 1393) 17.

1443 Wu (n 298) 18.

1444 Monteiro and Teh (n 1411) 47; Wu (n 298) 19.

1445 The most straightforward example can be found in the EU – Japan EPA where Article 8.81 stipulates 'The Parties shall reassess within three years of the date of entry into force of this Agreement the need for inclusion of provisions on the free flow of data into this Agreement'. This provision was allegedly prompted by the EU's internal ambiguity as to the protection of personal data (which was subsequently addressed in the GDPR, as discussed in Chapter 7 of this book). Other countries consistently include such provisions. For example, in a study on South Korean RTAs, it was found that 9 out of 10 Korean RTAs contained clauses on both consumer protection and personal data protection. Kim (n 1443) 95.

1446 Wu (n 298) 20.

1447 Examples of the latter can be found in the Australia – Singapore RTA, CPTPP and generally RTAs with Australia, Canada, New Zealand and Korea. ibid.

A very limited number of RTAs contain a provision recognising the importance of ensuring access to and use of digital products and services of the consumer's choice and/or the benefit of competition among network providers and content providers.[1448] Various RTAs include provisions on the liability of intermediary service suppliers, either in IPR or e-commerce chapters.[1449] Several RTAs also refer to international agreements. The UNCITRAL model law on electronic commerce[1450] seems to have been included most frequently, especially in RTAs involving Australia or New Zealand.[1451] The model law was one of the first instruments to include technological neutrality and the functional equivalence of paperless trading.[1452] Finally, several RTAs also include a prohibition on the disclosure of source code as a condition for conducting business in a party's territory.[1453]

8.2 Selection of RTAs and Method of Analysis

8.2.1 How the Relevant RTAs Were Selected

In this part of the book I perform an analysis, in the first instance, of the body of RTAs that contain e-commerce provisions, *inter alia,* on the basis of the parties' geographical location and income level and, in the second instance, of how certain specific RTAs address barriers to digital trade in services. To conduct this analysis, I compiled a list of relevant RTAs and analysed the texts of these RTAs. I limited the group of relevant RTAs studied in two ways: (i) only RTAs that are currently in force or are pending authentication are taken into account; and (ii) only RTAs that contain provisions related to e-commerce.

The WTO maintains the RTAs Information System (RTA-IS), which contains information on those RTAs that have been notified to the

1448 Monteiro and Teh (n 1411) 59.
1449 ibid 61.
1450 The UNCITRAL model law was adopted in 1996 with the aim to enable and facilitate commerce conducted through electronic means through rules aimed at removing legal obstacles and increasing legal predictability for electronic commerce. In 2020, 74 countries had adopted the model law. For more information see UNCITRAL, 'UNCITRAL Model Law on Electronic Commerce (1996)', available at <www.uncitral.org/uncitral/en/uncitral_texts/electronic_commerce/1996Model.html>.
1451 Wu (n 298) 14.
1452 ibid 13.
1453 For example: CPTPP, Australia – Singapore RTA, Japan – Mongolia RTA. ibid 24.

Table 8.1 *Classification of issues in e-commerce-related RTA provisions*[1454]

	Herman (2010)	Lopez-Gonzalez and Ferencz (2018)	Mitchell and Mishra (2018)	Monteiro and Teh (2017)	Wu (2017)
Chapter objective		X		X	
Scope		X		X	
Definition	X	X		X	X
Limitations of scope				X	
Nature of electronic transmissions		X		X	
No obligation to deliver products electronically				X	
Promotion of e-commerce		X		X	
Technological neutrality		X		X	
Trade rules	X				
Applicability WTO rules	x	X		X	X
Applicability RTA rules	x	X		X	
Customs duty moratorium	x	X	X	X	X
Transparency	x	X		X	
Non-discrimination	x	X	X	X	X
Domestic regulation	X				
Avoiding unnecessary barriers	x	X		X	
E-authentication and e-signature	x	X		X	X

[1454] Legend: X = separate category; x = included within a category (not a separate category in itself).

Table 8.1 (*cont.*)

	Herman (2010)	Lopez-Gonzalez and Ferencz (2018)	Mitchell and Mishra (2018)	Monteiro and Teh (2017)	Wu (2017)
Consumer protection	x	X	X	X	X
Data/privacy protection	x	X	X	X	X
Other provisions	X				
Paperless trade	x	X		X	X
Cooperation	x	X	X	X	X
IPRs	x				
Applicability DSM	x				X
Unsolicited commercial electronic messages		X	X	X	X
Access to and use of the Internet				X	
Use and location of computing facilities		X		X	X
Liability of intermediary service suppliers		X		X	
Software source code		X		X	X
Private sector participation		X		X	
Institutional arrangements		X		X	
UNCITRAL model law		X	X		X
Cross-border data flows		X	X		X

WTO.[1455] This database allows users to filter the notified RTAs on various bases, including the topics that they cover. The notified RTAs in this database were filtered on their inclusion of the topic 'E-Commerce', which yielded a list of ninety-one RTAs. To allow for a more detailed and nuanced analysis, I supplemented the list of RTAs to be studied with additional variables: the date of entry into force, the names of the parties to the RTA, the geographical region of each party and the income level of each party.

The list of RTAs procured from the RTA-IS was subsequently cross-checked against lists of RTAs containing e-commerce-related provisions that could be found in WTO documents and literature.[1456] Additionally, recently concluded RTAs (or those awaiting ratification) that had not yet been notified but that also contained e-commerce-related provisions were added to the list. Finally, a new phenomenon appeared in 2020, with countries concluding stand-alone digital trade agreements.[1457] Even though these agreements strictly speaking do not qualify as free trade agreements in the sense of Article V GATS, they have been included in the dataset and are considered 'RTAs' for the purpose of this chapter's analysis.[1458] This resulted in a final dataset of 105 RTAs.[1459] The analysis is conducted on the basis of the full text of the RTAs with the exception of the annexes and parties' schedules. However, specific annexes on e-commerce remain included.[1460] This delimitation of the studied text ensures that the analysis is focussed on the obligations and rights that have been included in the text of the agreement and that these do not get confounded by possible party-

1455 The Regional Trade Agreements Information System (RTA-IS) can be accessed at <http://rtais.wto.org/UI/PublicMaintainRTAHome.aspx>.

1456 Including WTO Work Programme on Electronic Commerce, 'Non-Paper for the Discussions on Electronic Commerce/Digital Trade from Japan', JOB/GC/100, 25 July 2016, 5–8; Mira Burri and Rodrigo Polanco Lazo, 'E-Commerce And Data Flows Provisions In Preferential Trade Agreements: Introducing A New Dataset' (2020) 23 Journal of International Economic Law 187; Lopez-Gonzalez and Ferencz (n 6); Monteiro and Teh (n 1411); Wu (n 298). Monteiro and Teh based their selection of relevant RTAs on their use of specific terms: 'computerized', 'cyber', 'digital', 'electronic', 'electronic commerce, 'e-commerce', 'e-government', 'information and communication', 'ITC', 'Internet', 'online', 'paperless' and 'telecommunication'.

1457 More specifically, this includes the Digital Economy Partnership Agreement between Chile, New Zealand and Singapore (DEPA) and the US–Japan Digital Trade Agreement.

1458 It is debatable whether a digital trade agreement has 'substantial sectoral coverage' in the sense of Article V:1(a) GATS.

1459 This list of relevant RTAs is up to date until 1 September 2020.

1460 See for example the EFTA RTAs.

specific carve-outs or commitments undertaken in services schedules.[1461]

8.2.2 Descriptive Statistics to Analyse E-commerce Provisions in RTAs

Various methods can be used to analyse the text of e-commerce provisions in RTAs. Monteiro and Teh, for example, use the Jaccard Index[1462] to measure the degree of similarity in e-commerce provisions and network analysis to study the similarity of provisions by income group. The combination of these two techniques is used to analyse the heterogeneity of e-commerce provisions in RTAs.[1463] On the basis of these approaches, they concluded that the level of similarity between the provisions is generally quite low, but that the level of similarity increases in tandem with the number of provisions that RTAs have in common.[1464] Interestingly, even the RTAs that have been negotiated by the same countries show significant divergence in their provisions.[1465] The dissimilarity of these provisions highlights the importance of using a number of different terms to detect the same type of provisions.[1466]

8.2.2.1 Term-frequency Analysis

This chapter utilises a term-frequency analysis to identify the presence of e-commerce provisions in the corpus of RTAs. The use of text-mining tools allows for an efficient and accurate summarisation of the e-commerce language used in RTAs. A corpus of text-data comprising the 105 RTAs constitutes the basis for the analysis in this chapter. The data of interest is generated from the corpus by identifying specific terms relating to various aspects of e-commerce provisions. Where relevant, the analysis is supplemented by covariates relating to the RTAs (entry into force) and the parties (geographical region and income level).

[1461] This is prompted by the inherent limitations to the text-mining technique applied in this chapter. As descriptive analysis of the presence of terms does not take account of the specific context for the terms, I tried to exclude mentions of these terms not in the context of parties' obligations. An additional reason to exclude schedules was to improve the readability of the texts by the program 'R'.

[1462] The Jaccard index is a statistic used for comparing the similarity and diversity of sample sets.

[1463] Monteiro and Teh (n 1411) 8–9.

[1464] ibid 9.

[1465] ibid 10.

[1466] As observed: '*[The] heterogeneity of e-commerce provisions in RTAs negotiated by the same countries foreshadows the difficulty in identifying strong commonalities in e-commerce provisions across agreements*'. ibid 11.

More specifically, the text-mining task performed in this research is term extraction. The text analysis performed was limited to information retrieval: the presence of certain specific terms in the corpus. The data used in this analysis is twofold: the texts of the 105 RTAs (excluding schedules and annexes) and the characteristics of the RTAs (parties, date of entry into force, region and income level). This data was processed and structured into a database, mapping the presence of the searched-for terms for each RTA. The structured data was compiled and analysed using the R software environment.

Machine-assisted text analysis, contrary to 'manual' searching, allows for an exhaustive and structured analysis of the use of several e-commerce-related terms in a relatively large corpus of agreements. As noted by Alschner, Pauwelyn and Puig, data-driven research can be used for descriptive and exploratory research, with the aim of better understanding a large corpus of texts.[1467] They, however, also note that data-driven research cannot substitute critical reflection or in-depth case studies but that it is a complementary research method.[1468] This chapter should therefore be considered as a preliminary venture into the analysis of the evolution of e-commerce-related provisions in RTAs.

The added characteristics of the RTAs allow for a more nuanced distinction and a comparison of trends between regions and income levels. Both the indication of the geographical region and of the income level was based on the World Bank's country-specific information.[1469] In the case of the RTAs at issue, seven separate geographical regions were identified: East Asia and Pacific, Europe and Central Asia, Latin America and Caribbean, Middle East and Northern Africa, North America, South Asia and Sub-Saharan Africa. The income levels identified are high income, upper middle income, lower middle income and low income. Finally, for the information on the year of entry into force, some of the RTAs included have not yet entered into force, but their legal text has already been agreed upon. On the timelines used in the graphs, these RTAs are indicated with 'NA'. One RTA already entered into force in 1994,[1470] all of the other RTAs studied entered into force between 2001 and 2020.

1467 Wolfgang Alschner, Joost Pauwelyn and Sergio Puig, 'The Data-Driven Future of International Economic Law' (2017) 20 Journal of International Economic Law 217, 223–225.

1468 ibid 230.

1469 The World Bank's country-specific information can be found at <https://data.worldbank.org/country>.

1470 The European Economic Area, between the EU, Iceland, Liechtenstein and Norway.

A merely terms-based analysis is confronted with several limitations, all of which should be taken into consideration when interpreting the outcome of this study. First, the presence of certain terms does not paint a conclusive picture as to how the terms are used in that RTA. Whether a term is being used to grant parties certain rights, to impose obligations or to exclude provisions from the scope of certain chapters cannot be deduced from the results of a term-frequency analysis. Second, an analysis of the terms does not clarify the extent of commitments parties have undertaken, as it does not take into account whether the terms are used in the context of a soft provision or a provision that imposes strict obligations. Nor does it clarify the meaning given to specific terms.[1471] It will therefore not always give an indication of whether the provisions impose considerable GATS+ obligations or not. The number of terms present in an RTA only says so much on the commitment that parties have undertaken. It is, however, maintained that the analysis of terms extracted from a large number of documents provides interesting insights into the historical evolution of e-commerce chapters in RTAs.

8.2.2.2 Selection of the Terms

The terms were selected on the basis of their specific relevance to certain e-commerce-related provisions by analysing a curated sample of RTAs with parties from various regions and income levels. This allows for the chosen terms to cover as many e-commerce-related provisions as possible. The curated list of terms is neither claimed to be exhaustive nor to allow for a complete picture of the content of the e-commerce chapters of these RTAs. Rather, it covers various elements that are generally present (or expected to be present) in such chapters.

For the choice of relevant terms, several considerations were taken into account. First, due to the wide disparity in RTA parties' approach to the e-commerce issues, many Members have used (slightly) different terms to refer to the same kinds of products, obligations and policy objectives. To address this issue, I grouped various related terms under several categories that map different types of e-commerce provisions that can be found in the RTAs. Second, the terms must be chosen in a way to ensure that they only relate to digital trade and not to other aspects of the RTAs. Because e-commerce-related provisions are not limited to what can be found in specific e-commerce chapters, this analysis looks into the use of specific terms throughout complete RTAs. To avoid 'false' reporting of the presence

[1471] For example, the meaning given to the term 'digital products' differs between Korea's different RTAs. Kim (n 1443) 88.

of certain terms in these RTAs, I limited the selected terms to those inextricably linked to e-commerce.[1472] Third, not all of the RTAs analysed in this study came with an English translation. The text of several RTAs could only be provided in Spanish. Therefore, the search terms have been translated into Spanish, to be able to include these agreements into the analysis as well.

The first category ('scope') includes the terms 'digital product', 'electronic commerce', 'electronic supply', 'information service' 'electronic means', 'electronic transmission' and 'carrier medium'.[1473] The aim of this category is to analyse the extent of the scope of the e-commerce provisions as well as the general extent of the e-commerce chapters (or provisions). The scope of the e-commerce provisions will partly be determined by the mention of terms such as 'digital product', 'by electronic means' and 'electronic transmission'. The general extent (and length) of the e-commerce chapter or provisions can partly be inferred from how often the terms related to basic e-commerce notions (such as 'electronic commerce' and 'electronic supply') are mentioned throughout the RTA. It is hypothesised that the more of these basic e-commerce-related provisions are included (and the longer an e-commerce chapter is), the more often the 'scope' terms will be mentioned.

The second group of terms relates to trade facilitation and covers the terms 'use of the Internet', 'electronic payment', 'electronic signature', electronic authentication', 'paperless' and 'digital certificate'.[1474] 'Use of Internet' is a term used in the context of enabling access to and use of the Internet to foreign service suppliers, which can be a practical obstacle for suppliers to supply their service within a market. The term 'electronic payment' is included as this is an essential element in enabling electronic commerce. Finally, the terms 'digital certificate', 'electronic authentication' and 'electronic signature' were included as these all contribute towards

[1472] To limit false reporting for 'customs duties' and 'cooperation', terms which can be found throughout any RTA and often not linked to e-commerce provisions, the script used a 'wildcard' for a limited amount of terms that could be in between the terms 'customs duties' and 'electronic transmission' on the one hand and 'cooperation' and 'electronic commerce' on the other hand. Through the use of these wildcards, it was possible to search for provisions on customs duties and cooperation in the context of electronic commerce.

[1473] These Spanish variations were included as well: 'producto(s) digital(es)', 'comercio electrónico', 'suministro electrónico', 'servicio(s) de información', 'transmisión electrónica', 'transmitido electrónicamente' and 'medio partador'.

[1474] Variations included: 'e-payment', 'e-signature', 'e-authentication', 'digital certifications'. Spanish translations used: 'use del Internet', 'pago electrónico', 'firma(s) electrónica(s)', 'autenticación electrónica', 'autenticación digital', 'sin papeles', 'sin papel' and 'certificado(s) digital(es)'.

paperless (and therefore facilitated) trade.[1475] Provisions containing these terms aim at facilitating trade in general but they are closely related to electronic commerce as the digitisation of customs procedures and provision of electronic versions of trade administration documents are key in order to allow for more seamless e-commerce (especially in its impact on MSMEs). 'Cooperation' on digital issues was added to this category as well. To this end, the term 'cooperation [. . .] electronic commerce' was included.[1476] This category is therefore referred to as 'trade facilitation and cooperation'.

The third category of terms aims to address and include some specific barriers to digital trade. The category of 'specific barriers' includes the terms 'source code', 'customs duties [. . .] electronic transmission' and 'unsolicited commercial electronic messages'.[1477] All of these terms are related to provisions addressing specific barriers to electronic commerce: the prohibition on the transfer of source code as a requirement to trade, the prohibition of customs duties on electronic transmission or electronic products, and provisions related to the prevention of spam. Their presence will provide an insight into whether parties have explicitly addressed some barriers specific to e-commerce in their RTA.

The fourth category, 'data flows', focusses on the most discussed specific barrier to e-commerce: barriers to cross-border data flows. Because these barriers are specific to electronic commerce and the provisions addressing them use very specific language, relevant provisions are relatively easily identifiable. The category includes 'location of computing facilities', 'transfer of information' and 'information flow' as terms that indicate the presence of provisions related to data flows.[1478] Whereas the first term indicates a provision on data localisation requirements, the latter two allow for the identification of a broader group of provisions related to cross-border data flows.

[1475] The distinction between electronic authentication and digital certificates lies in that the former is the confirmation or certification of electronic identities and works whereas the latter authenticates web credentials of (encrypted) data.

[1476] Variations included: 'co-operation [. . .] electronic commerce'. Spanish translations used: 'cooperación sobre comercio electrónico' and 'cooperación [. . .] comercio electrónico'.

[1477] Variations included: 'customs duties [. . .] electronic commerce', 'customs duties [. . .] delivered electronically' and 'unsolicited commercial electronic communications'. Spanish translations used: 'código fuente', 'derechos de aduana a las transmisiones electrónicas', 'derechos aduaneros [. . .] de productos digitales', 'aranceles aduaneros a productos digitales', 'mensajes electrónicos comerciales no solicitados', 'mensajes comerciales electrónicos no solicitados'.

[1478] Variations included: 'data flow'. Spanish translations used: 'ubicación de las instalaciones informáticas', 'flujos de información', 'corrientes de información', 'flujo transfronterizo de información'.

The fifth and final category includes the policy objectives that are related to e-commerce. The terms included in this category are 'cybersecurity', 'online consumer protection', 'privacy' and 'personal data protection'.[1479] These terms all indicate policy objectives that are of specific relevance when regulating electronic commerce. The presence of these terms indicates that parties have decided to explicitly acknowledge the importance of these policy objectives and that they probably have agreed to balance these objectives with the aim of removing barriers to e-commerce.

8.3 General Observations and Historical Perspective

So far, it has proven difficult to map the general evolution of e-commerce provision in all RTAs. Figure 8.2 displays all of the RTAs that have been notified to the WTO and which have entered into force between 1990 and

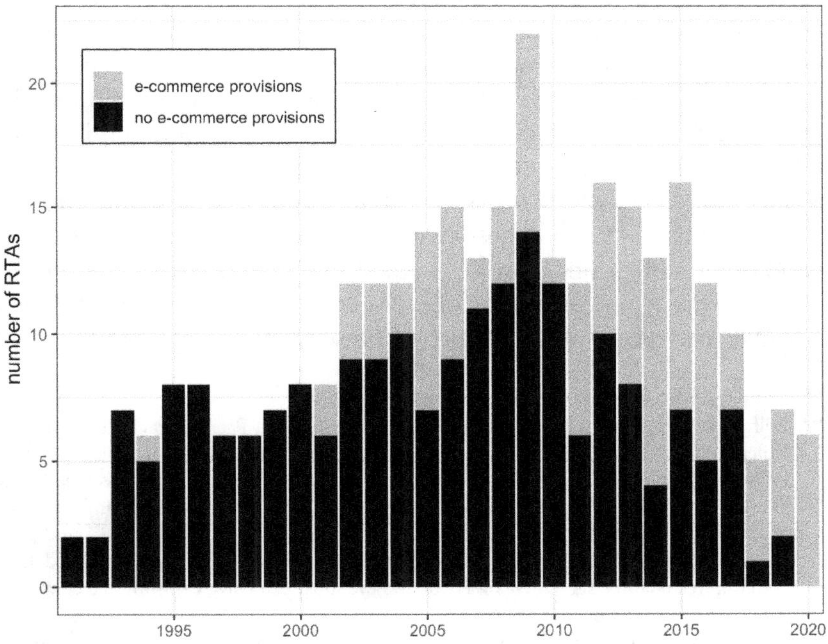

Figure 8.2 All RTAs that entered into force between 1990 and 2020

[1479] Variations included: 'cyber security', 'protection of online consumers', 'personal information protection', 'online data protection', 'protection of personal information' and 'protection of personal data'. Spanish translations used: 'ciberseguridad', 'protección al consumidor en línea', 'protección de los consumidores en línea', 'privacidad', 'protección de datos personales', 'protección de la información personal'.

2020, dividing them into those that contain e-commerce provisions and those that do not. The graph shows that the first RTA containing e-commerce provisions entered into force in 1994 but that e-commerce provisions have only been included in at least one RTA every year from 2001 onwards. Even though an increase in the number of e-commerce RTAs can be observed, this increase is hardly linear.[1480] Overall, more RTAs are concluded that do not contain any e-commerce references than those that do. From 2011 onwards, the pace of e-commerce RTAs entering into force, however, significantly picked up. In 2011, an equal number of e-commerce and non-e-commerce RTAs entered into force. In 2014, 2015, 2016, 2018 and 2019 more RTAs with e-commerce provisions entered into force than those without. This indicates that the trend to make e-commerce provisions a staple in modern RTAs is solidifying.

When studying Asian-Pacific RTAs, Weber notes that the inclusion of e-commerce provisions in RTAs has happened in discernible waves.[1481] During e-commerce's infancy (2000–2002), relevant provisions focussed on paperless trading. E-commerce chapters started to be included in RTAs from 2003 onwards[1482] and RTA parties have moved through more and less inclusion of e-commerce-related provisions until 2011: whereas some RTAs consistently included a basic chapter on e-commerce, others merely referenced paperless trading, cooperation or nothing at all.[1483] During that period, most extensive e-commerce provisions can be found in the Korea–Singapore RTA and the Singapore–India RTA. From 2014 onwards, a new generation of RTAs can be identified that considerably liberalise e-commerce.[1484] It has, however, been reported that the

[1480] Consider the low values in 2004, 2007, 2008 and 2010.

[1481] Rolf H Weber, 'The Expansion of E-Commerce in Asia-Pacific Trade Agreements' (International Centre for Trade and Sustainable Development (ICTSD) (2015) <http://e15initiative.org/blogs/the-expansion-of-e-commerce-in-asia-pacific-trade-agreements/>.

[1482] The pioneering RTA being the Australia – Singapore RTA, which included an extensive chapter on e-commerce for its time. This agreement was updated in 2017 and the Australia – Singapore Digital Economy Agreement as signed in 2020 updated the e-commerce chapter again. This RTA boasts the most extensive e-commerce chapters in RTAs at the time of writing.

[1483] For example, two ASEAN RTAs only include soft e-commerce cooperation references (due to this extremely limited scope, these RTAs were not included in the list of studied RTAs): Art. 7.3 of the China – ASEAN RTA indicates 'promotion of e-commerce' as an area for cooperation and Article 6 of the Framework Agreement on Comprehensive Economic Cooperation Between the Republic of India and the Association of Southeast Asian Nations (ASEAN) mentions electronic commerce as a sector of economic cooperation.

[1484] Even the historically reluctant Japan started including e-commerce-related provisions in its RTAs.

rules in these RTAs are generally unclear on their implementation and enforceability.[1485]

Looking more generally at the history of e-commerce provisions in RTAs, the two very first e-commerce-related provisions can be found in EU RTAs: the EEA Agreement in 1994 and the EU–Mexico Agreement in 2000. Both of these provisions required cooperation with regard to 'information services' and 'the information society', respectively.[1486] Other scholars have pointed to the New Zealand–Singapore RTA (2001) as the first to include a provision on paperless trading.[1487] This example was swiftly followed in the Japan–Singapore RTA (2002). The US–Jordan RTA (2001) was the very first RTA to include a dedicated e-commerce provision.[1488] This is a remarkable feat, especially considering the fact that the agreement only contains nineteen articles.[1489] The Australia–Singapore RTA (2003) was the first to include a dedicated chapter on electronic commerce.[1490] The United States started including e-commerce chapters and stronger obligations in its RTAs from 2004 onwards.[1491] In the US–Australia RTA (2005) provisions on authentication, digital products, online consumer protection and paperless trade were added.[1492] KORUS, concluded in 2012, was the first RTA to include specific language on the principle of open networks and the free flow of information in its e-commerce chapter.[1493]

E-commerce-related provisions are not necessarily gathered in a specific e-commerce chapter. Several RTAs, old and new, have scattered e-commerce provisions throughout the text of the agreement or grouped e-commerce provisions in broader (often trade in services-related)

1485 Weber (n 1483).

1486 Article 78 EEA Agreement and Article 20 EU – Mexico RTA. As the 2000 EU – Mexico RTA will soon be replaced by the newly agreed upon RTA between both parties, the 2000 RTA was not taken into account for the rest of the analysis in this Chapter (as the focus lies on the new EU – Mexico RTA).

1487 Monteiro and Teh (n 1411) 5.

1488 Jie Huang, 'Comparison of E-Commerce Regulations in Chinese and American FTAs: Converging Approaches, Diverging Contents, and Polycentric Directions?' (2017) 64 Netherlands International Law Review 309, 316.

1489 Article 7 on electronic commerce sets out that parties recognise the economic growth and opportunity provided by electronic commerce and the importance of avoiding barriers and that they seek to refrain from *inter alia* imposing customs duties and unnecessary barriers on electronic transmissions.

1490 Monteiro and Teh (n 1411) 5; Wu (n 298) 6.

1491 See the US – Chile RTA and the US – Singapore RTA, both of which entered into force on 1 January 2004.

1492 Huang (n 1490) 316.

1493 Aaronson and Leblond (n 116) 255; ibid 316–317. See Articles 15.7 and 15.8 KORUS.

chapters. One of the advantages of including e-commerce rules in a separate chapter of an RTA is that it avoids the discussion on the goods versus services classification and does not require Members to take an explicit position in this ongoing debate.[1494] Out of 339 RTAs currently in force, 105 contain e-commerce-related provisions, out of which 73 contain a chapter solely dedicated to e-commerce.[1495] Not a single RTA with a Sub-Saharan African country includes a separate e-commerce chapter. It is interesting to note that out of the six RTAs that China has concluded that contain e-commerce-related provisions, only three contain a separate e-commerce chapter.[1496] Additionally, whereas most e-commerce chapter-less RTAs were concluded in the early 2000s, in the last few years some RTAs have been concluded that contain e-commerce provisions but not in a separate chapter, notably the Chile–Thailand RTA, the Malaysia–Turkey RTA and the China–Georgia RTA. A remarkable amount of EU RTAs do not contain a separate chapter on e-commerce. Rather, they group e-commerce provisions in chapters together with investment and trade in services provisions.[1497]

In assessing these numbers, it should be taken into account that the presence of a separate RTA chapter does not necessarily entail more extensive provisions and/or obligations. For example, the Chile–Thailand RTA (no separate chapter) contains more of the searched-for terms than either the New Zealand–Taiwan RTA or the Hong Kong–Georgia RTA, both of which contain dedicated chapters. However, there is a clear general trend for considerably more inclusion of the e-commerce-related terms in RTAs that contain a separate chapter. The average term count for RTAs

[1494] Wunsch-Vincent and Hold (n 497) 202.

[1495] The following RTAs do not include a separate chapter on electronic commerce: the European Economic Area Agreement (EEA 1994), New Zealand – Singapore (2001), US – Jordan (2002), CARICOM Treaty (2002), Japan – Singapore (2002), Canada – Costa Rica (2003), China – Hong Kong (2003), China – Macao (2003), Gulf Cooperation Council Agreement (GCC 2003), EU – Algeria (2005), EU – Chile (2005), Trans-Pacific Strategic Economic Partnership Agreement (TPSEP 2006), Central European Free Trade Agreement (CEFTA 2007), Japan – Thailand (2007), Japan – Philippines (2008), EU – Korea (2011), EU – Eastern and Southern African States (ESA 2012), EU – Cameroon (2014), EU – Georgia (2014), EU – Moldova (2014), EU – Ukraine (2014), EFTA – GCC (2014), Chile – Thailand (2015), EU – Bosnia and Herzegovina (2015), Malaysia – Turkey (2015), EU – Ghana (2016), EU – Côte d'Ivoire (2016), China – Georgia (2018), EU – Armenia (2018), EU – Japan (2019), EU – Singapore (2020) and EU – Vietnam (NA).

[1496] And these three RTAs were concluded with high-income or upper-middle-income countries with a strong tradition of including e-commerce in their agreements: Australia, Chile and Korea.

[1497] Thereby taking an implicit position in the good v service debate.

without separate e-commerce chapter is twenty, compared to an average of seventy-four terms for RTAs with dedicated e-commerce chapters.[1498]

Focussing on the countries that have concluded e-commerce provisions in RTAs, it has been observed that the United States, Australia and Singapore RTAs have consistently included e-commerce provisions and thereby played a significant role in the proliferation of these provisions.[1499] At a later stage, they were joined by Canada, the EU, Japan and Korea.[1500] China has sparingly started including e-commerce-related provisions from 2003 onwards.

Not only high-income economies have pursued substantive e-commerce chapters in their RTAs.[1501] Countries like Colombia, Costa Rica, Mexico, Panama and Peru have concluded a considerable number of RTAs with e-commerce-related provisions.[1502] Already two-thirds of the WTO Membership is party to an RTA that includes e-commerce-related provisions.[1503] The discernible trends of e-commerce provisions in RTAs per region and income level are discussed in more detail *infra*.

Several authors have already indicated a significant heterogeneity in structure, language and scope of e-commerce provisions throughout RTAs.[1504] As to the most prevalent provisions, it has been reported that most RTAs include provisions on the elimination of customs duties, consumer protection, authentication methods, electronic signature and paperless trading.[1505] Provisions on data localisation, cross-border data flows and mandated transfer of source code are more rare. Both of these statements are confirmed by the results produced from the data frame created for this chapter's analysis.[1506] A considerable overlap exists

1498 Based on author's own calculations.

1499 Herman (n 1393) 14.

1500 Their first e-commerce chapters can respectively be found in the EU – CARIFORUM RTA (2008), Canada – Peru RTA (2009), Japan – Switzerland RTA (2009), and Korea – Singapore RTA (2006). Wu (n 298) 7.

1501 ibid 6.

1502 Based on author's own calculations: Colombia (9), Costa Rica (7), Mexico (6), Panama (6) and Peru (9).

1503 108 out of 164 WTO Members are party to an RTA that includes at least one e-commerce related provision. Calculations based on own database.

1504 Manfred Elsig and Sebastian Klotz, 'Data Flow-Related Provisions in Preferential Trade Agreements' (World Trade Institute 2018) 03/2018 4; Kim (n 1443) 97–98; Monteiro and Teh (n 1411) 71.

1505 ICTSD (n 895) 3.

1506 Provisions on customs duties in e-commerce can be found in 68 RTAs, provisions on consumer protection in 55 RTAs, provisions on e-authentication in 39 RTAs, provisions on e-signatures in 56 RTAs and provisions on paperless trade in 55 RTAs. This is very different for provision on data localisation and source code, which are counted in

between RTAs that contain provisions on data localisation and source code.[1507]

8.3.1 Use of All the Terms in the RTAs

Figure 8.3 sets out the total amount of terms that have been found in all of the 105 studied RTAs, ordered chronologically. Each RTA is indicated by the standardised two-letter code for the countries party to the RTA (ISO Alpha-2) or by its generally used abbreviation. This plot allows for an analysis of the general evolution of the use of the e-commerce-related terms in RTAs over time. It is presumed that a high amount of terms found in a single RTA indicates the presence of a highly developed e-commerce chapter.[1508]

Some observations can be made. First, there does not appear to be a clear linear trend of increased use of e-commerce terms over time. Even some of the earliest RTAs already contain a significant amount of e-commerce terms and low presence of terms happens throughout the whole timeline. Here, it should of course be taken into account that this graph only includes RTAs that include at least one e-commerce term. The plot would arguably look different if the RTAs that do not include any reference to e-commerce terms had also been included. The fact that e-commerce-related provisions can already be found in the early 2000s should not surprise though, as the discussions related to e-commerce at the WTO level have been ongoing since 1998. It is clear that from 2001 onwards, some Members considered that certain specific e-commerce provisions deserved inclusion in their RTAs.

Second, three very recent RTAs clearly tower above the rest: the CPTPP, the USMCA and the Australia–Singapore RTA. All three contain a much higher amount of e-commerce terms, compared to the other RTAs that have been included. The presence of CPTPP and USMCA among the top three already hints at the United States' influence on the inclusion of far-

10 RTAs each. Provisions mentioning data flows or data transfer are more prevalent and can be found in a total of 54 RTAs.

1507 The terms related to data localisation provisions were found in ten RTAs: the Japan – Mongolia RTA, the Australia – Singapore RTA, the CPTPP, the Singapore – Sri Lanka RTA, the USMCA, the Australia – Peru RTA, the Australia – Indonesia RTA, the Australia – Hong Kong RTA, DEPA and the US – Japan Digital Trade Agreement. Eight of these agreements also included a provision on the transfer of source code, together with the EU – Japan RTA and the EU – Mexico RTA.

1508 Or, if no chapter is present, indicates well-developed e-commerce provisions throughout the RTA.

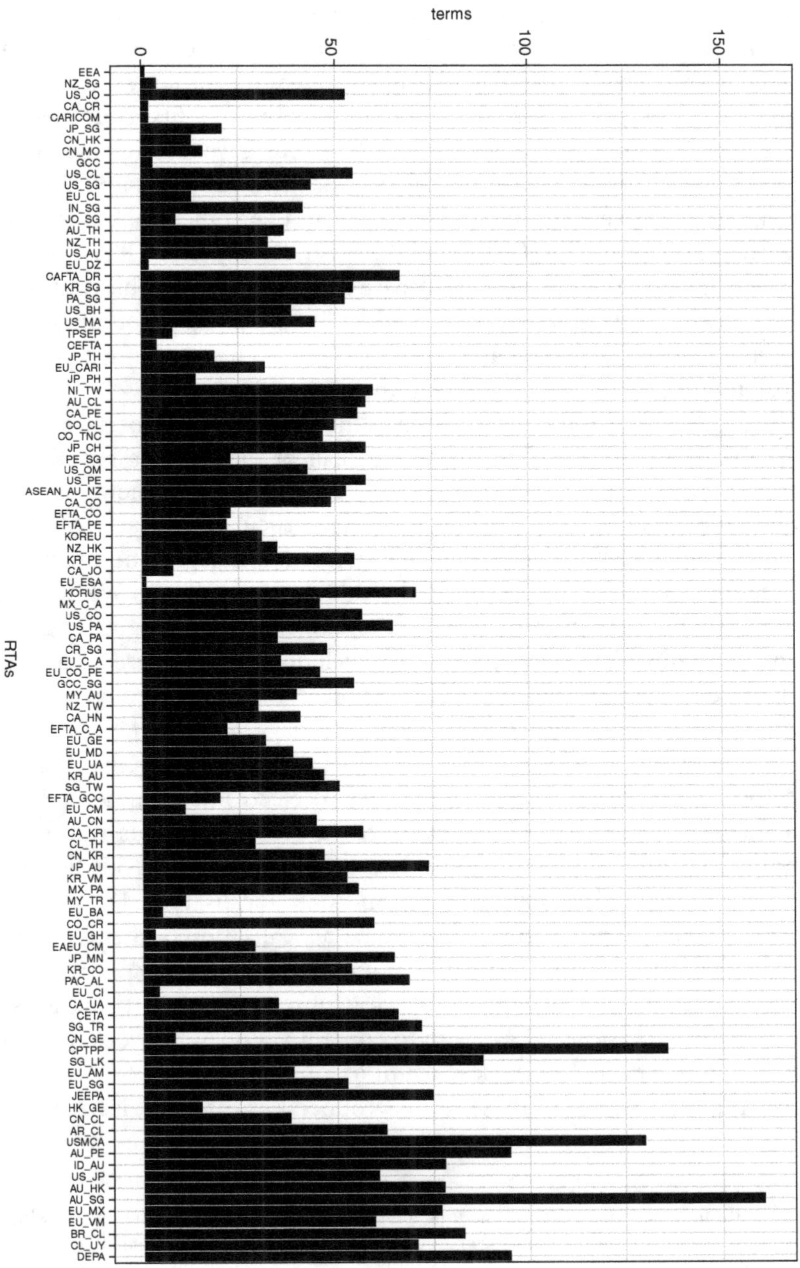

Figure 8.3 Total terms per RTA in chronological order

reaching e-commerce provisions in recent RTAs.[1509] On 6 August 2020, Australia and Singapore signed the Digital Economy Agreement, updating the e-commerce chapter that was already included in their RTA since 2003. Australia and Singapore were therefore not only the very first countries to include an e-commerce chapter in their RTA but have also updated this chapter to be the most extensive at the time of writing. Both countries also implement extensive e-commerce provisions in their other RTAs, like the Singapore–Sri Lanka RTA, DEPA and the Australia–Indonesia RTA, which complete the top six of the most extensive e-commerce RTAs. This confirms that, as already highlighted in the preceding literature study, countries like the United States, Singapore and Australia have been frontrunners in the inclusion of e-commerce provisions in their RTAs.

Third, interesting, but not surprising, is the fact that several of the lowest RTAs that were concluded in the second half of the timeline have been concluded with Sub-Saharan African countries. Over the last few years, it has become apparent that the digital divide particularly impacts African Members. Initially, the African group also refused to engage in negotiations on e-commerce-related provisions in the context of the WTO's WPEC.[1510] At the time of writing, the United States and Kenya are negotiating an extensive RTA, which is expected to also include an e-commerce chapter.

Figure 8.4 sets out the sum of the various terms used throughout all e-commerce RTAs, coloured in by term category.

It is interesting to note that the most often discussed issues in scholarship (policy objectives related to barriers to electronic commerce and data flows) are not that widely included in RTAs. Whereas the term 'privacy' is mentioned often, this is less so for consumer protection in e-commerce, data flows/data transfer and data localisation. Few countries have included provisions related to data localisation or the free flow of data. Neither do they explicitly point to cybersecurity as a chief consideration in the enactment of electronic commerce provisions. Additionally, almost no RTAs seem to contain an 'open network' provision, which is reflected in the low count of 'use of Internet'.

Looking into the use of these terms grouped per category, it becomes even more clear that whereas many RTAs include references to terms

[1509] Even though the United States is no longer a party to the CPTPP, it did negotiate (what was then called) the TPP and arguably considerably affected the final text of this agreement. Moreover, the text of the TPP was not significantly altered after the US withdrew from it.

[1510] WTO General Council, 'Draft Ministerial Decision on Electronic Commerce' Communication for the African Group, JOB/GC/155, 21 November 2017.

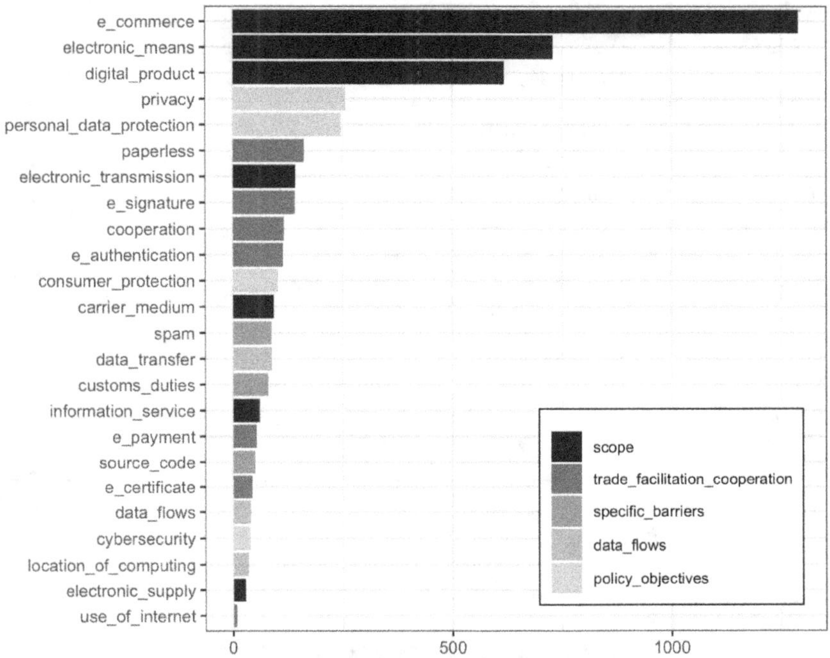

Figure 8.4 Number of mentions of each term in all RTAs

such as electronic commerce, digital product and electronic means, the amount of provisions addressing specific issues seems much more limited. The plot shows that only a limited number of RTAs have included provisions on data flows or certain specific barriers to digital trade. None of the other categories come close to being as widely represented as the scope category. The main explanation for this wide divergence is the fact that the terms that fall within the scope category will be mentioned multiple times within the provisions that contain terms of the other categories. For example, a provision that deals with e-signatures, customs duties on electronic transmission or cross-border data flows will also include terms such as e-commerce, electronic means, etc. This of course significantly inflates the count for the scope terms.

Figure 8.5 represents the total amount of terms that countries have mentioned throughout their RTAs. As was to be expected from our earlier observations, Australia, Singapore and the United States have included most e-commerce-related terms in their RTAs (and thus arguably, most e-commerce provisions). This confirms their position as the

Table 8.2 *Highest ranking countries in terms of number of RTAs*

	No. of RTAs	Countries			
1	21	European Union			
2	19	Singapore			
3	14	United States			
4	13	Australia	Chile		
5	11	Canada			
6	9	Colombia	Japan	Korea	Peru
7	8	New Zealand			
8	7	Costa Rica			
9	6	China	Mexico	Panama	Switzerland
10	5	Honduras	Iceland	Liechtenstein	Norway
		Thailand	Viet Nam		

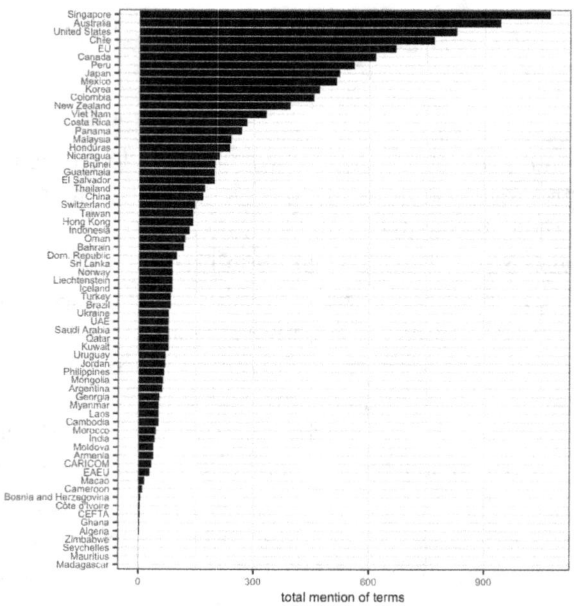

Figure 8.5 Total number of terms used per country

frontrunner in the international e-commerce debate. None of them concluded the highest number of e-commerce RTAs (see Table 8.2), the EU did. This, however, confirms that the e-commerce RTAs that they did negotiate all contain extensive e-commerce provisions.

The top of the table is further supplemented by the EU, Canada and a mix of South American and East Asian countries. When considering the high level of term inclusion for South American countries, it is interesting to take into account the lack of domestic framework on e-commerce, digital services or data flows in these countries. Therefore, many of them can commit to a high level of e-commerce liberalisation at the multilateral level without restrictions from domestic policies. This, however, creates a precarious situation. If and when these countries want to enact regulation at the domestic level in the future, such regulation could collide with the commitments they have made at the regional and bilateral level.

What is particularly interesting to note in Figure 8.6 is the low position of the EU. The EU ranks only as the forty-first out of sixty-seven RTA parties with an average level of term inclusion that is only marginally higher than China's. Even the United States has to relinquish its position as one of the leading e-commerce RTA negotiating parties. Here, it should, however, be

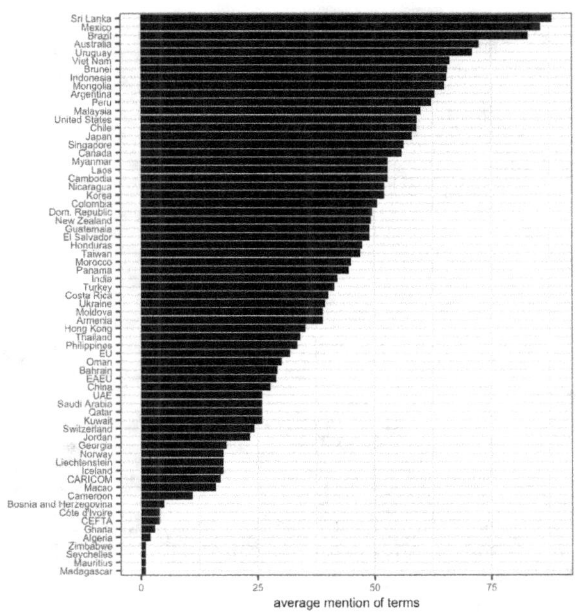

Figure 8.6 Average number of terms used per country

taken into account that the CPTPP was negotiated by the United States, but that it withdrew from the agreement. If the CPTPP provisions were also taken into consideration for the US' average count, it is hypothesised that it would rank closer to first place. Overall, the table with average use of the terms provides a much more balanced result, with less disparity between the different parties. Both Sri Lanka and Brunei owe their exceptional ranking to the fact that they are only party to, respectively, one and two very 'e-commerce heavy' RTAs: the Singapore–Sri Lanka RTA for Sri Lanka and the ASEAN–Australia–New Zealand RTA and the CPTPP for Brunei. In a similar vein, Brazil and Uruguay have only concluded one RTA with a (relatively extensive) e-commerce chapter, both with Chile.

8.3.2 Average Use of Terms over the Years

Figure 8.7 maps the average count per term category per year, which allows for an analysis of the evolution over time of the different types of e-commerce provisions in RTAs. In order to take into account the fact that in some years more RTAs have been included than in others, this plot displays the average

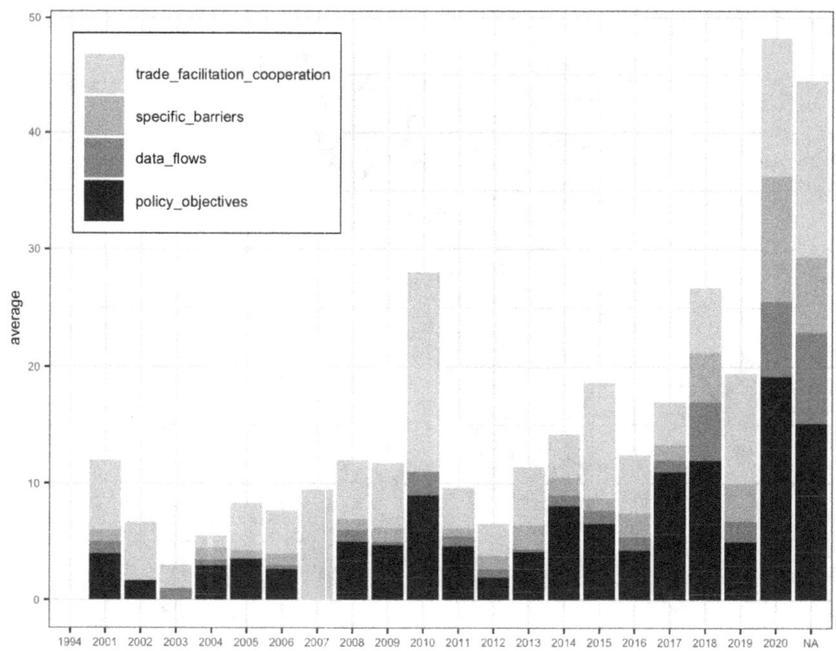

Figure 8.7 Average number of terms per category per year

number of terms that were mentioned in the RTAs concluded in that year. This offsets the distortion created by 'RTA-heavy years'. In addition, the 'scope' category was excluded from this plot, to allow for a more detailed analysis of the other categories. The somewhat anomalous high value for the 2010 RTAs is caused by the fact that only one 2010 RTA is included in the data set, the ASEAN–Australia–New Zealand RTA. This RTA includes a considerable amount of e-commerce-related terms and cannot be 'balanced out' by 'e-commerce light RTAs' since none entered into force that year. The unicolour bar for the year 2007 is explained by the fact that only two e-commerce RTAs entered into force that year (the CEFTA and the Japan–Thailand RTA), the former of which only included terms in the scope category and the latter only trade facilitation and cooperation terms.

At first sight, it can immediately be noted that the 1994 RTA only contained references to terms from the scope category. In 1994, the European Economic Area agreement entered into force, thereby incorporating three of the EFTA States (Iceland, Liechtenstein and Norway) into the EU's single market. Even though this agreement entered into force a year before the entry into force of the WTO Agreements, it already contained a reference to 'information services', in the context of further cooperation outside of the four freedoms.[1511] However, as can be expected, no other e-commerce-related provisions have been included in this RTA.

Moreover, some category-specific increases can be observed. Terms related to trade facilitation and policy objectives have been included throughout the years, in varying numbers. Interestingly, the average use of all of the identified terms does not show a clear linear increase over the years. It can be observed that the terms in the data flows category have actually been present throughout the years, but a steadier increase in the number of mentions can be seen from 2017 onwards. A very similar observation can be made about the terms related to the specific barriers to electronic commerce. Neither for data flows nor specific barriers can it be contended that they have only risen to RTA parties' attention in recent years. However, the relatively steep increase in their use in the most recent RTAs indicates a more widespread awareness of the specific barriers that electronic commerce is confronted with.

In order to allow for an analysis of the use of the specific terms over the years, a plot has been created, mapping the evolution of the average use of each term per category. For these plots, the average use per year is displayed, again to offset distortion created by 'RTA-heavy years'.

[1511] See Article 78 of the Agreement on the European Economic Area (EEA Agreement).

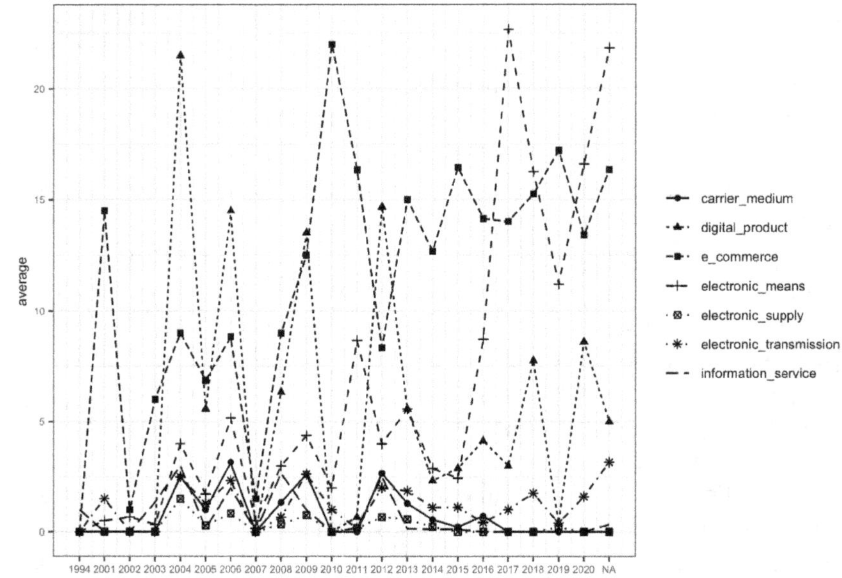

Figure 8.8 Average terms for 'scope' over time

The use of terms related to the scope of e-commerce provisions in regional agreements varies considerably (see figure 8.8). Whereas 'e-commerce' is widely used throughout the depicted timeline, this is not the case for other terms. For example, the use of the term 'digital product' is very prominent from 2004 to 2012. From 2013 onwards, the term is used considerably less, with a significant zero level in 2019. This could indicate that, whereas digital products were characterised as 'products' in the early years of e-commerce provisions in the RTAs, the focus has been shifting to digital trade as a specific means of supply. This is illustrated by the increased use of 'electronic means' from 2011 onwards, with a steep incline in the last few years. Closely linked to this argument is also the use of the term 'information service', which has always been used to a limited extent, but which has no longer been mentioned since 2013. This supports the abovementioned argument that Members are focussing less on the good versus service debate but rather focus on the *way* in which the product is being supplied. Any interpretations on evolutions in use of various terms should, however, be taken with a pinch of salt, as the focus of RTA negotiators is not necessarily on the use of specific terms but rather on agreeing on a formulation that is

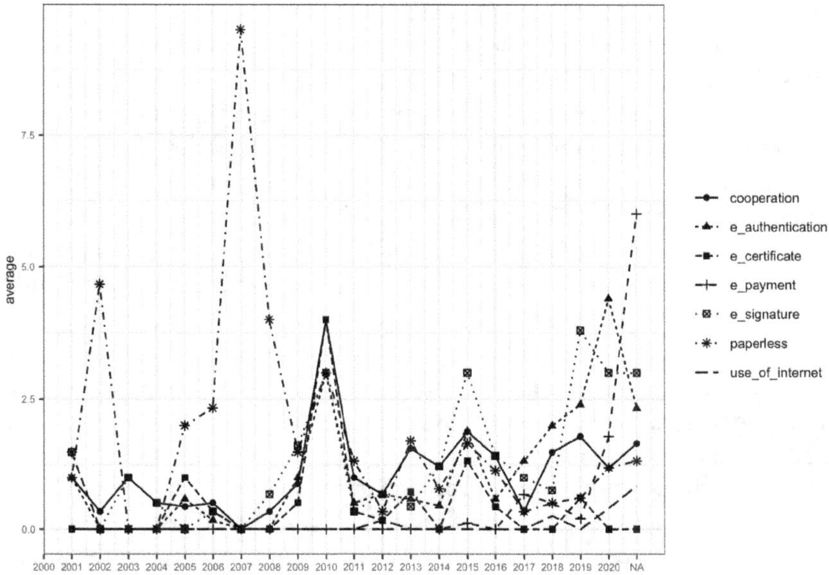

Figure 8.9 Average terms for 'trade facilitation and cooperation' over time

acceptable to all parties. This is definitely the case where the change in language does not impact the obligations agreed to.

The analysis of the terms related to trade facilitation and cooperation also provide interesting insights into the evolutions of the use of the specific terms (see figure 8.9). The strong decrease of the use of the term 'paperless' immediately grabs the attention. Whereas RTA parties used the term significantly in the 2000s, they do so to a much more limited extent in recent years. This can partially be explained by the fact that early RTAs contained limited provisions related to e-commerce and very often these early e-commerce-related provisions covered paperless trade. In fact, the inclusion of a provision on paperless trade was one of the first manifestations of e-commerce-related provisions in RTAs.[1512]

The recognition of electronic authentication, electronic certificates and electronic signatures facilitates trade. Even though it could be argued that these terms are closely related and deal with similar issues,[1513] we can observe different evolutions for the different terms. The use of terms related to electronic authentication has been fluctuating throughout the years but has slowly gained popularity from 2010 onwards. In recent

[1512] New Zealand – Singapore RTA (2001).
[1513] See *supra*, fn 1477.

years, RTAs seem to include standard provisions on electronic authentication. Terms related to electronic signatures have run an even bumpier track, having outlying results in 2010, 2015 and 2019.

The issue of electronic payment seems to be something of more recent concern, as the term was completely absent in RTAs that entered into force before 2015. E-payment provisions are very prevalent in RTAs that entered into force in 2020 and those that have been signed but have not yet entered into force ('NA'). Terms related to cooperation on electronic commerce are more or less steadily present throughout the timeline, with a slight increase in the last decade.

The term 'use of the Internet' represents provisions that mandate (or at least recognise the importance of) access to and use of the Internet, thereby requiring reasonable and open access to the Internet. Even though it could be argued that this term might be too specific to catch all of the 'open networks' provisions, the absence of other proposed terms such as 'open network' and 'open Internet access' supports the finding that barely any RTAs include such requirements of access to the Internet. The plot shows that only in the RTAs in 2012, 2017, 2018, 2020 and those not yet in force mention was made of this

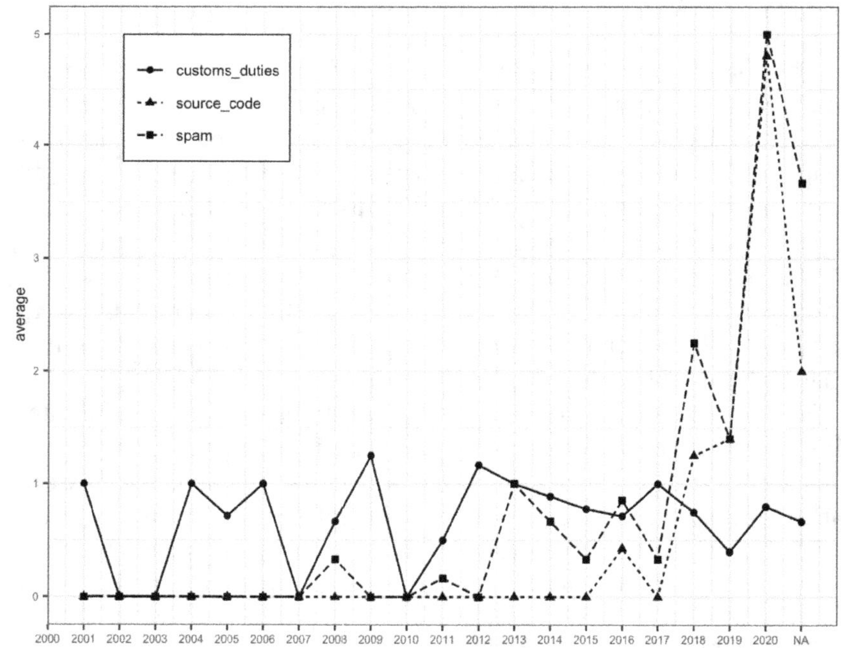

Figure 8.10 Average terms for 'specific barriers' over time

term. RTA parties have so far very rarely included provisions that mandate free access to and use of the Internet for service providers.

There is an overall increase in the use of terms related to specific barriers to electronic commerce in the last five years (see figure 8.10). The specific barrier that is mentioned most consistently in the RTAs is that of customs duties on electronic transmission or on products delivered electronically. This is not surprising, considering that one of the main outcomes of the WPEC is the (extended) moratorium on customs duties on electronic transmission.[1514] Various RTAs include a reference to this moratorium or reference a ban on customs duties on products transmitted or delivered electronically. However, the absolute number of RTAs that includes such a provision is still limited, as the average use of the number of terms is below one for most years (with a zero value in 2002, 2003, 2007 and 2010).

The increased use of terms related to source code indicates that RTA parties progressively include provisions that prohibit parties from requiring transfer of, or access to, source codes. Similarly, parties increasingly include provisions related to unsolicited commercial electronic messages (i.e. spam). Even though spam does not qualify as a substantial barrier to digital trade, it has been argued that limitations on the presence of spam boost consumers' trust and thereby benefit electronic commerce. For both of these provisions, it is easily understandable that parties would be willing to include them in their RTAs. Spam, on the one hand, is more and more curtailed domestically, in some forms even criminalised, as it is increasingly considered consumer harassment and an unacceptable business practice. Provisions on transfers of source code, on the other hand, are mainly prompted by China's practice of requiring the transfer of or access to source code in order for companies to be able to provide their services within Chinese territory. Very few other countries widely engage in the same practice, which allows for a (supposedly) easily found common ground. Both of these barriers are, however, relatively recent issues for RTA parties as provisions addressing spam and source code were only included more consistently from, respectively, 2013 and 2017 onwards.

Several authors have focussed on the provisions addressing data flows in RTAs. Burri observes that WTO Members' focus has shifted from stopping data from coming into the country towards keeping information from going out of the country, which has prompted the increase in data localisation requirements.[1515] Peng and Liu, however, highlight that

[1514] See *supra* Section 4.3.2.
[1515] See *supra* Section 3.2.1.

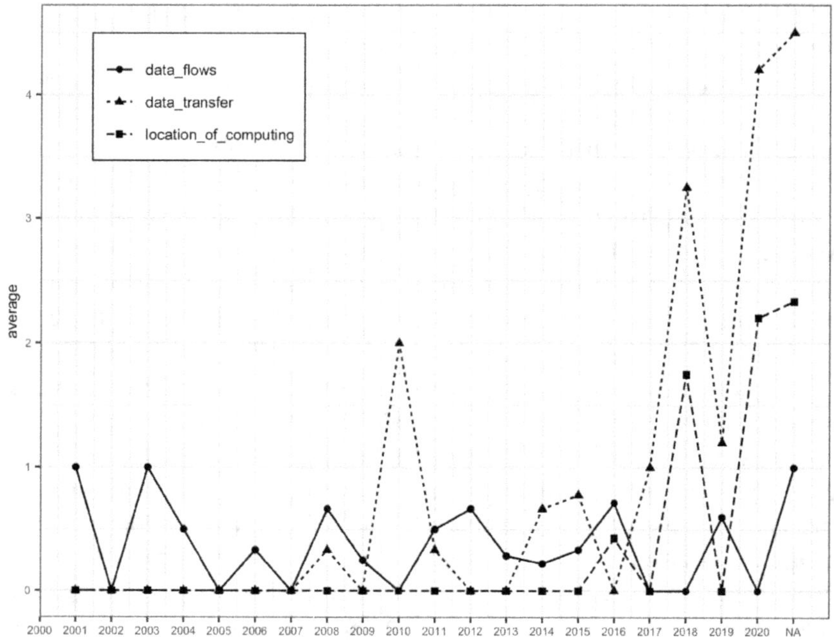

Figure 8.11 Average terms for 'data flows' over time

DLRs run counter to the underlying logic of the Internet, causing the balkanisation of the inherently global cyberspace.[1516] The combination of the increase in DLRs and the observation of its trade-distorting effects has led to some RTAs addressing these types of barriers head-on. Moreover, as discussed in Part III of this book, DLRs could amount to a violation of Members' GATS obligations. In the same line, Burri argues that if the EU, for example, would limit search engines' market access, discriminate against foreign search engine service suppliers or impose localisation requirements in domestic regulation, it could be argued that it is violating its GATS commitments.[1517]

Wu identifies two categories of data-related issues. First, several RTAs contain provisions on cross-border data flows. These range from requiring an 'endeavour to refrain from unnecessary barriers' in KORUS to the state-of-the-art recognition in the CPTPP of the right to transfer data across borders for the conduct of business. Such provisions, which have

1516 Peng and Liu (n 336) 187.

1517 Burri, 'The Governance of Data and Data Flows in Trade Agreements: The Pitfalls of Legal Adaptation' (n 177) 84–85.

been earmarked as 'cutting-edge', can also be found in RTAs between developing countries.[1518] Most other RTAs simply require regulatory cooperation between the parties on these issues.[1519] Secondly, by now, ten RTAs contain specific obligations on data localisation, either an endeavour or an obligation not to impose these barriers on trade between the RTA parties. As pointed out in Chapter 7, specific provisions targeting data localisation measures are not required to address these barriers to digital services trade (as GATS commitments can suffice). Wu points out that general language that prohibits unnecessary barriers to cross-border data flows should equally be able to address this issue.[1520]

Whereas terms related to data flows have been mentioned in some RTAs throughout the years, it is clear from figure 8.11 that this was only done in a handful of cases. This is different for terms related to data transfers, which were completely missing from RTAs until 2008.[1521] Considering the limited values on the y-axis, it becomes clear that, here as well, only a handful of RTAs have included such terms. Even though data flows are a prominent topic in scholarship nowadays, provisions dealing with such flows have been included surprisingly little. This likely relates to the difficulties surrounding the qualification of data flows and their position in the international trading system.

The terms related to location of computing facilities (i.e. related to DLRs) can only be found in RTAs that entered into force from 2016 onwards. This shows that even though DLRs are being discussed plenty nowadays, RTA parties have scarcely been able to agree on provisions dealing with the significant barrier to digital trade. It remains to be seen whether future RTAs will focus more on this issue, but it is clear that of all RTA parties, it is mainly the United States and East Asian and Pacific high-income countries that include provisions related to data localisation.[1522] As has been shown in previous chapters, the EU seems

1518 For example in the Mexico – Panama RTA, which contains binding commitments on cross-border data flows. Wu (n 298) 22.

1519 For examples see ibid 23.

1520 ibid 24.

1521 Even though it can be argued that 'data flows' and 'data transfers' refer to different kinds of data movement (i.e. the former indicating the continued moving of data over the Internet, whereas the latter signifies the more specific targeted transmission of (specific) data) nothing in the use of these terms by Members in their RTAs points towards them consciously distinguishing between both. For the purpose of this book, these terms are understood as more or less synonymous.

1522 The terms related to data localisation provisions were found in ten RTAs, see *supra* n 1508.

more reluctant to agree to an outright ban on data localisation due to its strong focus on consumer protection and data privacy domestically.

Figure 8.12 clearly shows that there is an increased inclusion of all terms on policy objectives related to e-commerce. Especially privacy and personal data protection (which are closely related) seem to be taking up an increasingly important role in RTAs and move more or less in sync on the graph. Even though they have been present from the start, both of them have seen a considerable increase in the last decade. This confirms that WTO Members are increasingly aware of the issues related to privacy and data protection. It should not be surprising that these terms have been included from the start though. As mentioned in Part III of this book, privacy is included as a general exception in Article XIV GATS and RTA parties seem to have continued the inclusion of this exception or policy concern in their agreements. Similarly, cybersecurity has been included to a very limited extent in RTAs from 2004 onwards but is gaining a more consistent presence since 2015. Consumer protection has been included on and off in the context of e-commerce, with a more or less steadily increasing presence since 2008.

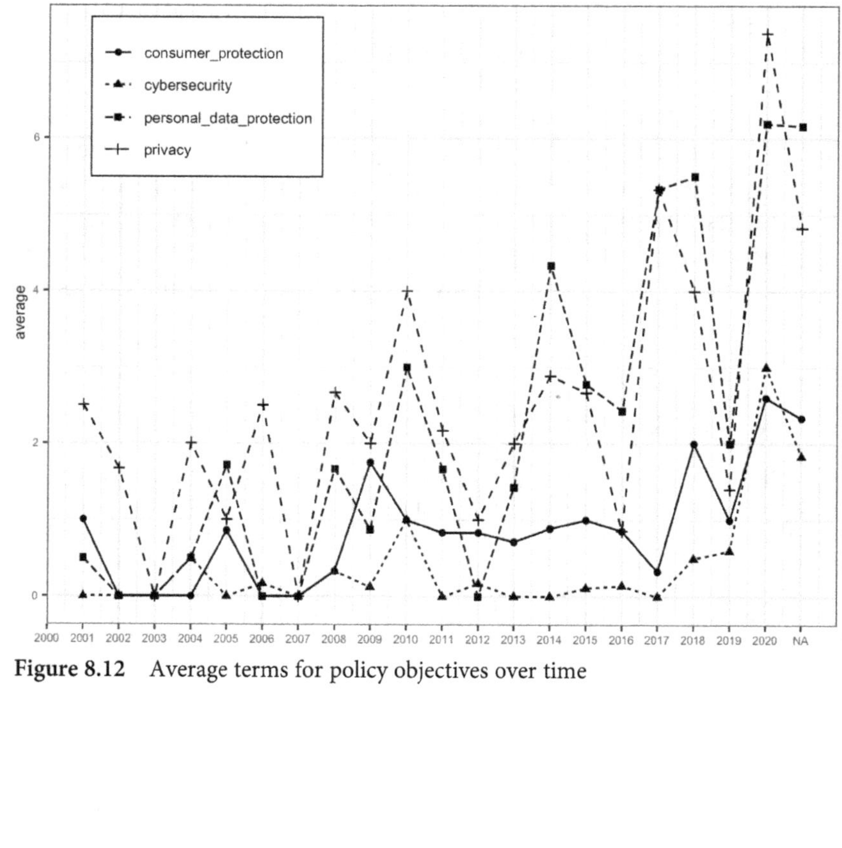

Figure 8.12 Average terms for policy objectives over time

8.4 Comparing E-commerce Terms on the Basis of Geographical Region and Income Level

It has been argued that existing e-commerce chapters fail to level the playing field between countries with different levels of development and that proper attention should be paid to the digital divide (through technical cooperation provisions, 'buffer language' and special and differential treatment).[1523] The accuracy of this statement will be assessed based on an analysis of the distribution of e-commerce RTAs based on the geographic regions they cover and their parties' income level.

To this date, not a single study has compared the extent of e-commerce chapters and provisions in RTAs on the basis of the parties' geographical location and their income level. This study plots the total number of e-commerce-related terms mentioned per RTA by geographical region and income level of the parties. The figures presented in this section shine a light on how countries from different geographical regions and with different income levels have approached the inclusion of e-commerce provisions in their RTAs. In considering these plots, it should be taken into account that most RTAs are inter-regional rather than intra-regional. This entails that an RTA will often be displayed in two or more regions (as more than one geographical region is involved in these RTAs). The same consideration goes for RTAs concluded between parties with different income levels.

Allocating weight to the inclusion of certain provisions in RTAs based on their region or income level does not take account of the relative negotiation power exercised by the different parties. In considering the distribution of these terms over the various regions and income levels, one cannot lose sight of the fact that, very often, one of the parties involved (e.g. United States, EU, Australia, Japan and China) will be able to push its own agenda more than the other party, ensuring inclusion of the provisions that it deems most important. Nonetheless, all of these RTAs remain the outcome of a negotiation process between sovereign states and the value of their inclusion of e-commerce provisions therefore remains relevant.

Figure 8.13 displays the number of terms (y-axis) per RTA concluded within each region, mapping them in chronological order (x-axis). The graph provides an insight into which regions are the front-runners in their inclusion of e-commerce-related terms in their RTAs and allows for a distinction between RTAs that have been concluded between countries

[1523] ICTSD (n 895) 4.

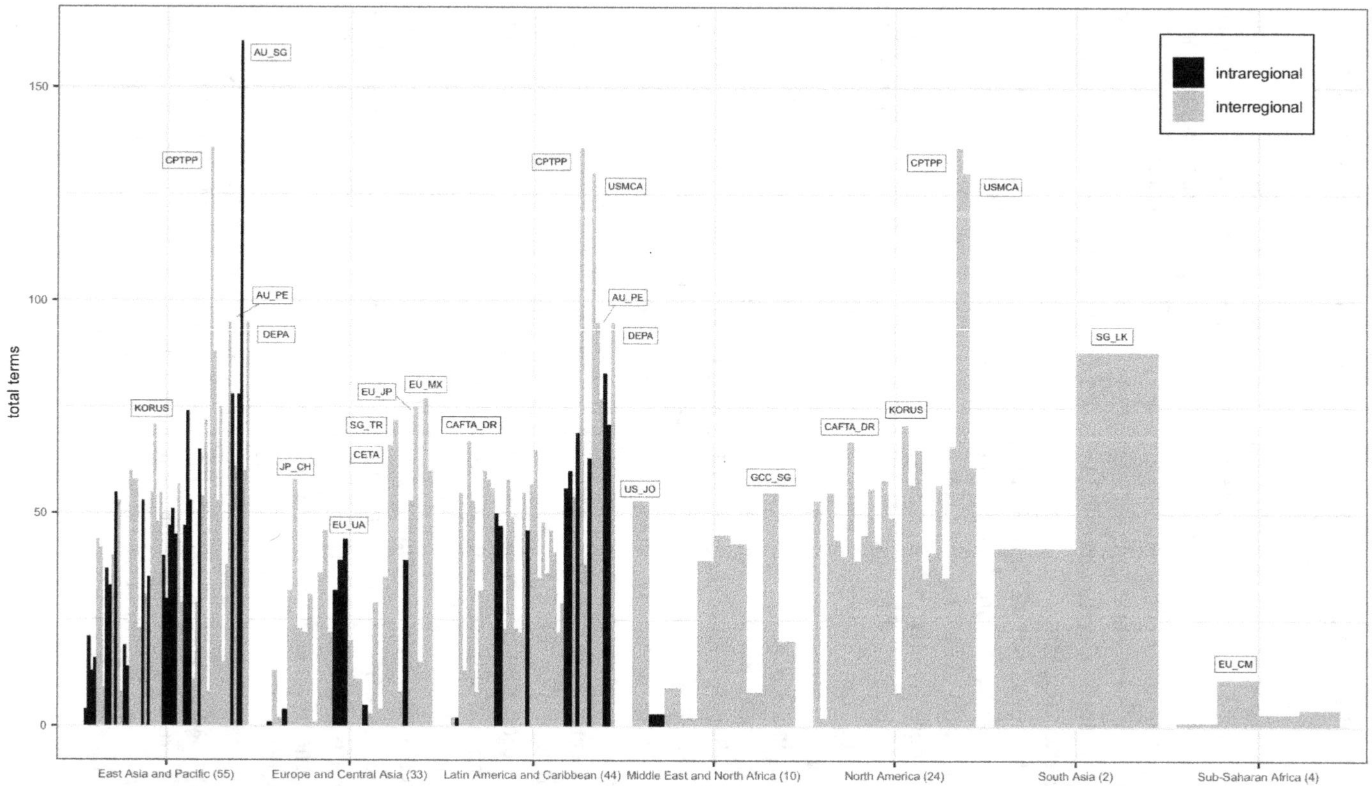

Figure 8.13 Use of terms per RTA per region

within the same region (intraregional RTAs) and those that have been concluded between countries from different regions (interregional RTAs). For each region, the number of RTAs with e-commerce provisions has been indicated as well. The figure shows that the East Asia and Pacific Region concluded considerably more RTAs than any other region, many of which are intraregional. The Latin American and Caribbean region also contains a considerable proportion of intraregional RTAs with e-commerce-related provisions. The intraregional RTAs concluded in both Europe and Central Asia and Latin America and the Caribbean vary considerably in their 'e-commerce heavy-ness'. This graph illustrates the disparate inclusion of e-commerce provisions in RTAs within regions and throughout the years.

Most e-commerce-related RTAs have been concluded in the East Asia and Pacific region, with a more or less even distribution of 'e-commerce heavy' and 'e-commerce light' RTAs. Clear outliers are the CPTPP and the Australia–Singapore RTA. Both contain considerably more e-commerce terms than others in this region, with the updated Australia–Singapore RTA having more than twice as many as other RTAs. Other recent agreements in this region, such as the Australia–Peru RTA and DEPA, also contain a high number of e-commerce terms. Noteworthy is also KORUS' position as a relatively 'e-commerce heavy' RTA for its time. East Asia and Pacific is the region with the highest proportion of intraregional e-commerce RTAs. These intraregional RTAs also generally display a relatively high number of e-commerce provisions (amounting to more than one-third of all terms for this region).

Like the East Asia and Pacific region, the European and Central Asian region (which most prominently includes the EU) sees a strong variation in the presence of e-commerce-related terms in its RTAs. The strongest e-commerce RTA pre-2010 for this region is the Japan–Switzerland RTA (2009). The block of consequent intraregional RTAs contains the EU's agreements with three Eastern European countries: Georgia, Moldova and Ukraine. The 'heaviest' e-commerce RTA concluded by the EU so far is the EU–Mexico RTA, which accounts for a considerably lower level of e-commerce-related terms than the outliers in other regions. Interesting to note is also the relatively 'e-commerce light' CETA. Even though CETA was presented as an important deep integration agreement between large (digital) trading partners, it arguably failed to deliver on the e-commerce front. The most 'e-commerce heavy' RTA in this region that doesn't include the EU was concluded between Singapore and Turkey.

The region of Latin America and the Caribbean also includes a considerable amount of agreements with e-commerce provisions which entered into force throughout the last two decades. Compared to the East Asia and Pacific Region, RTAs in Latin America and the Caribbean included quite a number of e-commerce-related terms early on. Additionally, the total number of e-commerce terms in these RTAs is higher than compared to the East Asian and European region. Most intraregional RTAs seem to fit within this trend and display a varying degree of term inclusion. Here again, two outliers can immediately be noticed. Again, the CPTPP, and the USMCA (or NAFTA 2.0) contain a very high amount of e-commerce terms. The Australia–Peru RTA and DEPA also attest to strong transpacific e-commerce agreements. An interesting early outlier is the CAFTA-DR, which contained a very high number of e-commerce terms for its time.

The number of RTAs concluded by the countries within the Middle East and North African region is much more limited, but interestingly almost all of them are relatively 'e-commerce heavy'. Only the relatively old (and only intraregional) agreement on the Gulf Cooperation Council is very 'e-commerce light'. It is interesting to note that most e-commerce RTAs in this region entered into force before 2010 and no new e-commerce RTAs were concluded after 2014.[1524] Moreover, the most 'e-commerce heavy' RTAs in this region were all concluded with the United States or Singapore, which confirms their position as e-commerce advocates.[1525]

As could be expected, the North American region (which only includes the United States and Canada) counts most 'e-commerce heavy RTAs'. Almost all of their RTAs can be qualified as 'e-commerce heavy', with USMCA and CPTPP dominating the graph. Interestingly, Canada's RTAs generally include significantly less e-commerce provisions than do the US' RTAs. This region does not contain an intraregional RTA as, according to the World Bank classification, Mexico is considered part of Latin America and the Caribbean. The very e-commerce-heavy USMCA therefore does not qualify as an intraregional RTA here.

Finally, there are only two and four RTAs that include e-commerce terms concluded by South Asian and Sub-Saharan African countries, respectively. Whereas both South Asian RTAs were concluded with Singapore, all four of the Sub-Saharan African RTAs have been concluded with the EU. This hints at both parties' role as e-commerce facilitators in these regions. Singapore's

[1524] US – Jordan RTA (2001), Gulf Cooperation Council Agreement (2003), Jordan – Singapore RTA (2005), EU – Algeria RTA (2005), US – Bahrain RTA (2006), US – Morocco RTA (2006), US – Oman RTA (2009), Canada – Jordan RTA (2012), GCC – Singapore RTA (2013) and EFTA – GCC RTA (2014).

[1525] Jordan – US RTA (2001), Morocco – US RTA (2006), Bahrain – US RTA (2006), Oman – US RTA (2009) and GCC – Singapore RTA (2013).

RTAs with South Asian countries are significantly more 'e-commerce heavy' than the EU's RTAs with Sub-Saharan African countries. As could be expected, the latter are all very 'e-commerce light' and contain a limited amount of e-commerce terms. Here, the digital divide clearly draws a line between Sub-Saharan Africa and the rest of the world.

WTO Members do not seem inclined to include more e-commerce-related provisions in their intraregional RTAs, rather the opposite: most of the strongest e-commerce RTAs have been concluded between countries from different geographical regions. Of course, this determination depends on the delineation of the regions. The USMCA and the CPTPP have been considered intraregional RTAs as they include parties from respectively North America (if Mexico is considered part of North America) and the Pacific Region.

Figure 8.14 provides an insight into how many e-commerce RTAs have been concluded by countries with different income levels. Here as well, the plot is divided into four sections (for each income level). Within each section, the term count for each RTA is displayed on the y-axis and the RTAs are ordered chronologically on the x-axis. The different colours indicate the different income levels of the parties to the RTAs.

The largest group of e-commerce RTAs have been concluded by at least one high-income country, totalling ninety-seven RTAs. There is a more or less equal distribution of 'e-commerce heavy' and 'e-commerce light' RTAs over time. Some of the earliest RTAs concluded between high-income countries already contained a high number of e-commerce-related terms. An early outlier is the CAFTA-DR, which grouped high-income, upper middle-income and lower middle-income parties. Of course, the same outliers can be identified here as in the figure on the regions: USMCA, CPTPP and the Australia–Singapore RTA. Of these three, the CPTPP is the only one that includes countries from high-income, upper middle *and* lower middle-income levels. The CPTPP thereby successfully involved lower middle-income countries into its very substantive e-commerce chapter. Studying the overall distribution of RTAs over the years, it is clear that high-income countries have concluded RTAs containing e-commerce provisions with countries that have various income levels. Most RTAs between high-income and lower middle-income countries were, however, concluded later on. It is interesting to note that there is no clear trend in number of e-commerce provisions based on the parties' income level. *Any* RTA concluded with high-income countries holds the potential of including a substantial number of e-commerce-related terms, but there is no guarantee of it being an 'e-commerce heavy' RTA either.

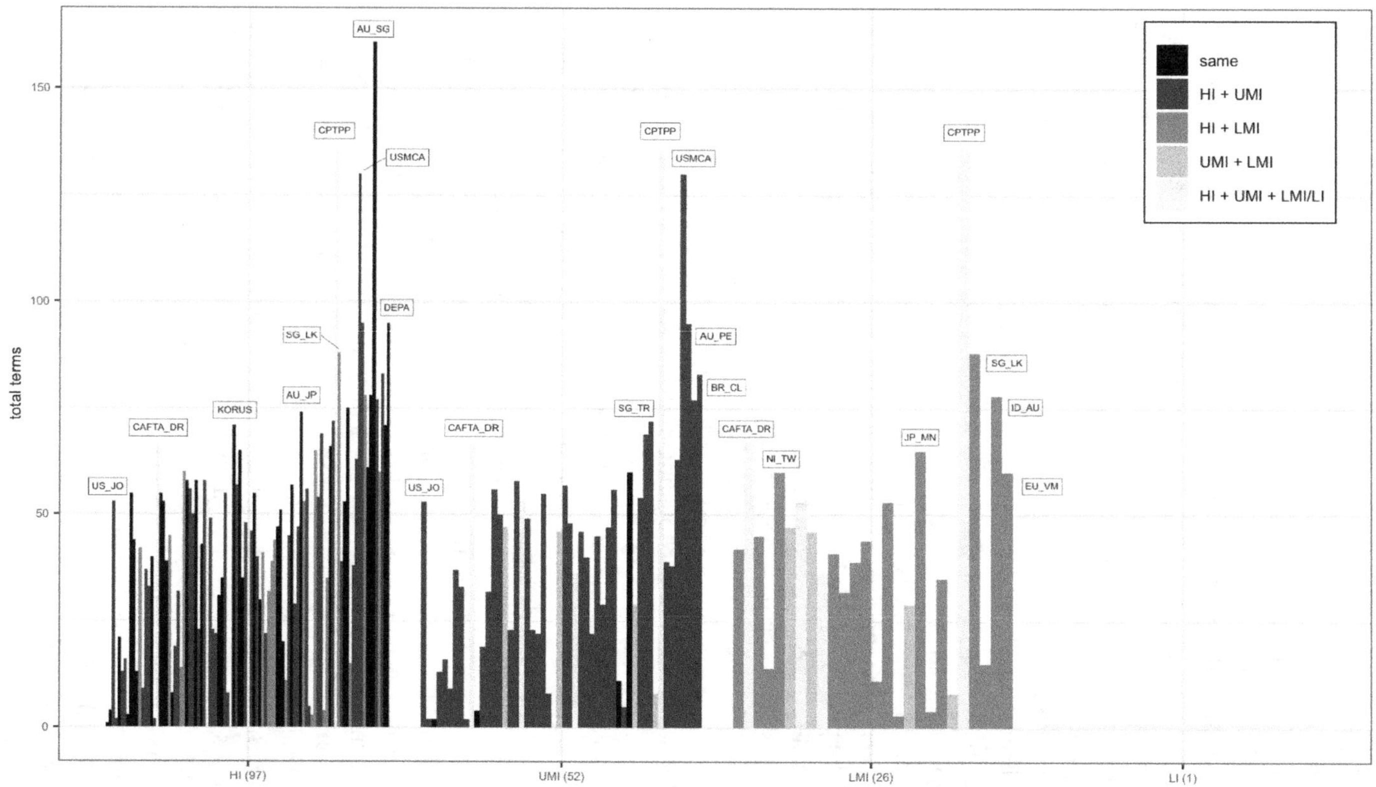

Figure 8.14 Use of terms per RTA per income level

Throughout the years, most of the upper middle-income countries' RTAs containing e-commerce provisions have been concluded with high-income countries. Four RTAs were concluded between upper middle-income countries and lower middle-income countries, all of which are relatively 'e-commerce light'.[1526] Only a handful of e-commerce-related RTAs have been concluded among upper middle-income countries, most of which turn out to be very 'e-commerce light' (CARICOM (2002), CEFTA (2007), Turkey–Malaysia (2015)), with the exception of the latest (Colombia–Costa Rica (2016)). The e-commerce-liberalising influence of high-income countries becomes apparent when considering the RTAs that were concluded between high-income, upper middle-income and lower middle-income countries, two of which (CAFTA-DR and CPTPP) are amongst the most 'e-commerce heavy' RTAs for upper middle-income countries. The average level of term inclusion for RTAs with high-income countries is higher than for those with other income level groups.

The group of e-commerce RTAs of lower middle-income countries is considerably smaller. Here as well, most RTAs have been concluded with high-income countries. The most 'e-commerce heavy' RTAs, however, also involve upper middle-income countries. Interestingly but not unexpectedly, lower middle-income countries so far did not conclude RTAs with e-commerce provisions amongst themselves. The overall level of e-commerce term inclusion is lower than for the first two income groups, especially when considering more recent RTAs (with the notable exception of CPTPP).

Not unexpectedly, only one RTA with e-commerce-related terms involves low-income countries (the EU–Eastern and Southern African RTA (with low-income countries Madagascar and Zimbabwe)).[1527] Moreover, the level of term inclusion for this RTA is very low. This again hints at the large unfulfilled potential of engaging low-income Sub-Saharan African countries into the e-commerce debate and making efforts at closing the digital divide.

In order to assess whether a linear trend can be observed, Figures 8.15 and 8.16 plot the level of term inclusion for each RTA per region and per income level over the years. A trend line is incorporated for each region

[1526] The Colombia – Northern Triangle RTA (2009), the Mexico – Central America RTA (2012), the EAEU – Vietnam RTA (2016) and the China – Georgia RTA (2018).

[1527] Comoros, also a low-income Sub-Saharan African country, joined this RTA in 2017.

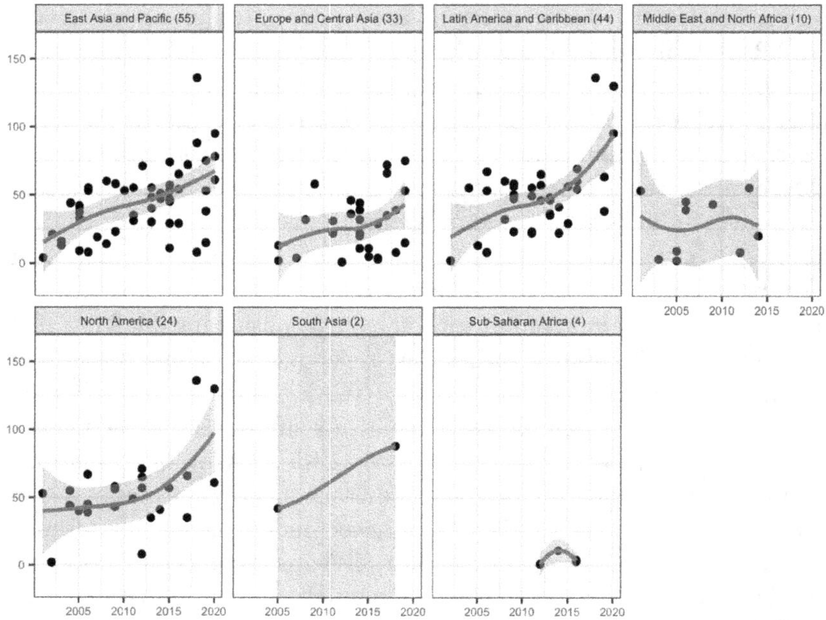

Figure 8.15 Trends in e-commerce term inclusion per region

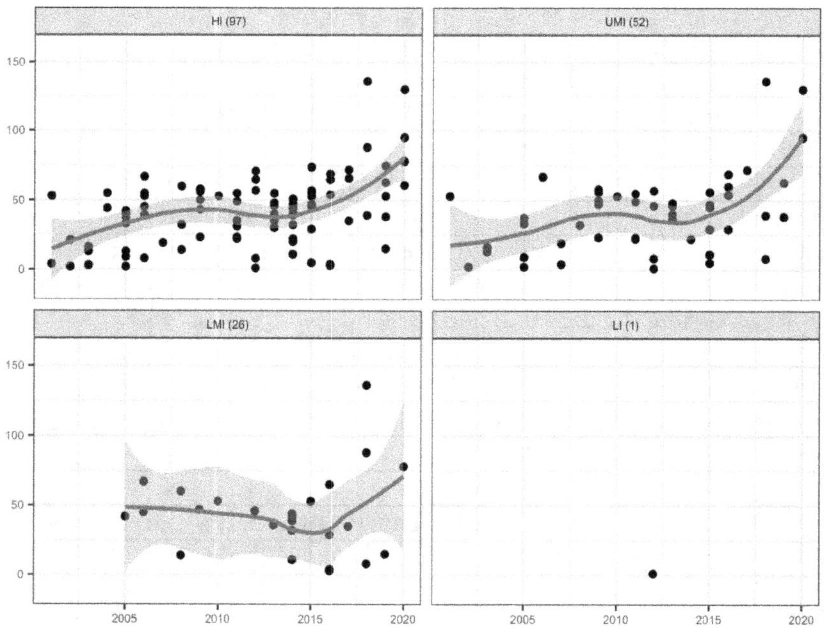

Figure 8.16 Trends in e-commerce term inclusion per income level

and income level, with varying degrees of confidence.[1528] The graphs show that for almost all regions, there is an increase over time in the total number of terms included. Only the Sub-Saharan and the Middle Eastern region have not included more e-commerce-related terms in their RTAs over the years. The increase over time is also clear when assessing the graphs for e-commerce RTAs concluded with high-income and upper middle-income countries. Lower middle-income countries see a certain variation of total term inclusion over the years, but on average only include slightly more e-commerce-related terms in their RTAs now than they did in 2005.

1528 The grey area displays the confidence interval (95 per cent confidence level) and thereby indicates the level of confidence that should be attributed to the trend line. The narrower the grey area, the more confidence can be attributed to the trend line. Confidence is determined by the amount of data available.

9

How Extensive E-commerce RTAs Address Barriers to Digital Services Trade

As illustrated in Part II, various barriers to digital trade in services exist but they are not explicitly addressed within the WTO legal framework. This raises the question whether RTAs are better positioned to deal with these emerging barriers to digital trade than the multilateral framework of the WTO (where most of the negotiation initiatives are deadlocked).[1529] As mentioned by the ASEAN countries in their submission to the General Council, international and regional legal frameworks are useful references in the development of digital trade provisions.[1530] The outcome of an extensive study of the content of provisions relevant to e-commerce in RTAs might lay the groundwork for substantive outcomes in the ongoing plurilateral negotiations at the WTO on the trade-related aspects of e-commerce.

9.1 Selection of RTAs for Deeper Examination

This chapter conducts a deeper analysis of a handful of RTAs. These RTAs have been selected on the basis of, amongst others, their high level of term-inclusion as found in Chapter 8 and their geographical disparity. Six RTAs are analysed in this chapter: the Korea–US FTA (KORUS, 2012), the China–Korea FTA (2015), the Australia–Singapore FTA (2020),[1531] the Comprehensive and Progressive Agreement for Trans-Pacific Partnership

[1529] Burri, 'The International Economic Law Framework for Digital Trade' (n 71) 66.

[1530] WTO General Council, 'ASEAN Reflections on Lunch Panel on "Can E-Commerce Trade Rules Help MSMEs from Developing Countries?" Held During the UNCTAD E-Commerce Week', 27 April 2017, JOB/GC/126, JOB/CTG/6, JOB/SERV/260, JOB/IP/23, JOB/DEV/44, 2 June 2017, p. 2.

[1531] The updated Australia–Singapore FTA entered into force in 2017. However, in 2020, Australia and Singapore signed the Australia–Singapore Digital Economy Agreement, which will amend the RTA and replace the existing Electronic Commerce chapter with a new Digital Economy chapter. This new Digital Economy chapter is analysed for this study.

(CPTPP, 2018),[1532] the EU–Japan Economic Partnership Agreement (2019) and the United States–Mexico–Canada Agreement (USMCA, 2020).

KORUS is part of the selection as it is considered a milestone in the inclusion of e-commerce provisions at the regional level. It was the first RTA to include a provision on cross-border flows of information and contains a quite complete set of model provisions on digital trade for its time, adequately reflecting the US' approach.[1533] The China–Korea RTA has been included as it is the Chinese RTA that contains most e-commerce-related terms. Considering China's important position on the digital market and its restrictive domestic approach to digital services trade, it is deemed worthwhile to assess its regional commitments on electronic commerce in more depth. The Australia–Singapore RTA emerged as the RTA with the most e-commerce-related terms in the study of Chapter 8 and is therefore included as a strong example of an intraregional RTA with (expected) extensive commitments. Both the CPTPP and the USMCA have been included in this selection because they are the two other most extensive e-commerce-related RTAs that are currently in force. Moreover, they together encompass a group of twelve countries that have committed to substantive obligations on e-commerce, thereby possibly setting the standard for future e-commerce chapters in RTAs. The CPTPP was the first RTA to reflect the US' Digital 2 Dozen principles.[1534] Finally, the EU–Japan RTA

[1532] Agreement between 11 Pacific Rim states: Australia, Brunei, Canada, Chile, Japan, Malaysia, Mexico, New Zealand, Peru, Singapore and Vietnam.

[1533] Barfield (n 471) 41–42; Burri, 'Designing Future-Oriented Multilateral Rules for Digital Trade' (n 96) 346.

[1534] Kelsey (n 437) 279. The Digital 2 Dozen principles are available on the website of the USTR: <https://ustr.gov/about-us/policy-offices/press-office/reports-and-publications/2016/digital-2-dozen>. These principles are: (1) promoting a free and open Internet; (2) prohibiting digital customs duties; (3) securing basic non-discrimination principles; (4) enabling cross-border data flows; (5) preventing localisation barriers; (6) barring forced technology transfers; (7) protecting critical source code; (8) ensuring technology choice; (9) advancing innovative authentication methods; (10) delivering enforceable consumer protections; (11) safeguarding network competition; (12) fostering innovative encryption products; (13) building an adaptable framework for digital trade; (14) promoting cooperation on cybersecurity; (15) preserving market-driven standardisation and global interoperability; (16) eliminating tariffs on all manufactured products; (17) securing robust market access commitments on investment and cross-border services, including those delivered digitally; (18) ensuring faster, more transparent customs procedures; (19) promoting transparency and stakeholder participation in the development of regulations and standards; (20) ensuring fair competition with state-owned enterprises; (21) promoting strong and balanced copyright protections and

was included as it is the EU's most extensive e-commerce RTA that was in force at the time of writing.

For all six of these RTAs several chapters were analysed in depth. This includes their chapters on e-commerce, (cross-border) trade in services, financial services and telecommunications services. Additionally, the annexes containing the parties' lists of non-conforming measures have been analysed. Where considered relevant, references to other RTAs are included throughout the comparison in this chapter.

The comparison of these RTAs is done in three parts. First, the definitions of terms relevant to digital trade in services is compared, together with their approach to the classification of digital products and whether the e-commerce chapter focusses on digital services or rather on the regulation of goods purchased through e-commerce and their approach to the principle of technological neutrality and new services. This provides a preliminary idea of the focus of the chapter and the extent to which it affects trade in digital services. In a second instance, the architectural features of the RTAs are assessed, together with the scope of the e-commerce chapters. This part addresses how the e-commerce chapters relate to the other parts of the RTAs and provides a view on the extensiveness of the chapters. Finally, it is assessed how these RTAs address the specific barriers to digital services trade that have been identified and discussed in Chapters 3 and 7. The aim of this chapter is to analyse how RTAs with extensive e-commerce provisions concluded by different important digital trading nations and from different geographical regions address the barriers to digital services trade. How do their provisions compare? Do the provisions go considerably further than the GATS framework? Do their provisions add binding obligations that can successfully address these barriers?

Table 9.1 sets out the presence of e-commerce provisions that are of specific interest for this research. The table provides a clear overview of the similarities and divergences in the provisions that are included in different RTAs. The table not only indicates the presence of certain provisions but, where useful, also indicates whether parties formulated a binding obligation, opted for a provision setting out an endeavour or recognition of importance or rather agreed to cooperate. Additionally, it has been indicated where relevant provisions were found outside of the e-commerce chapter.

enforcement; (22) advancing modern patent protection; (23) combatting trade secret theft; and (24) recognising conformity assessment procedures.

Table 9.1 *Comparing RTAs in depth*

	Definitions		Scope				Obligations							
	Digital product	**Carrier medium**	**WTO obligations apply**	**Other chapters RTA apply**	**Other chapters RTA prevail if conflict**	**Dispute settlement applies**	**New services included**	**MFN treatment**	**Market access**	**National treatment**	**Customs duties**	**E-authentication**	**Paperless trade**	**Transparency**
KORUS (2012)	x 15.9	x 15.9	x 15.1	x 15.2		x 22.4	FS 13.6	x 15.3.3	CBS 12.4	x 15.3.2	O 15.3.1	O 15.4	E 15.6	
China–Korea RTA (2015)			x 13.1		x 13.2	(x) 13.9			CBS 8.3	CBS 8.4	WTO 13.3	O 13.4	E 13.6	CBS 8.8
CPTPP (2018)	x 14.1			x 14.2.4		x 28.3	FS 11.7	x 14.4	CBS 10.5	x 14.4	O 14.3	O 14.6	E 14.9	CBS 10.11
EU–Japan RTA (2019)					x 8.70.6	x 21.2	FS 8.60	CBS 8.17	CBS 8.15	CBS 8.16	O 8.72	O 8.77		CBS 8.23
USMCA (2020)	x 19.1			x 19.2.4		x 31.2	FS 17.7	x 19.4	CBS 15.5	x 19.4	O 19.3	O 19.6	E 19.9	SC 29.2
Australia–Singapore RTA (NA)	x 14.1 (g)					x 16.1	CBS/FS 7.1(o)/ 9.7	x 14.6.1	CBS 7.3	x 14.6.1	O 14.5	O 14.9	O 14.12	x 14.14

Table 9.1 (*cont.*)

	Obligations (cont.)										Exceptions and policy objectives			
	Cooperation	**Unsolicited commercial electronic messages**	**Source code/ technology transfer**	**Access to and use of Internet**	**Cross-border data flows**	**Data localisation**	**Reference to international standards**	**Content liability**	**Technology transfer**	**Artificial intelligence**	**General exceptions**	**Consumer protection**	**Protection of personal data**	**Cybersecurity**
KORUS (2012)				E 15.7	E 15.8						SC 23.2	E 15.5		
China–Korea RTA (2015)	E 13.7												O 13.5	
CPTPP (2018)	E 14.15	O 14.14	O 14.17	E 14.10	O 14.11	O 14.13	x 14.5				SC 29.1	O 14.7.2	O/E 14.8	C 14.16
EU–Japan RTA (2019)	O 8.80	O 8.79	O/O 8.73/ 8.11						O 8.11		x 8.3	E 8.78		C 8.80
USMCA (2020)	E 19.14	O 19.13	O 19.16	E 19.10	O 19.11/ 17.17	O 19.12 / 7.18	x 19.5/ 19.8	O 19.17			SC 32.1.2	O 19.7	O 19.8	E 19.15
Australia–Singapore RTA (NA)	E 14.4/ 16/32/ 33	O 14.19	O 14.28	E 14.20	O 14.23	O 14.24	x 14.8/ 11/ 17/ 30	E 14.18	O 14.7.3	E/C 14.31	x 14.3	O 14.15	O 14.17	E 14.34

Legend:
E = endeavour or recognition of importance; O = obligation; C = cooperation; CBS = cross-border trade in services chapter; FS = financial services chapter; SC = separate (dedicated) chapter

9.2 Comparing Definition, Approach to Technological Neutrality and 'New Services'

KORUS defines digital products as '*computer programs, text, video, images, sound recording, and other products that are digitally encoded and produced for commercial sale or distribution, regardless of whether they are fixed on a carrier medium or transmitted electronically*'.[1535] The definition of 'digital products' in the CPTPP is almost identical to the one found in KORUS, but crucially omits the reference to products fixed on a carrier medium.[1536] The e-commerce chapter of the CPTPP thus only applies to digital products that are being transmitted electronically. The parties also explicitly exclude 'digitised representation of financial instruments, including money' from this definition.[1537] Both the Australia–Singapore RTA and the USMCA contain the same definition of 'digital product' as the CPTPP and also exclude the digitised representation of financial instruments.[1538] Neither the China–Korea RTA nor the EU–Japan RTA contains a definition of digital products (nor do they define other terms like electronic commerce, information services or digital services). Interestingly, only a handful of all the studied RTAs define 'electronic commerce'.[1539]

The China–Korea RTA explicitly does not take a position on whether deliveries by electronic means should be categorised as trade in services or goods.[1540] Similarly, footnote 4 to Article 15.9 KORUS clarifies that the definition of 'digital product' should not be understood to reflect the US' or Korea's view on whether digital products that are transmitted electronically

[1535] Article 15.9 KORUS. A carrier medium is defined as '*any physical object designed principally for use in storing a digital product by any method now known or later developed, and from which a digital product can be perceived, reproduced, or communicated, directly or indirectly, and includes, but is not limited to, an optical medium, a floppy disk, or a magnetic tape*'.

[1536] It thereby departs from previous US practice. Huang (n 1490) 319.

[1537] Footnote 1 to Article 14.1 Australia–Singapore RTA.

[1538] Article 14.1(g) Australia–Singapore RTA and Article 19.1 USMCA.

[1539] Including, Article 14.4 US–Morocco RTA ('*the production, distribution, marketing, sales, or delivery of products or services through electronic means*'), Article 16.1 CETA ('*commerce conducted through telecommunications, alone or in conjunction with other information and communication technologies*'), Article 15.01 Canada-Panama RTA ('*commerce conducted through telecommunications, alone or in conjunction with other information and communication technologies*'), Article 14.1 Mexico–Panama Agreement ('*todo acuerdo, transacción o intercambio de información con fines comerciales en la que las Partes interactúan utilizando Internet u otras tecnologías de la información y las comunicaciones*') and Article 13.2 EAEU–Vietnam RTA ('*trade with the use of electronic technologies*').

[1540] Footnote 46 to Article 13.3 China–Korea RTA.

are categorised as goods or services. Footnote 2 to Article 15.3 KORUS, however, appoints the Committee on Trade in Goods as the place to discuss classification matters related to the application of the prohibition on customs duties on digital products transmitted electronically.[1541] This hints at an inclination to deal with digital products as goods.[1542] The Australia–Singapore, the CPTPP and the USMCA contain a similar caveat on the classification of digital products as goods or services.[1543] Both in CPTPP and USMCA this disclaimer is repeated in a footnote to the provision that applies the general exceptions of the GATS (Article XIV GATS) to the chapter on electronic commerce.[1544]

The EU–Japan RTA is unique among the set of compared RTAs as it contains an explicit recognition of the importance (and therefore also existence) of the principle of technological neutrality.[1545] Only one (implicit) iteration of the technological neutrality principle can be identified in the e-commerce chapter of the China–Korea RTA. The first paragraph of Article 13.4 stipulates that parties have to ensure that the legal validity of a signature is not denied solely on the basis that the signature is in electronic form. Several similar implicit references to technological neutrality can be found throughout the other studied RTAs. Principally, the recognition of the applicability of the services chapters in KORUS, Australia–Singapore RTA, CPTPP and USMCA (as discussed *infra*) is also an implicit recognition of the principle of technological neutrality. Moreover, the recognition of equivalence of electronic signatures[1546] and electronically submitted trade documents[1547] also fits within this principle. The EU–Japan RTA also dedicates a separate provision to the equivalence of contracts concluded by electronic means.[1548]

Out of the six agreements analysed, only one explicitly addressed the phenomenon of 'new services' in its chapter on cross-border trade in

1541 Footnote 2 to Article 15.3 KORUS.

1542 KORUS did not establish a Committee on Trade in Services.

1543 Footnote 2 to Article 14.1 Australia–Singapore RTA, Article 14.1 CPTPP and Article 19.1 USMCA.

1544 Footnote 2 to Article 29.1.3 CPTPP and Footnote 2 to Article 32.1.2 USMCA. The GATT's general exceptions are not applied *mutatis mutandis* to the e-commerce chapter (Article 29.1.1 CPTPP).

1545 Article 8.70.3 EU–Japan RTA.

1546 Article 13.4.1 China–Korea RTA, Article 15.4(c) KORUS, Article 14.9 Australia–Singapore RTA, Article 14.6.1 CPTPP, Article 8.77.1 EU–Japan RTA and Article 19.6.1 USMCA.

1547 Article 13.6.2 China–Korea RTA, Article 15.6.2 KORUS, Article 14.12 Australia–Singapore RTA, Article 14.9 CPTPP and Article 19.9 USMCA.

1548 Article 8.76.1 EU–Japan RTA.

services.[1549] Australia and Singapore clarify that 'services' includes '*all services including new and variant services in any sector except services supplied in the exercise of governmental authority*'.[1550] It is, however, unclear what is meant by 'new services'. Does this entail services that were not supplied (through a certain mode of supply) in the parties' territory at the time of concluding the RTA? Does it refer to services that do not yet exist? Without further clarification, it is hard to imagine what kind of services the parties are referring to. Regardless of the exact interpretation of this definition, it is clear that the parties want to avoid the exclusion of services based on the argument that these services are new.[1551]

KORUS' financial services chapter requires parties to permit a financial institution of another party to supply any new financial service that it would permit its own financial institutions to supply. A new financial service is defined as '*a financial service not supplied in the Party's territory that is supplied within the territory of the other Party, and includes any new form of delivery of a financial service or the sale of a financial product*'. The same requirement with regard to new financial services is included in the Australia–Singapore RTA, the CPTPP, the EU–Japan RTA and the USMCA.[1552] These provisions all follow the wording of section 7 of the Understanding on commitments in financial services.

Other RTAs have explicitly carved out 'new services' from the scope of their services chapters. For example, CETA Annex 9-B contains the parties' agreement that the chapter on domestic regulation as well as the provisions on MFN treatment, market access and national treatment in the chapter on cross-border supply of services do not apply to measures relating to a new service that cannot be classified in the CPC 1991.[1553] The Annex, however, clarifies that it does not exclude '*existing service[s] that could be classified in the CPC 1991, but that could not previously be supplied on a cross-border basis due to lack of technical feasibility*'. Therefore, most (if not all) digital services as defined in Part II will fall within the scope of those obligations. Both Japan and Switzerland in their

1549 Many FTAs contain provisions on new financial services, following the Understanding on Commitments in Financial Services. For an analysis see Carlo M Cantore, '"Parallel Convergences" in Free Trade Agreements on Financial Services: Select Issues' in Markus Krajewski and Rhea Tamara Hoffman, *Coherence and Divergence in Services Trade Law* (Springer 2020) 202–203.

1550 Article 7.1(o) Australia–Singapore RTA.

1551 This aligns with the findings in Chapter 5 of this book.

1552 Article 9.7 Australia–Singapore RTA, Article 11.7 CPTPP, Article 8.60 EU–Japan RTA and Article 17.7 USMCA.

1553 Even though the CPCprov is considered to be exhaustive. See *supra* Section 5.1.1.

joint RTA have included a carve-out for 'new services' in their list of reservations to the trade in services chapter. In the second section of Annex III, Japan reserves the right to adopt measures in relation to new services in all service sectors for its MFN treatment, market access and national treatment obligations. Japan qualifies as new services '*services other than those recognised or that should have been recognised owing to the circumstances at the time of entry into force of this Agreement by the Government of Japan*'.[1554] It also includes 'services in any mode of supply in which those services were not technically feasible at the time of entry into force of this Agreement' in this reservation, which arguably targets services that could so far not have been provided through the Internet, but that can now be supplied online. Switzerland lists a limited number of service sectors for which it reserves the right to adopt measures for new services that might be inconsistent with the market access and the national treatment obligation.[1555] It clarifies that it reserves the right to introduce any new discriminatory measures with regard to cross-border trade and defines 'new services' very broadly as '*services that are not currently delivered on the Swiss market. It includes services related to existing or new products or the manner in which a product or service is supplied.*'

It can thus be concluded that the major e-commerce RTAs do not explicitly want to take a position on whether e-commerce affects trade in goods and/or services. It can, however, be deduced that all of these e-commerce chapters include digital services within their scope. None of the RTAs define digital services and only the RTAs with US or Australia/ Singapore involvement define 'digital products'. When defined, digital products are, however, described broadly, affecting a large group of

[1554] Japan–Switzerland RTA, Annex III, Appendix 1, Section 2, entry 3 (p 455).

[1555] Japan–Switzerland RTA, Annex III, Appendix 2, Section 2, entry 103 (p 619–620). It excludes the following service sectors: Programme transmission services (limited to new audiovisual services)(CPC 7524), radio and television cable services (limited to new audiovisual services)(CPC 75300), telecommunications services (limited to new telecommunications services)(CPC 752), other computer services n.e.c. (limited to new computer services)(CPC 8499), other advertising services (limited to new advertising services)(CPC 8719), other business services n.e.c. (limited to new auctioneering services)(CPC 87909), motion picture and video production and distribution services (limited to new audiovisual services)(CPC 9611), motion picture projection services (limited to new audiovisual services)(CPC 9613), radio and television services (limited to new audiovisual services) (CPC 9613), other entertainment services (limited to new entertainment services)(CPC 96199), other recreational services n.e.c. (limited to new entertainment services) and Internet-based services (limited to new services)(no CPC code mentioned).

products. Moreover, all of the RTAs contain at least an implicit iteration of the principle of technological neutrality, which furthers the applicability of provisions dealing with measures affecting trade in services to digital services. Finally, whereas all RTAs, except for the Chinese RTA, committed to allowing the provision of 'new' financial services, only Australia and Singapore were brave enough to address the issue of new services in their RTA head-on. Even though the effort to include new services is laudable, the provision seems to create more questions than it answers. Moreover, as has been argued in Part II, only very few services (if any) will qualify as truly new services. Most digital services already existed but can, because of the Internet, now be supplied through different means. The need for such a provision on 'new services' is therefore questionable. Where it clarifies the position of the parties on this political rather than legal matter, it does add value to the parties' commitments on trade in services.

9.3 Comparing Architectural Features and Scope

The electronic commerce chapter of the China–Korea RTA starts out with the general statement that the Parties recognise the applicability of the WTO Agreement to measures affecting electronic commerce. 'The WTO Agreement' arguably refers to the 1994 Agreement Establishing the World Trade Organization or 'Marrakesh Agreement', which incorporates the Covered Agreements as annexes.[1556] A reference to the applicability of 'the WTO Agreement' therefore entails the applicability of, *inter alia*, the GATS. KORUS also recognises the applicability of the WTO Agreement to measures that affect electronic commerce.[1557] The EU–Japan RTA confirms the applicability of their respective commitments under the WTO Agreement, but only their commitments 'for cooperation on electronic commerce'.[1558] Contrary to US and Singapore RTA practice, neither the CPTPP, the Australia–Singapore RTA nor the USMCA confirm applicability of WTO rules.[1559]

KORUS' e-commerce chapter does not explicitly define its scope. It does, however, define digital products (to which the substantive obligations in the e-commerce chapter apply) broadly.[1560] It additionally clarifies that measures affecting the supply of a service that is delivered or performed

[1556] Including GATT (Annex 1A), GATS (Annex 1B) and TRIPS (Annex 1C).
[1557] Article 15.1 KORUS.
[1558] Article 8.1 EU–Japan RTA.
[1559] Wu (n 298) 10.
[1560] See Articles 15.3 and 15.9 KORUS.

electronically are subject to the obligations contained in the services chapters of the RTA. This applicability, however, entails that digital services are also subject to any exceptions and non-conforming measures.[1561] Only one non-conforming measure explicitly related to digital services can be identified in the list of non-conforming measures: Korea reserves the right to promote access to digital audio or video content that is not (yet) available.[1562]

The Australia–Singapore RTA explicitly sets out the (broad) scope of its e-commerce chapter, stating that it applies to measures that affect trade by electronic means or that, by electronic means, facilitate trade.[1563] The reservations, non-conforming measures and exceptions that apply to the obligations on cross-border trade in services or financial services chapters also apply to the non-discrimination obligation and the obligations related to data flows and DLRs.[1564] The chapter does not apply to government procurement or (measures related to) information held or processed by or on behalf of a party.[1565] In its negative service sector list, two relevant entries should be highlighted. First, Australia retains the right to promote the availability of electronically transmitted audiovisual services.[1566] Second, Singapore limits its commitments on broadcasting services but clarifies that this does not include value-added network services such as electronic mail, voice-mail, online information and data base retrieval, electronic data interchange and/or data processing.[1567]

The CPTPP's e-commerce chapter applies to measures that affect trade by electronic means, but excludes from its scope government procurement and information held or processed by or on behalf of a party.[1568] It recognises the applicability of other services chapters to a service delivered or performed electronically, but with it also the list of non-conforming measures related to those chapters.[1569] Looking into the lists of

[1561] Article 15.2 KORUS.

[1562] KORUS Annex II-Korea, no. 33. It is additionally clarified what is understood under 'digital audio or video service': '*a service that provides streaming audio content, films or other video downloads or streaming video content regardless of the type of transmission (including through the Internet) but does not include broadcasting services*'.

[1563] Article 14.2.1 Australia–Singapore RTA.

[1564] Article 14.2.3 Australia–Singapore RTA.

[1565] Article 14.2.2 Australia–Singapore RTA.

[1566] Annex 4-II(A)-AUS-10 of the Australia–Singapore RTA.

[1567] Annex 4-II(B)-SGP-10 of the Australia–Singapore RTA.

[1568] Article 14.2 CPTPP.

[1569] Article 14.2.4 CPTPP.

non-conforming measures, there are again some noteworthy reservations related to culture. Australia reserves the right to adopt or maintain measures to make electronically transmitted audiovisual services available in Australia.[1570] Chile reserves the right to adopt discriminatory measures with respect to arts and cultural industries, which include printed and electronic newspapers, and with respect to cross-border trade of one-way satellite broadcasting of digital telecom services.[1571] Peru reserves the right to preferential treatment for cultural industries (including printed and electronic newspapers).[1572]

The e-commerce section in the EU–Japan RTA applies to 'measures by a Party affecting trade by electronic means' but it excludes quite some service sectors: gambling and betting services, broadcasting services, audiovisual services, services of notaries or equivalent professions and legal representation services.[1573] The lists of non-conforming measures annexed to this agreement do not contain any references to electronically supplied services or digital services.

The USMCA's chapter on electronic commerce applies to measures that affect trade by electronic means, with the exclusion of government procurement and information held or processed by or on behalf of a party.[1574] Like most of the studied RTAs, the applicability of the trade in services chapters to services that are delivered or performed electronically is explicitly recognised. This also entails the applicability of any exceptions or non-conforming measures applicable to those chapters.[1575] In its Schedule containing the improved market access commitments, the United States included 'information services (the offering of a capability for generating, acquiring, storing, transforming, processing, retrieving, utilising, or making available information via telecommunications, and includes electronic publishing)' committing fully to mode 1, 2 and 3.[1576] It additionally liberalised motion picture or videotape production (whether on fixed media or electronically).[1577] Mexico undertook the commitment to allow for the cross-border supply of electronic payment services if these services are

1570 Annex II – Australia – 9 CPTPP.
1571 Annex II – Chile – 11 and 4 CPTPP, respectively.
1572 Annex II – Peru – 6 CPTPP.
1573 Article 8.70.4 and 5 EU–Japan RTA.
1574 Article 19.2.2 and 3 USMCA.
1575 Article 19.2.4 USMCA.
1576 Annex II – United States – 13 USMCA.
1577 ibid.

supplied domestically in the other party's territory, in line with the Understanding on commitments in financial services.[1578]

Chapter 13 of the China–Korea RTA does not explicitly set out its scope of application, but does stipulate that other chapters prevail in case of conflict and that the provisions on dispute settlement do not apply to the provisions in Chapter 13.[1579] Similarly, the EU–Japan RTA states that, in case of conflict between the e-commerce provisions and other parts of the RTA, the other provisions prevail.[1580]

KORUS' provisions on dispute settlement apply to Chapter 15, with the exclusion of disputes brought with regard to benefits that a party expected to accrue to it.[1581] Similar stipulations can be found in Article 16.1 Australia–Singapore RTA, Article 28.3 CPTPP,[1582] Article 21.2 EU–Japan RTA and Article 31.2 USMCA. Both the CPTPP and the USMCA do not allow application of dispute settlement for claims of nullification or impairment of a benefit expected under the e-commerce chapters.[1583]

Most of the RTAs studied define the scope of their e-commerce chapter quite broadly, only excluding 'usual suspects' topics like subsidies, government procurement and government-held information from the scope of these rules. Notable exceptions to this are the China–Korea RTA and the EU–Japan RTA. While the former does not elaborate on the scope of its chapter (which only contains three substantive obligations and two endeavour clauses), the latter is the only agreement to exclude several service sectors from the scope of the e-commerce provisions. These are also the only two agreements that stipulate that other chapters prevail in case of conflict with the provisions in the e-commerce chapter.

Not a single RTA stipulates that the provisions on e-commerce override relevant reservations for non-conforming measures or limitations in Schedules. However, the measures listed as non-conforming in the RTAs' annexes that are relevant to digital services are relatively limited in scope and mainly relate to cultural and audiovisual services, which have historically been excluded by several WTO Members (with the EU as the most prominent example). Overall, it can thus be concluded that the scope of these chapters is quite broad. Moreover, the fact that only the China–

[1578] Annex III – Mexico – 22 USMCA.

[1579] Articles 13.2 and 13.9 China–Korea RTA.

[1580] Article 8.70.6 EU–Japan RTA.

[1581] Article 22.4 KORUS.

[1582] Article 14.18 CPTPP provides Malaysia and Vietnam with a two-year exemption from certain obligations being subject to dispute settlement.

[1583] Article 28.3.1(c) CPTPP and Article 31.2.1(c) USMCA.

Korea RTA excludes the applicability of the dispute settlement provisions adds to the conclusion that parties are serious about their commitment to these e-commerce obligations.[1584] It allows parties to bring cases alleging the inconsistency of the measures of other RTA parties with the e-commerce provisions before the RTA's dispute settlement bodies.

Finally, looking into the architectural structure of these six RTAs and how their e-commerce chapters relate to the other provisions in the RTA, it can be concluded that most of them do not isolate the e-commerce chapter from obligations in other chapters and rather seem to apply them in harmony. The explicit recognition of the applicability of the services chapters to services delivered electronically confirms the interlinkage between the e-commerce chapters and the rest of the agreement, which endorses the applicability of relevant provisions throughout the regional agreements to digital services.

9.4 Addressing Specific Barriers and Obstacles to Digital Services Trade in the Selected RTAs

9.4.1 Non-discrimination and Market Access Obligations

All agreements compared in this chapter reiterate the national treatment obligation contained in the GATS and many also include the MFN treatment and the market access obligation. KORUS explicitly sets out that its parties may not accord less favourable treatment to digital products originating in the territory of another party compared to like domestic digital products or like digital products from a non-party.[1585] These obligations do not apply to non-conforming measures and broadcasting. The national treatment obligation additionally does not apply to subsidies

1584 This statement should be nuanced for two reasons: (i) several of the provisions only contain best endeavour commitments, and (ii) regional dispute settlement is often not put into action. As NAFTA was an important exception to this rule, it could therefore be expected that the USMCA will continue this practice of organising effective regional dispute settlement. Overall, most RTAs with e-commerce provisions subject these to dispute settlement. Other RTAs which have excluded e-commerce chapters from the scope of dispute settlement include the Australia–China RTA, the Australia–Malaysia RTA, the Australia and New Zealand–ASEAN RTA, the New Zealand–Hong Kong RTA and the New Zealand–Taiwan RTA. It is interesting to see that Australia and New Zealand, which generally include a considerable amount of e-commerce provisions in their RTAs, have excluded the e-commerce chapters from dispute settlement in several of their RTAs.

1585 Thereby incorporating the national treatment obligation and the most-favoured-nation treatment obligation. Article 15.3.2 and 15.3.3 KORUS.

or services supplied in the exercise of governmental authority.[1586] The Australia–Singapore RTA likewise stipulates that the MFN treatment and national treatment obligation are applicable to digital products. However, it clarifies that these obligations shall not apply to the extent of any inconsistency with provisions on IPRs and shall not apply to subsidies or to broadcasting.[1587] Both the CPTPP and the USMCA include a provision on the non-discriminatory treatment of digital products, incorporating both the MFN treatment and the national treatment obligation.[1588] Whereas KORUS, CPTPP and USMCA explicitly state that no less favourable treatment will be accorded than to like products from non-parties,[1589] this clarification is omitted from the Australia–Singapore RTA.

Four of the studied RTAs slightly changed the language in their national treatment obligation (and sometimes also most-favoured-nation treatment obligation), not referring to like services and service suppliers, but rather to 'in like circumstances'.[1590] So far, neither panels nor the Appellate Body have interpreted the scope of 'in like circumstances'. Therefore, it is difficult to assess whether reference to 'in like circumstances' rather than to 'like services and service suppliers' changes the scope of the obligation. Some RTAs moreover clarify that findings on 'like circumstances' can depend on distinctions made on the basis of legitimate public welfare objectives, thereby arguably narrowing the scope of these obligations.[1591]

In addition to these obligations, it should be taken into account that other chapters applicable to services (including the chapter on cross-border services trade, financial services and telecommunications services) also apply to services that are delivered electronically.[1592] So even where

[1586] Article 15.3.4–6 KORUS.

[1587] Article 14.6 Australia–Singapore RTA.

[1588] Article 14.4 CPTPP. CPTPP excludes subsidies and broadcasting from the scope of this obligation. Moreover, in case of inconsistency with rights and obligations on IPRs, the latter prevail. Article 19.4 USMCA. USMCA only excludes subsidies from this obligation.

[1589] See Article 15.3.3 KORUS, footnote 4 to Article 14.4 CPTPP and footnote 3 to Article 19.4 USMCA.

[1590] See Article 12.2 KORUS, Article 7.4 Australia–Singapore RTA, Article 10.3 CPTPP and Article 15.4 USMCA.

[1591] See for example Article 15.4.3 USMCA and footnote 3 to Article 7.4 Australia–Singapore RTA. Mitchell, Voon and Hepburn (n 1376) 18.

[1592] As explicitly recognised in KORUS, the Australia–Singapore RTA, CPTPP and USMCA. Moreover, the fact that the provisions on cross-border trade in services, financial services, telecommunications services and electronic commerce are included in the same chapter in EU RTAs implies the interlinkage between these provisions and that all of them apply to services trade.

the e-commerce chapter does not specifically set out any non-discrimination obligations, the non-discrimination obligations contained in other services chapters apply to the measure affecting digital services. More generally, due to the principle of technological neutrality, the provisions applicable to trade in services should be considered to apply to measures affecting digital services, unless stated otherwise in the RTA.

For example, the e-commerce chapter in the China–Korea RTA does not include a reiteration of the non-discrimination principle. The China–Korea RTA also includes a trade in services chapter, which does not exclude digital services or services supplied through electronic means from its scope. The chapter on trade in services includes specific obligations on market access and national treatment, for which commitments have been undertaken in the annexed Schedules of Specific Commitments.[1593] These obligations will therefore also apply to services supplied through electronic means.

Similarly, the EU–Japan RTA does not reiterate the non-discrimination obligations applicable to e-commerce specifically. However, as it sets out these obligations in the section on cross-border trade in services of the same chapter and the application of other chapters to e-commerce is not excluded, it can be inferred that the non-discrimination obligations will also apply to digital services.[1594] The EU excludes, *inter alia*, audiovisual services from provisions on cross-border trade in services.[1595]

All RTAs confirm the applicability of general exceptions clauses to the obligations in the e-commerce chapters. The USMCA even clarifies what it understands under 'public morals' in the context of e-commerce.[1596] The Australia–Singapore RTA applies the GATT and GATS general exceptions

1593 Articles 8.3 and 8.4 China–Korea RTA. Korea's Schedule of Specific Commitments explicitly prohibits the sale of alcohol through electronic commerce. As regards basic telecommunications services (which includes commitments on digital cellular services) a full commitment was made for mode 2 and licensing limitations were scheduled for mode 1 and 3. Full commitments were undertaken for value-added telecommunications services, computer and related services and audiovisual services for mode 1, 2 and 3. See Annex 8-A-1. China has undertaken more limited commitments: for telecommunications services (both basic and value-added) mode 1 and 3 are limited to joint ventures with minority foreign shareholding. Computer and related services are fully liberalised for mode 1, 2 and 3 but it is explicitly stated that this does not cover 'the economic activity consisting of the provision of content services which require computer and related services as means of supply'. Several audiovisual services are fully committed for mode 1, but imports of motion pictures for theatrical release are limited to 20 on an annual basis. See Annex 8-A-2.

1594 Articles 8.16 and 8.17 EU–Japan RTA.

1595 Article 8.14.2(d) EU–Japan RTA.

1596 Annex 19-A, paragraph 4 lists online sex trafficking, sexual exploitation of children and prostitution as examples of measures necessary to protect public morals.

clauses *mutatis mutandis* to the digital economy agreement.[1597] Interestingly, only paragraphs (a), (b) and (c) of Article XIV GATS are transposed. The two other subparagraphs of that article, both of which relate to taxation, are not applied to the digital trade provisions in that RTA.[1598]

The applicability of non-discrimination and market access obligations to e-commerce or digital trade in RTAs entails that the GATS-consistency analysis as conducted in Chapter 7 will equally apply at the RTA level.[1599] Importantly, the liberalisation of trade in services in many RTAs goes considerably beyond their commitments under the GATS,[1600] which leads to a broader scope of application of the national treatment and market access obligations in these RTAs. Where RTAs apply the MFN treatment obligation, national treatment obligation and market access obligation to electronic commerce, barriers to e-commerce might violate these commitments. The following sections assess whether more specific obligations relating to these barriers have been included in the compared RTAs.

9.4.2 Restrictions on Cross-border Data Transfers

The China–Korea RTA contains very limited references to cross-border data flows. Firstly, in its financial services chapter it clarifies that parties are not required to disclose information relating to the affairs and accounts of individual consumers or any confidential or proprietary information in the possession of public entities.[1601] It thereby provides the parties with leeway to limit the transfer of personal data in the context of financial services. This, however, seems limited to information that is in possession of the government, as it applies to the party directly, not to its service suppliers. Secondly, analogous to the Annex on Telecoms, Article 10.3 of the China–Korea RTA requires parties to ensure that service suppliers of other parties may use public telecommunication networks or services for the movement of information in its territory or across its border. The scope of this obligation is, however, limited to what is in accordance with domestic laws and regulations.[1602] This obligation is mitigated by the subsequent

[1597] Article 14.3 Australia–Singapore RTA.
[1598] Article XIV(d) and (e) GATS.
[1599] Subject, however, to the interpretation of 'in like circumstances'.
[1600] Either through more comprehensive services schedules (positive lists) or the use of negative lists for services commitments.
[1601] Article 9.4 China–Korea RTA.
[1602] See paragraph 3 of Article 10.3 China–Korea RTA.

paragraph, which allows parties to take measures to protect personal information of end users of public telecommunications networks or services.[1603] The third and most specific provision in relation to cross-border data flows can be found in Article 13.5, which requires parties to '*adopt or maintain measures which ensure the protection of the personal information of the users of electronic commerce*'. Rather than mandate free cross-border flows of data, the e-commerce chapter in the China–Korea RTA focusses on the protection of personal information, which has been defined broadly in the context of the chapter on Telecommunications.

KORUS contains a soft provision on allowing data flows, merely recognising the importance of free flow of information to facilitate trade and an endeavour of the parties to refrain from imposing or maintaining unnecessary barriers to electronic information flows across borders.[1604] Non-binding as it may be, this article was the first reference to the free flow of data across borders in any RTA and seems to fit within the US' traditional preference for the deregulation of the Internet. KORUS did not yet contain a provision on the protection of personal information.

With regard to financial services, like the China–Korea RTA, parties are not required to provide access to information related to financial affairs and accounts of individual customers or confidential information of which disclosure would impede law enforcement or otherwise be contrary to public interest or prejudice legitimate commercial interest.[1605] But the parties do explicitly commit to allowing transfer of information by financial institutions for data processing in the ordinary course of business.[1606] In the telecommunications chapter, which covers not only access to and use of public telecoms services but also measures relating to the supply of value-added services,[1607] the parties reiterate the commitment to ensure that service suppliers from the other party may use public telecommunications services for the movement of information.[1608] Moreover, parties are required to take reasonable steps to protect the confidentiality of

[1603] Personal information is defined as: '*any information transmitted by electromagnetic means that identifies a natural person or is related to personal privacy*'. Article 10.18 China–Korea RTA.

[1604] Article 15.8 KORUS. See also Mattoo and Meltzer (n 149) 18–19.

[1605] Article 13.7 KORUS.

[1606] Annex 13-B, section B KORUS.

[1607] Broadcasting or cable distribution of radio and television programming are, however, excluded from the scope of this chapter. Article 14.1.2 KORUS.

[1608] Article 14.2.3 KORUS.

commercially sensitive information of suppliers and end users of public telecoms services obtained from interconnection arrangements.[1609]

The CPTPP includes the obligation for parties to allow the cross-border transfer of information by electronic means, including personal information, when this is done in the conduct of business of a covered person.[1610] Parties also included a prohibition on DLRs as a condition for conducting business.[1611] Both of these obligations are limited by the parties' right to adopt measures to achieve a legitimate public policy objective and the different regulatory approaches of countries are recognised.[1612] Moreover, chapter 14 of the CPTPP does not apply to government procurement or government-held information.[1613]

Regarding financial information, CPTPP parties agreed to allow financial institutions to transfer information in electronic or other form in the ordinary course of business.[1614] Here as well, parties are not required to allow access to information related to financial affairs and accounts of individual customers of financial institutions or to confidential information, the disclosure of which would be contrary to the public interest or prejudice legitimate commercial interests of particular enterprises.[1615] Like all other RTAs studied, the CPTPP incorporates the Telecoms Annex's obligation to ensure that service suppliers can move their information over public telecommunications networks.[1616]

Mattoo and Meltzer also set out the multitiered approach to enabling cross-border data flows and privacy protection in the CPTPP. They expect a heavy reliance on the exceptions linked to the obligation on cross-border data transfer and data localisation requirements and signal a need for mechanisms to develop common standards for privacy protection. They additionally point out that data destination countries are required to prevent fraud and deception and to protect personal information.[1617]

1609 Article 14.3.1(b) KORUS.

1610 Article 14.11 CPTPP.

1611 Article 14.13 CPTPP. Computing facilities are defined as '*computer servers and storage devices for processing or storing information for commercial use*'. Article 14.1 CPTPP.

1612 Like in the Australia–Singapore RTA, no limitative list of objectives was included. Peng and Liu (n 336) 195.

1613 Articles 14.2(3) CPTPP. The reference to government procurement and information held by the government was included to ensure that Canada's provincial laws, requiring data localisation, do not violate its CPTPP obligations. ibid 194.

1614 Annex 11-B, section B CPTPP.

1615 Article 11.8 CPTPP.

1616 Article 13.4.3 CPTPP.

1617 Articles 14.7 and 14.8 CPTPP. Mattoo and Meltzer (n 836) 783–784.

They consider that the approach taken by CPTPP, which is practically identical to the one taken in the Australia–Singapore RTA and the USMCA, functions as a potential model for further regulatory cooperation on trade in services in this regard.

The EU–Japan RTA stipulates that parties will reassess the need to include provisions on the free flow of data in the agreement within three years. At the time of writing, the agreement did not include provisions on the cross-border flow of data or on data localisation. On 23 January 2019, the European Commission implemented its Decision 2019/419, which recognises that Japan ensures an adequate level of protection of personal data transferred from the EU to personal-information-handling business operators in Japan.[1618] This adequacy decision was taken in the context of the GDPR and allows cross-border flows of personal data of EU citizens to Japan. On 16 July 2020, the Court of Justice invalidated the adequacy decision for data transfers to the United States (also known as the Privacy Shield).[1619] At the time of writing, it remains to be seen what the impact of this judgment will be on other adequacy decisions, including that regarding Japan.

Additionally, the EU–Japan RTA includes the requirement to ensure access to public telecoms transport networks for the movement of data (like the Telecoms Annex) and the obligation to allow transfer of information or processing of financial information, including transfers of data by electronic means, that are necessary for the conduct of ordinary business of a financial service supplier, subject to the right to protect personal data, personal privacy and confidentiality of individual records and accounts.[1620]

The USMCA prohibits parties from restricting cross-border transfer of data (including personal data) by electronic means if this is done for the conduct of ordinary business. This obligation is limited by the parties' right to adopt or maintain measures necessary to achieve a legitimate public policy objective.[1621] Additionally, USMCA parties cannot require the use or

[1618] Commission Implementing Decision (EU) 2019/419 of 23 January 2019 pursuant to Regulation (EU) 2016/679 of the European Parliament and of the Council on the adequate protection of personal data by Japan under the Act on the Protection of Personal Information, *OJ* L 76, 19 March 2019, 1–58. Other countries for which their personal data protection framework has been recognised as adequate so far are Andorra, Argentina, Canada, Faroe Islands, Guernsey, Israel, Isle of Man, Jersey, New Zealand, Switzerland, Uruguay and the US. Adequacy talks are ongoing with Korea (information up to date on 22 May 2019).

[1619] Judgment of 16 July 2020, *Data Protection Commissioner v Facebook Ireland and Maximillian Schrems ('Schrems II')*, Case C-311/18, EU:C:2020:559.

[1620] Respectively Article 8.44.3 and 8.63 EU–Japan RTA.

[1621] Article 19.11 USMCA. Again, no list of covered public policy objective is included.

location of computing facilities as a condition for conducting business. Contrary to the CPTPP and the Australia–Singapore RTA, parties cannot deviate from this obligation to achieve a legitimate public policy objective.[1622]

The USMCA parties also included a DLR prohibition in the financial services chapter. In Article 17.18, the parties commit not to require data localisation, '*so long as the party's financial regulatory authorities, for regulatory and supervisory purposes, have immediate, direct, complete, and ongoing access to information processed or stored on computing facilities that the covered person uses or locates outside the party's territory*'.[1623] Parties maintain the right to protect personal data, personal privacy and confidentiality of individual records and accounts, as long as they do not circumvent their obligations. In relation to financial services, the USMCA parties are required to allow transfer of information in electronic form for data processing in the ordinary course of business.[1624] Finally, like the other RTAs studied, the USMCA includes the Telecoms Annex's obligation to ensure that service suppliers can use public telecoms networks or services for the movement of data.[1625]

The Australia–Singapore RTA contains a broad definition of 'personal information' as '*any information, including data, about an identified or identifiable natural person*'.[1626] Australia and Singapore recognise that each party may have its own regulatory requirements concerning the transfer of information by electronic means. The parties have, however, committed to allowing cross-border transfer of information, including personal information, when this is done for the conduct of the business of a covered person.[1627] Parties can limit cross-border data flows to achieve

[1622] Article 19.12 USMCA.

[1623] The second element in this obligation might have partially been prompted by the Microsoft Case. In this case, the US issued a warrant to search a certain e-mail account controlled and maintained by Microsoft. The information was stored on servers established in Ireland, maintained by a Microsoft EU subsidiary. Microsoft did not want to turn over the data it had stored on its Irish servers, arguing the section 2703(a) of the Stored Communications Act (SCA) did not apply extraterritorially. While the district court held Microsoft in civil contempt for its failure to comply with the warrant, the second circuit court reversed that decision on the basis of non-extraterritorial applicability. Before the Supreme Court could rule on this issue, the 'Clarifying Lawful Overseas Use of Data Act (Cloud Act)' was enacted which modified the SCA to specifically include cloud storage regardless of the location of the servers. US Supreme Court, *United States v Microsoft Corp.*, No. 17–2, 584 U.S. (2018).

[1624] Article 17.17 USMCA.

[1625] Article 18.3.3 USMCA.

[1626] Article 14.1(w) Australia–Singapore RTA.

[1627] Article 14.23.2 Australia–Singapore RTA.

a legitimate public policy objective if the measure is not applied in a way that constitutes a means of arbitrary or unjustifiable discrimination or a disguised restriction on trade and meets the proportionality test.[1628] Finally, the updated digital trade chapter of the Australia–Singapore RTA contains a general prohibition on DLRs and a DLR prohibition for financial services.[1629] DLRs can only be maintained to achieve a legitimate public policy objective.[1630]

Australia and Singapore committed to allowing financial institutions of the other party to transfer information in electronic form for data processing in the ordinary course of business.[1631] This obligation is limited as parties are allowed to maintain measures to protect personal data and personal privacy and to require obtaining prior authorisation from the relevant regulator. Parties are, however, not required to provide access to confidential information the disclosure of which might be contrary to public interests or prejudice legitimate commercial interests of particular enterprises.[1632] In its telecommunications services chapter, the RTA includes the Annex on Telecoms' obligation to ensure that all service suppliers from the other party can use public telecoms networks for the movement of information.[1633]

The Australia–Singapore RTA, the CPTPP and the USMCA contain almost identical provisions on the protection of personal data, requiring their parties to adopt or maintain a legal framework that provides for the protection of the personal information of the users of electronic commerce.[1634] In all three RTAs, restrictions to cross-border data flows (including DLRs) are only allowed if three requirements have been cumulatively met: (i) the measures must achieve a legitimate public policy objective;[1635] (ii) the application of the measures cannot constitute a means

[1628] Article 14.23.3 Australia–Singapore RTA. There is no limitative list included of recognised public policy objectives.

[1629] Article 14.24 Australia–Singapore RTA. In this context 'computing facilities' are defined as '*computer servers and storage devices for processing or storing information for commercial use but does not include computer servers or storage devices of or used to access financial market infrastructures*'. Article 14.1(b) Australia–Singapore RTA. Article 14.25 Australia–Singapore RTA uses similar language to the USMCA.

[1630] Article 14.24.3 Australia–Singapore RTA.

[1631] Annex 9-B, section B of the Australia–Singapore RTA.

[1632] Article 9.8 Australia–Singapore RTA.

[1633] Article 10.3.3 Australia–Singapore RTA. This network includes the Internet (see footnote 2 to Article 10.1).

[1634] Article 14.17 Australia–Singapore RTA, Article 14.8 CPTPP and Article 19.8 USMCA.

[1635] Unlike in the GATS, these objectives are not listed, which opens up the possibility of a wide range of possible policy objectives that could justify a violation of these obligations.

of arbitrary or unjustifiable discrimination or a disguised restriction on trade; and (iii) it cannot impose greater restrictions than required to achieve the public policy objective. The USMCA clarifies that a measure is more restrictive than necessary if it accords different treatment to data transfers solely on the basis that they are cross-border in nature in a manner that modifies the condition of competition to the detriment of service suppliers of another party.[1636] EU RTAs generally do not contain similar provisions.

At first sight, RTAs containing prohibitions on DLRs go considerably beyond the provisions found in the GATS. However, the question remains whether prohibitions on DLRs substantively add to existing GATS obligations. Prohibitions on DLRs and obligations on cross-border data flows arguably prevent parties from maintaining these measures, whether they have scheduled commitments in the affected service sectors or not (as is the case under the GATS). Even though DLR prohibitions would not necessarily 'catch' all types of DLRs (especially not those that are more flexible[1637]), barriers to cross-border data flows can be addressed under free flow of data provisions, where these contain enforceable obligations. Enforceable obligations on cross-border data flows in RTAs are still rare. Additionally, prohibitions on local presence requirements in FTAs might amount to prohibitions on DLRs, depending on the interpretation of 'local presence'.[1638] Such provisions might be applicable to local storage requirements on digital service suppliers as those require the suppliers to establish or maintain servers in the party's territory.

Based on the observations above, it can be noted that the EU and the United States seem to take differing positions on cross-border data transfers and personal data protection. This is illustrated by the proposals both parties tabled in the (*de facto* frozen) Trade in Services Agreement (TiSA) and Transatlantic Trade and Investment Partnership Agreement (TTIP) negotiations. Whereas the United States reported that it is facing strong opposition in its broad proposals on the right for service suppliers to transfer data across borders, the EU stressed that it will not jeopardise privacy protection of data in the EU.[1639] The EU's aversion to agreeing to a prohibition on data localisation requirements is also illustrated by the fact that, while the EU–Japan RTA does not contain such a provision, it can be found in the

[1636] Footnote 5 to Article 19.11 USMCA.

[1637] See *supra* Section 3.2.1.

[1638] See Article 12.5 KORUS, Article 7.6 Australia–Singapore RTA, Article 10.6 CPTPP and Article 15.6 USMCA.

[1639] Peng and Liu (n 336) 202–203.

Japan–Mongolia RTA, which entered into force three years prior.[1640] The dichotomy between the EU and the United States on this topic has reportedly also complicated the ongoing e-commerce negotiations at the WTO.

9.4.3 *Web Filtering and Content Control*

Most of the studied RTAs explicitly address the issue of lack of reasonable and non-discriminatory access to the Internet. KORUS recognises that its parties should be able to access and use services and digital products of their choice, run applications and services of their choice, connect their choice of devices to the Internet and have the benefit of competition among network providers, application and service providers, and content providers.[1641] Using even less binding terms than KORUS, the Australia–Singapore RTA recognises the benefit of consumers having access to and the ability to use the services and applications of their choice and access to information on the network management practices of a consumers ISP.[1642] Using very similar language, Article 14.10 CPTPP recognises the benefits of access to and use of the Internet for e-commerce. Finally, the USMCA also sets out that the parties recognise the benefits for consumers to access and use services and applications of their choice on the Internet, to connect devices to the Internet and to access information on network management practices.[1643] Interestingly, the earliest RTA studied contains the clearest commitment on access to and use of the Internet. Even though it is still formulated in best-endeavour language, recognising that 'consumers should be able to access and use the Internet' is arguably somewhat stronger than recognising that 'access to and use of the Internet is beneficial for consumers'. No RTA includes an enforceable obligation to ensure free choice of online services and applications to consumers. China's blocking of a great deal of foreign services to Chinese consumers, as discussed in Chapter 7, constitutes an example of how this free choice can be hampered. Due to the filtering performed by China's Great Firewall, consumers are prevented from choosing freely between services and applications online.

[1640] Article 9.10 Japan–Mongolia RTA.

[1641] Article 15.7 KORUS RTA. It could be argued that this last element also goes against the US' abolishment of network neutrality as analysed in Chapter 7, as this abolishment enables network providers to discriminate against application and service providers as well as content providers.

[1642] Article 14.20 Australia–Singapore RTA.

[1643] Article 19.10 USMCA.

The USMCA contains a, so far, unique provision on the liability of suppliers or users of interactive computer services.[1644] Article 19.17 requires the parties '*not to adopt or maintain measures that treat a supplier or user of an interactive computer service as an information content provider in determining liability for harms related to information stored, processed, transmitted, distributed or made available by the service, except to the extent the supplier or user has, in whole or in part, created, or developed the information*'.[1645] Measures pertaining to intellectual property (infringement) are excluded from the scope of the obligation. This provision addresses content liability, exonerating suppliers and users of services that enable access to a server (ISPs and website hosts [including social media platforms][1646]) from bearing (civil) responsibility for the information that is stored on that server but created by a user of the platform or third-party posters.[1647] China's practices under the Great Firewall umbrella, including the requirement on ISPs to monitor and filter the content that is being published online (under the threat of sanctions), would arguably go against such an obligation.

The Australia–Singapore RTA does not include an obligation related to content liability, but its parties have recognised that industry (rather than the parties themselves) has a responsibility to adopt or maintain preventative measures to protect natural persons from harmful online experiences.[1648]

As could be expected, no provisions have been included in the China–Korea RTA that explicitly address the issues related to web filtering and content control. However, as has been shown in Chapter 7, web filtering practices can be challenged under Members' market access and the national treatment obligations. In as far as the market access and national treatment obligations in the trade in services chapter apply to digital services trade between China and Korea, these obligations could be used

[1644] Article 19.1 defines an interactive content provider as '*a person or entity that creates or develops, in whole or in part, information provided through the Internet or another interactive computer services*' and an interactive computer service as '*a system or service that provides or enables electronic access by multiple users to a computer server*'.

[1645] This obligation is modelled after Section 230 of the United States Communications Decency Act of 1996, 47 U.S.C. § 230.

[1646] *Klayman v Zuckerberg*, 910 F. Supp. 2d 314, 318 (D.D.C. 2012), which found Facebook to qualify as an interactive computer service.

[1647] For an analysis of the interpretation of Section 230 of the Communications Decency Act, see: Amanda Cecil L, 'Taking Back the Internet: Imposing Civil Liability on Interactive Computer Services in an Attempt to Provide an Adequate Remedy to Victims of Nonconsensual Pornography' (2014) 71 Washington and Lee Law Review 2513, 2538–2547.

[1648] Article 14.18.3 Australia–Singapore RTA.

to address China's web filtering practices.[1649] This same consideration applies to all other RTAs that included such provisions. The EU–Japan RTA, for example, also does not to contain an explicit provision requiring the parties to ensure consumers' access to and choice of online services and applications, so recourse to more general obligations could be warranted.

The compatibility of practices of web filtering and content-control with the obligations in the Annex on Telecommunication was already put into question in Chapter 7. All of the RTAs studied reiterated the obligations in the Telecoms Annex to a certain extent. The telecommunications chapter in the China–Korea RTA, for example, requires parties to ensure access to and use of public telecommunications networks, in the same way as the GATS' Annex on Telecommunications.[1650] Moreover, significant obligations with regard to interconnection have been included, requiring both parties to ensure interconnection on non-discriminatory terms, of decent quality and in a timely fashion.[1651] Parties have additionally agreed to maintain measures to prevent suppliers of public telecom network or service suppliers from engaging in anti-competitive practices, such as cross-subsidisation, abusing information obtained and predatory pricing.[1652] The telecommunications chapter thereby also incorporates the competitive safeguards and requirements on interconnection as formulated in the Reference Paper on Basic Telecommunications.

In its telecommunications chapter, KORUS includes a provision that incorporates the obligations of the Telecoms Annex, including the requirement to ensure that service suppliers of the other party have access to and use of any public telecommunications network or service on reasonable and non-discriminatory terms and conditions. Additionally, the obligations contained in the Reference Paper have also been included throughout this chapter. Also the CPTPP, the EU–Japan RTA and the USMCA reiterate the obligations in the Annex on Telecommunications and the Reference Paper.[1653] Interestingly, the Australia–Singapore RTA also incorporates the obligations in the Annex on Telecoms and the Reference Paper into its telecommunications chapter, but it is the only studied RTA that clearly states that 'public telecommunications services' include Internet routing and

[1649] Considering that recourse to the dispute settlement chapter applies to obligations arising from chapter 8 (Trade in Services).

[1650] Article 10.3 China–Korea RTA.

[1651] Article 10.4 China–Korea RTA.

[1652] Article 10.6 China–Korea RTA.

[1653] Articles 13.4 and 13.11 CPTPP, Articles 8.44 and 8.48 EU–Japan RTA and various Articles in chapter 18 USMCA.

connectivity services.[1654] By including this clarification, the RTA provides an effective solution to the ongoing debate as to whether the Annex on Telecommunications also applies to the Internet.[1655]

9.4.4 Digital Taxes

All of the RTAs studied explicitly address the issue of customs duties in the context of electronic commerce. The China–Korea RTA confirms that both parties will maintain the WTO practice of not imposing customs duties on electronic transmissions.[1656] Parties retain the right to adjust the practice consistent with any changes made to this issue in WTO Ministerial Decisions.[1657] The agreement therefore explicitly does not (plan to) go further than WTO practice.

KORUS prohibits parties from imposing customs duties, fees or other charges on or in connection with the importation or exportation of digital products fixed on a carrier medium or digital products transmitted electronically.[1658] It is clarified that parties are still allowed to impose internal taxes or other internal charges on digital products if they are imposed in conformity with the rest of the agreement.[1659]

The Australia–Singapore RTA clearly prohibits the parties from imposing customs duties on electronic transmissions, including content transmitted electronically between persons of the parties.[1660] Compared to KORUS, the provision omits reference to 'fees or other charges' and digital products on carrier mediums but, like KORUS, it does not preclude parties from imposing internal taxes, fees or other charges on content transmitted electronically if in conformity with the rest of the agreement. The CPTPP includes a prohibition on the imposition of customs duties that is almost identical to the one in the Australia–Singapore RTA, also referring to the content of the transmission being included in the moratorium and allowing imposition of internal taxes.[1661]

[1654] Footnote 2 to Article 10.1(t) Australia–Singapore RTA.

[1655] For this discussion see Section 6.1.3.1.

[1656] In doing so, it refers to WTO Ministerial Conference Bali, 'Work Programme on Electronic Commerce - Ministerial Decision of 7 December 2013', WT/MIN(13)/32, WT/L/907, 11 December 2013.

[1657] Footnote 48 to Article 13.3 China–Korea RTA.

[1658] Article 15.3.1 KORUS.

[1659] Footnote 1 to Article 15.3 KORUS.

[1660] Article 14.5 Australia–Singapore RTA.

[1661] Article 14.3 CPTPP.

The EU–Japan RTA very concisely prohibits parties from imposing customs duties on electronic transmission.[1662] It does not refer to fees or other charges nor does it address digital products stored on carrier mediums or whether this electronic transmission includes taxation of the content of the transmission. It does not reserve the parties' right to amend this practice in accordance with any changes made to it at the WTO level nor does it clarify that imposition of internal taxes or charges is still allowed.

The language used in the USMCA to prohibit customs duties on digital products leans more closely to the terms used in KORUS than it does to the provision in the CPTPP. Parties commit not to impose customs duties, fees or other charges on or in connection with the importation or exportation of digital products transmitted electronically between two parties. However, the USMCA does not include a reference to digital products stored on carrier mediums. This obligation does not limit parties' right to impose internal taxes, fees or other charges in electronically transmitted digital products.[1663]

Even though all of the studied RTAs contain a provision on customs duties in their e-commerce chapters, all of them use (slightly) different wording. It is, however, not immediately clear what the omission of references to 'fees or other charges' would change to the substance of the obligation. It has become clear that parties to these agreements, except for KORUS, only target (the content of) electronic transmission and not the digital content that crosses the border on a carrier medium. It is unclear whether the obligations in the China–Korea RTA and the EU–Japan RTA cover the content of the transmission or only the transmission itself. Based on the interpretation of the WTO moratorium given by most Members, the taxation of content transmitted electronically should also fall within this obligation.[1664]

Overall, the inclusion of digital products stored on carrier mediums in this obligation is limited to a couple of agreements.[1665] The WTO Committee on Customs Valuation already set out that Members can choose to value data or software stored on carrier media either according to its full transaction value or on the basis of the cost or value of the carrier medium

[1662] Article 8.72 EU–Japan RTA.
[1663] Article 19.3 USMCA.
[1664] See *supra* Section 4.3.2.
[1665] Including, apart from some US RTAs, Article 12.3 Colombia–Chile RTA, Article 16.3 Colombia–Costa Rica RTA, Article 14.4 of the Northern Triangle RTA, Article 10.4 of the Singapore- India RTA, Article 7.4 of the GCC–Singapore RTA, Article 14.03 Nicaragua–Taiwan RTA and Article 15.4 of the Mexico–Central America RTA.

alone.[1666] KORUS clarifies that digital products fixed on carrier mediums are only subject to this obligation if they constitute an originating *good*. Moreover, as mentioned *supra* (Section 9.2), the Committee on Trade in Goods is appointed to resolve classification issues related to digital products transmitted electronically.[1667] In contrast, several EU RTAs state that electronic transmissions should be considered as the provision of services, which entails that they cannot be subject to customs duties.[1668] Whereas such statements were no longer present in most recent EU RTAs (e.g. CETA and the EU–Japan RTA), they are again present in the proposed digital trade chapters for the agreements with Australia and New Zealand.[1669]

9.5 Summary

The study conducted in Chapter 8 has shown how the inclusion of e-commerce provisions differs between RTAs, not only over time but also based on the geographical regions and income levels of the parties. The study thereby adds to existing scholarship on e-commerce provisions in RTAs, as it adjusts and nuances some assumptions as to how different countries approach the issue of a changing global trade landscape because of digitisation in their regional agreements.

It has been shown that, unlike what might be expected, it is not only high-income countries that have pioneered and pushed the move towards inclusion of e-commerce provisions in RTAs. Over the years, there has been a successful engagement of lower middle-income countries in RTAs that contain provisions related to e-commerce. Moreover, many of the frontrunners on e-commerce-related provisions can be found in the Latin American and the East Asian and Pacific region. The United States, Australia and Singapore have come to the fore as

1666 WTO Committee on Customs Valuation, 'Proposal for updating the "Decision on the Valuation of Carrier Media Bearing Software for Data Processing Equipment" – Revision', G/VAL/W/241/Rev.1, 2 May 2014.

1667 Footnote 2 to Article 15.3 KORUS.

1668 Article 119.3 of the EU–CARICOM RTA, Article 16.2.3 of the EU–Colombia, Ecuador and Peru RTA, Article 127.3 of the EU–Georgia RTA, Article 254.3 of the EU–Moldova RTA and Article 139.3 of the EU–Ukraine RTA. The accuracy of such statements can, however, be questioned as services can definitely be subject to customs duties, especially if they cross borders on physical carriers.

1669 See Article 7 of both of the proposed chapters on digital trade for the EU–Australia RTA and the EU–New Zealand RTA, available at <http://trade.ec.europa.eu/doclib/press/index.cfm?id=1865> and <http://trade.ec.europa.eu/doclib/press/index.cfm?id=1867>.

the e-commerce champions, having included extensive e-commerce provisions in most of their RTAs.

The East Asian and Pacific Region has concluded more intraregional RTAs than any other region, and many of them contain a significant amount of e-commerce-related provisions. The lack of 'e-commerce heavy' RTAs in the European and Central Asian region is also noteworthy. The EU only started including more extensive e-commerce provisions in its most recent RTAs, most of which have not yet entered into force. Based on the results of the text-based analysis, the EU trails considerably behind other high-income countries when it comes to e-commerce provisions. It remains to be seen whether it will be able to close this gap in its future RTAs.

RTAs concluded with high-income countries generally contain most e-commerce provisions. The CPTPP has played an unprecedented role in committing lower middle-income countries to substantive obligations on electronic commerce. It has, however, also been observed that, so far, low middle-income and low-income countries have not concluded RTAs amongst themselves that include e-commerce provisions. At the same time, the almost complete lack of inclusion of low-income countries as well as Sub-Saharan African countries sends an important message on the persistence of the digital divide.

It can hardly be contended that we see a strong convergence in WTO Members' approach to e-commerce issues in their RTAs. There is still a considerable disparity between what types of provisions are included, even between three of the leading digital nations (China, the EU and the United States). Even though there is an increase over time of inclusion of e-commerce provisions in RTAs concluded with lower middle-income countries, 'e-commerce light' RTAs are still commonplace in every geographical region. Considering this persistent regional disparity, one can only call for more clarification and guidance on e-commerce from the multilateral level. It remains to be seen whether an outcome from the ongoing plurilateral negotiations on e-commerce at the WTO will lead to a more streamlined and inclusive regulation of e-commerce at the regional level.

Chapter 9 has shown that quite some overlap can be observed in the six extensive e-commerce RTAs studied. Three RTAs stand out in their level of commitment and the number of obligations undertaken relevant to digital services and e-commerce more generally: the Australia–Singapore RTA, the CPTPP and the USMCA all include several provisions that are, at least on their face, considerably 'GATS+'. It is especially interesting to note the considerable overlap in language between the e-commerce/digital trade chapters in these three RTAs.

The China–Korea RTA contains considerably fewer obligations compared to other RTAs that were studied. This is not surprising and is more or less in line with how China has approached the e-commerce discussion at the multilateral level. Nonetheless it is remarkable that China did commit to certain provisions that go beyond GATS language, including obligations on electronic authentication and on protection of personal data.

The EU's provisions on electronic commerce are more limited than those found in the RTAs that involve the United States. This is of course largely due to the EU's strong domestic policy on privacy and personal data protection on the one hand, and its strong historical protection of audiovisual services on the other hand. These policy considerations prevent the EU from undertaking commitments on the free cross-border flow of data as well as general non-discrimination obligations with regard to digital products. From the EU's perspective, data protection and privacy should not be bartered with light-heartedly. These values are considered more than a commodity and precondition for trade and the EU considers them fundamental rights that need to be protected in themselves.[1670] The EU's (and other countries') concerns and reservations should not be tossed aside lightly and it should be considered whether such policy concerns can adequately be addressed in the context of trade agreements.

This does not mean that the EU has not committed to any provisions on data flows in its RTAs. First, the European Commission explicitly endorsed horizontal provisions for cross-border data flows in its RTAs.[1671] Second, the EU has proposed provisions addressing restrictions on cross-border data flows, which identify and prohibit various forms of DLRs, in its negotiations with Australia and New Zealand.[1672] These proposed obligations are, however, limited by broad exceptions. Article

[1670] European Commission, 'Exchanging and Protecting Personal Data in a Globalised World' Communication from the Commission to the European Parliament and the Council, COM(2017) 7 final, Brussels, 10 January 2017, 6.

[1671] Preferably in the context of 'adequacy decisions'. European Commission, 'European Commission Endorses Provisions for Data Flows and Data Protection in EU Trade Agreements', *Daily News*, 31 January 2018, available at <http://europa.eu/rapid/press-release_MEX-18-546_en.htm>.

[1672] This is an interesting approach as other RTAs with data localisation prohibitions so far used more general formulations prohibiting 'requirements to use or locate computing facilities for conducting business in a party's territory'.

6 of the proposed chapters on digital trade recognises the protection of personal data and privacy as a fundamental right and preserve the parties' right to adopt and maintain the safeguards they deem appropriate to ensure the protection of personal data and privacy. This exception is not subject to chapeau-like qualifications or requirements of proportionality or necessity. The EU thereby maintains its strong position on privacy protection, even in its newest, more elaborate e-commerce chapters. The EU proposed very similar provisions in the context of the ongoing plurilateral negotiations on trade-related aspects of electronic commerce.[1673]

More generally, it is worth asking the question whether the electronic commerce chapters and provisions actually add to the rights and obligations Members have already agreed to, multilaterally, in the GATS. Preliminarily it should be noted that most, if not all, RTAs add considerably to the commitments undertaken in service sectors that are related to digital services trade. Part II has shown that most service sectors are implicated in digital services trade. RTAs that include GATS+ services commitments will therefore automatically lead to an increased liberalisation of trade in digital services between the parties to the RTA, whether they have included specific e-commerce-related provisions or not. Secondly, it is true that some of the RTAs (successfully or not) try to clarify some of the issues that have arisen in the application of the GATS to digital services. The clear recognition of the principle of technological neutrality in the EU–Japan RTA is one example. The explicit inclusion of new services in the Australia–Singapore RTA is another. It should however be borne in mind that, so far, such provisions are exceptional, and some RTAs even move in the other direction (for example, the exclusion of new services in CETA and the Japan–Switzerland RTA). Certain RTAs arguably even diminish the obligations that they have agreed to multilaterally. For example, Korea included a reservation on digital audio and video content in KORUS whereas it committed fully to sound and video production and distribution in its GATS Schedule.[1674]

The RTAs studied contain some provisions that specifically target or are related to the barriers to digital services trade. For example, three out of six RTAs studied contain obligations for parties to allow cross-border

[1673] WTO, Joint Statement on Electronic Commerce, 'EU Proposal for WTO Disciplines and Commitments Relating to Electronic Commerce – Communication from the European Union', INF/ECOM/22, 26 April 2019.

[1674] WTO GATS, 'Republic of Korea – Schedule of Specific Commitments', GATS/SC/48, 15 April 1994, 19.

data flows in the ordinary course of business. Such commitments arguably allow for effective addressing of various barriers to data flows, including regulatory requirements for cross-border data flows. Moreover, where parties have agreed not to require the localisation of computing facilities, DLRs can no longer be applied to the trade between the parties (of course, data localisation can still be required of third-party countries). It could therefore be argued that these provisions adequately address the issue of barriers to cross-border data flows. However, one should be cautious in allocating too much weight to these obligations as they are considerably limited by the exceptions linked to them. None of the RTAs include a limitative list of legitimate public policy objectives, which entails that a wide range of policy considerations could prompt a regulatory limitation of cross-border data flows. Even though these exceptions can be criticised for the wide policy margin they leave to the parties, it should also be acknowledged that data flows inherently entail privacy and security concerns. Pending full understanding of the implications of data flows on personal privacy, competition, security and public morals, parties are wise to allow for a broad group of policy concerns that allow for deviation from this obligation. The strict requirements of proportionality and the chapeau-like requirement of avoiding arbitrary or unjustifiable discrimination and disguised restrictions on trade should be able to sufficiently safeguard against abuses of these exceptions.

For both the barriers of web filtering and digital taxes, explicit provisions can also be found in the RTAs, but their implications for these barriers are less clear-cut. Will endeavours on access to and use of the Internet have any impact on web filtering practices? How should the moratorium on customs duties on electronic transmissions be interpreted and what are the implications of the different language used by different parties? Neither the Chinese nor the EU RTA studied contained significant obligations on these issues nor do they successfully clarify the obligations that have been undertaken when it comes to customs duties in the context of e-commerce. That is not to say that no relevant obligations can be found in these RTAs, but those are limited to reiterations of what can already be found in the GATS and its Annexes. Where the applicability of WTO Agreements is recognised, the exact same analysis as conducted in Chapter 7 applies identically at the regional/bilateral level. Moreover, where the applicability of the trade in services chapters is explicitly confirmed, a similar analysis to Chapter 7 can be conducted as these chapters reiterate the obligations contained in the GATS and its Annexes.

It can thus be concluded that the value added by the specific e-commerce chapters to addressing three specific barriers to digital services trade that have been the focal point of this research is quite limited. The added value in these e-commerce chapters can be found in the explicit provisions on cross-border data flows and data localisation and any provisions that clarify elements that are still under discussion at the multilateral level. One should, however, dare to question the desirability of extensive liberalisation of cross-border data flows and the focus on avoiding government intervention in electronic commerce.[1675] It is imperative that an optimal balance is struck between trying to liberalise electronic commerce and safeguarding the necessary policy space to address the privacy, cybersecurity and other legitimate concerns related to the Internet.

It is important to acknowledge the continued importance of the obligations and commitments undertaken in the GATS, also at the regional and bilateral level. The WTO's key contribution to the ongoing debates on the trade-related aspects of digital services is exactly the fact that it can build upon the relevant provisions that are already present. In the ongoing plurilateral negotiations, Members should ask themselves whether it is really necessary to create a new instrument dedicated to addressing 'trade-related aspects of electronic commerce' or whether the Membership would benefit more from building on and expanding the existing obligations and commitments.[1676] The main benefit of the latter approach is that it would take a clear position on how new provisions relate to existing provisions and it would require much less 'new legislation', as clarifying the applicability of the existing framework to digital trade would already enable parties to successfully address many of the barriers to digital services trade, while allowing for sufficient policy space to safeguard important policy concerns. This research

[1675] Neeraj, for example, rejects the CPTPP as a normative benchmark for multilateral negotiations, arguing that it is too focussed on minimising or eliminating government interventions in the e-commerce market. Neeraj (n 95) 141.

[1676] In its communication in the context of the plurilateral negotiations on trade-related aspects of electronic commerce, the EU explicitly requests increased market access. It does so by calling for Members to join the Information Technology Agreement and its expansion, more commitments on computer services and more commitments on telecommunications services. WTO, Joint Statement on Electronic Commerce, 'EU Proposal for WTO Disciplines and Commitments Relating to Electronic Commerce – Communication from the European Union', INF/ECOM/22, 26 April 2019.

has shown that the GATS framework already applies to digital services trade and that most specific barriers to digital services trade can already be addressed under the existing provisions. In addressing concerns related to digital services, RTAs should focus on clarifying and building on these existing obligations.

Conclusions

This book set out to answer the research question: 'Can the specific barriers to digital services trade be addressed within the existing international legal framework applicable to trade in services?' The final conclusion that can be drawn from this research is that the specific barriers that were identified can be addressed under Members' existing GATS obligations. It can therefore suffice for Members to clarify their understanding of the scope of the GATS in relation to digital services and the interpretation of their specific commitments without needing to negotiate new substantive provisions in order to address these barriers.

The book has sought to preliminarily clarify the phenomena that influenced twenty-first-century trade and that help to explain the rise of trade in services in general and trade in digital services in particular. The digitisation of trade and production, combined with the importance of services in proliferating GVCs, has led to digital services being traded at an unprecedented level. This prompts an enquiry into the applicable rules, especially due to the fact that the multilateral obligations related to services trade date back to the early 1990s when services were scarcely traded through electronic means.

The final conclusion on the applicability of the legal framework was reached by answering a number of preliminary questions as formulated in the introduction. First, digital services were defined as services supplied digitally or through electronic means. This broad definition clarifies the large group of services that are implicated in the discussions on electronic commerce. Second, it is established that the GATS is applicable to digital services trade, due to its broad scope (as established in Article I) and the applicability of the principle of technological neutrality. The applicability of the GATS to trade in digital services directly entails the applicability of the GATS' general obligations (including the MFN treatment obligation). Third, a clear and consistent classification methodology was proposed. The teleological or functional approach to services classification allows for a clear identification of the service sectors at issue, in line with existing jurisprudence and practice as proposed by the WTO Secretariat. The clear classification of digital services is a prerequisite for establishing the applicability of GATS obligations subject to Members' specific commitments (including the market access and national treatment obligations as well as the obligations contained in the Annex on Telecommunications). Where Members have scheduled commitments in relevant service sectors, their measures affecting trade in digital services are subject to these commitments.

Fourth, several types of specific barriers to digital services trade (or with a specific impact on digital services) were identified. These include restrictions on cross-border data flows, web filtering and content control, and digital taxes. It was established that domestic regulation amounting to these types of barriers considerably hinder digital trade, mainly to the detriment of foreign service suppliers. Fifth, the GATS obligations were applied to illustrative case studies for four of these barriers. The GATS inconsistency of several of these case studies was established. For example, it was shown that Russia's data localisation requirements likely violate its national treatment obligation for any digitally enabled service for which it has scheduled specific commitments and that it also violates its market access obligation on data processing services. Additionally, China's practice of web filtering through the maintenance of the Great Firewall is arguably inconsistent with its national treatment obligation. The United States' removal of net neutrality rules seem to constitute an 'as such' violation of the obligations contained in the Telecoms Annex. France's digital services tax arguably violates its national treatment commitments. The research thereby established that Members should be aware of the fact that their measures which affect trade in digital services are possibly inconsistent with those obligations.

Sixth, the research established that most e-commerce RTAs do not contain considerable GATS+ provisions. Through a general, quantitative analysis it was established that e-commerce RTAs generally contain little language that addresses specific barriers to digital trade. This preliminary finding was confirmed by an in-depth analysis of six extensive e-commerce RTAs. Only with regard to limitations on cross-border data flows do some RTAs contain obligations that go beyond the GATS and that make it even less likely that such limitations are consistent with Members' international obligations. Provisions addressing other specific barriers are hardly included in e-commerce chapters. Moreover, as it was established that these barriers can already be addressed under existing GATS commitments, the main contribution of these RTAs to dealing with barriers to digital services trade is limited to the fact that they extend commitments on market access and national treatment beyond their level of commitment at the WTO and that some of them clarify the parties' understanding on certain outstanding issues at the multilateral level. This entails a higher level of liberalisation of digital services as well.

The final conclusion of the research is therefore that the GATS is applicable to digital services trade, that certain specific barriers to digital services trade can adequately be addressed under the GATS and that the majority of e-commerce chapters in Members' RTAs do not substantively contribute towards addressing most of the specific barriers. In the context of the ongoing plurilateral negotiations on the trade-related aspects of electronic commerce, Members should be mindful of their existing obligations and the added complexity that might result from a new agreement that addresses issues that can already (at least partially) be addressed under existing WTO obligations. Multilateral obligations on digital services would benefit most from a (political) clarification of what already exists.

This research presented an in-depth legal analysis, aiming to clarify the applicable legal framework to trade in digital services. The legal analysis in this book is an important starting point for policy makers in their consideration of how to regulate digital services trade. Any exercise in regulating new phenomena should be based on a thorough understanding of the existing (international) legal rights and obligations. For clarity the main findings of this book are listed and explained below.

The phenomena of trade in global value chains and digitisation have transformed the global economy and caused the proliferation of trade in digital services

Two evolutions in the global trade landscape have contributed significantly to the exponential growth of trade in digital services: the important role that services play in GVCs both as enablers and as inputs and the increased tradability of services through electronic transmission because of the Internet. Increased digital services trade also created new challenges as Members try to regulate these intangibles. In trying to regulate Internet access, cross-border data flows and digital services (with the aim of protecting important policy considerations such as privacy and national security), WTO Members are erecting barriers to digital services trade, to the detriment of foreign service suppliers, consumers and MSMEs. This prompts the need to assess the legality of such barriers under the international legal framework applicable to digital services trade.

No blanket statement can be made on the classification of digital products. Classification should, however, be based on the *nature* of these products

The discussion on the classification of digital products should not be dictated by liberalisation considerations. It is rather the nature of the product (as advocated by the US and the WTO Secretariat) that should determine whether a digital product is a good or a service. It is impossible to make a blanket statement on the outcome of such an analysis for all digital products. I argue that, based on their nature, products like e-books, packaged software and online movies should be considered as goods. The availability of a new means of delivery does not alter the nature of these products. However, service suppliers can of course supply services that allow access to these goods (e.g. VOD services). In considering this discussion, it should be kept in mind that it is the measure at issue that will determine the applicable agreement in case of a dispute.

Classification of (digital) services should be done on the basis of the teleological or functional approach

The teleological or functional approach to the classification of services leads to the most consistent and true classification as it will depend on what final service is being supplied to the consumer. In applying this classification approach, one should depart from the question 'what function is achieved by the service?' This also entails an assessment of *who* the service is being supplied to and what the service's output is. Classification should happen regardless of the means of supply, the (marketing) name given to the service, the service's components or inputs or the supplier's source of revenue.

The phenomenon of 'new digital services' is vastly overestimated: the means of supply is new, not the function of the service

Even though no blanket statement can be made on the existence of 'new services', which are not classifiable within the existing classification, it can be concluded that the phenomenon of 'new services' is vastly overestimated. Most digital services are not new in their function, they are only new in the way in which they are being supplied. However, the means of supply do not alter the nature of the product. Finally, the phenomena of increased convergence between goods and services, integrated services and service suppliers supplying different services (to different types of consumers) at the same time should not obfuscate the approach to classifying digital services.

Digital services trade is confronted with a myriad of different barriers, some of which are specific to this type of trade

Digital services trade is confronted with a wide array of different kinds of barriers. With the creation of a 'new' means to supply services also came new variations of trade barriers as governments want to regulate the Internet and protect consumers, their privacy, national security or, simply, the domestic industry. This research elaborated on several barriers that carry specific relevance to digital services trade, including restrictions on cross-border data transfers, web filtering and content control, lack of access to infrastructure and digital taxes. The trade-restrictive impact of these barriers should not be underestimated.

The GATS' obligations apply to digital services trade

Due to the broad scope of the GATS and the fact that the Agreement does not make any distinctions on the basis of different means of supply, the GATS applies to digital services trade. It is important that Members acknowledge that the principle of technological neutrality applies to the GATS. Especially the market access and national treatment obligation are relevant in addressing measures that affect trade in digital services for which Members have undertaken specific commitments. It can therefore not be argued that the GATS does not contain adequate obligations to address barriers to digital services trade. Members should be aware of the applicability of the GATS to digital services trade and ensure the WTO consistency of any measure taken to regulate digital services trade.

Various existing barriers to digital services trade are inconsistent with those Members' commitments under the GATS

Three existing barriers to digital services trade have been found inconsistent with the GATS. Russia's amended Law on Personal Data likely violates its market access obligations regarding data processing services, violates its national treatment obligations regarding other digitally enabled services and possibly violates its obligations under Section 5(c) of the Telecoms Annex. China's 2016 Cybersecurity Law (in the context of it maintaining the Great Firewall) arguably violates its national treatment obligations as well as its obligations under the Telecoms Annex and risks violating its market access obligations if it effectively prevents any cross-border supply in a whole service (sub)sector. France's Digital Services Tax arguably violates its national treatment obligation. Members additionally have a positive obligation to address another obstacle to digital services trade: the lack of access to (Internet) infrastructure. The United States effectively failed to adequately address this obstacle as it abolished existing network neutrality rules through its Restoring Internet Freedom Order. It thereby violates its obligation to ensure non-discriminatory access to and use of public telecommunications transport networks and services. The barriers and obstacle assessed in this book are only illustrative of the broader problem of Members maintaining measures that are inconsistent with their WTO obligations when regulating digital services trade.

There is an overall increase in the number of RTAs that include e-commerce related provisions, but their extensiveness diverges considerably

More and more e-commerce RTAs are being concluded but only a handful contain substantive obligations that address barriers to digital services trade. Even though there is an overall increase of e-commerce RTAs, many RTAs still do not address digital trade. Of all the RTAs that have been concluded in the last few years (at which point digital services have become *incontournable*), at least half do not contain provisions on electronic commerce. Most e-commerce RTAs do not undertake substantial commitments or formulate GATS+ obligations. This indicates that, even in their bilateral trade relations, WTO Members are unsure on how to address digital services trade or are unwilling to do so. The increased inclusion of provisions addressing specific barriers to digital trade and DLRs in a number of RTAs that were concluded in the last five years, however, points to a growing awareness of the barriers to digital trade and an increased willingness by a handful of Members to address them outright.

The digital divide is clearly visible in how RTAs address electronic commerce

Only a handful of RTAs concluded with Sub-Saharan African countries include provisions related to e-commerce. None of these provisions contain substantive obligations related to electronic commerce. This illustrates the persistence of the digital divide and the lack of opportunity seizing by Sub-Saharan African countries to facilitate electronic commerce in the future. It is clear that the digital divide, in its various forms, persists.

The RTAs with the most extensive e-commerce chapters contain some GATS+ provisions, but they are not necessary to address the three identified specific barriers to digital services trade

Several of the extensive e-commerce RTAs that were studied contained GATS+ provisions in relation to electronic commerce. They create new specific obligations related to the cross-border flows of data and elaborate on the prohibition to impose customs duties on electronic transmissions. Such GATS+ provisions can, however, only be found in a small group of RTAs, often concluded between high-income countries. It can additionally be questioned whether these provisions add substantially to the existing obligations in the GATS. The specific barriers studied can all be addressed under the GATS and while the new substantive obligations on electronic commerce can be valued for their clarification of some of the issues discussed in this book, it cannot be contended that they are necessary to address these barriers to digital services trade.

BIBLIOGRAPHY

Aaronson SA and Leblond P, 'Another Digital Divide: The Rise of Data Realms and Its Implications for the WTO' (2018) 21 Journal of International Economic Law 245

Adler R, 'Towards a Better Understanding of Internet Economics' (Internet Association 2018) <https://internetassociation.org/publications/towards-better-understanding-internet-economics/>

Ahmed U and Aldonas G, 'Addressing Barriers to Digital Trade' (International Centre for Trade and Sustainable Development (ICTSD) 2015) <http://e15initiative.org/publications/addressing-barriers-to-digital-trade/>

Alexander K and Andenas M (eds), *The World Trade Organization and Trade in Services* (Martinus Nijhoff 2008)

Alschner W, Pauwelyn J and Puig S, 'The Data-Driven Future of International Economic Law' (2017) 20 Journal of International Economic Law 217

Antimiani A and Cernat L, 'Liberalizing Global Trade in Mode 5 Services: How Much Is It Worth?' (2018) 52 Journal of World Trade 65

Baldwin R, 'Stepping Stones or Building Blocs? Regional and Multilateral Integration' (2004) Paper prepared for G-20 workshop on 'Regional Economic Integration in a Global Framework'

Barfield C, 'When Trade and Tech Collide. Digital Policy Challenges and Solutions for 2016 and Beyond' (American Enterprise Institute 2015) AEI Technology Policy Working Paper, 12–13 <www.aei.org/research-products/report/when-trade-and-tech-collide/>

Bauer M and others, 'The Costs of Data Localisation: Friendly Fire on Economic Recovery' (ECIPE 2014) ECIPE Occasional Paper 3/2014 <https://ecipe.org/publications/dataloc/>

Benz S, Khanna A and Nordas HK, 'Services and Performance of the Indian Economy: Analysis and Policy Options' (OECD Publishing 2017) OECD Trade Policy Papers 196

Berry R and Reisman M, 'Policy Challenges of Cross-Border Cloud Computing' (2012) Journal of International Commerce and Economics 1

Bhagwati J, 'US Trade Policy: The Infatuation with FTAs' in Jagdish Bhagwati and Anna O Krueger (eds), *The Dangerous Drift to Preferential Trade*

Agreements (AEI Press 1995) <https://academiccommons.columbia.edu/doi/10.7916/D8CN7BFM>

Botta A, Digiacomo N and Mole K, 'Monetizing Data: A New Source of Value in Payments' (McKinsey 2017) <www.mckinsey.com/industries/financial-services/our-insights/monetizing-data-a-new-source-of-value-in-payments>

Bukht R and Heeks R, 'Defining, Conceptualising and Measuring the Digital Economy' (Centre for Development Informatics, Global Development Institute, SEED, University of Manchester 2017) 68 <www.gdi.manchester.ac.uk/research/publications/di/di-wp68/>

Burri M, 'The Global Digital Divide as Impeded Access to Content' in Mira Burri and Thomas Cottier (eds), *Trade Governance in the Digital Age* (Cambridge University Press 2012)

'The International Economic Law Framework for Digital Trade' (2015) 135 Zeitschrift für Schweizerisches Recht 10

'Designing Future-Oriented Multilateral Rules for Digital Trade' in Pierre Sauvé and Martin Roy (eds), *Research Handbook on Trade in Services* (Edward Elgar Publishing 2016)

'The Governance of Data and Data Flows in Trade Agreements: The Pitfalls of Legal Adaptation' (2017) 51 UC Davis Law Review 65

Burri M and Polanco Lazo R, 'E-Commerce and Data Flows Provisions in Preferential Trade Agreements: Introducing a New Dataset' (2020) 23 Journal of International Economic Law 187

Burri M and Schär R, 'The Reform of the EU Data Protection Framework: Outlining Key Changes and Assessing Their Fitness for a Data-Driven Economy' (2016) 6 Journal of Information Policy 479

BusinessEurope, 'The Proposal for a Free Flow of Data Regulation' (BusinessEurope 2017) position paper <www.businesseurope.eu/publications/proposal-free-flow-data-regulation-businesseurope-position-paper>

Cantore CM, '"Parallel Convergences" in Free Trade Agreements on Financial Services: Select Issues' in Rhea T. Hoffmann and Markus Krajewski (eds), *Coherence and Divergence in Services Trade Law* (Springer 2020)

Castro D and McQuinn A, 'Cross-Border Data Flows Enable Growth in All Industries' (Information Technology and Innovation Foundation 2015) <www2.itif.org/2015-cross-border-data-flows.pdf>

Cecil AL, 'Taking Back the Internet: Imposing Civil Liability on Interactive Computer Services in an Attempt to Provide an Adequate Remedy to Victims of Nonconsensual Pornography' (2014) 71 Washington and Lee Law Review 2513

Cernat L and Kutlina-Dimitrova Z, 'Thinking in a Box: A "Mode 5" Approach to Services Trade' (2014) 48 Journal of World Trade 1109

Chander A, 'The Internet of Things: Both Goods and Services' (2019) 18 World Trade Review 9

Choi C, 'The Effect of the Internet on Service Trade' (2010) 109 Economics Letters 102

Chung C-M, 'Data Localization: The Causes, Evolving International Regimes and Korean Practices' (2018) 52 Journal of World Trade 187

Clarke GRG and Wallsten S, 'Has the Internet Increased Trade? Developed and Developing Country Evidence' (2006) 44 Economic Inquiry 465

Cook G, 'The Illusion of "Evolutionary Interpretation" in WTO Dispute Settlement' in Georges Abi-Saab and others (eds), *Evolutionary Interpretation and International Law* (Hart Publishing 2019)

Crosby D, 'Analysis of Data Localization Measures Under WTO Services Trade Rules and Commitments' (International Centre for Trade and Sustainable Development (ICTSD) 2016) <https://e15initiative.org/publications/analysis-of-data-localization-measures-under-wto-services-trade-rules-and-commitments/>

Czernich N and others, 'Broadband Infrastructure and Economic Growth' (2011) 121 The Economic Journal 505

De Meester B, *Liberalization of Trade in Banking Services: An International and European Perspective* (Cambridge University Press 2014)

Delimatsis P, 'Don't Gamble with GATS – The Interaction between Articles VI, XVI, XVII and XVIII GATS in the Light of the US – Gambling Case' (2006) 40 Journal of World Trade 1059

'Due Process and "Good" Regulation Embedded in the GATS – Disciplining Regulatory Behaviour in Services Through Article VI of the GATS' (2007) 10 Journal of International Economic Law 13

'Trade in Services and Regulatory Flexibility: 20 Years of GATS, 20 Years of Critique' in Marc Bungenberg and others (eds), *European Yearbook of International Economic Law 2016* (7th edn, Springer 2016)

Delimatsis P and Hoekman B, 'National Tax Regulation, Voluntary International Standards, and the GATS: Argentina – Financial Services' (2018) 17 World Trade Review 265

Delimatsis P and Molinuevo M, 'Article XVI GATS' in Rüdiger Wolfrum, Peter-Tobias Stoll and Clemens Feinäugle (eds), *WTO – Trade in Services*, vol 6 (Brill 2008)

Diebold NF, *Non-Discrimination in International Trade in Services – 'Likeness' in WTO/GATS* (Cambridge University Press 2010)

Drake-Brockman J and Stephenson S, 'Implications for 21st Century Trade and Development of the Emergence of Services Value Chains' (International Centre for Trade and Sustainable Development (ICTSD) 2012) <https://ictsd.iisd.org/themes/services/research/implications-for-21st-century-trade-and-development-of-the-emergence-of>

Dreyer I and Hindley B, 'Trade in Information Technology Goods: Adapting the ITA to 21st Century Technological Change' (ECIPE 2008) ECIPE Working Paper 06/2008 <https://ecipe.org/publications/trade-in-information-technology-goods-adapting-the-itata-to-21st-century-technological-change/>

Erixon F, Hindley B and Lee-Makiyama H, 'Protectionism Online: Internet Censorship and International Trade Law' (ECIPE 2009) ECIPE Working Paper 12/2009 <https://ecipe.org/publications/protectionism-online-internet-censorship-and-international-trade-law/>

Ezell SJ and Atkinson RD, 'The Good, the Bad, and the Ugly (and the Self-Destructive) of Innovation Policy: A Policymaker's Guide to Crafting Effective Innovation Policy' (Information Technology and Innovation Foundation 2010) <https://itif.org/publications/2010/10/07/good-bad-and-ugly-innovation-policy>

Farrokhnia F and Richards C, 'E-Commerce Products Under the World Trade Organization Agreements: Goods, Services, Both or Neither?' (2016) 50 Journal of World Trade 793

Ferracane M, 'Restrictions on Cross-Border Data Flows: A Taxonomy' (ECIPE 2017) ECIPE Working Paper 1/2017, 2 <https://ecipe.org/publications/restrictions-to-cross-border-data-flows-a-taxonomy/>

Ferracane MF and Lee-Makiyama H, 'China's Technology Protectionism and Its Non-Negotiable Rationales' (ECIPE 2017) <http://ecipe.org/publications/chinas-technology-protectionism/>

Freund C and Weinhold D, 'The Internet and International Trade in Services' (2002) 92 American Economic Review 236

'The Effect of the Internet on International Trade' (2004) 62 Journal of International Economics 171

Gao H, 'Annex on Negotiations on Basic Telecommunications' in Rüdiger Wolfrum, Peter-Tobias Stoll and Clemens Feinäugle (eds), *WTO – Trade in Services*, vol 6 (Martinus Nijhoff 2008)

'Annex on Telecommunications' in Rüdiger Wolfrum, Peter-Tobias Stoll and Clemens Feinäugle (eds), *WTO – Trade in Services*, vol 6 (Martinus Nijhoff 2008)

'Fourth Protocol to That General Agreement on Trade in Services' in Rüdiger Wolfrum, Peter-Tobias Stoll and Clemens Feinäugle (eds), *WTO – Trade in Services*, vol 6 (Martinus Nijhoff 2008)

'Google's China Problem: A Case Study on Trade, Technology and Human Rights under the GATS' (2011) 6 Asian Journal of WTO & International Health Law and Policy 347

'Googling for the Trade-Human Rights Nexus in China: Can the WTO Help?' in Mira Burri and Thomas Cottier (eds), *Trade Governance in the Digital Age* (Cambridge University Press 2012)

Gasser U and Palfrey J, 'Fostering Innovation and Trade in the Global Information Society: The Different Facets and Roles of Interoperability' in Mira Burri and Thomas Cottier (eds), *Trade Governance in the Digital Age* (Cambridge University Press 2012)

Hahn RW and Wallsten S, 'The Economics of Net Neutrality' (American Enterprise Institute and Brooking Institution 2006) RP06–13 <www.cato.org/sites/cato.org/files/serials/files/regulation/2012/6/v34n4-4.pdf>

Herman L, 'Multilateralising Regionalism: The Case of E-Commerce' (OECD Publishing 2010) 99 <www.oecd-ilibrary.org/trade/multilateralising-regionalism_5kmbjx6gw69x-en>

Hoekman B, 'Tentative First Steps: An Assessment of the Uruguay Round Agreement on Services' (World Bank 1995) WPS1455

Hoekman B and Mavroidis PC, 'A Technical Barriers to Trade Agreements for Services?' (European University Institute – Robert Schuman Centre for Advanced Studies 2015) RSCAS 2015/25 <https://cadmus.eui.eu/handle/1814/35419>

Huang J, 'Comparison of E-Commerce Regulations in Chinese and American FTAs: Converging Approaches, Diverging Contents, and Polycentric Directions?' (2017) 64 Netherlands International Law Review 309

ICTSD, 'Updating the Multilateral Rule Book on E-Commerce' (ICTSD 2018) Policy brief <https://ictsd.iisd.org/themes/services-and-digital-economy/research/updating-the-multilateral-rule-book-on-e-commerce>

International Monetary Fund, 'Measuring The Digital Economy' (International Monetary Fund 2018) <www.imf.org/en/Publications/Policy-Papers/Issues/2018/04/03/022818-measuring-the-digital-economy>

Irion K, Yakovleva S and Bartl M, 'Trade and Privacy: Complicated Bedfellows? How to Achieve Data Protection-Proof Free Trade Agreements' (Institute for Information Law, University of Amsterdam 2016) <www.ivir.nl/projects/trade-and-privacy-complicated-bedfellows-how-to-achieve-data-protection-proof-free-trade-agreements/>

Kariyawasam R, *International Economic Law and the Digital Divide: A New Silk Road?* (Edward Elgar Publishing 2007)

'Better Regulation of Digital Markets: A New Look at the Reference Paper' in Mira Burri and Thomas Cottier (eds), *Trade Governance in the Digital Age* (Cambridge University Press 2012)

Kelsey J, 'How a TPP-Style E-Commerce Outcome in the WTO Would Endanger the Development Dimension of the GATS Acquis (and Potentially the WTO)' (2018) 21 Journal of International Economic Law 273

Kim EY, 'E-Commerce in South Korean FTAs: Policy Priorities and Provisional Inconsistencies' (2019) 18 World Trade Review 85

Kox H and Lejour A, 'Regulatory Heterogeneity as Obstacle for International Services Trade' (CPB Netherlands Bureau for Economic Policy Analysis2005)

Krajewski M, *National Regulation and Trade Liberalization in Services: The Legal Impact of the General Agreement on Trade in Services (GATS) on National Regulatory Autonomy* (Kluwer Law International 2003)

National Regulation and Trade Liberalization in Services: The Legal Impact of the General Agreement on Trade in Services (GATS) on National Regulatory Autonomy (Kluwer Law International 2003)

'Article VI GATS' in Rüdiger Wolfrum, Peter-Tobias Stoll and Clemens Feinäugle (eds), *WTO – Trade in Services*, vol 6 (Martinus Nijhoff 2008)

Lapid K, 'Outsourcing and Offshoring Under the General Agreement on Trade in Services' (2006) 40 Journal of World Trade 341

Larouche P, 'Network Neutrality: The Global Dimension' in Mira Burri and Thomas Cottier (eds), *Trade Governance in the Digital Age* (Cambridge University Press 2012)

Leal-Arcas R, 'The GATS in the Doha Round: A European Perspective' in Kern Alexander and Mads Andenas (eds), *The World Trade Organization and Trade in Services* (Martinus Nijhoff 2008)

Lee-Makiyama H, 'Future-Proofing World Trade in Technology: Turning the WTO IT Agreement (ITA) into the International Digital Economy Agreement (IDEA)' (Ecipe 2011) ECIPE Working Paper 04/2011 <https://ecipe.org/publications/future-proofing-world-trade-in-technology-turning-the-wto-it-agreement-ita-into-the-international-digital-economy-agreement-idea/>

'Cross-Border Data Flows in the Post Bali Agenda' in Simon Evenett and Alejandro Jara (eds), *Building on Bali: A Work Programme for the WTO* (CEPR 2013)

Lester S and Barbee I, 'The Challenge of Cooperation: Regulatory Trade Barriers in the Transatlantic Trade and Investment Partnership' (2013) 16 Journal of International Economic Law 847

Liu C, 'Internet Censorship as a Trade Barrier: A Look at the WTO Consistency of the Great Firewall in the Wake of the China-Google Dispute' (2011) 42 Georgetown Journal of International Law 1199

Lopez-Gonzalez J and Ferencz J, 'Digital Trade and Market Openness' (OECD 2018) Working Party of the Trade Committee TAD/TC/WP(2018)3/FINAL

Luff D, 'Telecommunications and Audio-Visual Services: Considerations for a Convergence Policy at the World Trade Organization Level' (2004) 38 Journal of World Trade 1059

'Convergence: A Buzzword to Remain?' in Mira Burri and Thomas Cottier (eds), *Trade Governance in the Digital Age* (Cambridge University Press 2012)

Lund S and Manyika J, 'How Digital Trade Is Transforming Globalisation' (International Centre for Trade and Sustainable Development (ICTSD) 2016) <https://e15initiative.org/publications/how-digital-trade-is-transforming-globalisation/>

Manyika J and others, 'Digital Globalization: The New Era of Global Flows' (McKinsey Global Institute 2016) <www.mckinsey.com/business-functions/digital-mckinsey/our-insights/digital-globalization-the-new-era-of-global-flows>

Marchetti J, 'Addressing E-Payment Challenges in Global E-Commerce' (World Economic Forum 2018) White Paper <www.weforum.org/whitepapers/addressing-e-payment-challenges-in-global-e-commerce>

Mattoo A and Meltzer JP, 'International Data Flows and Privacy: The Conflict and Its Resolution' (World Bank 2018) Policy Research Working Paper 8431 <https://documents.worldbank.org/en/publication/documents-reports/documentdetail/751621525705087132/international-data-flows-and-privacy-the-conflict-and-its-resolution>

'International Data Flows and Privacy: The Conflict and Its Resolution' (2018) 21 Journal of International Economic Law 769

Mattoo A and Schuknecht L, 'Trade Policies for Electronic Commerce' (World Bank 2000) 2380 <https://elibrary.worldbank.org/doi/abs/10.1596/1813-9450-2380>

Mattoo A and Wunsch S, 'Pre-Empting Protectionism in Services: The WTO and Outsourcing' (World Bank 2004) WPS3237 <https://openknowledge.worldbank.org/handle/10986/14438>

Mavroidis PC, 'And You Put the Load Right on Me: Digital Taxes, Tax Discrimination and Trade in Services' (2020) 12 Trade, Law and Development 75

Meijers H, 'Does the Internet Generate Economic Growth, International Trade, or Both?' (2014) 11 International Economics and Economy Policy 137

Meltzer JP, 'Supporting the Internet as a Platform for International Trade Opportunities for Small and Medium-Sized Enterprises and Developing Countries' (Brookings 2014) 69 <https://papers.ssrn.com/sol3/papers.cfm?abstract_id=2400578>

'A New Digital Trade Agenda' (International Centre for Trade and Sustainable Development (ICTSD) 2015) <https://e15initiative.org/publications/a-new-digital-trade-agenda/>

'Maximizing the Opportunities of the Internet for International Trade' (International Centre for Trade and Sustainable Development (ICTSD)

2016) <https://e15initiative.org/publications/maximizing-opportunities-internet-international-trade/>

'The Internet and International Data Flows in the Global Economy' (International Centre for Trade and Sustainable Development (ICTSD) 2016) <http://e15initiative.org/blogs/the-internet-and-international-data-flows-in-the-global-economy/>

'Governing Digital Trade' (2019) 18 World Trade Review 23

Miroudot S, 'The Value of Market Access and National Treatment Commitments in Services Trade Agreements' (OECD 2018) Working Party of the Trade Committee TAD/TC/WP(2016)22/FINAL <www.oecd-ilibrary.org/trade/the-value-of-market-access-and-national-treatment-commitments-in-services-trade-agreements_d8bfc8d8-en>

Mishra N, 'Privacy, Cybersecurity, and GATS Article XIV: A New Frontier for Trade and Internet Regulation?' (2019) 19 World Trade Review 341

Mitchell AD and Hepburn J, 'Don't Fence Me In: Reforming Trade and Investment Law to Better Facilitate Cross-Border Data Transfer' (2018) 19 Yale Journal of Law and Technology 182

Mitchell AD and Mishra N, 'Data at the Docks: Modernizing International Trade Law for the Digital Economy' (2018) 20 Vanderbilt Journal of Entertainment & Technology Law 1073

Mitchell AD, Voon T and Hepburn J, 'Taxing Tech: Risks of an Australian Digital Services Tax Under International Economic Law' (2019) 20 Melbourne Journal of International Law 88

Monteiro J-A and Teh R, 'Provisions on Electronic Commerce in Regional Trade Agreements' (World Trade Organization, Economic Research and Statistics Division 2017) ERSD–2017–11 <www.wto.org/english/res_e/reser_e/ersd201711_e.htm>

Mueller M, 'Convergence: A Reality Check' in Damien Geradin and David Luff (eds), *The WTO and Global Convergence in Telecommunications and Audio-Visual Services* (Cambridge University Press 2004)

Muller G, 'Troubled Relationships under the GATS: Tensions between Market Access (Article XVI), National Treatment (Article XVII), and Domestic Regulation (Article VI)' (2017) 16 World Trade Review 449

Munin N, *Legal Guide to GATS* (Kluwer Law International 2010)

Natens B, *Regulatory Autonomy and International Trade in Services: The EU under GATS and RTAs* (Edward Elgar Publishing 2016)

National Board of Trade, 'E-Commerce – New Opportunities, New Barriers: A Survey of e-Commerce Barriers in Countries Outside the EU' (National Board of Trade 2012) 2012–4

'No Transfer, No Production – a Report on Cross-Border Data Transfers, Global Value Chains, and the Production of Goods' (National Board of Trade 2015) 2015–4

'Data Flows. A Fifth Freedom for the Internal Market?' (National Board of Trade 2016) 2016–8

'The Servicification of EU Manufacturing – Building Competitiveness in the Internal Market' (National Board of Trade 2016) 2016–4

Neeraj RS, 'Trade Rules for the Digital Economy: Charting New Waters at the WTO' (2019) 18 World Trade Review 121

Nihoul P, 'Audio-Visual and Telecommunications Services: A Review of Definitions under WTO Law' in Damien Geradin and David Luff (eds), *The WTO and Global Convergence in Telecommunications and Audio-Visual Services* (Cambridge University Press 2004)

Noam E, 'Overcoming the Three Digital Divides' in Damien Geradin and David Luff (eds), *The WTO and Global Convergence in Telecommunications and Audio-Visual Services* (Cambridge University Press 2004)

Nordas HK, 'Domestic Regulation: What Are the Costs and Benefits for International Trade in Services?' in Aik Hoe Lim and Bart De Meester (eds), *WTO Domestic Regulation and Services Trade: Putting Principles into Practice* (Cambridge University Press 2014)

'Services Trade Restrictiveness Index (STRI): The Trade Effect of Regulatory Differences' (OECD Publishing 2016) 189 <www.oecd-ilibrary.org/trade/services-trade-restrictiveness-index_5jlz9z022plp-en>

Nuzzo S, 'Tackling Diversity Inside WTO: GATT Moral Clause after Colombia – Textiles' (2017) 10 European Journal of Legal Studies 267

OECD, 'OECD Communications Outlook 192013' (OECD Publishing 2013)

'The OECD Privacy Framework ' (OECD 2013)

Measuring the Digital Economy: A New Perspective (OECD Publishing 2014)

OECD, UNCTAD and WTO, 'Discussion Paper on E-Commerce for the G20' (2016) 2016/TMM /12

OECD and WTO, 'Aid for Trade at a Glance 2017. Promoting Trade, Inclusiveness and Connectivity for Sustainable Development' (WTO/OECD Publishing 2017)

OECD Directorate for Financial and Enterprise Affairs, 'The Digital Economy' (OECD 2012) Hearings Competition Committee DAF/COMP(2012)22 <www.oecd.org/daf/competition/The-Digital-Economy-2012.pdf>

Pauwelyn J, 'Squaring Free Trade in Culture with Chinese Censorship: The WTO Appellate Body Report on China – Audiovisuals' (2010) 11 Melbourne Journal of International Law 1

Pélissié du Rausas M and others, 'Internet Matters: The Net's Sweeping Impact on Growth, Jobs and Prosperity' (McKinsey Global Institute 2011) <www.mckinsey.com/industries/high-tech/our-insights/internet-matters>

Peng S, 'Trade in Telecommunications Services: Doha and Beyond' (2007) 41 Journal of World Trade 293

'Renegotiating the WTO Schedules of Commitments: Technological Development and Treaty Interpretation' (2012) 45 Cornell International Law Journal 403

'Cybersecurity Threats and the WTO National Security Exceptions' (2015) 18 Journal of International Economic Law 449

'GATS and the Over-the-Top Services: A Legal Outlook' (2016) 50 Journal of World Trade 21

Peng S and Liu H, 'The Legality of Data Residency Requirements: How Can the Trans-Pacific Partnership Help?' (2017) 51 Journal of World Trade 18

Perset K, 'The Economic and Social Role of Internet Intermediaries' (OECD 2010) OECD Digital Economy Papers No. 171 <www.oecd.org/sti/ieconomy/44949023.pdf>

Porges A and Enders A, 'Data Moving Across Borders: The Future of Digital Trade Policy' (International Centre for Trade and Sustainable Development (ICTSD) 2016) <https://e15initiative.org/publications/data-moving-across-borders-the-future-of-digital-trade-policy/>

Primo Braga CA, 'E-Commerce Regulation: New Game, New Rules?' (2005) 45 The Quarterly Review of Economics and Finance 541

Qiang CZ-W, Rossotto CM and Kimura K, 'Economic Impacts of Broadband', *2009 Information and Communications for Development: Extending Reach and Increasing Impact* (World Bank 2009) <https://openknowledge.worldbank.org/handle/10986/2636>

Riker D, 'Internet Use and Openness to Trade' (US International Trade Commission 2014) Office of Economics Working Paper 2014–12 c

Santana R and Jackson LA, 'Identifying Non-Tariff Barriers: Evolution of Multilateral Instruments and Evidence from the Disputes (1948–2011)' (2012) 11 World Trade Review 462

Sauve P and Roy M (eds), *Research Handbook on Trade in Services* (Edward Elgar Publishing 2016)

Schloemann HL and Ohlhoff S, '"Constitutionalization" and Dispute Settlement in the WTO: National Security as an Issue of Competence' (1999) 93 American Journal of International Law 424

Sen N, 'Understanding the Role of the WTO in International Data Flows: Taking the Liberalization or the Regulatory Autonomy Path?' (2018) 21 Journal of International Economic Law 323

Suominen K, 'Fuelling Trade in the Digital Era: Policy Roadmaps for Developing Countries' (International Centre for Trade and Sustainable Development (ICTSD) 2017) Issue Paper <www.ictsd.org/sites/default/files/research/suominen_fuelling_trade_in_the_digital_era_0.pdf>

Trachtman JP, 'Mutual Recognition of Services Regulation at the WTO' in Aik Hoe Lim and Bart De Meester (eds), *WTO Domestic Regulation and Services Trade: Putting Principles into Practice* (Cambridge University Press 2014)

Tuthill L, 'Cross-Border Data Flows: What Role for Trade Rules?' in Pierre Sauve and Martin Roy (eds), *Research Handbook on Trade in Services* (Edward Elgar Publishing 2016)

Tuthill L and Roy M, 'GATS Classification Issues for Information and Communication Technology Services' in Mira Burri and Thomas Cottier (eds), *Trade Governance in the Digital Age* (Cambridge University Press 2012)

Tuthill L and Sherman L, 'Telecommunications: Can Trade Agreements Keep up with Technology?' in Juan Marchetti and Martin Roy (eds), *Opening Markets for Trade in Services: Countries and Sectors in Bilateral and WTO Negotiations* (Cambridge University Press 2009)

UNCTAD, '2009 Information Economy Report. Trends and Outlook in Turbulent Times' (United Nations Publications 2009) UNCTAD/IER/2009

'2015 Information Economy Report' (United Nations Publications 2015) UNCTAD/IER/2015

'Data Protection Regulations and International Data Flows: Implications for Trade and Development' (United Nations Publications 2016) UNCTAD/WEB/DTL/STICT/2016/1/iPub

'2017 Information Economy Report. Digitalization, Trade and Development' (United Nations Publications 2017) UNCTAD/IER/2017/Corr.1

'Fostering Developments Gains from E-Commerce and Digital Platforms' (United Nations Conference on Trade and Development 2018) TD/B/EDE/2/2

'The Value and Role of Data in Electronic Commerce and the Digital Economy and Its Implications for Inclusive Trade and Development' (United Nations Conference on Trade and Development 2019) Note by the UNCTAD Secretariat TD/B/EDE/3/2

United States Trade Representative, 'Key Barriers to Digital Trade' (USTR 2017) Fact Sheets <https://ustr.gov/about-us/policy-offices/press-office/fact-sheets/2017/march/key-barriers-digital-trade>

USITC, 'Digital Trade in the U.S. and Global Economies, Part 1' (US International Trade Commission 2013) USITC Publication 4415

'Digital Trade in the U.S. and Global Economies, Part 2' (US International Trade Commission 2014) USITC Publication 4485

Van Damme I, 'The Interpretation of Schedules of Commitments' (2007) 41 Journal of World Trade 1

Van den Bossche P and Zdouc W, *The Law and Policy of the World Trade Organization. Text, Cases and Materials* (4th edn, Cambridge University Press 2017)

Vemuri VK and Siddiqi S, 'Impact of Commercialization of the Internet on International Trade: A Panel Study Using the Extended Gravity Model' (2009) 23 The International Trade Journal 458

Walden I and Angel J (eds), *Telecommunications Law and Regulation* (second, Oxford University Press 2005)

Weber R, 'Regulatory Autonomy and Privacy Standards Under the GATS' (2012) 7 Asian Journal of WTO & International Health Law and Policy 25

Weber R and Burri M, *Classification of Services in the Digital Economy* (Springer 2013)

Weber RH, 'The Expansion of E-Commerce in Asia-Pacific Trade Agreements' (International Centre for Trade and Sustainable Development (ICTSD) 2015) <http://e15initiative.org/blogs/the-expansion-of-e-commerce-in-asia-pacific-trade-agreements/>

Willemyns I, 'Disciplines on State-Owned Enterprises in International Economic Law: Are We Moving in the Right Direction?' (2016) 19 Journal of International Economic Law 657

'Addressing Digital Services in PTAs: Only Convergence in the 11th Hour?' in Rhea Tamara Hoffmann and Markus Krajewski (eds), *Coherence and Divergence in Services Trade Law* (Springer 2020)

Wolfe R, 'Learning about Digital Trade: Privacy and E-Commerce in CETA and TPP' (2019) 18 World Trade Review 63

Wolfrum R, Stoll P- T and Feinäugle C (eds), *WTO – Trade in Services*, vol 6 (Martinus Nijhoff 2008)

Wouters J and Coppens D, 'GATS and Domestic Regulation: Balancing the Right to Regulate and Trade Liberalization' in Kern Alexander and Mads Andenas (eds), *The World Trade Organization and Trade in Services* (Martinus Nijhoff 2008)

Wu M, 'Digital Trade-Related Provisions in Regional Trade Agreements: Existing Models and Lessons for the Multilateral Trade System' (ICTSD and IDB 2017) <http://e15initiative.org/publications/digital-trade-related-provisions-in-regional-trade-agreements-existing-models-and-lessons-for-the-multilateral-trade-system/>

Wu T, 'The World Trade Law of Censorship and Internet Filtering' (2006) 7 Chicago Journal of International Law 263

Wunsch-Vincent S, 'WTO, E-Commerce, and Information Technologies – From the Uruguay Round through the Doha Development Agenda' (Markle Foundation 2004)

'Trade Rules for the Digital Age' in Marion Panizzon, Nicole Pohl and Pierre Sauvé (eds), *GATS and the Regulation of International Trade in Services* (Cambridge University Press 2008)

Wunsch-Vincent S and Hold A, 'Towards Coherent Rules for Digital Trade: Building on Efforts in Multilateral versus Preferential Trade Negotiations' in Mira Burri and Thomas Cottier (eds), *Trade Governance in the Digital Age* (Cambridge University Press 2012)

Yoo JY and Ahn D, 'Security Exceptions in the WTO System: Bridge or Bottle-Neck for Trade and Security' (2016) 19 Journal of International Economic Law 417

Zacharias D, 'Article I General Agreement on Trade in Services (GATS): Scope and Definition' in Rüdiger Wolfrum, Peter-Tobias Stoll and Clemens Feinäugle (eds), *Max Planck Commentaries on World Trade Law, Vol. 6: WTO – Trade in Services* (Martinus Nijhoff 2008)

Zhang R, 'Covered or Not Covered: That Is the Question – Services Classification and Its Implications for Specific Commitments under the GATS' (World Trade Organization 2015) WTO Staff Working Paper ERSD–2015–11 <www.wto.org/english/res_e/reser_e/ersd201511_e.htm>

INDEX

For EU product safety concerns, contact us at Calle de José Abascal, 56–1°, 28003 Madrid, Spain or eugpsr@cambridge.org.

www.ingramcontent.com/pod-product-compliance
Lightning Source LLC
LaVergne TN
LVHW011659200926
848484LV00004B/1000
* 9 7 8 1 1 0 8 8 3 7 5 3 8 *